Substance Abuse Counseling: Theory and Practice

SECOND EDITION

Patricia Stevens
University of Colorado

Robert L. Smith
University of Colorado

Merrill
Prentice Hall

Upper Saddle River, New Jersey
Columbus, Ohio

Library of Congress Cataloging in Publication Data

Stevens, Patricia.

    Substance abuse counseling : theory and practice / Patricia Stevens, Robert L. Smith.—2nd ed.

      p.   cm.

    Includes bibliographical references and index.

    ISBN 0-13-021285-7

    1. Substance abuse—Treatment. 2. Substance abuse—Patients—Counseling of.   I. Smith, Robert L. (Robert Leonard) Title.

    RC564.S624   2001

    362.29'186—dc21

00-025322

Vice President and Publisher: Jeffery W. Johnston
Executive Editor: Kevin M. Davis
Editorial Assistant: Christina M. Kalisch
Development Editor: Heather Doyle Fraser
Production Editor: Linda Hillis Bayma
Copyeditor: Laura Larson
Design Coordinator: Diane C. Lorenzo
Cover Designer: Jason Moore
Text Designer: Ed Horcharik/Pagination
Cover art: © Image Bank
Production Manager: Laura Messerly
Electronic Text Management: Marilyn Wilson Phelps, Karen L. Bretz, Melanie N. Ortega
Illustrations: Christine Haggerty
Director of Marketing: Kevin Flanagan
Marketing Manager: Amy June
Marketing Services Manager: Krista Groshong

This book was set in Galliard by Prentice Hall. It was printed and bound by R.R. Donnelley & Sons Company. The cover was printed by Phoenix Color Corp.

10 9 8 7 6 5 4 3 2

ISBN: 0-13-021285

Preface

Substance abuse itself still ranks as one of the major public health issues in today's society. The use and abuse of substances cross gender, socioeconomic levels, ethnicity, age, religion, profession, geography, and most dimensions of human existence and background. Comprehensive programs at undergraduate and graduate levels are now in place in many settings, systematically studying substance abuse and subsequent treatment modalities. Everyone during their lifetime will be touched by substance abuse or addiction; therefore, clinicians should be adequately trained to recognize the enormity of this problem, how to assess it, and, ultimately, how to treat individuals and families who come for assistance.

Contributors to this edition have extensive backgrounds in substance abuse work as well as a special knowledge in a particular segment of the field. Space and time limitations prevented us from examining many of the issues in the field: public policy, working in a school setting, substance abuse in the workplace, and a more in-depth study of the dual-diagnosis issues of mental illness and substance abuse. This text was developed to be helpful for the general clinician as well as the beginning substance abuse counselor. It is intended to serve as the major text for substance abuse classes and as an adjunct to, not a replacement for, counseling theory and techniques texts and coursework.

This textbook takes the reader through the process of working with substance-abusing clients. Chapters build on each other but yet can be used independently as resource information. Chapter 1 provides the foundation for the text by presenting a history of drug use, basic terminology, references to subsequent chapters, and case studies that are used throughout the text. Chapter 2 examines major drugs and their addictive properties, providing essential knowledge for anyone entering this field. Chapter 3 presents the etiology and theories common to drug use and abuse. The beginning of treatment starts with Chapter 4 by emphasizing assessment and diagnosis, again using cases from earlier chapters to understand assessment and diagnosis on a more applied basis.

Treatment is emphasized in Chapters 5 and 6. First, treatment settings are discussed, followed by a closer look at treatment modalities most often used alone or with other methods in treating substance abuse clients. "Family Therapy in Substance Abuse Treatment," Chapter 7, is new to this text and emphasizes the importance of systemic work with substance abusers. Chapters 8 and 9 provide an in-depth analysis of substance abuse prevention and intervention with selected cultures and specific groups: women, children and adolescents, people with disabilities, the elderly, African Americans, American Indians, Asian Americans, and Hispanics. Relapse is seen as an element of the treatment process and is the focus of Chapter 10. Chapter 11, "Prevention," was also added to this edition, emphasizing a proactive approach to substance abuse. Finally, Chapter 12 presents a synopsis of research findings as well as contemporary issues in the field that are currently being studied.

Because it was impossible to portray a "real" client, case histories were developed and are used in selected chapters to offer a sense of the practical application of information in each chapter. These case histories provide a sample of the types of issues presented when working with this population.

ACKNOWLEDGMENTS

The first edition of *Substance Abuse Counseling* evolved after a detailed survey was conducted with professors across the country who teach in the areas of substance abuse counseling, addictions, and chemical dependency. This second edition continues to build on earlier responses, as well as feedback from those who used the first text. Special thanks and appreciation go to the professors and their institutions who helped shape this text. Furthermore, we appreciate the insights and comments from the reviewers of this edition: Michael Cohn, University of Phoenix; Tom Cornille, Florida State University; Mary C. Fitzgerald, Loyola Marymount University; Loren H. Froehlich, Chadron State College; Charles L. Guest, University of South Alabama; Mark L. Kilwein, Clarion University of Pennsylvania; John F. Koscinlek, University of Missouri–Columbia; and James F. Scorzelli, Northeastern University. We appreciate also the still valuable input from the reviewers of the first edition: David Couch, Southwest Texas State University; J. Scott Hinkle, University of North Carolina–Greensboro; Gerald A. Juhnke, University of North Carolina–Greensboro; Richard C. Page, University of Georgia; Michael J. Taleff, Pennsylvania State University; and R. Craig Williams, Northern Illinois University.

We wish again to thank our contributors for their efforts. We express appreciation to each of the students who have used the first edition as part of their coursework and subsequently provided suggestions and feedback. We would also like to thank Kevin Davis for his patience and perseverance. A special thanks to Linda Bayma, senior production editor, and to Laura Larson for a magnificent editing job. And, again, we thank family and friends who have been supportive throughout this process.

Discover the Companion Website
Accompanying This Book

The Prentice Hall Companion Website:
A Virtual Learning Environment

Technology is a constantly growing and changing aspect of our field that is creating a need for content and resources. To address this emerging need, Prentice Hall has developed an online learning environment for students and professors alike—Companion Websites—to support our textbooks.

In creating a Companion Website, our goal is to build on and enhance what the textbook already offers. For this reason, the content for each user-friendly website is organized by topic and provides the professor and student with a variety of meaningful resources. Common features of a Companion Website include:

For the Professor—

Every Companion Website integrates **Syllabus Manager**™, an online syllabus creation and management utility.

- **Syllabus Manager**™ provides you, the instructor, with an easy, step-by-step process to create and revise syllabi, with direct links into Companion Website and other online content without having to learn HTML.
- Students may logon to your syllabus during any study session. All they need to know is the web address for the Companion Website and the password you've assigned to your syllabus.

- After you have created a syllabus using **Syllabus Manager**™, students may enter the syllabus for their course section from any point in the Companion Website.
- Class dates are highlighted in white and assignment due dates appear in blue. Clicking on a date, the student is shown the list of activities for the assignment. The activities for each assignment are linked directly to actual content, saving time for students.
- Adding assignments consists of clicking on the desired due date, then filling in the details of the assignment—name of the assignment, instructions, and whether or not it is a one-time or repeating assignment.
- In addition, links to other activities can be created easily. If the activity is online, a URL can be entered in the space provided, and it will be linked automatically in the final syllabus.
- Your completed syllabus is hosted on our servers, allowing convenient updates from any computer on the Internet. Changes you make to your syllabus are immediately available to your students at their next logon.

For the Student—

- **Topic Overviews**—outline key concepts in topic areas
- **Electronic Bluebook**—send homework or essays directly to your instructor's email with this paperless form
- **Message Board**—serves as a virtual bulletin board to post—or respond to—questions or comments to/from a national audience
- **Web Destinations**—links to www sites that relate to each topic area
- **Professional Organizations**—links to organizations that relate to topic areas
- **Additional Resources**—access to topic-specific content that enhances material found in the text

To take advantage of these and other resources, please visit the *Substance Abuse Counseling: Theory and Practice* Companion Website at

www.prenhall.com/stevens

About the Authors

Patricia Stevens, Ph.D., is the director of the Marriage and Family Training in the Counseling Psychology and Counselor Education Division at the University of Colorado at Denver. She is currently the president of the International Association of Marriage and Family Counselors (IAMFC), a past board member of the Council for Accreditation of Counseling and Related Educational Programs, the past chair of the Ethics Committee of the IAMFC, and the past cochair of the Women's Mentoring and Interest Network of the Association for Counselor Education and Supervision. Dr. Stevens is a Fulbright Scholar who spent several months in Malaysia developing a marriage and family curriculum at the Universiti Kenbangsaan. She has presented extensively at the local, regional, national, and international levels in the areas of marriage and family training, substance abuse, gender issues, and ethical and legal issues in marriage and family training. She is the author of four books and numerous professional articles in the counseling field.

Robert L. Smith, Ph.D., is the chair of the Counseling Psychology and Counselor Education Division at the University of Colorado at Denver. He completed his Ph.D. at the University of Michigan. As a licensed psychologist, he has worked as a private practitioner and has taught and administered graduate-level courses. He is the author of three books and more than 50 professional articles in counseling and family therapy and the field of mental health. He is the executive director of the International Association of Family Counseling and founder of the National Academy for Certified Family Therapists. Dr. Smith's professional research interests include the efficacy of treatment modalities in individual psychotherapy, family therapy, and substance abuse counseling.

Linda Chamberlain, Psy.D., is a clinical psychologist in private practice and the coordinator of clinical training for the Licensed Professional Counselor program at Regis University in Denver, Colorado. She has authored numerous articles and coauthored several books related to addictions, chaos theory, family therapy, and compulsive gambling.

Sharon H. Erickson, Ph.D., is a marriage and family therapist in private practice in Bozeman, Montana. She is former director of the Human Development Training and Research Clinic and adjunct professor at Montana State University. Dr. Erickson is a member of the Ethics Committee for the International Association of Marriage and Family Counseling, is a member of the Standards and Policies Board for the Ethics Committee of AAMFT, is on the editorial board of *The Family Journal,* and is a former board member of the Mississippi Association for Marriage and Family Therapy. She is a clinical member and approved supervisor in the American Association for Marriage and Family Therapy and a trained clinical hypnotist with training and experience in crisis intervention and disaster counseling. She worked as a pediatric and school nurse prior to receiving her master's degree in marriage, family, and child counseling and her Ph.D. in counselor education.

Cynthia L. Jew, Ph.D., is the director of the Pupil Personnel Services Counseling program and an assistant professor at the University of Redlands (Redlands, CA). Her professional research interest is in resiliency. She is the author of Resiliency Skills and Abilities Scale (RSAS). Dr. Jew is a licensed psychologist and a certified school psychologist.

Oliver J. Morgan, Ph.D., NCC, is associate professor and chair of the Department of Counseling and Human Services at the University of Scranton (Scranton, PA). He has worked in the area of substance abuse prevention for almost 20 years. Dr. Morgan is a National Certified Counselor (NCC), a clinical member of the American Association for Marriage and Family Therapy (AAMFT), and a diplomate in the American Psychotherapy Association (DAPA). He has a number of publications in the area of substance abuse and addiction.

John Joseph Peregoy, Ph.D., is a member of the confederated Salish and Kootenai Tribes of Montana (Flathead Nation). He is an assistant professor in the Department of Educational Psychology at the University of Utah and has over 15 years of experience in diversity issues. He is a past member of the executive board of directors for the Indian Recovery Center and Health Clinic of Salt Lake City, Utah. Research interests include minority identity development, issues in American Indian/Alaskan Native mental health, ethnic/minority experiences in the educational system (K–12), and how people seek assistance when in crisis (help-seeking pathways). He received his doctorate in counselor education, with a specialty in multicultural counseling, from Syracuse University.

Philip J. Perez, Ph.D., is a Colorado and Florida licensed marriage and family therapist currently residing in Fort Lauderdale, Florida, with expertise in family system approaches to substance abuse, lesbian/gay marginalization issues, and HIV/AIDS-impacted families.

Connie Schliebner Tait, Ph.D., is an assistant research professor in the Department of Health Promotion and Education at the University of Utah. She holds a doctorate from Syracuse University in counselor education with a concentration in multicultural counseling. Her research interests include high-risk youth, women, substance-abusing families, and culturally appropriate counseling for ethnic and nonethnic minorities.

Brief Contents

Contents

CHAPTER 4
Assessment and Diagnosis   113

CHAPTER 11
Prevention   299

CHAPTER 12
Research and Contemporary Issues   321

Introduction to Substance Abuse Counseling

PATRICIA STEVENS, PH.D.

Drug use and abuse is a commonplace event in our lives today—so commonplace that it is often not considered a problem. Probably everyone has used/abused, has an abuser in the family, has a close friend that has abused, or knows someone who uses alcohol or other drugs inappropriately. In the United States the tobacco industry denied addiction while people were dying from lung cancer and others continued to smoke. Alcoholism continues to be a major problem among adolescents and is a major contributor to fatal automobile accidents and domestic violence situations. Smoking is on the increase in children ages 12 to 13.

America has had campaigns and drug busts to stop the explosion of use, but to no avail. For professionals in the helping professions, drug abuse and dependency continue to be a major concern. As professionals, anecdotally, we know substance use is intertwined with the majority of other problems that clients present in therapy. Statistics support that belief.

At any given time in the United States, substance abuse is either directly or indirectly related to up to 50% of emergency room admissions, one-third of psychiatric emergencies, completed suicide attempts (25% of completions are people addicted to alcohol), psychiatric conditions in adolescents, 56% of domestic violence cases, half of all homicides, and ischemic stroke in adults (illicit drug use is the major cause of this problem) (Cohen, 1995; Evans & Sullivan, 1990; Gentillelo, Donovan, Dunn, & Rivera, 1995; Hyman & Cassem, 1995; Martin, Enevoldson, & Humphrey, 1997; National Foundation for Brain Research, 1992).

Franklin (1987) offered an estimate that in the mid-1980s, one in five Americans were "hopelessly addicted to something—and another one or two steady users [of drugs]" (p. 59). Other studies have not confirmed his estimate, but indeed present data come close to Franklin's numbers (Kessler et al., 1997; Warner, Kessler, Hughes, Anthony, & Nelson, 1995). Some studies present significantly different data. The *Harvard Mental Health Letter* ("Treatment of Drug Abuse and Addiction—Part 1," 1995) estimates that 5% to 10% of adults have a serious alcohol problem and another 1% have a serious illicit drug problem.

This controversy of data brings to light some of the serious problems in the field. Research may define *use, abuse,* and *dependency* differently, leading to a problem when comparing data collected. The second problem is an outgrowth of the first: the question of how to collect data. Not only do definitions differ, but the nature of the problem leads to isolation and hiding of facts about the problem. These two issues leave us without a clear idea of the actual number of recreational users and those with more serious problems but with a sincere belief that "ours is a drug-centered society and that recreational substance abuse extracts a terrible toll from everyone living in this country" (Doweiko, 1999, p. 2).

THE CONTEXT OF SUBSTANCE USE/ABUSE

Humankind has used mind- or mood-altering drugs since the beginning of recorded history. The use of substances goes back to prehistoric times. Over the centuries, drugs have been used medicinally, religiously, and socially. In tribal societies, mind-altering drugs were commonly used in healing practices and religious ceremonies. Alcohol consumption was recorded as early as the Paleolithic times of the Stone Age culture with the discovery that drinking the juice of fermented berries created a pleasant feeling. Cocaine was part of the original Coca-Cola recipe. Alcohol, cocaine, marijuana, opium, and caffeine have all been used for medical purposes through the years.

An examination of the historical perspective of humankind's use of substances for both analgesic and mind-altering purposes and the multidimensional functions that drugs have played throughout history may provide a context for understanding today's substance abuse issues and ensuing ramifications. History may also provide some rationale for the treatment methods used with substance abusers over the past 50 years.

A perusal of some of the early legends that relate to the discovery of substances as well as the development of other drugs may add a perspective to the current context of drug use in our society. The following is not intended to be a thorough history, but a historical overview of early use.

Alcohol

It has been documented that early cave dwellers drank the juices of mashed berries that had been exposed to airborne yeast. When they found that the juice produced pleasant feelings and reduced discomfort, they began to produce a crude wine (Ray & Ksir, 1990). By the Neolithic Age, approximately 8000 B.C. (or 10,000 years ago), liquor in the form of beer, wine, or mead was abundant. Egyptian records dating back to 300 B.C. give testimony to beer production. Homer's *Iliad* and *Odyssey* both discuss drinking wine, while Egypt and Rome had gods or goddesses of wine. The Bible also has many references to the use of wine in sacrificial ritual; in fact, Noah was perhaps the first recorded inebriate.

A 4,000-year-old Persian legend tells the story of the discovery of wine. A king had vats of grapes stored, some of which developed a sour liquid at the bottom. The king labeled these vats as poison but kept them for future use. One lady of the court was prone to severe headaches that no one could remedy. Her pain was so severe that she decided to kill herself. She knew of the poisoned grape juice, went to the storage area, and drank the poison. Needless to say, the lady didn't die but in fact found relief. Over the next few days, she continued to drink the "poison" and only later confessed to the king that she had been in the vats. In the 10th century an Arabian physician, Phazes, who was looking to release the "spirit of the wine," discovered the process of distillation (Kinney & Leaton, 1991).

By the Middle Ages, alcohol was used in ceremonies for births, deaths, marriages, and religious celebrations. Monasteries offered wine to weary travelers who stopped for rest and safety. In Europe, it was known as the "water of life" and considered the basic medicine for all human ailments.

In addition to being used in rituals and then for its convivial effect, alcohol was one of the few chemicals consistently available for physicians to use to induce sleep and reduce pain. Alcohol has been used as an antiseptic, an anesthetic, and in combinations of salves and tonics. As early as A.D. 1000 Italian winegrowers were distilling wine for medicinal purposes.

When European settlers brought alcoholic beverages in the form of wine, rum, and beer to the Americas, native cultures were already producing homegrown alcoholic beverages. The *Mayflower's* log reports, "We could not take time for further search or consideration, our victuals having been much spent, especially our bere" (as cited in Kinney & Leaton, 1991, p. 82). Spanish missionaries brought grapevines, and the Dutch opened the first distillery in 1640. By the Civil War, alcoholic beverages were a portion of each soldier's daily ration.

This brief history of alcohol use indicates the consistent presence of alcohol in human history from before written records were kept. It has been used in every aspect of our lives—social, medicinal, religious. The impact of this history cannot be ignored.

Cocaine

Like alcohol, coca has been around for thousands of years, but the active agent, cocaine, was not isolated until 1857. Cocaine was added to wine and tonics in the mid-19th century as well as to snuff, advertised as a cure for asthma and hay fever. Freud experimented with cocaine as a cure for depression and digestive disorders, hysteria, and syphilis. He also recommended cocaine to alleviate withdrawal from alcohol and morphine addiction. Freud himself used cocaine daily for a period of time. However, when he became aware of the addictive effects, he discontinued use for himself and his patients. An American named John Pemberton created a medicine that contained cocaine and caffeine. He advertised this product as an "intellectual beverage" or "brain tonic." This product, later known as Coca-Cola, contained about 60 milligrams of cocaine in an 8-ounce serving until 1903, when the cocaine was voluntarily removed (Louis & Yagyian, 1980).

In the 20th century, cocaine grew in popularity as it decreased in cost and then became available in the intensified form of "crack." The 1995 National Household Survey on Drug Abuse indicates an estimated 1.5 million current cocaine users (identified as having used once in the past month), with 0.3% (or more than half a million) of the U.S. population estimated to be frequent users (defined as having used more than 51 days in the past year). Sixty percent of cocaine users are between the ages of 18 and 34 (Substance Abuse and Mental Health Services Administration [SAMHSA], 1993).

Marijuana

Marijuana has been used recreationally and medicinally for centuries. The earliest account of its use is in China in 2737 B.C. (Scaros, Westra, & Barone, 1990). Use of marijuana has been controversial since the beginning.

In Europe in the mid-19th century, cannabis (marijuana) was used extensively by members of the French romantic literary movement, and through their writings, American writers became aware of the euphoric effects attributed to the drug. Although knowledge of its existence was almost ignored, the primary interest in this drug has been for its euphoric effects. With the beginning of Prohibition, individual use increased as a substitute for alcohol. After Prohibition, its use declined until the 1960s, when it gained significantly in popularity along with LSD and "speed." It has been used as an analgesic, a hypnotic, an anticonvulsant, and recently as an antinausea drug for individuals undergoing chemotherapy for cancer treatment (Jaffe, 1990).

Marijuana is now the fourth most commonly used drug after nicotine, caffeine, and alcohol. In the 1970s, *Playboy* reported that the Asthma and Allergy Foundation had examined air samples in Los Angeles. A reported 40% of the pollen came from marijuana plants being grown in the area (cited in Resnick, 1979).

Opioids

Opium is a derivative of the poppy plant, and early humans learned that by splitting the top of the *Papaver somniferum* (poppy) plant, they could extract a thick resin. Later it was discovered that the dried resin could be swallowed to control pain. By the Neolithic Age, there is evidence that the plant was being cultivated (Doweiko, 1999; Spindler, 1994).

As early as 7000 B.C., opium was used to quiet crying children. In A.D. 129–199 there are reports of opium cakes being sold in the streets of Rome. In 1729 China found it necessary to outlaw opium smoking because of the increasing number of opium addicts. Morphine, a derivative of opium, was freely used in the Civil War and in other wars both for pain as well as for dysentery. The resulting addiction was known as "soldier's disease." In the last half of the 19th century, a wave of opiate abuse hit the United States. The drug was brought to America by Chinese laborers who came to work on the railroads. At this same time, morphine could still be obtained without a prescription and was thought to be nonaddictive.

U.S. statistics on opium imports were not kept until the mid-1840s. Domestic use increased until the 1890s, when the annual importation of crude opium was half a million pounds (Terry & Pellens, 1928).

Amphetamines

Amphetamines were discovered in 1887 and used in World War II by U.S., British, German, and Japanese soldiers for energy, alertness, and stamina. After the war, amphetamines were prescribed for depression, weight loss, and heightened capacity for work. Soon it was realized that these capsules could be broken open and their contents injected into the body with a needle, heightening the effect of the drug. Amphetamines also replaced high-priced cocaine. By 1970, 8% of all prescriptions in the United States were for some form of amphetamines.

Hallucinogens

Hallucinogens have been around for about 3,500 years. Central American Indian cultures used hallucinogenic mushrooms in their religious ceremonies. When the New World was discovered, Spanish priests, in an effort to "civilize" the Indians, tried to eliminate the use of the "sacred mushrooms." In 1938 the active ingredient that caused hallucinations was isolated for the first time by a Swiss chemist. He was studying a particular fungus in bread that appeared to create hallucinations. The substance he synthesized during this research was LSD (d-lysergic acid diethylamide). Between 1950 and the mid-1970s, LSD was well researched by the government in the hope that it could be used to understand the psychotic mind and to view the subconscious. LSD was used in the treatment of alcoholism, cancer, and schizophrenia. It was also one of the drugs of choice during the drug epidemic that began in the 1960s.

Tobacco

Tobacco was being used by the Indians in the New World over 2,000 years ago. Sailors who had visited that land and taken up the habit carried it home across the Atlantic. Smoking because quite popular in Europe and Asia, but it faced harsh opposition from the church and government. Public smoking was punishable by death in Germany, China, and Turkey and by castration in Russia (Berger & Dunn, 1982). Despite this early response, people continued to smoke and eventually were at least moderately accepted into society.

With the Industrial Age came the invention of machinery to make the cigarette a smaller, less expensive, neater way to smoke (Doweiko, 1999), making the price affordable to almost everyone. Laws were passed that allowed the decrease in price, and after 1910 public health officials began to campaign against chewing tobacco and for smoking tobacco. Smokers also realized that, unlike cigars, cigarette smoke could be inhaled, entering the lungs and the bloodstream (Jaffe, 1990). A few hours of smoking are all that is needed for tolerance to develop. The body immediately begins to adapt to protect itself from the toxins found in tobacco. This results in a rapid development of the need to smoke to feel "normal" (Inaba & Cohen, 1991).

Over time the view of smoking has taken various forms. Early in its use, tobacco was seen as medicinal. In recent history, smoking has been seen as sophisticated. Currently, the view of tobacco use has shifted again. The highly addictive nature of nicotine was acknowledged as a health hazard by the surgeon general of the United States in his 1964 report on tobacco. In his report, the surgeon general outlined the various problems that could be related to, or caused by, smoking tobacco. Since then, the relationship between smoking and cancer has continued to be researched and, on the whole, is substantiated.

This information has required individuals to rethink their position on cigarette smoking. Many cities now ban smoking in public buildings. The number of smokers has declined since that report, but an estimated 61 million people in the United States, or 19% of the population age 12 and above, continue to smoke regularly, and 6.9 million people use smokeless tobacco. An alarming 4.5 million of our children, ages 12 to 17, smoke regularly (SAMHSA, 1993).

Caffeine

The legend of the initial caffeine use lies with a goatherder in Arabia about 1,000 years ago, who observed the energetic behavior of his goats and wondered what was happening. He noticed that this started after they ate the berries of a particular bush. So he tried the berries himself and liked the effect. Usage spread from Arabia to China and to Europe. As more easily ingested versions became available, such as coffee, usage increased.

Tea was first mentioned in writing in A.D. 3560 but is believed to have been available in China as early as 2700 B.C. Tea came to Europe in A.D. 1600. Both tea and coffee have had their advocates and detractors throughout history, with debates about usage. Whether it should be categorized as a "drug" comparable to alcohol and opioids continues to be discussed (Greden & Walters, 1992).

In low doses, caffeine is a mild stimulant that dissipates drowsiness or fatigue, speeds up the heart rate, raises blood pressure, and irritates the stomach. Tolerance and withdrawal are associated with long-term use. Of the 100 million coffee drinkers in the United States, 20% to 30% drink five to seven cups a day. Some researchers report overdose and lethality at 1 gram (Inaba & Cohen, 1991). An average cup of coffee contains 85 to 100 milligrams of caffeine; cola beverages contain 50 to 100 milligrams per 12 ounces. Chocolate has about 25 milligrams per ounce.

This brief overview of drug use indicates that the desire or need to alter one's consciousness has always been an element of the human experience. It also provides a sense of the changing attitudes toward drug use and different drugs through the years.

PATTERNS OF USE AND SOCIETAL COSTS OF SUBSTANCE USE/ABUSE

Patterns of Use

The National Institute on Drug Abuse (NIDA) *Director's Report to the National Council on Drug Abuse* (1998) gives some interesting demographics of drug use in the United States. This report makes the following statements (see also Figure 1.1):

In the Past 6 Months

- Heroin indicators have shown increases in many cities, in some cases overshadowing cocaine.
- Marijuana indicators have continued to escalate across the country.
- Cocaine indicators have continued to level or decline, except for some isolated potentially emerging problems (in Miami and Texas).
- Methamphetamine indicators have increased in most western areas, following some declines last year.

Additionally, the report states that crack cocaine remains the nation's predominant illicit drug problem but that cocaine-related deaths were down or stable in the majority of the areas where such information was reported.

FIGURE 1.1   Types of drugs used by past month illicit drug users, 1997

Note: From the National Clearinghouse for Alcohol and Drug Information site: www.health.org

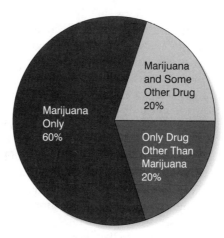

Marijuana and Some Other Drug 20%

Marijuana Only 60%

Only Drug Other Than Marijuana 20%

13.9 Million Illicit Drug Users

Heroin now overshadows cocaine in some cities: it ranks first among mentions in three cities, and it is the primary drug of abuse among treatment admissions in six areas. More than 10% of male arrestees tested heroin-positive in six of the surveyed cities. Heroin continues to increase among new and young users in a number of cities because of its easy availability, low price, high purity, and favorable reputation compared with crack. Younger heroin users tend to snort the drug.

Marijuana accounted for more than 10% of total emergency department mentions in four cities, and it was the primary drug of abuse among treatment admissions in Denver, Minneapolis, and Seattle. Treatment admissions remained at elevated levels: percentages increased in five cities, remained stable in nine, and decreased in one. Among adult male arrestees, marijuana-positive findings exceeded cocaine-positives in seven cities. Despite declines in nine cities between 1996 and 1997, marijuana levels in this population were generally higher than in 1995. Qualitative and quantitative data indicate widespread marijuana use among youth. For example, among primary marijuana treatment admissions, the average age at first use was 13.9 in Minneapolis and 14 in Denver. In Washington, DC, the number of marijuana treatment admissions in the 12 to 17 age group increased 70% between 1995 and 1997. In each of the seven test cities, the percentage of positive urinalyses was much higher for juveniles than for adults.

Indicators of methamphetamine use continue to show increases in the West. Smoking remains the primary route of administration for methamphetamine in San Diego and for "ice" in Hawaii, and it has become more common in Denver and San Francisco, although injecting still predominates. Inhalation still predominates in Los Angeles. In San Francisco, "speed" use is increasing among blue-collar workers, young professionals, and college students. In Denver, where methamphetamine is often used with crack, some former crack users may have crossed over to exclusive methamphetamine use.

Methylphenidate (Ritalin) abuse is reported, mostly among school-age adolescents, in Boston, Detroit, Minneapolis/St. Paul, Phoenix, Seattle, Washington, DC, and areas of Texas; in Chicago, it is the drug of choice for some stimulant users or is mixed with heroin as a "speedball." Methylenedioxymethamphetamine (MDMA, or "ecstasy") availability is reported in several areas, primarily as a club drug at raves and dance parties. Increases are reported in Boston. Ephedrine-based products remain a concern, with products such as "herbal ecstasy" widely available at convenience stores and truck stops in many areas. Treatment admissions, however, remain low for all hallucinogens.

The potency pill sildenafil citrate (Viagra) may be appearing in the club scene. Los Angeles treatment officials describe "Viagra parties" at gay bars and report that three young men have died after combining the drug with "poppers," a recreational nitrate.

This is a graphic description of the extensiveness of use throughout the country as well as the variety of ways and means used to administer the drug. This report also highlights the concern of younger adult use increasing, while older adult use stays stable (see also Figure 1.2).

Another excellent source of demographic information concerning drug abuse, and perhaps the largest collection of data, is the National Household Survey on Drug

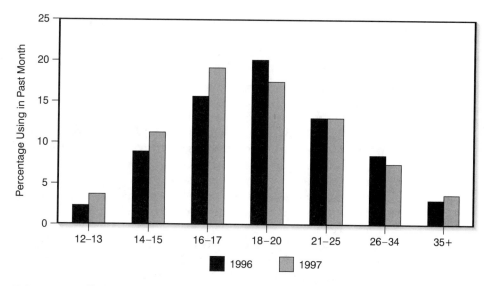

FIGURE 1.2   Past month use of any illicit drug by age, 1996–1997
Note: From the National Clearinghouse for Alcohol and Drug Information site: www.health.org

Abuse conducted by the Substance Abuse and Mental Health Services Administration. The preliminary results of the 1997 study describe the following patterns of use:

- An estimated 13.9 million Americans are current illicit drug users (in all categories "current" is defined as having used within the previous 30 days). This does not indicate a significant change from 1995.

- Of youth ages 12 to 17, 11.4% reported current illicit drug use. Although this figure was stable from 1995 to 1996, the current illicit drug use for youth ages 12 to 13 increased significantly from 2.2% to 3.8%.

- One in 10 youth are current marijuana users, with the prevalence of use doubling between 1992 and 1997 and significantly increasing from 1996 to 1997. Marijuana remains the most commonly used drug—used by 80% of current illicit drug users.

- An estimated 1.5 million Americans are current cocaine users.

- Approximately 111 million Americans ages 12 and above are current alcohol drinkers. Thirty-two million are binge drinkers (five or more drinks on one occasion in the past month), and 11 million are heavy drinkers (five or more drinks on 5 or more days in the past month). This demographic has remained stable since 1988.

- Eleven million current drinkers are between the ages of 12 and 20.

- Currently 64 million Americans are tobacco smokers; 20% percent of youth ages 12 to 17 are current smokers, with a significant increase in the 12 to 13 age group from 7.3% to 9.7%.

Enlightening information concerning race/ethnicity, gender, education, and employment as they correlate to drug use also is reported. Among youth, the current rates of illicit drug use are about equal for whites, Hispanics, and blacks. Most illicit drug users were white. Men continue to have a higher rate of illicit drug use than women. Illicit drug use is highly correlated with educational status, with those who have not finished high school having the highest rate of current use and college graduates having the lowest rate. Employment is also highly correlated with illicit drug use. An estimated 13.8% of unemployed adults are current illicit drug users, while only 6.5% of full-time employed adults are current users (see Figure 1.3).

Whites continue to have the highest rate of alcohol use: 85% of men and 45% of women are current alcohol drinkers. In contrast to findings for illicit drugs, the higher the educational level, the more likely the person is a current alcohol drinker. However, there seems to be a high correlation between heavy drinking and illicit drug use (see Figure 1.4).

Current tobacco smokers tend to be white, male, and with less than a high school degree. Significantly, youth (ages 12 to 17) who smoke tobacco are 12 times as likely to use illicit drugs and 23 times as likely to drink heavily than nonsmoking youth (see Figure 1.5). Stacy and Newcomb (1995) also state that a general factor of

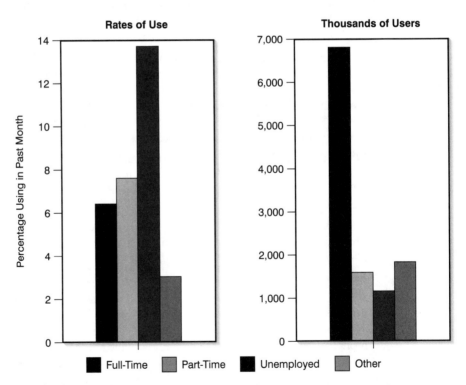

FIGURE 1.3   Past month illicit drug use by current employment status, 1997
Note: From the National Clearinghouse for Alcohol and Drug Information site: www.health.org

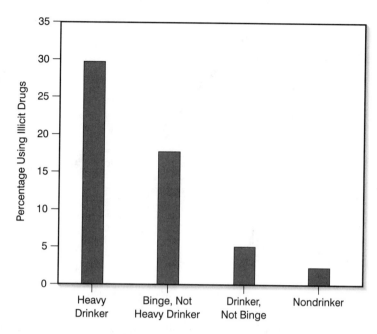

FIGURE 1.4   Past month illicit drug use by past month alcohol use, age 12 and older, 1997

Note: From the National Clearing-house for Alcohol and Drug Information site: www.health.org

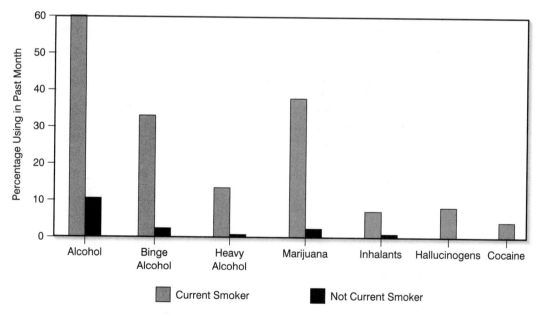

FIGURE 1.5   Use of illicit drugs and alcohol by 12- to 17-year-old smokers and non-smokers, 1997

Note: From the National Clearinghouse for Alcohol and Drug Information site: www.health.org

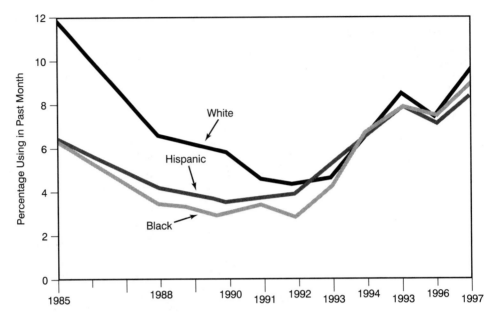

FIGURE 1.6   Past month marijuana use among youth, age 12–17, 1985–1997
Note: From the National Clearinghouse for Alcohol and Drug Information site: www.health.org

drug use in adolescence (rather than use of only certain, specific drugs) significantly predicted criminal deviance in adulthood.

These demographics give an overview of who is using what drugs but no sense of what is spent to purchase these drugs (see also Figures 1.6 and 1.7). One estimate is that the "annual expenditure for illicit recreational chemicals in the United States is greater than the total combined income of the 80 poorest Third World countries" (Corwin, 1994, as cited in Doweiko, 1999, p. 9). And this estimate does not include alcohol and tobacco purchases!

Societal Costs

The National Clearinghouse for Alcohol and Drug Information (1996) reports that

> expenditures for treatment of mental health and abuse of alcohol and other drugs (MHAOD) were $79.3 billion in 1996. Of the total, $66.7 billion was for treatment of mental illness, $5.0 billion was for treatment of alcohol abuse, and $7.6 billion for treatment of other drug abuse. Out of $79.3 billion in total MHAOD treatment expenditures, $46.9 billion (59.1%) comprised treatment by specialty providers. Specialty providers include organized and dedicated MHAOD settings ($33.2 billion) such as psychiatric hospitals, mental health clinics, specialty substance abuse clinics, as well as specialized independent practitioners ($13.6 billion) such as psychiatrists, psychologists, counselors, and social workers. [See Table 1.1.]

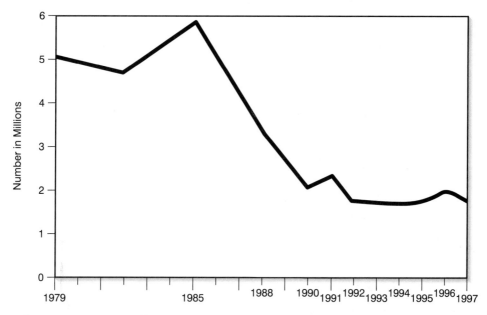

FIGURE 1.7   Number of persons age 12 and older using cocaine in the past month, 1979–1997

Note: From the National Clearinghouse for Alcohol and Drug Information site: www.health.org

   Hospital settings accounted for the largest share of MHAOD expenditures in 1996 (33.4%). The second largest share went to expenditures on independent practitioners (26.2%). The public sector paid for the majority of MHAOD treatment (54.2%). Among the public sector payers, state/local government sources other than Medicaid paid for the greatest share of MHAOD treatment (18.7%), followed by Medicaid (18.2%), and Medicare (13.4%). Other federal government programs accounted for only 3.8% of all MHAOD payments. Private insurance accounted for 26.3% of total MHAOD treatment expenditures, out-of-pocket expenditures 16.0%, and other private spending 3.5%. The average annual growth of expenditures for treatment of MHAOD was 7.2% between 1986 and 1996. MHAOD spending growth was notably slower than the 8.3% average annual growth rate for national health care expenditures. The public sector's share of MHAOD expenditures increased from approximately 49% in 1986 to 54% in 1996. This was countered by a decreasing share of expenditures paid out-of-pocket (23% decreasing to 16%). The private insurance share of MHAOD expenditures remained relatively constant between 1986 and 1996. MHAOD expenditures were 8.1% of the $942.7 billion in national health expenditures in 1996. This represents a decrease from 1986, when MHAOD treatment expenditures were 9.0% of total national health expenditures. Public payers played a proportionately larger role in MHAOD treatment than in all health problems (56% versus 47%, when MHAOD is estimated with methods equivalent to the National Health Accounts). (p. 1)

   In addition to the cost of treatment, there are multitudes of other costs associated with chemical use. These include the lost productivity that results from workers'

TABLE 1.1   Economic costs of alcohol and drug abuse in the United States, 1992 (millions of dollars)

Economic Costs	Total	Alcohol	Drugs
Health Care Expenditures			
Alcohol and drug abuse services	9,973	5,573	4,400
Medical consequences	18,778	13,247	5,531
Total, Health Care Expenditures	28,751	18,820	9,931
Productivity Effects (Lost Earnings)			
Premature death	45,902	31,327	14,575
Impaired productivity	82,201	67,696	14,205
Institutionalized populations	2,990	1,513	1,477
Incarceration	23,356	5,449	17,907
Crime careers	19,198	——	19,198
Victims of crime	3,071	1,012	2,059
Total, Productivity Effects	176,418	106,997	69,421
Other Effects on Society			
Crime	24,282	6,312	17,970
Social welfare administration	1,020	683	337
Motor vehicle crashes	13,619	13,619	——
Fire destruction	1,590	1,590	——
Total Other Effects on Society	40,511	22,204	18,307
Total	**245,680**	**148,021**	**97,659**

Note: Analysis by The Lewin Group. Components may not sum to totals because of rounding. From "The Economic Costs of Alcohol and Drug Abuse in the United States" [On-line], by National Institute on Drug Abuse, 1992, available: www.165.112.78.61/EconomicCosts/Index.html

abuse of drugs and alcohol, the losses to society from premature deaths, fetal alcohol syndrome, costs involving the criminal justice system (see Table 1.2), social welfare administration, property losses from alcohol-related motor vehicle crashes, and costs related to HIV/AIDS.

Estimates of a cost range from $98.6 billion per year (Rice, 1993) to a high of $130 billion a year (Angell & Kassirer, 1994) for alcohol abuse/dependency have been suggested. The estimates for the cost of drug abuse/addiction vary from $160 billion (Hyman, 1996) to $300 billion (White, 1993) when one includes all of the categories mentioned earlier.

Alcohol use was a factor in 41% of automobile fatalities in 1995, 40% of all cases of traumatic injury, and estimated to account for 15% of money spent for health care (Doweiko, 1999). Tresh and Aronow (1996) estimate the annual cost of direct health care for smokers to be an estimated $65 billion per year. Approximately 36% of AIDS cases diagnosed in 1992 were attributable to intravenous drug abuse. It is estimated that drug abuse-related HIV and AIDS cases cost $3.7 billion.

Certainly all of these figures are estimates. It would be difficult if not impossible to account accurately for the multitude of interacting factors that need to be consid-

TABLE 1.2   Total costs of alcohol and drug abuse for specific and related crime, 1992 (millions of dollars)

Type of Cost	Total	Alcohol	Drugs
Criminal Justice Expenditures and Victim Health Care			
Economic Costs to Victims			
Medical expenses for victims of violent crimes	505	400	105
Property damage	221	28	193
Total, Economic Costs to Victims	726	428	298
Criminal Justice System			
Police protection	6,191	1,547	4,644
Legal and adjudication	1,701	491	1,210
State and federal correction	8,483	1,790	6,693
Local correction	3,517	2,326	1,191
Total, Criminal Justice System	19,892	6,154	13,738
Federal Drug Traffic Control	3,753	62	3,691
Subtotal, Public Expenditures	23,645	6,216	17,429
Private Legal Defense	416	68	348
Subtotal	24,787	6,712	18,075
Crime-Related Productivity Losses			
Homicide victims (premature death)	8,016	6,589	1,427
Other victims of crime	3,071	1,012	2,059
Incarcerated offenders	23,356	5,449	17,907
Crime careers	19,198	——	19,198
Subtotal	53,641	13,050	40,591
Total	78,428	19,762	58,666

Note: Analysis by The Lewin Group. Components may not sum to totals because of rounding. From "The Economic Costs of Alcohol and Drug Abuse in the United States" [On-line], by National Institute on Drug Abuse, 1992, available: www.165.112.78.61/EconomicCosts/Index.html

ered when estimating these costs. Nonetheless, the price of substance use is very high one (see Tables 1.2, 1.3, and 1.4).

WORKING IN THE FIELD OF SUBSTANCE ABUSE COUNSELING

As indicated, substance misuse, abuse, and addiction is a multifaceted problem that varies across cultures and families as well as with individuals. It is a problem that affects everyone, and the costs are staggering. The complexity of the problem has resulted in

TABLE 1.3   Where the burden of alcohol and drug problems falls, 1992 (billions of dollars)

	Alcohol	Drugs
Abusers and households	66.8	42.9
Government	57.2	45.1
Private insurance	15.1	3.1
Victim losses	8.9	6.5
Total	**148.0**	**97.7**

Note: Analysis by The Lewin Group. Components may not sum to totals because of rounding. From "The Economic Costs of Alcohol and Drug Abuse in the United States" [On-line], by National Institute on Drug Abuse, 1992, available: www.165.112.78.61/EconomicCosts/Index.html

no single treatment method evolving as most effective for health-distressed individuals experiencing the consequences of substance abuse. In fact, empirical research does not support the efficacy of many approaches. However, current research does find that some approaches are more effective than others and that family treatment approaches for substance abusers and their families may be one of those approaches.

All counselors, whether they work in the field of substance abuse counseling or in the general field of psychotherapy, will encounter issues of substance abuse with many of their clients. Considering the economic costs and the price in human suffering of substance use and abuse, it seems imperative that counselors be trained in all

TABLE 1.4   Updated cost estimates: 1992 estimates and inflation- and population-adjusted costs of alcohol and drug abuse for 1995 (millions of current-year dollars)

	Alcohol		Drugs	
	1992	1995	1992	1995
Health Care Expenditures				
Specialty alcohol and drug services	5,573	6,660	4,400	5,258
Medical consequences	13,247	15,830	5,531	6,623
Productivity Impacts				
Lost earnings—premature death	31,327	34,921	14,575	16,247
Lost earnings—illness	69,209	7,150	15,682	17,481
Lost earnings—crime/victims	6,461	7,231	39,164	43,829
Other Impacts				
Crashes, fires, criminal justice, etc.	22,204	24,752	18,307	20,407
Total	**148,021**	**166,543**	**97,659**	**109,832**

Note: Analysis by The Lewin Group. Components may not sum to totals because of rounding. From "The Economic Costs of Alcohol and Drug Abuse in the United States" [On-line], by National Institute on Drug Abuse, 1992, available: www.165.112.78.61/EconomicCosts/Index.html

aspects of substance abuse intervention and prevention. It is essential that all mental health professionals understand the process of abuse and addiction, the etiology of addiction, and the treatment modalities that are considered to be effective. It is also important that the professional be aware of the psychological and physiological effects of drugs on the human brain and thereby on human behavior. *Substance Abuse Counseling* has been written to guide mental health professionals in their recognition, assessment, and treatment of substance abuse or dependency in their clients.

For consistency throughout this book, we have used the terms *substance abuse* and *substance dependency* whenever possible. These terms coincide with the *Diagnostic and Statistical Manual* (1994) (DSM-IV) definitions and criteria. Being consistent with the DSM-IV allows for measurable and consensually defined diagnosis. We are aware that a variety of terms are used in the field, including *chemical addiction, chemical dependency, drug abuse, addiction,* and *ATOD* (alcohol, tobacco, and other drugs). Our choice of *substance abuse* and *dependency* is in no way intended to imply that other terms do not have validity but is merely a way to develop consistency of terminology and meaning throughout the text.

The authors also have used the term *substance* or *chemical* to include alcohol, nicotine, caffeine, prescription drugs, and illegal drugs. We may, however, at times refer to alcohol and other drugs when the distinction is necessary to maintain clarity. It is, of course, relevant to acknowledge that alcohol, nicotine, and caffeine are legal and societally accepted drugs. This lends a different dynamic to the use, abuse, and even dependency issues related to these substances that does not exist for illegal drugs. It is imperative, however, to also acknowledge that these drugs represent a major threat to physical as well as psychological health.

AN OVERVIEW OF THIS BOOK

Physiology, Drugs, and the Brain: Chapter 2

The discovery of enkephalins in 1974 by John Hughes and Hans Kosterlitz introduced a new dimension to the understanding of human behavior and the physiological aspect of drug use. These enkephalins and related components, endorphins, are naturally produced pain-killing molecules in the brain. Alcohol and opiates bear a strong molecular resemblance to these neurotransmitters in the brain and may fool the brain. Drugs such as cocaine, caffeine, and other stimulants mimic the structure of other neurotransmitters, creating an increased metabolism or false "high" in the brain.

Chapter 2 describes the different drugs of use and abuse and details the effects these drugs have on the central nervous system and the brain. This chapter also gives an overview of how the brain functions and the effect that each particular drug has on that functioning. No matter which theory of etiology one believes, with today's medical technology, it is impossible to ignore the chemical effects that any drug has on the brain's functioning. These chemical effects must be considered in detoxification, treatment, and aftercare planning.

It is also important to understand the various routes by which a drug can be delivered into the human body. Different routes create both different problems and different "highs." A drug can be delivered into the body (a) by mouth, (b) through inhalation, (c) through injection, (d) through contact absorption, and (e) through "snorting."

Oral ingestion is probably the most familiar method of delivery. When someone drinks a beer or swallows a pill, the substance passes through the esophagus and into the stomach. It is then passed into the small intestine where it is absorbed into the blood vessels lining the walls of the intestines. Any substance taken orally passes through enzymes and acids in the mouth and stomach so that its effect is weakened. The reaction time for chemicals taken in this manner is 20 to 30 minutes.

Smoking marijuana or crack, freebasing cocaine, or "huffing" paint are examples of delivering a drug through inhalation. The vapors enter the lungs and are rapidly absorbed by the tiny blood vessels lining the air sacs of the bronchi. This blood is pumped to the heart and directly through the body and to the brain. This is the fastest method of chemical delivery, creating a reaction in 7 to 10 seconds.

Cocaine, heroin, speed, and some barbiturates can be delivered into the body with a needle (injection). Drugs can be injected into the bloodstream, the muscle tissue, or under the skin. Reaction time varies from 15 to 30 seconds if injected into the bloodstream to 3 to 5 minutes under the skin or in the muscle. This method of delivery also poses the highest health risk. Individuals who inject drugs are exposed to many potential problems such as hepatitis, abscesses, septicemia, and HIV/AIDS.

Some drugs can be absorbed into the body through contact. A small amount of LSD can be dropped into the eye or on a moist part of the body to be absorbed. Cocaine powder is sometimes rubbed on gums or on the soft tissue of the female genital area. Medicinally, morphine is given in a suppository form to terminally ill patients who are too weak for other methods of medication. Reaction time for this method of delivery is 5 to 10 minutes.

Cocaine and heroin are often snorted into the nose and absorbed through the mucus membranes lining the nasal passage. Reaction time is 3 to 5 minutes, and the effect is more intense than ingesting the chemical (Inaba & Cohen, 1991).

The Etiology of Drug Use: Chapter 3

As documented by the involvement of humans with drugs throughout history, drug use is a part of human behavior. As such, it functions by the rules of human behavior. Behavior, in general, persists when it increases an individual's pleasure or decreases an individual's discomfort. Drugs are used to achieve one of these purposes.

A number of theories are related to the etiology of substance abuse, factors that perpetuate this abuse, and influence methods of treatment. These are discussed at length in Chapter 3. Until recently, substance abuse etiology was viewed from two opposite polarities, somewhat akin to the nature/nurture argument. The first model was the disease concept, which sees addiction as a progressive, terminal disease over which the individual has no control as long as the use continued. Treatment aligned with this model emphasizes the biological implications of addiction and requires complete abstinence. The second model is a social learning systems model that regards substance abuse as a learned coping behavior that is regulated and maintained by interacting systems, including the family and society. These systems influence the individual in both covert and overt ways. Abstinence is preferential in this model also, but not a necessity.

A third model, the biopsychosocial model has emerged as a holistic way to examine the unproductive behavior of abuse and addiction. This model incorporates all aspects of the individual's life and examines the interactive influences of the physical, emotional, familial, and societal on a person's growth and development. This model allows for the effects of each of these areas individually and collectively in maintaining (as well as treating) abuse and addiction.

Evidence of genetic inclination to addiction certainly exists as well as evidence that supports addiction as a learned behavior. Some authors believe that the only way to prevent drug abuse is for the individual never to come into contact with the drug. Seever (1968) believes that the powerful immediate reinforcement achieved by the use of drugs, if offered freely to the population, would be disastrous. Today this argument continues as society debates the consequences/benefits of legalization of drugs. One contention is that legalization would dramatically decrease drug use, while the other side argues Seever's point of 30 years ago. Many believe that abuse and addiction are a combination of nature and nurture and that the "frightening part of heredity and environment is that . . . parents provide both" (Milkman & Sunderwirth, 1987, p. 14).

Assessment and Diagnosis: Chapter 4

Chapter 4 discusses the assessment instruments and techniques used to diagnose substance misuse, abuse, or dependence. Assessment is an integral part of the treatment plan and includes the processes of information gathering, clinical evaluation, and diagnosis. Understanding the terminology, as well as the criteria for assessment and diagnosis, is necessary to develop an effective treatment plan for the client.

The terminology used in the field of substance abuse counseling may be somewhat confusing to beginning therapists—and at times to both the seasoned counselor and the client! This confusion speaks to the changing conceptualization of addiction. Where once we saw individual abuse as either/or—that is, either not a problem or addiction/alcoholism—we now understand that substance use exists on a continuum and that individuals are different in their history, pattern of use, and treatment needs. This continuum requires terminology to define the different positions along this spectrum of use. These definitions are provided here for your understanding of future references in this text and in the field.

Definitions: *Drug, Use, Abuse, Dependence*

The definition of *drug* is one that changes with fluctuations in social mores as well as with shifts in the law (Smith, 1970). Cultures also differ considerably on classification of substances such as foods, poisons, beverages, medicines, and herbs (Schilit & Gomberg, 1991). In this text, *drug* will be defined as any nonfood substance whose chemical or physical nature significantly alters structure, function, or perception (vision, taste, hearing, touch, and smell) in the living organism (Ray & Ksir, 1990). Legality of a substance has no bearing on whether it is defined as a drug. Alcohol, nicotine, and caffeine are legal but considered drugs in the same way as marijuana, hallucinogens, and narcotics. A *drug user* or *substance abuser* is a person who intentionally takes legal or illegal drugs to alter his or her functioning or state of consciousness. A drug might be instrumental but still abused. Instrumental drugs are used to reduce anxiety, induce sleep, stay awake, and so on. However, instrumental drugs are often abused and serve as an entry to other drugs.

A term that is closely associated with drug use is *drug of choice*. "A person's drug of choice is just that: Of all the possible drugs available—of all the drugs a person may have used over the years—what specific drug(s) would this person use if given the choice?" (Doweiko, 1999, p. 6). This concept is of particular importance as the number of polydrug users increases. In assessment, diagnosis, and treatment, drug of choice may play an important role.

Drug use, misuse, and *abuse* are also somewhat difficult to define. In this text, *drug use* refers to the intake of a chemical substance and does not distinguish whether the drug is used therapeutically, legally, or illegally. *Abuse* is defined by Merriam-Webster (1994) as "improper use" (p. 47) or excessive use; therefore, *substance abuse* would be excessive use of a drug or drug use without medical justification. Further defined, *to abuse* is seen as "to will to injure or damage"—all phrases and language that are easily understood. Whereas *misuse* is using a substance in a manner that causes detrimental effects in some area of the person's life, *abuse* is more specifically defined as the continued use of a psychoactive drug despite the occurrence of major detrimental effects associated with its use, such as, social, vocational, health, scholastic, or economic difficulties (Resnick, 1979).

The World Health Organization in 1974 defined *addiction* or *dependence* as

> a state, psychic and sometimes also physical, resulting from the interaction between a living organism and a drug, characterized by behavioral and other responses that always include a compulsion to take the drug on a continuous or periodic basis in order to experience its psychic effects, and sometimes to avoid the discomfort of its absence.
>
> Tolerance may or may not be present. A person may be dependent on more than one drug. (p. 14)

The DSM-IV, the primary diagnostic tool for the profession, defines *substance abuse* and *dependency* with varying criteria for each of these categories. It is of interest to note that the DSM-IV further divides dependence as "with physiological dependence or "without physiological dependence." This distinction is an addition to the criteria for dependence. Many designer drugs show psychological dependence but may, in fact, cause little or no physical dependence.

Two components separate the diagnostic categories of "abuse" from "dependence": tolerance and withdrawal. *Tolerance* means that a higher dosage of the drug is needed to produce the same level of effect over a period of time. The length of time may be influenced by the amount and frequency at which the drug is administered.

Schuckit (1989) defines two types of tolerance: (1) metabolic tolerance and (2) pharmacodynamic tolerance. *Metabolic tolerance* refers to liver function. Drugs are a foreign substance to the body, and the liver will assign chemicals to break down or metabolize these chemicals. If the liver is continuously exposed to the chemical, then more cells are assigned the task of metabolizing this chemical. The result is that the chemical is metabolized faster and therefore eliminated from the body more rapidly.

Pharmacodynamic tolerance is the central nervous system's increasing insensitivity to a chemical. As the nerve is bombarded with a continuous amount of a chemical, the nerve makes minute changes in its structure to continue normal functioning. The nerve becomes less sensitive to the chemical's effect, creating the need for an increased dosage to achieve the same effect (Doweiko, 1999).

Withdrawal refers to a specific set of symptoms that occur when use of the drug is discontinued—that is, withdrawn from the central nervous system. The particular nature of the withdrawal is contingent on the class or type of drug being taken, the length of time taken, the amount of the chemical taken, and the health of the individual.

Each class or type of drugs produces certain physical withdrawal symptoms. As the nerves endeavor to readapt to their original state of functioning and the body learns to function again without the chemical, the person experiences the physical symptoms of withdrawal. This *withdrawal syndrome,* also with criteria in the DSM-IV, is strong evidence of dependence or addiction.

It is important to see drug use, misuse, abuse, and addiction as a continuum of behavior. Although this will make assessment and diagnosis more difficult, it will also result in more effective treatment for the individual. An either/or diagnosis may lead to a generalized treatment plan that may be ineffective and usually meets the needs of only the most chronic substance abusers (Lewis, Dana, & Blevins, 1994).

A continuum model does not imply progression of drug use. It *does* imply that some users may progress but that others may fixate at a particular position on the continuum. This position may, in fact, be problematic for the client but not at a level that could be clinically diagnosed as "abuse" or "dependence."

Looking at substance use on a continuum allows the counselor to design individualized treatment plans. An adolescent who begins to use drugs may need only facilitation in good decision-making skills. An adult who is abusing a substance to cope with a recent loss may need facilitation in improvement of coping skills as well as support in a new life stage. These individuals need significantly different clinical intervention than do longtime, daily users who have developed a tolerance to a particular drug.

Treatment Settings and Modalities: Chapters 5, 6, and 7

Treatment settings ranging from outpatient care to long-term residential care are discussed in detail in Chapter 5. Settings include halfway houses where clients remain for approximately 3 to 6 months and therapeutic communities where individuals may live for 2 years or longer. As in all areas of health care, the type and length of treatment available is impacted by both managed health care for individuals with insurance and the continual decrease in federal money available for subsidized programs for uninsured individuals.

Multiple factors are necessary to assess the type of treatment setting that will produce the best treatment results for an individual. Familiarity with the assessment instruments discussed in Chapter 4 will enable the clinician to make a practiced and professional evaluation of the client's needs. The client's familial and social environment needs also to be assessed. Many practitioners in the field believe that the best method of explaining the etiology as well as devising a treatment strategy is the biopsychosocial (familial) model. Therefore, in assessing the client's needs, not only an individual assessment but also an assessment of the individual's support systems need to be completed. These support systems include but are not limited to the family, the school, the church, the workplace, and social relationships.

Treatment modalities are presented in Chapters 6 and 7. Chapter 6 discusses individual treatment issues. Intervention techniques and cautions are given, as are individual and group therapy techniques. Chapter 7 focuses on the systemic view of working with substance-abusing clients. Although family therapy and the addictions field have long been at odds, the use of the systemic approach appears to be effective in creating change not only in the current family but also in generations to come.

In discussing individual, group and family treatment modalities in Chapters 6 and 7, the author develops the treatment alternatives based on the belief that abuse/addiction is a result of many complicated factors in an individual's life. Therefore, to facilitate lasting changes, it is necessary to therapeutically engage not only the individual but also the existing systems in which the individual exists. It is also necessary to help the individual develop new, supportive systems outside the context of the client's drug-related social system.

Substance Abuse in Diverse Populations and Cultures: Chapters 8 and 9

Chapters 8 and 9 discuss assessment of individuals from diverse cultures and selected populations. Social and familial as well as personal characteristics that impact treatment are outlined. The multivariate dimensions that these facets add to the equation of assessment, diagnosis, and treatment planning create a kaleidoscope of information and consequences.

Other Issues in Substance Abuse: Chapters 10, 11, and 12

Chapter 10 discusses an important component of recovery: relapse prevention. Models of relapse planning and control are discussed along with behavioral, psychological, and emotional indicators of relapse. This aspect in treatment planning is often neglected but must be addressed carefully to maintain clean and sober living.

Prevention has become an essential component in the substance abuse field. Chapter 11 offers a broad introduction to the foundational terms, concepts, and currently accepted approaches to the ATOD prevention field. An effective prevention model and necessary resource information are presented.

Research in the area of substance abuse is presented in Chapter 12. Much of the research on which treatment planning has continued to be based was completed on an adult white male population in public treatment facilities in the mid-1970s to 1980s. This makes the assumptions that white male behavior can be generalized to all other individuals and that those people in treatment represented a sampling of the general population. Certainly these two design flaws are a cause of concern. It is of interest to note, also, that the research failed to differentiate between abuse and dependence (Peele, 1991). Another important factor omitted from the research is examination of individuals who have abused or been dependent on chemicals and have stopped using drugs without treatment intervention. These individuals might provide valuable insight into the process of recovery. Based on these observations, it would appear that many of our prevailing assumptions concerning etiology, assessment, diagnosis, and treatment of substance abuse/dependency are flawed.

The need to consider cultural and gender norms within the assessment process is an imperative. These factors effect the client's development of the problem as well as recovery issues such as access to services, likelihood of completing treatment, and ability to maintain long-term recovery (Lewis, Dana & Blevins, 1994). The context of society, the media, and the family must also be considered in assessment of a client (Stevens-Smith, 1994). It is obvious from these facts that research on diverse populations is desperately needed. There is a dearth of research on women, children, adolescents, and the elderly, as well as research that addresses differentiation of type of drug used and frequency of use.

Research also indicates that treatment methods in the area of substance abuse have been slow to change. Traditional treatment methods such as Alcoholics Anonymous, alcoholism education, confrontation, group therapy, individual counseling, and medications such as Antabuse, which creates a physical reaction (fever, vomiting, etc.) if one drinks, continue to be the norm in treatment programs.

The recent research in the genetics of addiction are fascinating and certainly an adjunct to working with this population of clients. Although this research also has its limitations, it has given us extensive physiological knowledge of the effect of drugs on the CNS.

OTHER ISSUES RELATED TO SUBSTANCE ABUSE

HIV/AIDS, Sexuality, and Drug Use

We would be remiss if we did not discuss the related higher incidence of HIV infection among drug users. Of the approximately 270,000 reported live AIDS cases in the United States at the end of 1997, about 10% are intravenous (IV) drug users. Adding to this figure their spouses, sexual partners, and/or their children might increase the number exposed through IV drug use to about one-third (Centers for Disease Control and Prevention, 1993, 1997). The use of crack appears to be associated with increased sexual activity, not only by women but by men as well, and crack use is common among all types of drug users including needle users. Obviously, this increase in sexual activity creates a greater risk for HIV infection. Studies also indicated that female drug users are involved not only in property crime and drug dealing but also in prostitution to support their habit (Inciardi, Lockwood, & Pottieger, 1991; Siegal et al., 1992). In the context of HIV infection, prostitution and drug use take on a particularly lethal significance. Because of the effects of drug use on the brain, drug use inhibits the ability of the individual to make rational decisions. Some drugs lower our inhibitions and give the illusion of increasing sexual desire. Because this combination of drugs and sexuality can be lethal, some information concerning sexuality and drug use seems appropriate.

Numerous factors may affect the sexual arousal process of individuals using drugs. Some of these are the same factors used to discuss drug effects on an individual. These include (a) the specific drug being used, (b) the specific amount of drug in the body and bloodstream, (c) body size, (d) food intake, (e) frequency and duration of use, (f) expectation of effect, and (g) potential interactions of drugs in the body. Given these factors, it is apparent that determining the effect of the drug on sexual desire, performance, or satisfaction is difficult. Although research consistently shows that chemical use is likely to interfere with performance and satisfaction if not desire, the myth continues that one or another drug is an aphrodisiac, a substance that enhances sexual pleasure and/or performance.

Alcohol

As early as Shakespeare's time, the observation that alcohol "provokes the desire but . . . takes away the performance" (*Macbeth,* act 2, scene 3) had been made. Alcohol is a disinhibitor, and low doses reduce anxiety and fear. In this case, sexual excitement may increase (Flatto, 1990). With lower anxiety and heightened sexual excitement, individuals tend to engage in sexual activities at a higher rate when intoxicated. Because of this disinhibiting effect, individuals also tend to engage in unsafe sex more frequently when intoxicated than when not intoxicated. This is particularly problematic in the adolescent population, who may be experimenting with both drugs and sex. Research also indicates that this experimentation is happening more frequently at the preadolescent age.

But in moderate to high doses, alcohol interferes with desire, performance, and satisfaction (Gold, 1988). Tests show that serum testosterone levels in males decrease as alcohol levels increase (Gold, 1987). Chronic use of alcohol results in a consistently low testosterone level (Flatto, 1990; Gold, 1988), nerve damage to the extremities (including the penis), and possible atrophy of the testicles (Geller, 1991). Male alcoholics also seem to experience a disruption of spinal cord nerves involved in penile erection.

Women who drink have lowered levels of vaginal vasocongestion, which will inhibit sexual desire and performance (Flatto, 1990). Chronic female alcoholics also experience menstrual disturbances, infertility, and a loss of secondary sexual characteristics, such as body and facial hair, bone-muscle density, body form, and voice pitch (Geller, 1991).

Amphetamines and Cocaine

Both of these drugs have a reputation as aphrodisiacs. Kolodny (1985) suggests that they may be mistaken for aphrodisiacs because they produce a physiological response similar to sexual excitement (increased blood pressure, increased heart rate, and an increase in blood flow to the genitals). Additionally, they bring about a feeling of well-being. It is also possible that CNS stimulators might increase compulsive sexual behaviors such as masturbation, sadism, exhibitionism, and possible mutilation of the penis (Lieberman, 1988). Because of the manner in which cocaine affects the brain's pleasure center, cocaine can intensify sexual thoughts, feelings, and fantasies, and "[m]any users experience increased sexual desire, prolonged sexual endurance, and markedly reduced inhibitions when high on cocaine" (Washton, 1989, p. 34).

Female cocaine users may develop a condition known as *anorgasmia,* the inhibition of orgasm. It is also known that some women or their partners rub cocaine on the clitoris prior to intercourse, believing that this will enhance the woman's pleasure. Conversely, cocaine is rubbed on the penis for the opposite effect, to reduce responsiveness. Since cocaine is a local anesthetic, it would seem apparent that it would function to reduce responsiveness, not to increase pleasure. Therefore, the user's expectation plays a significant role in the outcome or effect.

Marijuana

Marijuana alters the individual's perceptions, and it is believed that the individual expectations or subjective perception of the drug's effects is of greater consequence than the actual physiological effects. Another explanation is that marijuana, like alcohol, is a disinhibitor. Sexual feelings normally inhibited may be experienced with the use of the drug. However, physiological problems also result with marijuana use. Males who use it on a daily basis report erectile problems, lowered testosterone levels, and a disruption of normal sperm production. For females, prolonged use may result in abnormal menstruation and/or failure to ovulate (Mayo Clinic Letter, 1989). Female marijuana users report vaginal dryness, which may cause pain with intercourse as well as disruption of the menstrual cycle and egg production (Kolodny (1985).

Amyl Nitrate

Amyl nitrate is a prescription drug used to reduce the pain of angina pectoris (chest pain indicating heart disease). It is a quick-acting (30 seconds in some cases) drug used to cause the blood vessels to the heart to dilate for approximately 5 minutes. It has also been used at orgasm to prolong the moment, perhaps by altering the individual's perception of time. It is used frequently in the homosexual population (Masters,

Johnson, & Kolodny, 1986). The side effects are nausea, vomiting, headache, and a loss of consciousness. Overuse may result in nitrate poisoning (Lieberman, 1988).

Process Addictions

Another area related to substance abuse that should be addressed is the issue of "process addictions" (Donovan, 1988; McGurrin, 1994; Miller & Rollnick, 1991; Zweben, 1987). Process addiction refers to eating disorders, gambling, sexuality, shopping, working, and/or any other process (or behavior) in which one's behavior fits the criteria for "dependence." Although there may be some differences in each of these behavioral manifestations, the similarity of behaviors leads many in the field to address these issues as abuse and dependency issues. A great deal of evidence also suggests that individuals who have these process addictions come from families with a background of substance abuse and/or have a dual diagnosis of substance abuse/dependency with their process addiction (Carlton & Manowitz, 1988; McGurrin, 1994; Ramirez, McCormick, Russo, & Taber, 1984)

The prevalence of eating disorders has increased by epidemic proportions. Recent studies show that 1% of all adolescent girls develop anorexia nervosa and 2% to 3% develop bulimia nervosa (National Institute of Mental Health [NIMH], 1996). The obvious commonalties of eating disorders with other dependent behaviors is the compulsive behavior, the sense of powerlessness, the obsessive thought of food, and the learned ability to avoid feeling through the abuse of food (NIMH, 1996). Bulimics also describe having blackouts during their purging episodes. One major dissimilarity between an eating disorder and a substance abuse problem, of course, is that food is necessary to survive. Treatment, therefore, must be directed toward management of the problem, not abstinence.

Pathological gambling is another process disorder that has much in common with substance dependency. Individuals cannot resist the urge to wager money. The process is chronic and progressive, resulting in unmanageable debt and loss of friends, family, and possibly work. Both eating disorder individuals and pathological gamblers have a high degree of denial as a symptom of the problem.

Although this book focuses on substance abuse and dependence, psychotherapists today must broaden the lens of abuse and dependence to include processes or behaviors other than those involving substances. In assessment, it is clear that examining the possibility of cross-dependence is appropriate. In treatment, the substance abuse/dependency issue or the process issues may only be one component of the problem that must be addressed.

CONCLUSION

We have endeavored to organize the material in this text in a manner that presents a logical progression of knowledge about substance abuse and counseling. As a supplement to the knowledge base, we have incorporated the following three brief cases throughout the book to illustrate concepts discussed in each clinical chapter. The cases assist in understanding the process of assessment and diagnosis, treatment, and relapse prevention planning. Since a "live" case was not an option, the written cases will allow you to integrate the many concepts presented in the text.

CASE 1	Sandy and Pam

Sandy, age 42, and Pam, age 23, came into counseling to work on their relationship as well as their relationships with men. Sandy is Pam's mother. They have noticed patterns in their relationships that are similar to each other.

History

Sandy was the child of two alcoholic parents and the middle child. She took on the role of the rebellious child from an early age, drinking, sneaking out of the house, and finally getting pregnant at 18. She married Joe, the baby's father who was also an alcoholic and a violent man. She had two children: Pam and Henry. Henry is 2 years younger than Pam. When Pam was 5 years of age, her parents separated. Pam has had a distant and often disappointing relationship with her father since. Sandy admits to continuing to abuse alcohol in her adulthood. She remembers leaving Pam and her brother at home when she thought they were asleep so that she could go to bars. She brought home numerous men and would be sexual with them. Pam remembers hearing her mother in the bedroom with strangers and feeling frightened and alone. Sandy stopped drinking 2 months ago and has been trying to make amends to Pam. Pam voices forgiveness but finds herself in similar patterns.

Pam drinks "too much" but "not as much as a couple of years ago." She is living with a cocaine abuser, Sam, who also drinks and is emotionally abusive to her. She has used cocaine on "several occasions" with him but says she prefers to drink alcohol. Pam says she is tempted to "sleep around to get even" with Sam.

Pam is a bright young woman. She has a high school degree and 2 years of study at a community college. Her career counseling indicated that her best fit was in a people-oriented position, but she has been uninspired by any job she has held. Her job history is sporadic, holding jobs for an average of about 3 months as a waitress, receptionist, and bank teller. She then quits her job because she "hates it" and usually drinks heavily for several weeks before "getting it together" and finding another job.

Pam recently moved out of her boyfriend's house and back in with her mother. She is attempting to stay away from him, but he is pursuing her. She states that she "feels drawn to him and wants to make it work."

Pam believes her problem is her inability to commit to anything. Sandy says that this issue is her problem also, so that must be "where Pam learned it." Pam has recently begun to experience anxiety attacks that she attributes to her fear of being alone, stating that drinking helps relieve the fear.

CASE 2	The Smith Family

Joe and Jane Smith are in their mid-40s, with a stepdaughter, Sarah, age 13, and birth daughter, Karen, age 6. The family came into therapy due to conflict between Joe and Sarah.

Joe and Jane both admit to alcohol and cocaine abuse. Jane works as a bartender and receives free cocaine from her patrons. Joe worked as a bartender at the same place for almost 2 years but has changed professions. He is currently working as a contractor and is fairly successful.

Both have abused alcohol for approximately 23 years. Jane stopped drinking 5 years ago for health reasons and remained sober for 1 year before beginning to drink beer and then wine again. She states that she only drinks after the children are in bed and does not think that Sarah or Karen has ever seen her drunk. Joe drinks mostly beer every evening after work and smokes some "pot" on the weekends. He admits to drinking in front of the girls but not smoking pot until they were in bed or not around.

History

Jane reported a traumatic childhood with an alcoholic and abusive mother. Her father died before she was born. She recalls being sexually abused by an older brother around age 11 or 12 and then left home at age 13 and was placed in a foster home that was loving and supportive. Jane states that she is grateful for the 5 years she had in the foster home and that she has made peace with her mother.

Joe is the oldest of five children and had to parent the younger children from about age 10. Both parents drank "a lot," but Joe does not see them as alcoholics. He also left home at an early age and has no relationship with his parents or siblings.

Sarah is beginning to act out both at home and in the classroom. Her grades are dropping, and she is sneaking out of the house at night. She admits to yelling and screaming at Joe and turning up the stereo too loud "just to bug him." She also says he drinks too much, and when he is drunk, he tells her how much he loves her and how he hates that they fight all the time. Sarah says he yells at her, tells her to get out of his face, and calls her friends "dummies." Joe's response to Sarah's behavior (when sober) is to tighten the rules.

Karen is visibly sad. She is quiet and withdrawn from the family fights. She spends lots of time in her room playing with her stuffed animals.

Both Joe and Jane admit that being off drugs and alcohol would be difficult but express a desire to stop. The longest they have been able to stop (except for Jane's 1 year) was 9 days. When they started again, both drank to intoxication. Jane is somewhat reluctant to give up drugs altogether. She says she feel more socially upbeat when she "does a line or two" and, since she gets it free and has "no ill effects," sees no reason to abstain.

CASE 3	Leigh

Leigh, age 17, has been referred because of problems at school and a shoplifting charge. She admits to "smoking some dope" every now and then and having a drink or two with her friends. She is dressed in black with pierced ears, nose, and lip. Her appearance is disheveled and her hygiene poor. She appears to be overly thin.

History

Leigh's parents were divorced when she was 5 years old. She has a brother who is 5 years older. They used to live with their mother in the same town as their father. Leigh saw him frequently although she says he was "always busy with work" and she could never talk to him about much of anything. Leigh states that her mother was also busy but would "usually" stop and listen. She reports that her mother has a temper and is stressed all the time about money and work. She also reports that her mom and dad still fight about money and "us kids." She feels like she is in the middle and is always being asked to choose.

Leigh and her mother and brother recently moved to this area, and Leigh is at a new school this year. She is currently in 11th grade and has average grades. Her new friends are "different" from her old friends, but they "accept her for what she is."

REFERENCES

American Psychological Association. (1994). *Diagnostic and statistical manual* (4th ed.). Washington, DC: Author.

Angell, M., & Kassirer, J. P. (1994). Alcohol and other drugs—Toward a more rational and consistent policy. *New England Journal of Medicine, 331,* 537–539.

Berger, P. A., & Dunn, M. J. (1982). Substance induced and substance use disorders. In J. H.

Griest, J. W. Jefferson, & R. L. Spitzer (Eds.), *Treatment of mental disorders*. New York: Oxford University Press.

Carlton, P. L., & Manowitz, P. (1988). Physiological factors as determinants of pathological gambling. *Journal of Gambling Behavior, 3,* 274–285.

Centers for Disease Control and Prevention. (1993). *HIV/AIDS surveillance report, October, 1993*. Atlanta: Author.

Centers for Disease Control and Prevention. (1997). *HIV/AIDS surveillance report* (Vol. 5, no. 1). Atlanta: Author.

Cohen, M. S. (1995). HIV and sexually transmitted diseases. *Postgraduate Medicine, 98*(3), 52–64.

Donovan, D. M. (1988). Assessment of addictive behaviors: Implications of an emerging biopsychosocial model. In D. M. Donovan & G. A. Marlatt (Eds.), *Assessment of addictive behaviors* (pp. 3–48). New York: Guilford.

Doweiko, H. (1999). *Concepts of chemical dependency* (4th ed.). Pacific Grove: Brooks/Cole.

Evans, K., & Sullivan, J. M. (1990). *Dual diagnosis: Counseling the mentally ill substance abuser.* New York: Guilford.

Flatto, E. (1990). Alcohol and impotence from the doctor's casebook. *Nutrition Health Review, 53,* 19.

Franklin, J. (1987). *Molecules of the mind.* New York: Dell.

Geller, A. (1991). Sexual problems of the recovering alcoholic. *Medical Aspects of Human Sexuality, 25*(3), 60–63.

Gentillelo, L. M., Donovan, D. M., Dunn, C. W., & Rivera, F. P. (1995). Alcohol interventions in trauma centers: Current practice and future directions. *Journal of the American Medical Center, 274,* 1043–1048.

Gold, M. S. (1987). Sexual dysfunction challenges today's addictions clinicians. *Alcoholism & Addictions, 7*(6), 11.

Gold, M. S. (1988). Alcohol, drugs, and sexual dysfunction. *Alcoholism & Addictions, 9*(2), 13.

Greden, J. F., & Walters, A. (1992). Caffeine. In J. H. Lowenson, P. Ruiz, R. Milkman, & J. G. Langnod (Eds.), *Substance abuse: A comprehensive text* (pp. 357–370). Baltimore: Williams & Wilkins.

Hyman, S. E. (1996). Drug abuse and addiction. In E. Rubenstein & D. D. Federman (Eds.), *Scientific American medicine.* New York: Scientific American Press.

Hyman, S. E., & Cassem, N. H. (1995). Alcoholism. In E. Rubenstein & D. D. Federman (Eds.), *Scientific American medicine.* New York: Scientific American Press.

Inaba, D. S., & Cohen, W. (1991). *Uppers, downers, and all arounders: Physical and mental effects of drugs of abuse.* Ashland, OR: CNS Productions.

Inciardi, J. A., Lockwood, D. & Pottieger, A. E. (1991). Crack-dependent women and sexuality: Implications for STD acquisition and transmission. *Addiction & Recovery, 11*(4), 25–28.

Jaffe, J. H. (1990). Drug addiction and drug abuse. In A. G. Gilman, I. S. Goodman, T. W. Rall, & F. Murad (Eds.), *The pharmacological basis of therapeutics* (8th ed.). Upper Saddle River, NJ: Prentice Hall.

Kessler, R. C., Crum, R. M., Warner, L. A., Nelson, C. B., Schulenberg, J., & Anthony, J. C. (1997). Lifetime co-occurrence of DSM-III-R alcohol abuse and dependence with other psychiatric disorders in the National Comorbidity Survey. *Archives of General Psychiatry, 54,* 313–321.

Kinney, J., & Leaton, G. (1991). *Loosening the grip.* St. Louis: Mosby Year Book.

Kolodny, R. C. (1985). The clinical management of sexual problems in substance abusers. In T. E. Bratter & G. G. Forrest (Eds.), *Alcoholism and substance abuse: Strategies for clinical intervention* (pp. 475–489). New York: Free Press.

Lewis, J. A., Dana, R. Q., & Blevins, G. A. (1994). *Substance abuse counseling: An individualized approach.* Pacific Grove, CA: Brooks/Cole.

Lieberman, M. L. (1988). *The sexual pharmacy.* New York: New American Library.

Louis, G. C., & Yagyian, H. Z. (1980). *The cola wars.* New York: Everest House.

Martin, P. J., Enevoldson, T. P., & Humphrey, P. R. (1997). Causes of ischaemic stroke in the young. *Postgraduate Medical Journal, 73,* 8–16.

Masters, W. H., Johnson, V. E., & Kolodny, R. C. (1986). *Human sexual response.* Boston: Little, Brown.

Mayo Clinic Letter. (1989). *America's drug crisis.* Rochester, MN: Mayo Foundation for Medical Education and Research.

McGurrin, M. C. (1994). Diagnosis and treatment of pathological gambling. In J. A. Lewis (Ed.),

Addictions: Concepts and strategies for treatment (pp. 123-142). Gaithersburg, MD: Aspen.

Merriam-Webster. (1994). *Merriam-Webster dictionary*. Springfield, MA: Merriam-Webster.

Milkman, H., & S. Sunderwirth. (1987). *Cravings for ecstasy*. New York: Lexington.

Miller, W. R., & Rollnick, S. (1991). *Motivational interviewing: Preparing people to change addictive behavior.* New York: Guilford.

National Clearinghouse for Alcohol and Drug Information. (1996). *National expenditures for mental health, alcohol and other drug abuse treatment* [Online]. Available: http://www.health.org/mhaod/spending.htm.

National Foundation for Brain Research. (1992). *The cost of disorders of the brain*. Washington, DC: Author

National Institute of Mental Health. (1996). *Eating disorders*. Washington, DC: Author.

National Institute on Drug Abuse. (1991). *An economical approach to addressing the drug problem in America*. Rockville, MD: Author.

National Institute on Drug Abuse. (1997). *National household survey on drug abuse: Population estimates 1997*. Rockville, MD: Author.

National Institute on Drug Abuse. (1998, September). *Director's report: Epidemiology, etiology, and prevention* [On-line]. Available: http://165.112.78.61/DirReports?DirRep998/DirectorReport5

Peele, S. (1991). What we know about treating alcoholism and other addictions. *Harvard Mental Health Letter, 8*(6), 5–7.

Ramirez, L. F., McCormick, R. A., Russo, A. M., & Taber, J. I. (1984). Patterns of substance abuse in pathological gamblers undergoing treatment. *Addictive Behaviors, 8*, 425–428.

Ray, O. S., & Ksir, C. (1990). *Drugs, society, and human behavior*. St. Louis: Mosby.

Resnick, H. S. (1979). *It starts with people: Experiences in drug abuse prevention* (NIDA Publication No. ADM 79-590). Rockville, MD: National Institute on Drug Abuse.

Rice, D. P. (1993). The economic cost of alcohol abuse and alcohol dependence: 1990. *Alcohol Health & Research World, 17*(1), 10–11.

Scaros, L. P., Westra, S., & Barone, J. A. (1990). Illegal use of drugs: A current review. *U.S. Pharmacist, 15*(5), 17–39.

Schilit, R., & Gomberg, E. S. L. (1991). *Drugs and behavior: A sourcebook for the helping professions*. Newbury Park, CA: Sage.

Schuckit, M. A. (1989). *Drug and alcohol abuse: A clinical guide to diagnosis and treatment*. New York: Plenum.

Seever, M. H. (1968). Psychopharmacological elements of drug dependence. *Journal of the American Medical Association, 206*, 1263–1266.

Siegal, H. A., Carlson R. G., Falck, R., Forney, M. A., Wang, J., & Li, L. (1992). High-risk behaviors for transmission of syphilis and human immunodeficiency virus among crack cocaine-using women: A case study from the Midwest. *Sexually Transmitted Disease, 19*, 266–271.

Smith, J. P. (1970). Society and drugs: A short sketch. In P. H. Blachly (Ed.), *Drug abuse data and debate* (pp. 169-175). Springfield, IL: Thomas.

Spindler, K. (1994). *The man in the ice*. New York: Harmony.

Stacy, A. W., & Newcomb, M. D. (1995). Long-term social psychological influences on deviant attitudes and behavior. In H. B. Kaplan (Ed.), *Drugs, crime and other deviant adaptations*. New York: Plenum.

Stevens-Smith, P. (1994). Contextual issues in addiction. In J. A. Lewis (Ed.), *Addictions: Concepts and strategies for treatment* (pp. 11–21). Gaithersburg, MD: Aspen.

Substance Abuse and Mental Health Services Administration. (1993, September). *Estimates from the drug abuse warning network* (Advance Report No. 4). Rockville, MD: Department of Health and Human Services.

Terry, C. E., & Pellens, M. (1928). *The opium problem*. New York: Bureau of Social Hygiene.

Treatment of drug abuse and addiction—Part 1. (1995). *Harvard Mental Health Letter, 12*(2), 1–4.

Tresh, D. D., & Aronow, W. S. (1996). Smoking and coronary artery disease. *Clinics in Geriatric Medicine, 12*, 23–32.

Warner, L. A., Kessler, R. C., Hughes, M., Anthony, J. C., & Nelson, C. B. (1995). Prevalence and correlates of drug use and dependence in the United States. *Archives of General Psychiatry, 51,* 219, 229.

Washton, A. M. (1989). Cocaine abuse and compulsive sexuality. *Medical Aspects of Human Sexuality, 23*(12), 32–39.

White, R. J. (1993). Washington figuring out it has fought drug war on wrong fronts. *Minneapolis Star-Tribune, XI*(351), 23A.

World Health Organization Expert Committee on Drug Dependence. (1974). *Twentieth report* (Tech. Rep. Series No. 5[51]). Geneva: Author.

Zweben, J. E. (1987). Eating disorders and substance abuse. *Journal of Psychoactive Drugs, 19,* 181–192.

The Major Substances of Abuse and the Body

Sharon Erickson, Ph.D., R.N.

The causes of substance use, abuse, and addiction in U.S. society are complex, involving many factors. In the course of a typical month in a recent year, 13 million Americans used illicit drugs. Of these, 10 million used marijuana and 1.4 million used cocaine (Winick, 1997). Legal drug usage is also significant. More than 100 million adult Americans drink alcohol, with 12% to 13% of them meeting the criteria for alcohol abuse, dependence, or both (Substance Abuse and Mental Health Services Administration [SAMHSA], 1995). Even more significant, currently approximately 46 million people smoke in the United States (Doweiko, 1999), with more than 90% of this population considered dependent or "hooked" on the drug nicotine (National Institute on Drug Abuse, 1989; U.S. Department of Health and Human Services, 1990). This chapter will explore physical factors in addiction—the chemical makeup of commonly abused substances, the incidence of their use, their effects on the body and brain, addictive factors, and symptoms of withdrawal and overdose.

THE BRAIN

It has taken hundreds of millions of years for the human brain to evolve to its modern-day complex form. The center of human function and process, its convolutions and inner structures reveal traces of its evolutionary past

(Hooper & Teresi, 1986). The complexity of the brain and its interactions with all other systems of the body (i.e., endocrine, muscular, vascular) continue to challenge researchers as they attempt to find causes and more effective treatments for substance use, abuse, and addiction.

The brain is divided into two sections called *hemispheres*. The body of the corpus callosum forms the fissure dividing them and connects them with fibers. The left hemisphere is basically concerned with thinking and intellectual functions. It is the site of logic and verbal ability. The right hemisphere is the creative side and houses the intuitive and creative processes. It uses pictures, while the left hemisphere uses words (Andreasen, 1984). The sex of an individual, which is determined hormonally in the brain before birth, will influence the development, organization, and basic shape of the brain (Moir & Jessel, 1991).

The brain consists of three basic parts: the *hindbrain* contains the cerebellum and lower brain stem, the *midbrain,* which houses relay areas from the upper brain stem, and the *forebrain* (see Figures 2.1 and 2.2) (Hooper & Teresi, 1986). Although substance use affects the brain overall, the forebrain houses the mechanisms that most often interact with substances that can cross the blood-brain barrier. The forebrain includes the cerebral hemisphere and the rind or outer covering (about 2 millimeters thick) called the *cortex*. Most higher states of consciousness take place in the cortex, including thought, perception, motor function, sensory data processing, and vision. The brain also includes the *limbic system* and the structures of the *diencephalon*, which contains the *thalamus* and the *hypothalamus* (Fischbach, 1992; Hooper & Teresi, 1986). The limbic system lies just below and interconnects with the cortical area. It is involved in emotional behavior and long-term memory, while the hypothalamus regulates more basic, autonomic (primitive) functions such as hormonal activity, thirst, hunger, temperature, sex drive, and sleep.

The brain interfaces with all of these systems in a space about the size of a grapefruit. It accomplishes this through *neuronai* (nerve cell) networking (Cohen, 1988).

FIGURE 2.1   The human brain

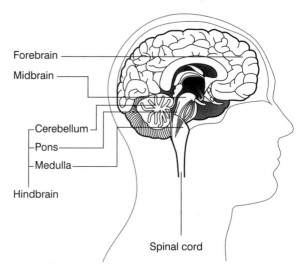

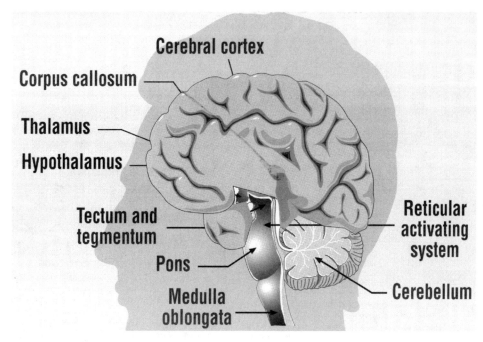

FIGURE 2.2   Cross section of the brain

From *Abnormal and Clinical Psychology, Series II* (Transparencies) by David Steele, 1996, Upper Saddle River, NJ: Prentice Hall.

The brain is composed of about 100 billion neurons (see Figure 2.3), and an astounding amount of structural variation and functional diversity can be found in brain cells (Fischbach, 1992; Shatz, 1992). About one-tenth of these neurons are nerve cells that have actual or potential links with tens of thousands of others. They compose cellular clusters that form highly specialized centers. These centers are interconnected by bundles of nerve fibers called *tracts*, which link up the different switchboards of the brain.

The tracts all conduct information in much the same way. Chemical messengers (molecules) called *neurotransmitters* are released by electrical impulses (action potentials) that reach the presynaptic membrane of a given synapse. These pathways can send thousands of electrochemical messages per second and yet work in harmony, because each cell in a tract responds like a complex, megamicroscopic information processor. It is this process of electrical "blipping" and chemical "dripping" that allows the brain to communicate. Newly sensed experiences (*imprints*) are sifted, rejected, or passed onto appropriate pathways. These imprints are matched to ones already encoded in the data banks directing conscious and unconscious feelings, thoughts, and actions. A bulk of this encoding is stored at an unconscious level.

Each neuron has a central body, from which wispy tendrils called *dendrites* appear to sprout at one end, and a long slender thread called an *axon* at the other. When stimulated, the axon and dendritic branches generate electrical impulses by the

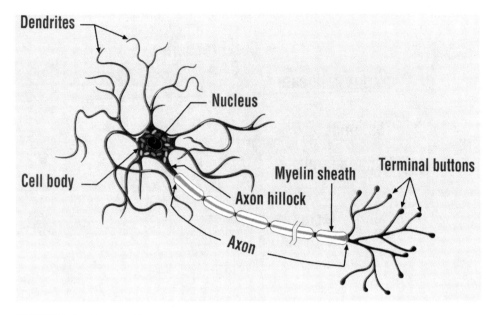

FIGURE 2.3   Nerve cell

From *Abnormal and Clinical Psychology, Series II* (Transparencies) by David Steele, 1996, Upper Saddle River, NJ: Prentice Hall.

exchange of electrically charged sodium and potassium atoms through ionic channels in the cellular membrane (Cohen, 1988; Hooper & Teresi, 1986). This creates a reversed polarity that allows the impulse to zoom down the axon at speeds up to 300 miles per hour.

A neuron's cell membrane can reverse its polarity from negative to positive and back again in one-thousandth of a second. A strongly stimulated neuron can easily fire 1,000 times per second. When the impulse reaches the button (*terminal*) at the end of the axon, it causes tiny sacs (*vesicles*) to fuse with the membrane (via calcium release) and discharge chemical molecules called (neuro-) *transmitters* and *peptides* (Cohen, 1988; Hooper & Teresi, 1986) (see Figure 2.3).

It is believed that most neurons contain multiple transmitters. The chief chemical messenger may be a neurotransmitter (amine/amino acid) but it acts in conjunction with a neuropeptide to modulate the transmission and/or a neurohormone to prolong the transmission (Cohen, 1988). There are several main neurotransmitters: *acetylcholine* (Ach), *dopamine* (DA), *norepinephrine* (NE), *epinephrine* (E), *serotonin* (5-HT), *histamine* (H), *gamma-amino-butyric acid* (GABA) as well as *glycine*, *glutamate*, *adenosine*, and *adenosine triphosphate* (Cohen, 1988) (see Table 2.1). These neurotransmitters discharge from the terminal of one neuron (presynaptic), cross a small gap called the *synapse*, and find their way into "receptor" sites on the adjoining neuron (postsynaptic) (see Figure 2.4). Each neurotransmitter, peptide, or hormone has a particular shape that allows it to fit into the appropriate receptor site, much like a key fitting into a lock. If the key fits the lock, it will turn on a message in the adjoin-

TABLE 2.1   Drugs related to neurotransmitters

Drug	Neurotransmitter
Alcohol	Gamma amine butyric acid (GABA), serotonin, met-enkephalin
Marijuana	Acetylcholine
Cocaine/amphetamines	Epinephrine (adrenaline), norepinephrine (noradrenaline), serotonin, dopamine, acetylcholine
Heroin	Endorphin, enkephalin, dopamine
Benzodiazepines	GABA, glycine
LSD	Acetylcholine
PCP	Dopamine, acetylcholine, alpha-endopsychosine
MDMA (ecstasy)	Serotonin, dopamine, adrenaline
Nicotine	Adrenaline, endorphin, acetylcholine
Caffeine	Dopamine, norepinephrine

ing neuron. The receptors exhibit a self-regulatory capacity, changing their sensitivity during excessive or infrequent use (Cohen, 1988). The classic neurotransmitters tend to have more than one receptor (Gilbert & Martin, 1978).

The neurotransmitter interaction functions for the well-being of the individual, insuring the basic survival of that organism. Survival is accomplished by the recall of memory imprints that have been stored in the neocortex of the brain. These survival skills become more sophisticated as the organism develops and uses them repeatedly in day-to-day functions. The human brain has many abilities. One of these is the ability to conceptualize and formulate future possibilities, including dangers. In early childhood, the brain forms pathways based on the raw data it receives from the environment. The mind wires up these pathways quickly so that it can avoid or survive potential dangers. For instance, if a child is repeatedly exposed to "fight or flight" situations, whether real or perceived, the association to this stimuli will cause the mind to strengthen developing excitatory pathways. This will allow the organism to be more vigilant and foster its survival.

Researchers have discovered that the feeling of pleasure is one of the most important emotions connected to survival. The feeling of pleasure is produced and regulated by a circuit of specialized nerve cells in a limbic structure called the *nucleus accumbens*. Dopamine-containing neurons relay pleasure messages through this part of the brain via a circuit that spans the brain stem, the limbic system, and the cerebral cortex (National Institutes of Health, 1996). Research scientists know this feeling of pleasure or reward is a strong biological force. If something elicits strong pleasure within the brain, it is wired so that its owner will develop behaviors that will reinforce this good feeling. Basic drives such as eating, sexual activity, and the need for power are activities that evoke rewards in the brain. We learn quickly to reproduce events that bring us pleasure, and such rewards become one of the brain's most powerful learning mechanisms (Siegel, 1989).

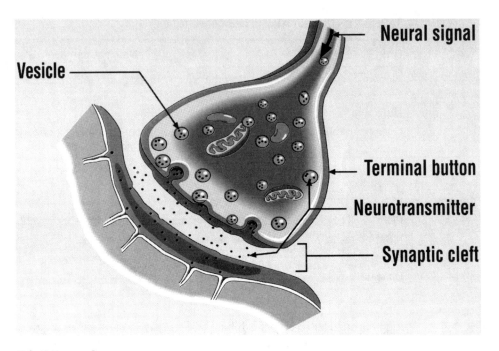

FIGURE 2.4 Synapse

From *Abnormal and Clinical Psychology, Series II* (Transparencies) by David Steele, 1996, Upper Saddle River, NJ: Prentice Hall.

Psychoactive Substances and the Brain

The brain has been the recipient of psychoactive substances allowing human beings to cope with both internal and external stressors for centuries. These substances have offered the user a variety of effects, including pain relief, pleasure, mystical insight, escape, relaxation, stimulation, and ecstasy, as well as a sense of social and spiritual connectedness (Siegel, 1989). It has been proposed that the pursuit of intoxication is as powerful a drive in human beings (and many animal species) as the innate survival drives of hunger, thirst, and sex (Siegel, 1989; Wise, 1988). A "barrier," known as the blood-brain barrier, acts to keep certain substances in the blood and away from brain cells. Although not well understood, a factor in the barrier is the nonpermeability of capillaries in the brain. Brain capillaries have no pores, preventing water-soluble molecules from passing through capillary walls. Only lipid-soluble substances can pass through the lipid capillary wall. The blood-brain barrier is not completely developed in humans until age 1 to 2 and can be damaged by head trauma or cerebral infection (Ray & Ksir, 1993).

Substances are considered psychoactive when they can cross the blood-brain barrier and create changes in the brain and, therefore, in the mind and behavior. The primary use of psychoactive substances is to change the neurochemistry of the brain and alter one's consciousness. Substances accomplish this by exciting, quieting, or distorting the chemical and electrical state (Milkman & Sunderwirth, 1986; Siegel, 1989). Substance addiction can include intoxicating substances such as caffeine, ethanol (ethyl alcohol), marijuana, crack cocaine, or heroin that produce rapid neuro-chemical shifts (8 seconds to 20 minutes) or nonintoxicating substances such as nicotine, caffeine, and refined carbohydrates.

Specific sites in the brain demonstrate a possible neurochemical basis for the ongoing use of substances (Esposito, Porrino, & Seeger, 1987; Wise, 1991). These sites include the *medial forebrain bundle* (MFB), the *ventral tegmental area* (VTA), the *nucleus accumbens*, the hypothalamus, and the *locus coeruleus* (LC).

The hypothalamus houses multiple nerve centers that are necessary for the main-tenance of life. Among them is the "pleasure center" that converges with the MFB as well as the nucleus accumbens and the VTA. There is a profuse convergence of cell bodies, axons, and synaptic terminals among these systems (Bozarth, 1987; Broekkamp, 1987; Khachaturian, Lewis, & Schafer, 1985; Mansour, Khachaturian, Lewis, Akil, & Watson, 1988). The MFB region has been associated with the posi-tive reinforcement associated with drugs of addiction by the release of dopamine (DA). Survival drives such as eating, drinking, copulation, and shelter produce a state of positive reinforcement in the brain. Likewise, it has been found that several categories of abusable substances have a *synergistic*, or enhancing, effect on the brain stimulation reward thresholds that involve DA systems (Gold, 1997). This includes all major drugs of abuse except some of the hallucinogenics (Gardner, 1997).

CONTROLLED SUBSTANCES SCHEDULES

In an effort to control the growing consumption of both the types and quantity of drugs that were being abused in the 1960s, the Comprehensive Drug Abuse Preven-tion and Control Act was passed in 1970. In it, the Drug Enforcement Agency (DEA) was established in the Department of Justice to enforce drug policy. Another of its provisions established a schedule of controlled substances that, by federal law, regulates the sale of certain drugs. They vary from low potential for abuse, with cur-rently accepted medical use (Schedule V), to those with a high potential for abuse and no currently acceptable medical use (Schedule I). Schedule V drugs include some over-the-counter medications, while Schedule I drugs are prohibited from medical and most research uses (Ray & Ksir, 1993) (see Table 2.2).

The remainder of the chapter will discuss specific classifications of abusable sub-stances. Substances in each classification with their properties, incidence of use, effects of the substance, and withdrawal symptoms will be presented. The chapter is summarized in Table 2.3, which begins on page 70.

DEPRESSANTS

Depressants of the central nervous system (CNS) include *ethanol, barbiturates, methaqualone, meprobamate*, and all *benzodiazepines*. At usual doses, they dampen CNS activity while displaying a weak analgesic effect. All drugs in this class can

TABLE 2.2   Summary of controlled substances schedules

Schedule	Criteria	Examples
Schedule I	a. High potential for abuse b. No currently acceptable medical use in treatment in the U.S. c. Lack of accepted safety for use under medical supervision	Heroin Marijuana LSD
Schedule II	a. High potential for abuse b. Currently accepted medical use c. Abuse may lead to severe psychological or physical dependence	Morphine Cocaine Injectable methamphetamine
Schedule III	a. Potential for abuse less than I and II b. Currently accepted medical use c. Abuse may lead to moderate physical dependence or high psychological dependence	Amphetamine Most barbiturates PCP
Schedule IV	a. Low potential for abuse relative to III b. Currently accepted medical use c. Abuse may lead to limited physical or psychological dependence relative to III	Barbital Chloral hydrate Paraldehyde
Schedule V	a. Low potential for abuse relative to IV b. Currently accepted medical use c. Abuse may lead to limited physical or psychological dependence relative to IV	Mixtures having small amounts of codeine or opium

Note: From *Drugs, Society, and Human Behavior,* by O. Ray and C. Ksir, 1993, St. Louis: Mosby–Year Book. Used with permission.

become physically addictive, can be lethal in overdose, and demonstrate a cross-tolerance and potentiation of one another. *Cross-tolerance* refers to the ability of one classification of drugs to produce a tolerance to the effects of another pharmacological classification, and *potentiation* to the ability of the combined action of some drugs used together to be greater than the sum of the effects of each drug being used alone. Depressants also have the ability to induce severe depressions as well as promote extreme anxiety during withdrawal (Radcliffe, Rush, Sites, & Cruse, 1985).

Alcohol

Ethyl alcohol (ethanol) is a clear liquid with a bitter taste. It can be used as an anesthetic, a poison, a foodstuff, an antiseptic, or a surface blood vessel dilator. It is an unstable CNS depressant while producing euphoria in some drinkers by activating the endorphin reward system within the brain (Doweiko, 1999). For many, alcohol becomes an addictive substance (Blum & Payne, 1991).

Incidence

Approximately 90% of adults in the United States have consumed alcohol at some time during their lives. Yearly per capita consumption peaked in 1980 with 2.76 gallons of pure alcohol consumed, falling 15% to 2.35 gallons in 1996 (Doweiko, 1999). However, to put these figures in perspective, many drink alcohol less than one time per week, leaving 50% of the alcohol to be consumed by only 10% of those who drink in this country (Doweiko, 1999; Goodwin & Gabrielli, 1997). The *National Household Survey on Drug Abuse,* in 1992, reported that 7.4% of Americans either abused (3.0%) or were dependent on (4.4%) alcohol (National Institute on Drug Abuse, 1999c). This reflected a reported drop of alcohol use from 76% in 1979 to 59% in 1992 among 18- to 25-year-olds and from 61% in 1979 to 50% in 1992 among adults over the age of 25 (National Institute on Drug Abuse, 1999c). However, alcohol use has climbed slightly since then (National Institute on Drug Abuse, 1999c).

Psychoactive Effects

Ethanol is a small organic molecule consisting of only two carbon atoms surrounded by hydrogen atoms, with a hydroxyl group attached to one of the carbons (CH_3-CH_2-OH). This molecular arrangement provides ethanol with water-soluble properties as well as lipid- (fat-) soluble properties (Valenzuela & Harris, 1997). As it passes the blood-brain barrier after ingestion and affects the cerebral cortex, most people feel their inhibitions quickly disappear and sense a more relaxed social attitude concerning their interactions with others. Although an individual may believe it to be so, experiments have proved that alcohol does not improve mental or physical capabilities (Liska, 1994). Individuals who continue to drink for an extended period of time (two to three drinks per hour for several hours) will disregard their own pain, exhibit poor judgment, and endanger their own or other's safety (Blum & Payne, 1991).

Alcohol, as a depressant, has a relaxing and disinhibiting effect. Many people erroneously assume that alcohol is a powerful aphrodisiac and a sexual stimulant. The assumption is based on observing people who appear to have a heightened sexual response when drinking (Liska, 1994). This reaction is due to the disinhibiting factor of ethyl alcohol and its immediate influence on the frontal lobes of the brain where the neurochemical mechanisms for exercising judgment are located.

Effects on the Body

One ounce of pure ethyl alcohol contains about 210 calories that can convert to energy at the cellular level but contains no nutrients to nourish the cell. It can pass through every tissue cluster in the brain and body if enough is consumed. Immediately after drinking, the mouth and esophagus begins to absorb small amounts via the mucous membranes. The stomach will rapidly assimilate about one-quarter of a dose, followed by complete absorption through the walls of the small intestine within 20 to 30 minutes (Liska, 1994).

The cardiovascular system is affected by low doses of alcohol through the dilation of peripheral blood vessels, while severe alcohol intoxication will create a depression of the entire cardiovascular system. Alcohol irritates the gastrointestinal tract through direct contact, as well as by stimulating the secretion of stomach acid and pepsin, which can cause gastritis and injury to the mucous membranes of the stomach lining. The presence of food can modify these effects to some extent and also slows the absorption rate of alcohol. Because alcohol is a diuretic, it overstimulates the production of urine in the kidneys (Liska, 1994).

The liver is the primary organ of alcohol detoxification. This 3-pound organ is the central filter for the blood and is the site of 90% of alcohol metabolism. The major pathway for such conversion involves the enzyme *alcohol dehydrogenase* and occurs in two phases in the liver. The first phase produces the metabolite *acetaldehyde*, and the second converts acetaldehyde to *acetic acid*. With continued heavy intake of alcohol, the liver cells begin to accumulate fatty deposits that destroy the cells and produce scarring called *cirrhosis*. This disease occurs in, and is fatal to, about 10% of chronic alcoholic patients (Liska, 1994; National Institute on Alcohol Abuse and Alcoholism, 1990).

Nearly every organ in the body is affected by heavy use of alcohol. Gastritis, diarrhea, and gastric ulcers are commonly associated with heavy drinking. A single heavy drinking episode can cause the pancreas to hemorrhage. The consumption of large amounts of alcohol can depress the respiratory center in the medulla, causing death (Doweiko, 1999). Alcohol can be deadly for individuals with epilepsy because it can promote convulsive seizures due to a hyperexcitable rebound condition in the brain after drinking has ceased (Liska, 1994).

Strong evidence indicates links between alcohol and cancers that occur in the upper digestive tract, respiratory system, mouth, pharynx, larynx, esophagus, and liver, and there is evidence suggesting a link between alcohol and cancer of the pancreas, stomach, large intestine, rectum, and breast (Doweiko, 1999). Recent studies suggest that alcohol is typically ingested with cocarcinogens such as tobacco, accounting for 3% of the cancer deaths that occur in the United States annually (Liska, 1994).

Besides liver damage (cirrhosis), alcoholics may develop a pathology of the nervous system due to vitamin deficiencies, as well as experience neurological complications such as the Wernicke-Korsakoff syndrome. This chronic brain syndrome is the result of thiamin deficiency from poor absorption, metabolism, and storage of the vitamin in the prolonged presence of alcohol, as well as poor diet while drinking (Goodwin & Gabrielli, 1997). It has as its most striking feature a dementia characterized by permanent short-term memory loss coupled with the telling of "fanciful" tales in an effort to fill in blanks in the memory (confabulation) (Goodwin & Gabrielli, 1997).

Tolerance and Dependence

In the presence of repeated drinking, tolerance to the effects of alcohol begins as the body adapts to try to maintain normal function in the continual presence of the foreign chemical. The liver becomes more efficient in detoxifying alcohol, the cells of the brain become less and less sensitive to the intoxicating effects of the chemical, and the chronic drinker exhibits fewer of the behavioral effects of intoxication. However, even in the presence of tolerance, the lethal dose of alcohol does not change (Doweiko, 1999).

Risk of dependence on alcohol is low to moderate, both physically and psychologically. The etiology is complicated and appears to be affected by such factors as genetics, biological changes, brain reward systems, and stress relief mechanisms (see Chapter 3). It is suggested that the younger the onset of drinking, the greater the chance of that person developing a clinically defined alcohol disorder (National Institute on Drug Abuse, 1999c).

Withdrawal

The acute withdrawal syndrome generally appears within 12 to 72 hours after drinking has subsided and lasts from 5 to 7 days. During this time, the alcoholic can experience symptoms of profuse sweating, shakes, anxiety, nausea, diarrhea, transitory hallucinations, and/or general disorientation. This syndrome is often referred to as *delirium tremens* (DTs), although this term more accurately describes certain characteristics of the syndrome. DTs are often associated with concurrent medical conditions that may have been induced by chronic heavy alcohol use accompanied by poor diet (Goodwin & Gabrielli, 1997). In severe cases, the alcoholic may suffer seizures and cardiovascular collapse.

Toxic and Lethal Effects

Coma usually occurs at blood alcohol concentrations (BACs) of 0.40%, and it can be lethal in higher concentrations by depressing the respiratory center in the medulla (Doweiko, 1999).

Gender Differences

Early studies on the effects of alcohol had only men as subjects, assuming that their findings could be generalized to women. Since the 1970s and 1980s, it has been found that, under standard conditions, BACs in women reach higher levels, for several reasons. First, men have a greater average body water content (65% ± 2%) than women (51% ± 2%). Since alcohol is absorbed into total body water, a standard dose of alcohol will be more concentrated in women (Blume, 1997). Second, women have a lower level of gastric alcohol dehydrogenase (ADH), thus metabolizing only about a quarter as much alcohol as men under standard conditions (Blume, 1997). A 1990 study by Frizza et al. (Blume, 1997) further found that, while alcoholics of both sexes had less gastric ADH, the level in alcoholic women was extremely low, and virtually all of the alcohol consumed was absorbed.

Fetal Alcohol Syndrome

Alcohol ingested during pregnancy easily passes through the placental barrier and can result in fetal alcohol syndrome (FAS). Doctors first recognized and reported

FAS in 1973 as a pattern of birth defects emerged in children born to alcoholic mothers (Jones, Smith, & Ulleland, 1973). Since that time, numerous studies have established ethanol as a *teratogenic* agent, producing defects in utero. FAS is characterized by distinct symptoms that can generally be observed in the newborn. The child will exhibit fetal growth retardation and is at high risk to suffer craniofacial deformities, incur central nervous system damage, and have major organ malformations. Eighty-five percent will exhibit mental retardation (Finnegan & Kandall, 1997). The symptoms can range from gross *morphological* defects (defects to the structure or form of the body) to more subtle cognitive-behavioral problems. FAS is one of the leading causes of mental retardation in newborns, with a societal cost of more than $320 million annually in the United States (Finnegan & Kandall, 1997). Despite this growing body of evidence, FAS, as a syndrome caused by alcohol consumption in the mother, remains controversial, largely because alcoholic women often smoke heavily, are malnourished, and have unhealthy lifestyles. The effect of these factors has not yet been conclusively separated from the possible effects of alcohol (Goodwin & Gabrielli, 1997).

Barbiturates

Until recently, barbiturates were considered primary drugs of abuse by "street people." Currently, benzodiazepines (e.g., Halcion, Librium, Valium, Xanax, Rohypnol) have largely replaced short-acting barbiturates in therapeutic medicine, as well as on the streets. Furthermore, controls have been placed on the availability of barbiturates (Wesson, Smith, Ling, & Seymour, 1997), listing them as II, III, or IV on the DEA Controlled Substances Schedule. They are still present in today's society, however, and deserve a cursory look.

Incidence

From 1950 to 1970, barbiturates were second only to alcohol as drugs of abuse. Although abuse of barbiturates has decreased significantly since benzodiazepines have largely replaced them in medical use for insomnia and anxiety, certain populations continue to abuse them. Among individuals 40 and older, subgroups became addicted when they were younger, sometimes on prescribed barbiturates. And the effects of low-level heroin have, for years, been bolstered by barbiturates (Wesson et al., 1997).

Psychoactive Effects

Barbiturates are used medically for their anesthetic, sedative, hypnotic, and anticonvulsant effects. They are short-acting sedative-hypnotics that can be administered as recreational drugs orally or by injection to produce an intoxication similar to that of alcohol. This intoxicated state produces "disinhibition," elevated mood, a reduction of negative feelings and negative self-concept, and an increase in energy and confidence. The euphoric mood can shift quite suddenly to sadness. Someone who is intoxicated on barbiturates may possess an unsteady gait, slurred speech, eye twitching, and exercise poor judgment (Wesson et al., 1997).

The most commonly used barbiturates include thiopental (sodium pentothal), amobarbital (Amytal), pentobarbital (Nembutal), secobarbital (Seconal), amobarbital in combination with secobarbital (Tuinal), butabarbital (Butisol), and phenobarbital (Luminal). On the street, the drug may be assigned a name that correlates with the color of the capsule such as yellow jackets (Nembutal), red birds (Seconal), or rainbows (Tuinal).

Barbiturates are lipid-soluble compounds, which allows them to pass the blood-brain barrier. They are also capable of passing the placental barrier and affecting the fetus. Barbiturates depress the CNS and inhibit neuronal activity, ranging from anxiety reduction to coma. This depressant action is achieved by potentiation of GABA-ergic transmission, which creates a diminished calcium ionic channel action resulting in a decreased state of neurotransmitters. Barbiturates also reverse the action of glutamate, which induces depolarization and adds to the CNS depression. Barbiturates and any of the other CNS depressants, such as narcotic-based analgesics, benzodiazepines, or alcohol (Cohen, 1988), potentiate the effects of each other, causing dangerous combinations or even death. In potentiation, each drug interferes with the biotransformation of the other chemical by the liver, allowing for the toxic effects of each drug to be at a higher level than expected from each drug alone (Doweiko, 1999).

Nonbarbiturate Sedative-Hypnotics

Other sedative-hypnotics that have an abuse potential similar to barbiturates include Quaalude, Chloral Hydrate, and meprobamate. Methaqualone (Quaalude) is chemically distinct from the barbiturates but is a prime example of drug approved by the Food and Drug Administration (FDA) that became a severe social hazard. Through its depression of the CNS, a dramatic reduction in heart rate, respiration, and muscular coordination results from its use (Liska, 1994).

Tolerance and Dependence

Like all sedative-hypnotic drugs, barbiturates can create tolerance in the user with a single dose. Although tolerance to barbiturates builds quickly, it is not uniform to all of its actions. For example, those taking a barbiturate for control of epileptic seizures may develop tolerance to its sedative effects but not to the anticonvulsant effect. Risk of both physical and psychological dependence on barbiturates is high to moderate.

Withdrawal

Withdrawal symptoms generally begin 12 to 24 hours after the last dose and peak in intensity between 24 and 72 hours. These symptoms include anxiety, tremors, nightmares, insomnia, anorexia, nausea, vomiting, delirium, and seizures. Death from overdose can occur owing to respiratory arrest when centers of the brain that control oxygen intake are severely depressed (Doweiko, 1999).

Benzodiazepines

Benzodiazepines are the most widely prescribed group of drugs in the treatment of anxiety and insomnia. They are considered less lethal than the barbiturates unless used in combination with other drugs such as alcohol and have better anxiety specificity than barbiturates (Preston, O'Neal, & Talaga, 1997). Many are capable of achieving a daytime anxiolytic response without excessive drowsiness. However, drugs from the benzodiazepine family interfere with the normal sleep cycle, and upon withdrawal after prolonged use, the patient may experience rapid eye movement (REM) rebound, with a greatly increased need for REM sleep, often accompanied by vivid, frightening dreams (Preston et al., 1997).

Incidence

The incidence of benzodiazepine abuse depends partly on the definition of substance abuse used. If the criterion is any nonmedical use, then benzodiazepine abuse is common. If, however, the DSM-IV criterion is used, the incidence of abuse is much lower (Wesson et al., 1997). Benzodiazepines are not primary drugs of abuse; they are rarely used to induce intoxication. Although incidence of abuse is relatively low when compared to their availability, certain subgroups, such as those on methadone maintenance, experience significant problems (Wesson et al., 1997).

Dependency

The use and abuse of benzodiazepines continues to generate controversy. As a result, the American Psychiatric Association reviewed the issue of benzodiazepine dependency and published its findings in 1991 (Wesson et al., 1997). Although risks to both physical and psychological dependency appear to be low when compared to other substances, benzodiazepine dependency can result from prolonged use (over 6 months) in several scenarios: (a) self-administration to produce intoxication, (b) therapeutic doses prescribed by a doctor over a long period of time that eventually develops into physical dependency, (c) patients' escalating their prescribed dosage, and (d) self-administration by heroin or cocaine addicts to treat symptoms of withdrawal or toxicity (Wesson et al., 1997).

Psychoactive Effects

There are more than a dozen varieties of benzodiazepines. The most notorious and controversial are diazepam (Valium), chlordiazepoxide (Librium), and triazolam (Halcion). Alprazolam (Xanax) has been found very effective in the treatment of panic attacks (Nightingale, 1990). Benzodiazepines are considered very safe and effective in the short-term treatment of anxiety, regardless of the cause (Preston et al., 1997). Long-term use, however, requires careful monitoring by a physician to prevent physical dependency.

Effects on the Body

Gamma-aminobutyric acid (GABA) is considered the most important inhibitory neurotransmitter in the brain. It is thought that benzodiazapines make the receptor site on the neuron more sensitive to GABA by binding to one of the GABA receptor sites and also to a chloride channel on the neuron surface (Doweiko, 1999). This inhibitory action produces anxiolytic, anticonvulsant, and sedative effects, useful in treating seizures, short-term insomnia, preoperative sedation and anesthesia, and anxiety disorders (Wesson et al., 1997).

The benzodiazepines are lipid-soluble and absorbed into the gastrointestinal tract after oral ingestion. They can also pass the blood-brain barrier and the placental barrier. Peak effects from use occur within 2 to 4 hours. By virtue of their specific recognition sites, the benzodiazepines act by potentiating the action of GABA, which increases neural inhibition.

Withdrawal

Withdrawal symptoms from low dosages of benzodiazepines can allow symptom reemergence (a return of the symptoms such as anxiety or panic attacks, for which the benzodiazepines were originally prescribed). For others, including those on higher doses, withdrawal symptoms may include anxiety, mood instability, sleep disturbance, agitated depression, seizures, or schizophrenia. It is important for treatment to differentiate between symptom reemergence and withdrawal symptoms. Over time, withdrawal symptoms gradually subside, while those of reemergence do not (Wesson et al., 1997). Because of the long half-life of some of these drugs, withdrawal symptoms may persist for weeks beyond the last dose (Doweiko, 1999).

Benzodiazepines are rarely used alone to induce intoxication; they are most commonly used for reduction of anxiety or sleep induction. On the street, they are often self-administered by drug addicts to reduce symptoms of withdrawal from heroin, alcohol, and other drugs or to lessen the side effects of cocaine or methamphetamine intoxication. Addicts also may use benzodiazepines to enhance the effects of heroin, alcohol, or marijuana (Wesson et al., 1997).

Opiates

Opium is derived from the poppy flower (*Papaver sominiferum*). It possesses a variety of pharmacological activities that have been studied by scientists for years (Simon, 1997). The main active ingredient is *morphine alkaloid*, which is widely used because it is the most effective and most powerful painkiller (analgesic) available (Gitlin, 1996). Other effects and signs of usage include euphoria, drowsiness, constricted pupils, nausea, possible respiratory distress, coma, and death. Other derivatives include heroin, codeine, hydromorphone (Dilaudid), hydrocodone (Hycodan), oxymorphone (Numorphan), and oxycodone (Percodan), as well as a number of synthetic medical compounds, including mesiridine (Demerol), methadone (Dolophine), fetanyl (Sublimaze), and Propoxyphene (Darvon). At least 20 drugs are available in the United States that have opioid actions (Cohen, 1998; Jaffe, 1992), and they may differ in the way they are absorbed, metabolized, and eliminated from the body. According to some sources, the most abused opioid substance is heroin (Liska, 1994). Opioids are listed on the DEA Controlled Substance Schedule as Schedule I (heroin) to Schedule II, III, and IV (codeine, morphine, and methadone), depending on the substance.

Incidence

A 1991 survey reported that 1.3% of the American population has tried heroin (American Psychiatric Association [APA], 1994). It appears to be gaining in popularity again, especially among the young, who may be lured by inexpensive, high-purity heroin that can be sniffed or smoked instead of injected, and among the affluent. The 1996 *National Household Survey on Drug Abuse* reported an estimated 141,000 new heroin users in 1995, reflecting an increasing trend since 1992 (National Institute on Drug Abuse, 1999e). The 1996 Drug Abuse Warning Network (DAWN) reported that 14% of drug-related emergency episodes in 21 metropolitan areas involved heroin, an increase of 64% from the time period of 1988 to 1994. NIDA's Community Epidemiology Work Group reported in December 1996 that heroin was the primary drug of abuse related to drug abuse treatment admissions in Newark, San Francisco, Los Angeles, and Boston, and it ranked a close second to cocaine in New York and Seattle (National Institute on Drug Abuse, 1999e).

Psychoactive Effects

Injection continues to be the predominant method of heroin use, with intravenous injection providing the greatest intensity and most rapid onset of euphoria (7 to 8 seconds). Intramuscular injection produces euphoria in 5 to 8 minutes, while sniffing or smoking require 10 to 15 minutes for peak effects to occur. Although nasal ingestion does not produce as intense or as rapid a rush, all forms of heroin administration are addictive (National Institute on Drug Abuse, 1999e).

Recent scientific demonstration of receptors in the central nervous systems of both animals and humans, followed by the discovery that the body makes its own opiate-like substances, has greatly enhanced the understanding of the action of opioids. Administered opioids are thought to act at the neuronal synapses, either by acting as a neurotransmitter decreasing the transynaptic potential or by modulating the release of a neurotransmitter postsynaptically (Simon, 1997). This appears to be the basis of their analgesic effect and may be similar to the action of the body's endogenous opioids.

Effects on the Body

There is evidence that chronic morphine use produces marked structural changes in the dopamine neurons in the brain's ventral tegmental area (VTA) (National Institutes of Health, 1996). In research studies with mice, the size of mesolimbic dopamine neurons originating in the VTA showed a dramatic decrease, and the shape of the neurons also changed. No changes were observed in nondopaminergic neurons. Thus, the opioids affected exactly those brain cells implicated in continuing drug use (National Institutes of Health, 1996).

Tolerance and Dependence

The risk of dependence of opioids, both physical and psychological, is high. Physiological tolerance and dependence results from brain changes after prolonged use, while psychological tolerance and dependence are a result of linking learned associations between drug effects and environmental cues. These phenomena of tolerance to and physical dependence (neuroadaption) on opioids appear to be receptor site–specific. In 1975, several endogenous molecules were identified with opioid activity (Hughes et al., 1975). Since then, at least 12 peptides have been discovered, including the beta-endorphins (Bradbury, Smyth, Snell, Birdsall, & Hulme, 1976) and dynorphines (Goldstein, Tachiban, Lowney, Hunkapiller, & Hood, 1979). These particular long-chain peptides bind to their own specific opioid receptors (Simon, 1997). Stimulation of opioid receptors located in critical cells, such as those located in the locus coeruleus, produces a decrease in cell firing, ultimately causing the cells to be come hyperexcitable (Jaffe, Knapp, & Ciraulo, 1997).

Tolerance to opioids can develop quite rapidly in frequent users, and experiments have verified that a clinical dose of morphine (60 milligrams a day) in an individual can be increased to 500 milligrams per day in as little as 10 days (Jaffe, 1990). Over time, the brain substitutes administered chemical opiates for natural endorphins, causing effects such as euphoria to become less intense. As the body accommodates to the presence of chemical opioids, long-term usage produces a "threshold effect," after which time the chronic opioid user will use the drug just to function in a normal state, no longer getting high (Simon, 1997).

Withdrawal

The symptoms of withdrawal from opioids include feelings of dysphoria, nausea, repeated yawning, sweating, tearing, and a runny nose (Jaffe et al., 1997). It is during this period that subjects experience craving or "drug hunger" for repeated exposure to the drug. Abundant literature suggests that the symptoms of opiate withdrawal are the result of interactions between the opioid and other neurotransmitter systems (Simon, 1997).

Recent research has led to promising developments in the understanding of narcotic addiction, although the molecular basis of narcotic addiction remains unknown. Specific CNS receptor sites for opiate narcotic analgesics were found, followed by the discovery that the body produces its own opiate-like substances (Simon, 1997). These discoveries may increase not only our ability to control pain but also our ability to prevent and treat narcotic addiction.

STIMULANTS

This section focuses on drugs of arousal, which include all forms of cocaine, amphetamine, prescription weight-reducing products, amphetamine-like drugs such as methylphenidate (Ritalin), some over-the-counter (OTC) weight-reducing drugs, and the minor stimulant drugs, nicotine and caffeine. The potential difficulties with frequent use of these drugs include possible overdoses, physical addiction, psychoses, severe depressions, and all anxiety syndromes, including panic attacks and obsessions.

Minor psychoactive stimulants include caffeine and nicotine. These substances are considered minor because they can induce and exacerbate anxiety but usually are not capable of producing the more intense psychiatric syndromes such as psychosis and major depression (Liska, 1994; Siegel, 1989).

Cocaine

Cocaine is an alkaloid drug compound that creates intense CNS arousal. It is processed from an organic source, the coca leaf (Liska, 1994; National Institute on Drug Abuse, 1999c). The natural source for the leaf (*Erythroxylon coca*) comes from two varieties of flowering coca shrubs, the *huanuco* and *truxillo*, which can exist only in the fertile soil of South America. They are grown and cultivated in the mountainous regions of Peru, Bolivia, Ecuador, and Colombia. During the last decade, new plantations have been developed in Venezuela and Brazil as a result of the huge demand for cocaine in the United States and Europe.

To convert the coca leaf into a substance that can be used psychoactively, various chemical processes involving mixtures of alcohol, benzol, sulfuric acid, sodium carbonate, and kerosene or gasoline baths combined with several shaking and cooling segments convert the coca leaf into a paste. The final product is a precipitate of crude cocaine called *bazooko*. With the addition of acetone, potassium permanganate, and hydrochloric acid, this pasty sulfate becomes powdery flakes or rocks of nearly pure *cocaine hydrochloride*. At this point it is a white, odorless, crystalline powder that is a member of the tropane family. Most bazooko is converted into cocaine hydrochloride in the jungle laboratories around Colombia and then smuggled out through the networks of organized crime to various destinations including the United States, Europe, and Asia. While en route, it is diluted several times ("stepped on") with various additives such as lactose or dextrose (sugar), inositol (vitamin B), mannitol (baby laxative), and even cornstarch, talcum powder, and flour to stretch the quantity. This "stretching" process increases profits as the now-diluted cocaine finds its way onto the streets of major cities throughout the world (Doweiko, 1999).

During the past few years, drug dealers have developed new marketing strategies by processing bazooko or cocaine hydrochloride (powder) into a potentiated form of prefabricated, freebase cocaine called *crack*. The term *crack* refers to the crackling sound made when the substance is smoked (National Institute of Drug Abuse, 1999c). This inexpensive method of psychoactive stimulant conversion can be accomplished in one's own kitchen by applying heat to cocaine cooked in a mixture of water, ammonia, baking soda, or liquid drain opener. Crack intensifies the bio-chemical experience in the brain but also increases the toxic effect on neurological tissue that is involved with cocaine stimulation (Gold, 1997). Cocaine is listed as a Schedule II drug on the DEA Controlled Substance Schedule.

Incidence

Cocaine use in the United States peaked in 1985 at 5.7 million (3% of the population 12 or older). In 1997, 1.5 million (0.7%) were current users, relatively unchanged since 1992 (National Institute on Drug Abuse, 1999c).

Crack cocaine remains a serious problem in the United States. In 1997, the number of current users was estimated to be 604,000, relatively unchanged since 1988 (National Institute on Drug Abuse, 1999c). In 1998, 3.2% of eighth grade students reported having used crack at least once, up from 2.7% in 1997 (National Institute on Drug Abuse, 1999a).

Psychoactive Effects

The quality of the cocaine experience is dependence on a number of variables, such as the strength of the drug, the setting, the circumstances under which it is taken, and the user's attitude, emotional state, drug-taking history, and expectation of what the drug should produce. Most users will experience at least a mild euphoria, an increased heartbeat, and a subtle sense of excitement. Some may get little or no reaction from using the drug, common most frequently as tolerance builds, and cocaine is required to maintain the body in a relatively normal state.

Cocaine is a tremendous mood elevator, filling the user with a sense of exhilaration and well-being. It melts away feelings of inferiority while loosening inhibitions and evaporating tensions. It relieves fatigue and imparts the illusion of limitless power and energy. Many compulsive users "treat" themselves for obesity, lack of energy, depression, shyness, and low self-esteem. High doses may be associated with rambling speech, headache, tinnitus, paranoid ideation, aggressive behavior, disturbances in attention and concentration, auditory hallucinations, and tactile hallucinations (coke bugs) (Gold, 1997).

Cocaine can be ingested through inhalation through the nose, commonly called *snorting* or *tooting*; injection under the skin, into a muscle or a vein; and smoking freebase or crack. Death has been reported from all forms of cocaine ingestion (Liska, 1994). Cocaine usage may also indirectly lead to the user's premature death through suicide resulting from cocaine-induced depression or aggressive or risk-taking behaviors. For example, in one New York City study, Marzuk and other researchers found that one-fifth of all suicides in people under the age of 60 were cocaine related and that cocaine was found to be a factor in 26.7% of all deaths for people in New York city between the ages of 15 and 44 in the period between 1990 and 1993 (Doweiko, 1999).

When cocaine is snorted, the moist nasal membranes quickly dissolve the powder into microscopic molecules that flood the circulatory system within 1 to 2 minutes (Gold, 1997). These molecules encounter and pass through the protective blood-brain barrier, penetrating the cortical tissue that surrounds the deeper layers of brain. The molecules find their way into stimulatory pathways in the limbic system, which regulate emotion and connect to primitive pain/pleasure centers deep within the brain (Gold, 1997). These pathways are normally indirectly activated by pleasurable activities such as eating, drinking, and sex. So powerful is the reward/pleasure stimulus by cocaine that responsibilities, family, job, morality, sleep, and safety may be ignored in its pursuit (Gold, 1997).

Effects on the Body

Cocaine acts directly on the heart muscle, causing the heart to beat inefficiently and its vessels to narrow, restricting the oxygen needed for peak performance. The heart has to work harder to keep up with the restricted blood flow in the rest of the body. Heavy use can cause angina, irregular heartbeat, and even a heart attack. As cocaine constricts blood flow, it can injure cerebral arteries. The acute hypertension brought on by cocaine use has been known to burst weakened blood vessels or produce strokes in young people (Liska, 1994).

It is not uncommon for chronic users to experience seizures that result in a constant tingling sensation of the jaw and neck region. The seizures are a result of neurons firing in bursts, creating uncontrollable electrical storms in the brain. They can cause a general diminution of alertness and mental functioning and can induce epilepsy, even in those with no previous signs of it (Liska, 1994).

Many other potential difficulties may ensue with the chronic use of cocaine, both physical and psychological. Physical dangers include possible overdose and physical addiction; psychological effects may manifest themselves as severe depression, paranoid psychosis, and anxiety syndromes including panic attacks and obsessions (Gold, 1997). The most common causes of death from cocaine are heart attacks, strokes, respiratory failure, paralysis, heart rhythm disturbances, and repeated convulsions, usually from massive overdoses or at the end of a binge (Dressler, 1990; Gold, 1997).

Tolerance and Dependence

Physical dependence on cocaine is possible, while the risk of psychological dependence is high. Smoking cocaine as coca paste, freebase, or crack has the highest addictive potential. An intense high, described by some as a "full-body orgasm," occurs within 8 to 10 seconds after inhaling the smoke. Effects of the drug only last 5 to 10 minutes, and the symptoms of withdrawal (anxiety, depression, and paranoia) are in proportion to the high obtained, leading to intense craving (Gold, 1997). The intense high occurs when cocaine blocks the reuptake of dopamine, greatly increasing the availability of the neurotransmitter. This flooding allows dopamine to stimulate the receptors more intensely, acting directly on the reward pathways of the brain. The pattern of rapid onset of intense euphoria, followed in a few minutes by intense dysphoria that can be quickly relieved by another self-administered dose of more cocaine, establishes a highly addictive cycle. This neurochemical response creates a rapid tolerance and dependence (drug hunger) for almost anyone who uses this drug (Doweiko, 1999). Each time the effects of cocaine wear off, dopamine levels drop, sending the user into a serious state of withdrawal. Normally, the brain replenishes dopamine from proteins in food, but in cocaine addicts, dopamine is quickly depleted, partly because of poor diet and partly because cocaine blocks the mechanism that recycles the neurotransmitter for future use (Gold, 1997). Chronic cocaine use can deplete the normal stores of dopamine in the brain, causing serious depression, not infrequently leading to suicide. Many individuals depress the action of the central nervous system with alcohol or benzodiazepines to temporarily counter the loss of the brain's dopamine supply. In the long run, this only heightens the need for more cocaine.

Effects on the Fetus

Recent studies suggest that 12% to 20% of children born at inner-city hospitals have been exposed to cocaine in utero (Forman, Klein, & Barks, 1994). Many of the abnormalities that have been identified in the offspring of pregnant cocaine users, including low birthweight, are more related to lifestyle of the drug user than to the pharmacological effect of cocaine (Karch, 1996). There is no doubt, however, that the drug constricts the blood vessels of the placenta, reducing the supply of blood and oxygen that reaches the fetus (Ganapathy & Leibach, 1994). Cocaine is also thought to contribute to premature and stillborn births, because of both vasoconstrictive effects on the developing fetus and its ability to induce intrauterine contractions (Doweiko, 1999; Saraf, Dombrowski, & Leach, 1995). Babies born to cocaine-using women may have persistently elevated cocaine levels for days, and the possibility exists that the enzymatic pathway for conversion of cocaine into metabolites may not be fully developed in the newborn (Karch, 1996). In spite of the dire predictions expressed in the 1980s of a generation of "crack babies" (Blume, 1997), many of the effects of prenatal crack use appears to be the result of poor nutrition, related to the lifestyle of the mother, polydrug use, lack of prenatal care, and premature birth (Doweiko, 1999). The exact nature of cocaine itself on the developing fetus remains unknown (Doweiko, 1999).

Amphetamines

Amphetamines are psychomotor stimulants that were first investigated in 1927 as a treatment for asthma. Their actions on the CNS were not reported until 1933, followed by the first reports of amphetamine abuse (Radcliffe, Rush, Sites, & Cruse, 1985). Methylphenidate (Ritalin) is chemically related to amphetamines and was first synthesized in 1944. Although its major medical use is for treatment of hyperactive (attention deficit disordered) children, it is frequently abused. Amphetamines can be orally ingested, intravenously injected, snorted, or smoked, creating intense CNS arousal.

Amphetamines and methamphetamines have a similar but slightly different molecular structure (Liska, 1994). Methamphetamine is making inroads into the United

States from the Pacific Basin and is considered the most hypercharged analog of this family of drugs (King & Ellinwood, 1997).

During the last three decades, "speed" epidemics have been reported in Japan, Sweden, and the United States (King & Ellinwood, 1997). In the United States, this situation led to a change in laws when amphetamines were restricted to medical use by the Controlled Substances Act of 1970. They are listed as Schedule II drugs on the Controlled Substances Schedule, and their use is strictly enforced by the DEA. In recreational use, amphetamines can be "snorted," smoked, administered by injection, or taken orally. In recent years, the explosive use of methamphetamines by bisexual and homosexual men is of grave concern, as the disinhibiting and sexual stimulating effects of the drug place homosexual male users at high risk for HIV infection (Cabaj, 1997).

The underground production of amphetamines in North America is largely accomplished through small, clandestine laboratories. They produce more then $3 billion worth of illegal amphetamines per year with a huge profit margin. Law enforcement officials believe these "speed labs" are financed by motorcycle gangs who distribute the final product (King & Ellinwood, 1997).

Methamphetamine is the most potent form of amphetamine. Illicit forms of methamphetamine sold on the street may be called *speed, crystal (meth), crank, Btu, slate, glass,* or *ice* (Liska, 1994). Ice is an odorless, colorless form of crystal methamphetamine, up to 100% pure, resembling a chip of ice or clear rock candy (Doweiko, 1999; National Institute on Drug Abuse, 1999i).

Incidence

Amphetamine abuse in the United States peaked in the late 1960s or early 1970s, declining to a low in the late 1980s or early 1990s. Since then, it has gradually been increasing. About 800,000 people in the United States are thought to use some form of amphetamine each month (Doweiko, 1999).

Methamphetamine spread from Japan to Hawaii after World War II and has remained endemic there. Methamphetamine has long been the dominant drug problem in the San Diego, California, area and has spread to other sections of the West and Southwest, as well as to both rural and urban sections of the South and Midwest. As it has spread, the traditionally blue-collar user has given way to a more diverse user population (National Institute on Drug Abuse, 1999i). At least 4 million people in the United States are thought to have used methamphetamine at least once in their lives (Doweiko, 1999).

Effects on the Body

Amphetamines cross the blood-brain barrier easily after oral ingestion. Once the amphetamine molecules pass through the stomach, they absorb into the blood via the intestines where they are able to reach peak levels within one hour. After absorption, the lipid-soluble molecules are distributed into the brain, lung, and kidney. Brain levels reach about 10 times the blood levels, which accounts for the intense CNS effect. Some of the metabolites are active and, if present in sufficient quantity, can cause high blood pressure and hallucinations (King & Ellinwood, 1997).

In the CNS, amphetamines mimic cocaine, acting on the neurotransmitters, dopamine, and norepinephrine. They cause a tremendous release of newly synthesized dopamine from the presynaptic neuron to bind and stimulate the postsynaptic neurons (King & Ellinwood, 1997). They also inhibit the action of monoamine oxidase (MAO), the enzyme that ends the action of these neurotransmitters, allowing them to remain active in the synapse for a longer time. Amphetamines also act on the sympathetic nervous system (SNS) through the stimulation and release of norepinephrine while blocking the reuptake of norepinephrine back into the presynaptic terminal. This action elicits a "fight or flight" response. Thus, the psychostimulants are called *sympathomimetic* drugs in that they mimic the action of the SNS (Ray & Ksir, 1993). High doses of amphetamines have also been found to have a direct effect on serotonergic receptors. Electroencephalogram (EEG) recordings have shown that amphetamine accelerates and desynchronizes neuronal firing rates in the brain, a possible explanation for some of the behavioral effects of amphetamines (King & Ellinwood, 1997).

With large doses of amphetamines, extreme symptoms may occur, including rapid heartbeat, hypertension, headache, profuse sweating, and severe chest pain. This generally occurs when dosages exceed 50 to 100 milligrams per day on a continuous basis, and the user may appear psychotic or schizophrenic. Severe intoxication also can produce delirium, panic, paranoia, and hallucinations. Murders and other violent offenses have been attributed to amphetamine intoxication, and some studies have shown increased aggression in humans after ingestion of amphetamines (King & Ellinwood, 1997).

Tolerance and Dependence

Tolerance develops to specific actions of amphetamines including euphoria, appetite suppression, wakefulness, hyperactivity, and heart and blood pressure effects. The risk of physical dependence on amphetamines is possible, and the risk of psychological dependence is high.

Withdrawal

During withdrawal, there is a reduction of available neurotransmitters due to depletion and reduced reuptake, causing a period of depression, fatigue, increased appetite, and prolonged sleep accompanied by REM (dream sleep) following the cessation of use (Preston et al., 1997). Death occurs from extreme heat elevation, convulsions, and circulatory collapse (King & Ellinwood, 1997).

Minor Stimulant: Nicotine

Nicotine is not listed as a controlled substance on the DEA's Controlled Substances Schedule. However, nicotine has had its share of controversy. In recent years, it has come to light that cigarette manufacturers have long known that the psychoactive agent in cigarettes is nicotine and that they have "long viewed cigarettes as little more than a single-dose container of nicotine that will quickly administer the chemical to the user" (Doweiko, 1999, p. 206). Lawsuits won by several states have held tobacco manufacturers liable for health problems caused by tobacco use because of their awareness of the addictive nature of nicotine.

Incidence

Tobacco smoking may have been prevalent for thousands of years. Modern use in the United States peaked in the mid-1960s, when 52% of adult males and 32% of adult females were cigarette smokers (Doweiko, 1999). Following the surgeon general's report on the health hazards of smoking, published in 1964, the incidence of smoking in the United States began to drop, to an estimated level of 25% in 1997 (Schmitz, Jarvik, & Schneider, 1997).

Psychoactive Effects

Nicotine is both a stimulant and a sedative to the central nervous system. The absorption of nicotine is followed almost immediately by a "kick" because it causes a discharge of epinephrine from the adrenal cortex. This, in turn, stimulates the CNS and other endocrine glands, producing a sudden release of glucose. As the effects of the sudden release of epinephrine and glucose wear off, depression and fatigue follow, leading the abuser to seek more nicotine (National Institute on Drug Abuse, 1999a).

Effects on the Body

Nicotine is readily absorbed in the body from every site with which it comes into contact, including the skin. It is both water- and lipid-soluble, allowing it to cross over the blood-brain barrier quickly to reach the brain and virtually every other blood-rich tissue in the body (Doweiko, 1999). Inhaled nicotine reaches the brain within 7 to 19 seconds of puffing (Schmitz et al., 1997). Once in the bloodstream, a portion is carried to the liver where it is metabolized into cotinine (90%) and nicotine-N-oxide (10%). It has a wide range of effects on the peripheral and CNS, including increased blood pressure and heart rate, cardiac output, coronary blood flow, and cutaneous vasoconstriction.

Women who smoke tend to have an earlier menopause, and those who use oral contraceptives, particularly those older than 30, are more prone to cardiovascular and cerebrovascular diseases than are other smokers (National Institute on Drug Abuse, 1999a).

Cigarette smoking is a profound contributor to mortality (Schmitz et al., 1997). Cigarette smoking and smokeless tobacco use claim more than 400,000 lives every year in the United States. Tobacco-related health problems include cardiovascular disease, cancer, chronic obstructive lung disease, and complications during pregnancy. Nonsmokers exposed to environmental tobacco smoke (passive smokers) also appear to be at an increased risk for the same diseases as smokers (Schmitz et al., 1997).

Tobacco smoke contains many toxic compounds. Nicotine is the major reinforcing agent, while tar and carbon monoxide have been identified as physiologically active chemicals. Cigarette tar exposes the user to a high expectancy rate of lung cancer, emphysema, and bronchial disease, while carbon monoxide increases the risk of cardiovascular disease (National Institute on Drug Abuse, 1999a).

Tolerance and Dependence

Tolerance occurs as the body becomes accustomed to the presence of nicotine and accommodates to its presence and appears to be linked to the number of binding sites (Schmitz et al., 1997). Nicotine accumulates in the body, and regular use causes it to remain in body tissues 24 hours a day. Nicotine is high in potential for both physical and psychological dependency.

Withdrawal

When chronic smokers are deprived of cigarettes for 24 hours, they experience increased anger, hostility, aggression, and loss of social cooperation, and they take longer to regain emotional equilibrium following stress. During periods of craving or abstinence, smokers experience impairment across a wide range of cognitive and psychomotor functioning (National Institute on Drug Abuse, 1999a).

Minor Stimulant: Caffeine

Caffeine belongs to a chemical class of alkaloids known as *xanthine derivatives,* and it was chemically isolated more than 170 years ago (Greden & Walters, 1997). It is found in coffee, tea, cocoa, chocolate, and a number of soft drinks, as well as hundreds of prescription and OTC drugs. Caffeine is not listed as a controlled substance on the Controlled Substances Schedule.

Incidence

Caffeine is the most widely consumed psychoactive agent in the world. About 80% of the adults in the United States use caffeine regularly, a per capita intake of 220 to 240 milligrams per day. The chronic overuse of this substance is called "caffeinism." Clinical and epidemiological data show that its overuse induces an intoxication of the CNS that includes habituation, tolerance, and a withdrawal syndrome (Greden & Walters, 1997).

Effects on the Body

Caffeine is rapidly absorbed into the gastrointestinal tract, and peak plasma levels occur within 30 to 45 minutes after ingestion. It crosses the blood-brain barrier very quickly and concentrates in brain plasma relative to the amount that is ingested (Greden & Walters, 1997).

Caffeine and other xanthines block the brain's receptors for adenosine (Ray & Ksir, 1993), a neuromodulator (Greden & Walters, 1997). Adenosine has sedative, anxiolytic, and anticonvulsant actions (Greden & Walters, 1997). When caffeine occupies adenosine-binding sites, these actions cannot occur and there is a stimulating or anxiogenic effect.

Two hundred milligrams of caffeine (the equivalent of two cups of coffee) will activate the cortex of the brain, showing an arousal pattern on an EEG. At this level, caffeine acts directly on the vascular muscles, causing dilation of the blood vessels. The CNS stimulation is also responsible for "coffee jitters" and increases the time it takes to fall asleep.

At higher dose levels (500 milligrams and above), autonomic centers of the brain are stimulated, causing increased heart rate and respiration and constriction of the blood vessels in the brain (Ray & Ksir, 1993). Caffeine increases heart rate and contraction, physiologically creating arrhythmias and mild tachycardia. It increases gastric acidity and is contraindicated for patients with ulcers. Caffeine directly acts on the kidneys to increase urine output and also increases salivary flow (Ray & Ksir, 1993).

Caffeine is generally not considered a toxic drug. Approximately 15% of circulating caffeine is metabolized an hour, with a half-life of 3.5 to 5 hours. A lethal dose for an average adult male would be 5 to 10 grams, the equivalent of 50 to 100 cups of regular coffee, probably necessitating ingestion in a nonbeverage form (Greden & Walters, 1997).

Tolerance and Dependence

Many researchers believe the key reinforcing factor may be caffeine's effects on the pleasure and reward centers found in the hypothalamus and the median forebrain bundle. Stimulation of the brain's reward center may be the most powerful reason that people move from a controlled phase of caffeine ingestion to the stage of caffeine dependency, or caffeinism (Greden & Walters, 1997).

Children do not seem to possess an innate craving for caffeine, and most people in our society seem to be exposed to it gradually as their intake eventually progresses to a pattern of frequent or daily use. Moreover, there appears to be an age-related rate of metabolism of caffeine, leaving newborns, infants, and small children more vulnerable to its effects (Greden & Walters, 1997).

The potential for both physical and psychological dependence on caffeine is small. However, a large number of variables make it difficult for researchers to determine users' responses to varying doses of caffeine intake. These include a subject's age, body mass, other psychoactive substances in use, amount of stress, level of fatigue, sleep disorders, and varying degrees of sensitivity to the drug. Furthermore, the acute use of caffeine produces very different biological consequences when compared with chronic use (Greden & Walters, 1997).

Withdrawal

Caffeine withdrawal may precipitate such symptoms as craving for caffeine, headache, fatigue, nausea or vomiting, or marked anxiety or depression (Greden & Walters, 1997).

CANNABIS

Marijuana and hashish are produced from the hemp plant, cannabis. As a psychoactive agent, it is used primarily to produce euphoria followed by relaxation. Cannabis is known by many names—*Indian hemp, marijuana, hashish, pot, grass,* or *dope*—and is a controversial drug in U.S. society (Grinspoon & Bakalar, 1997). Cannabis can be smoked, eaten, or drunk. The strengths of the end products that come from the hemp plant vary owing to the climate and soil in which it is grown and the method of cultivation and preparation. Its potency and quality depend mainly on the type of plant that is grown. Experienced growers identify potency by grading the plant with Indian names. *Bhang* is identified as the least potent and cheapest and is made from the cut tops of uncultivated plants that contain a low resin content. *Ganja* is derived from the flowering tops and leaves of selected, carefully cultivated plants that have a high content of resin and, therefore, is more potentiated to the user. *Charas* is the highest grade and is produced from the resin itself, obtained from fully mature plants. This highly potentiated source is generally referred to as *hashish* (Grinspoon & Bakalar, 1997; Liska, 1994).

The potency of marijuana, a Schedule I substance on the Controlled Substances Schedule, has drastically increased in the United States as California growers have successfully cultivated an unpollinated plant known as *sinsemilla*. Imported products from Thailand, Hawaii, and the Netherlands have also been tested with incredibly high amounts of tetrahydrocannabinol (THC), the active ingredient in marijuana. Additionally, clandestine laboratories have developed a method of producing a liquid called "hash oil," which has been found to have more than 60% THC content (Liska, 1994), compared with an average 30% in regular hashish and 7% to 15% in sinsemilla.

Incidence

Marijuana is the most frequently used illicit drug in the United States (National Institute on Drug Abuse, 1999b, 1999d). Its use reached a peak in the 1970s and has declined since. The 1992 *National Household Survey on Drug Abuse* reported that marijuana and hashish use dropped from 35% in 1979 to 11% in 1992 among 18- to 25-year-olds, and from more than 6% in 1982 to 3% in 1992 among adults over the age of 25 (National Institute on Drug Abuse, 1999d). In real numbers, 17.4 million persons in the United States in 1992 had used marijuana or hashish the previous year. This figure continued to drop, according to the 1997 *National Household Survey on Drug Abuse*, when more than 11 million people reported smoking marijuana within the last month in 1997 (National Institute on Drug Abuse, 1999b).

Psychoactive Effects

Smoking of cannabis can produce relaxation following euphoria, loss of appetite, impaired memory, concentration, and knowledge retention, loss of coordination, and more vivid sense of taste, sight, smell, and hearing. Stronger doses cause fluctuation of emotions, fragmentary thoughts, disoriented behavior, and psychosis. It may also cause irritation to the lungs and respiratory system and cancer (National Institute on Drug Abuse, 1999h).

Effects on the Body

In the United States, cannabis is generally smoked in a cigarette called a *joint* or a *doobie*. A marijuana cigarette contains 421 chemicals before ignition. There are 61 cannabanoids, including delta-1 tetrahydrocannabinol, which is believed to be the psychoactive agent. There are also 50 different waxy hydrocarbons, 103 terpines, 12 fatty acids, 11 steroids, 20 nitrogen compounds, as well as carbon monoxide, ammonia, acetone, benzene, benzathracene, and benzoprene. When ignited, these chemicals convert into more then 2,000 other chemicals. As these are metabolized by the body, they convert to about 600 chemical metabolites. Cannabinoids have a half-life of 72 hours in the human body. When ingested, effects appear to be dose-dependent. Cannabinoids are lipid-soluble and store at megamicroscopic levels for indefinite periods of time in the body (Liska, 1994).

The research findings on cannabis are mixed. Some research shows that the chemicals found in marijuana and hashish interfere with the cell's ability to manufacture pivotal molecules, which grossly affects the substances necessary for cell division including DNA, RNA, and proteins. This causes an "aging process" in particular clusters of cells found in the brain, liver, lungs, spleen, lymphoid tissues, and sex organs. These suggestions of long-term damage come almost exclusively from laboratory work with animal models (Liska, 1994).

Observations of human marijuana users from several studies conducted in this country and abroad do not confirm these findings. Several human studies in the past 20 years reveal little disease or organic pathology found in cannabis-using populations (Grinspoon & Bakalar, 1997; Gold, 1997; Liska, 1994). Unfortunately, many of these studies were conducted at a time when the THC content of cannabis was extremely low (0.05% to 4%). With some strains of the drug reportedly reaching THC content that extend into the teens (sinsemilla, 14%) and even the 20s (neiterweit, 27%), there is concern that cannabis may be doing more damage than previously realized.

One well-confirmed danger of heavy, long-term use is its ability to damage the lungs due to the fact that it burns 16 times "hotter" than tobacco and produces twice as many mutagens (agents that cause permanent changes in genetic material). Biopsies have confirmed that cannabis smokers may be at an extremely high risk for the development of lung diseases including bronchitis, emphysema, and cancer (Gold, 1997; Liska, 1994).

It has been believed that long-term marijuana use causes mental or emotional deterioration; however, studies have yet to support this premise. Amotivational syndrome, which includes symptoms of passivity, aimlessness, apathy, uncommunicativeness, and lack of ambition, has been attributed to prolonged marijuana use (Grinspoon & Bakalar, 1997). Do these symptoms result from the use of marijuana, or do they reflect the personality characteristics of heavy drug users—bored, depressed, listless, cynical, rebellious?

Marijuana has also been looked on as the "gateway drug," or precursor to use of other, more dangerous drugs. Anyone who uses one drug may be interested in others, for the same reasons. And users of one drug may find themselves in the company of users of other drugs, making them readily available. However, no research evidence directly links marijuana itself to escalation to more dangerous drug use (Grinspoon & Bakalar, 1997). Reliable, long-term studies on cannabis use of different populations are needed to determine the physiological, psychological, emotional, and medical outcomes.

Tolerance and Dependence

It is difficult to distinguish between marijuana use as a cause of problems or as the consequence of problems. For example, many people who develop a dependency on marijuana are susceptible to other dependencies because of anxiety, depression, or feelings of inadequacy (Grinspoon & Bakalar, 1997). In general, however, there appears to be a moderate psychological potential for dependency, while the risk of physical dependency is unknown.

Signs of possible misuse of marijuana include animated behavior and loud talking, followed by sleepiness, dilated pupils and bloodshot eyes, distortions in perception, hallucinations, distortions in depth and time perception, and loss of coordination. An overdose of marijuana can cause fatigue, lack of coordination, paranoia, and psychosis. Withdrawal can cause insomnia, hyperactivity, and a decrease in appetite (National Institute on Drug Abuse (1999b).

Withdrawal

Studies since the 1970s have suggested a marijuana withdrawal syndrome, characterized by insomnia, restlessness, loss of appetite, and irritability. A 1999 study conducted at Harvard Medical School confirmed higher levels of aggression in marijuana users during withdrawal when compared to the infrequent or former marijuana user (National Institute of Drug Abuse, 1999b).

Medical Use

Cannabis use for treatment of some medical ailments has held the interest of some in recent years, particularly in obtaining relief from glaucoma and asthma, as well as from the side effects of chemotherapy used in the treatment for some types of cancer. Some have experimented with its usefulness in treating the physical wasting that can occur with advanced AIDS. Its effectiveness over other methods of treatment remains controversial, partly because of legal complications involved in doing such research (Grinspoon & Bakalar, 1997).

Marijuana has been used by humans for thousands of years (Doweiko, 1999). It gained great popularity in the 1970s, although current use has declined. Currently a controversial drug, some fear it is a "gateway drug," leading to abuse of other substances. Others see no harm in it, even espousing its medicinal value. There continues to be political movement to legalize marijuana, and several states, such as California and Oregon, have passed initiatives to legalize the prescription of marijuana for medical use. However, the medical community, as a whole, remains skeptical of its medical value over other drugs, and research supporting each position is scarce.

HALLUCINOGENS

Hallucinogenic substances include the *indoles*, which include (a) lysergic acid derivatives and (b) substituted tryptamines such as dimethyltryptamine (DMT) and psilocybin and psilocin. All the indole-type hallucinogens have a structure similar to the neurotransmitter serotonin, while the substituted phenylethylamine-type hallucinogens are structurally related to the neurotransmitter norepinephrine. It is believed that the mechanism of action occurring in the indole-type hallucinogens involves the alteration of serotonergic neurotransmission. Lysergic acid diethylamide (LSD) is probably the best known of the indole-type hallucinogens and is most abused by white males between the ages of 10 and 29 years (Liska, 1994). A few of the indole-type such as psilocybin and psilocin are found in nature, while mescaline is a naturally occurring hallucinogen derived from the peyote cactus (Pechnick & Ungerleider, 1997).

The overall effects of many of the hallucinogens are similar, although there is a multitude of variables involving the rate of onset, duration of action, and the intensity of the drug experience. This is due to the wide range of potency available and the amount of the drug that is ingested relative to its specific dose-response characteristics. Because the goal of this text is to give an overview of the topic of substance abuse, a discussion of LSD and PCP (phencyclidine) will represent the hallucinogenic substances used for recreation.

Lysergic Acid Diethylamide (LSD)

LSD is between 100 and 1,000 times more powerful than natural hallucinogens but weaker than synthetic chemicals such as DOM and STP (for a discussion of DOM and STP, see Doweiko, 1999). Confiscated street samples of LSD can range from 10 to 300 micrograms in a single dose. LSD is listed as a Schedule I substance on the Controlled Substances Schedule.

Incidence

It is difficult to accurately estimate the number of users of hallucinogenic drugs. Both the use and availability of LSD decreased between the mid-1970s and the 1980s. However, that trend seems to be reversing itself (Doweiko, 1999; Pechnick & Ungerleider, 1997). It was reported that 2.8 million people in the United States in 1994 used LSD at least once a year (Doweiko, 1999). In 1994, 7% of high school students and 5% of college students used LSD at least once a year (Pechnick & Ungerleider, 1997). The next year, 1995, 11.7% of high school seniors admitted to using LSD during their lifetime, a significant increase in a year (Doweiko, 1999).

Psychoactive Effects

LSD triggers behavioral responses in some individuals after doses as low as 20 micrograms. Psychological and behavioral effects begin about an hour after oral ingestion and generally peak between 2 and 4 hours. There is a gradual return to the predrug state within 6 to 8 hours. The subjective effects can be somatic with symptoms of dizziness, weakness, and tremor, followed by perceptual changes of altered vision and intensified hearing, which gradually changes into visual distortions, dreamlike imagery, and synesthesia that includes "seeing" smells and "hearing" colors (Liska, 1994; Pechnick & Ungerleider, 1997). LSD is metabolized mainly at the site of the liver to various transformation products, and very little is eliminated as an unchanged product (Liska, 1994).

Tolerance and Dependency

There appears to be no potential for physical dependence on LSD, and the risk of psychological dependency for it is unknown.

Phencyclidine (PCP)

Phencyclidine (PCP, "angel dust") is considered a hallucinogenic drug. It was originally developed as a general anesthetic for human application but was found to be unstable. It was then offered as an anesthetic for veterinary applications until 1986 (Liska, 1994; Zukin, Sloboda, & Javitt, 1997). At that time, PCP and its chemical analogs were placed in the classification of Schedule I drugs under the Anti-Drug Abuse Act. There are extreme penalties for trafficking PCP or attempting to purchase piperidine, a major chemical used in the manufacture of PCP (Liska, 1994).

In its pure form, PCP is a water-soluble white powder. It is often adulterated or misrepresented as a variety of other drugs, including THC, cannabinol, mescaline, psilocybin, LSD, amphetamine, or cocaine. On the street, it can be found in powder, tablet, and liquid form. A typical street dose (one pill, joint, or line) is about 5 milligrams, but confiscated street samples have revealed that purity can run from 5% to 100% depending on the form. This wide variance can create a tremendous risk to the user (Liska, 1994)

Incidence

PCP use peaked, reaching epidemic proportions in the years between 1973 and 1979, and again between 1981 and 1984 (Zukin et al., 1997). In 1979, 14.5% of 18- to 25-year-olds had ever used PCP, compared to 9.5% in 1976. In 1988, these figures were 4.4% and have continued to decline. Whites are more likely to use PCP than other groups, followed by Hispanics and then African Americans (Zukin et al., 1997).

Psychoactive Effects

PCP can be ingested orally, smoked, snorted, intravenously injected, and even inserted vaginally. The mode of administration can drastically alter the onset of effects. Smoking and injection create a rapid onset of effects that usually peak within 30 minutes. The "highs" last from 4 to 6 hours. For typical chronic users, PCP is generally the primary drug of choice, whereas users of other substances may occasionally combine PCP with other substances they are using. "Runs" of staying high on PCP may last two to three days, during which time the user remains sleepless. Chronic users may also exhibit persistent cognitive memory problems, speech difficulties, mood disorders, weight loss, and decrease in purposeful behavior for up to a year after cessation of use. Coma can occur at any time during intoxication (Zukin et al., 1997). When used in this fashion, many of these chronic users may need emergency room treatment to overcome the residual effects of the drug (Zukin et al., 1997).

PCP is a potent compound and extremely lipid-soluble. Its psychological/behavioral effects are dose-dependent. The dose range for PCP effect on brain stimulation reward enhancement is relatively narrow. At low doses, it produces reward enhancement or a "good trip"; at high doses, it inhibits the brain reward system and may produce a "bad trip." It is believed that PCP binds to specific sites in the human brain and blocks the reuptake of several major neurotransmitter systems. It also disrupts electrophysiological activity by blocking the ionic exchange of sodium and potassium (Zukin et al., 1997). These serious actions on major brain systems probably account for PCP's symptoms of dissociative anesthesia and its ability to create coma and lethal complications. Currently, there is no PCP antagonist available to block its effects, and treatment for overdose must address the symptoms of toxicity. Close observation of the PCP-toxic patient must continue for days, as PCP levels may continue unevenly for hours or days (Zukin et al., 1997).

Tolerance and Dependence

PCP appears to have no potential for physical dependency but shows a high potential for psychological dependency.

DESIGNER DRUGS

"Designer drugs" are essentially synthetic (manufactured) substances that are used for their psychoactive properties. Their action is similar to many of the botanical psychoactive substances, and they have gained in popularity during the past decades because of their ease of manufacture, availability of precursors of the final chemical compound, and ease of sale (Morgan, 1997). The Controlled Substances Analogues Enforcement Act was passed in 1986, making illegal on Schedule I or II those synthetic substances "substantially similar" to the chemical structure of a substance already listed under those categories in the Controlled Substances Act (Morgan, 1997). Because of the many possible chemical variations of synthetic psychoactive substances, only MDMA, probably the most common in this category, will be discussed.

MDMA (Ecstasy)

MDMA, or 3, 4-methlenedioxymethamphetamine, also known as Ecstasy, is typical of the designer drugs: a synthesized psychedelic, with a history of recreational use beginning in the 1970s. Some feel that it more accurately should be called "Intimacy," since its psychoactive effects are mild, with loosening of social inhibitions (Grob & Poland, 1997).

Incidence

Popularity of MDMA spread from the United States to England in the 1980s and rapidly through Europe, becoming a popular feature at "rave" dance parties. In 1993, 2% of all college students in the United States admitted to taking MDMA in the previous 12 months (Grob & Poland, 1997). However, either this figure may be misleading, or there are pockets of population with much greater usage. For example, 39% of Stanford students reported that they had taken MDMA at least once in their lives (Grob & Poland, 1997). It is felt that the potential for growth of abuse of MDMA is large, particularly among the young, and fostered by the rave scene.

Psychoactive Effects

Early medical experimentation with MDMA reported relatively mild effects when compared to LSD, producing decreased anxiety and depression while heightening a sense of introspection and intimacy. A variety of treatment applications for MDMA were explored, including the physical pain and emotional distress associated with severe medical illness, post-traumatic stress disorders, depression, psychosomatic disorders, and relationship problems. However, before it could undergo rigorous scientific studies to validate its legitimate use, MDMA was placed in the most restrictive Schedule status, making use or research of it illegal (Grob & Poland, 1997).

Effects on the Body

The behavioral and psychological effects of MDMA appear to be the result of an acute, but reversible, depletion of serotonin in the brain. Dopamine systems can also be affected. Although low doses produce few side effects, larger doses, particularly when taken with alcohol or other drugs, have produced fatalities. Cardiovascular events (heart attacks) have occurred, as have cerebrovascular accidents (strokes). Liver disease, hyperthermia, panic disorder, paranoid psychosis, and depression have been reported to have been precipitated by MDMA use (Doweiko, 1999).

Some evidence indicates that people who take MDMA, even just a few times, may be risking permanent problems with learning and memory. Animal studies done at Johns Hopkins University found that serotonin neurons in some parts of the brain, specifically those that use the chemical serotonin to communicate with other neurons, were permanently damaged. Areas particularly affected were the neocortex (the outer part of the brain where conscious thought occurs) and the hippocampus (which plays a key role in forming long-term memories) (National Institute on Drug Abuse, 1999g).

VOLATILE SUBSTANCES OR INHALANTS

This group contains several chemicals that can be "sniffed," "snorted," "huffed," "bagged," or inhaled. Current use includes volatile organic solvents, such as those found in paint and fuel, aerosols, such as hair sprays, spray paints, and deodorants, volatile nitrites (amyl nitrite and butyl nitrite), and general anesthetic agents, such as nitrous oxide (Doweiko, 1999). Volatile substances, as ordinary household or medical items, are not listed on the DEA Controlled Substances Schedule.

Incidence

Abuse of inhalable substances is a much larger problem than most people realize. About 17% of adolescents in the United States say they have sniffed inhalants at least once in their lives, and "sniffing" has been found to occur in almost every country of the world (Sharp & Rosenberg, 1997). Although drug use in general has declined in the United States, the use of inhalants in adolescent and preadolescent populations has increased or held constant. It seems to occur at about the same frequency for females as for males. The level of use of inhalants in preadolescents and adolescents is exceeded only by marijuana, alcohol, and cigarettes (Sharp & Rosenberg, 1997).

Psychoactive Effects

Inhalants are widely available, readily accessible, inexpensive, and legally obtained, making them attractive to youths. The toxic vapors make users forget their problems as they obtain a quick high with a minimal hangover. Disruptive and antisocial behavior as well as self-directed aggression is associated with individuals who abuse inhalants. However, it is not clear whether there is a cause-and-effect relationship—that is, whether inhalant use promotes antisocial and self-destructive tendencies or, conversely, whether those youths who have antisocial or self-destructive tendencies tend to use inhalants (Sharp & Rosenberg, 1997).

Effects on the Body

Acute symptoms associated with the use of inhalants include excitation turning to drowsiness, disinhibition, lightheadedness, and agitation. With increasing intoxication, the user may develop ataxia, dizziness, and disorientation. Extreme intoxication may create signs of sleeplessness, general muscle weakness, nystagmus, hallucinations, and disruptive behavior. After the high wears off, the user may sleep, appear lethargic, and experience headaches. Chronic abusers may experience continued weight loss, muscle weakness, general disorientation, inattentiveness, and lack of coordination. These physical conditions can be complicated by the use of other drugs (mainly alcohol, cigarettes, and marijuana), malnutrition, and respiratory illness.

Toxicity

Neurotoxicity is predominantly related to the type of substance inhaled and the dose and duration of exposure. Acute, high-level exposure to solvents will induce short-term effects on brain function but appear to be reversible (Sharp & Rosenberg, 1997). Chronic, high-level exposure over a longer time slowly produces irreversible neurological syndromes (Doweiko, 1999; Sharp & Rosenberg, 1997). Severe damage to the brain and nervous system can occur, and use can cause death by starving the body of oxygen or forcing the heart to beat more rapidly and erratically (National Institute on Drug Abuse, 1999f). There is increasing concern over the rising number of deaths caused by the direct toxic effects of inhalants, particularly in young people (Sharp & Rosenberg, 1997).

ANABOLIC-ANDROGENIC STEROIDS

Anabolic-androgenic steroids (AASs), although strictly not psychoactive or mood-altering drugs, are included in this chapter because of the increasing incidence of abuse and their widespread effects on the body. The use of AASs to enhance athletic performance and muscular appearance is widespread today, both in world-class athletes and nonathletes, such as adolescents, law enforcement and corrections officers, and physical fitness devotees. They are listed as Schedule III drugs on the DEA Controlled Substances Schedule.

Incidence

Use of AASs has become a silent epidemic. A SAMHSA report in 1995 showed 1,084,000 Americans as ever having used AASs, with 312,000 (29%) using in the previous year, compared with a lifetime heroin use of 2,083,000 Americans and 281,000 (13%) having used in the previous year (Galloway, 1997).

Several factors contribute to the high incidence of repeated AAS use. The most obvious is the reinforcing effects of increased muscular strength, attainment of improved physique, improvement in athletic performance, and increased self-confidence. Some coaches and parents of young athletes exert pressure to use AASs to become more competitive. In addition, certain groups seem more associated with AAS use. Recent research suggests that histrionic, narcissistic, antisocial, and borderline personality disorder groups have a higher incidence of use, as do those with dissatisfaction of body image (Galloway, 1997).

Effects on the Body

Anabolic describes the action of this category of drugs to increase the speed of growth of body tissues, while steroids refers to their chemical structure (Doweiko, 1999). Anabolic-androgenic steroids are only one in the classification of steroids, produced naturally in the body. Testosterone and similar altered steroids are androgenic, having masculinizing effects on the body, increasing muscle mass, aggression, and self-confidence. Testosterone has the disadvantage of having a brief elimination half-life, making it available to the body only for short periods of time. Alteration of testosterone to increase oral bioavailability, absorption half-life, elimination half-life, and ratio of anabolic to androgenic effects has produced new AASs through esterification of the 17-ß-hydroxyl group, alkylanation of the 17-α-position, and modification of the steroid nucleus (Galloway, 1997).

Administration of AASs is oral or, more commonly, by injection. Dosing is usually done with a pyramid-dosing schedule, in which a cyclic building to a peak followed by a gradual reduction in dosage is maintained. Cycles typically run 4 to 18 weeks on AASs with 1 month to 1 year off the drugs. Alternatively, the intermittent use of up to eight AASs concurrently may be used (Galloway, 1997).

AASs affect many body systems. Unwanted effects may include cardiovascular conditions, such as myocardial infarction, myocarditis, cardiac arrest with enlargement of the heart and death of heart cells, cerebrovascular accident (stroke), and severe restriction of blood flow to the lower limbs of the body. Liver changes may also occur. Testosterone and other AASs are metabolized in part by estrogen antagonists, such as estradiol. The estrogen antagonists can cause breast pain in men and gynecomastia (enlargement and development of breast tissue) requiring medical or surgical intervention. Testicular atrophy in men is common, as is voice deepening, clitoral hypertrophy, shrinking of breasts, menstrual irregularities, and excessive growth of hair in women. These changes are largely irreversible in females, while the sexual side effects in males are often reversible. The masculinizing effects of testosterone are achieved by its binding to intracellular receptors in target cells. This forms an androgen-receptor complex that binds to chromosomes, leading to increases in proteins and RNAs within the chromosome (Galloway, 1997). Mood disturbances of hypomania, mania, irritability, depressed mood, major depression, elation, recklessness, feelings of power and invincibility, and both increased and decreased libido have been reported during use of AASs. It is suspected that extremely high dosage levels may cause psychotic symptoms in the chronic user (Doweiko, 1999).

The first reports of psychological dependence on AASs emerged in the late 1980s. Loss of control and interference with other activities have been reported during use. Withdrawal symptoms include the desire to take more AASs, fatigue, dissatisfaction with body image, depressed mood, restlessness, anorexia, insomnia, decreased libido, and headache. Suicidal thoughts have been reported after cessation of use (Galloway, 1997).

CONCLUSION

The human brain is the major site for all psychoactive drug interactions. All psychoactive substances manipulate the biochemistry of the brain to some degree and change the neuron's process of communication within its existing structural framework.

These changes can alter the user's perceptions, emotions, thoughts, and behaviors over time. In addition, drugs have effects on many other body organs. (Table 2.3 summarizes the characteristics of various drugs.) Research is making significant strides in determining the biological actions that make people reliant on drugs. Future research involving the neurosciences, psychopharmacology, and new therapeutic strategies with chemically dependent populations will, it is hoped, produce new insights and actions to successfully tackle the problem of illicit drugs in our society.

TABLE 2.3   Summary of characteristics of drugs

Classification	Trade or Other Names	Dependence Physical	Dependence Psychological	Possible Effects	Effects of Overdose	Withdrawal Syndrome
Depressants						
Ethanol	Alcohol (beer, wine, liquor, etc.)	Low–Moderate	Low–Moderate	Tolerance, diminishment of inhibitions, Fetal Alcohol Syndrome, poor judgment, staggering, slurred speech	Severe CNS depression, black-outs, death Prolonged use: damage to all organs of body, Wernicki-Korsakoff Syndrome	Delerium tremens, profuse sweating, shakes, anxiety, nausea, diarrhea, hallucinations, general disorientation. In severe cases, seizures, cardiovascular collapse, death
Barbiturates	Sodium Pentothal, Amytal, Nembutal (yellow jackets), Seconal (red birds), Tuinal (rainbows), Butisol, phenobarbital, Quaalude (ludes), chloral hydrate, meprobamate	High–Moderate	High–Moderate	CNS depression, disinhibition, elevated mood, increased self-concept, increased energy and confidence, decreased anxiety	Unsteady gait, slurred speech, nystagmus, vomiting, poor judgment, coma	CNS hyperactivity, hand tremor, insomnia, nausea, hallucinations, illusions, rebound anxiety, panic attacks, delirium, psychosis, mania, paranoia, psychomotor agitation
Benzodiazepines	Diazepam (Valium), Librium, Halcion, Xanax, Buspar, Klonopin	Low	Low	Anticonvulsant, anxiety reduction, muscle relaxant. Reduces adverse effects of cocaine, methamphetamine, heroin, and alcohol	Similar to barbiturates	Anxiety, tremors, nightmares, insomnia, anorexia, nausea, vomiting, delirium, seizures, respiratory arrest, death
Opiates	Opium, morphine, heroin (horse, smack), Dilaudid, Demerol, Hycodan, Numorhphan, Percodan, Darvon, Dolophine, Sublimaze, black tar	High	High	Analgesia, rapid tolerance, euphoria, drowsiness, respiratory distress, constructed pupils, nausea	Slow and shallow breathing, clammy skin, convulsions, runny nose, possible coma, death	Dysphoria, nausea, repeated yawning, sweating, tearing, craving, "drug hunger"

Stimulants

Cocaine	Coke, crack, snow	Possible	High	Psychological: Intense CNS arousal—tremendous mood elevation, exhilaration, feeling of well-being, decreased inhibitions, relief of limitless power and energy, impaired judgment Physiological: increased or decreased pulse and blood pressure, insomnia, pupillary dilation, nausea or vomiting, weight loss, muscular weakness, respiratory depression, chest pain, cardiac arrhythmias, confusion, seizures	Acute hypertension, angina, irregular heartbeat, heart attack, injury to cerebral arteries, seizures, coma, possible death	Dysphoria, seizures, hypotension, depression, anxiety, panic attacks, insomnia or hypersomnia, obsessions
Nicotine	Cigars, cigarettes, chewing tobacco, snuff	High	High	Euphoria, cardiac acceleration	Long-term effects: Lung disease, cardiac disease, linked to several cancers	Weight gain, negative emotions, interpersonal conflicts, depression, insomnia, irritability, frustration or anger, anxiety, difficulty concentrating
Caffeine	Ingredient in tea, coffee, cocoa, chocolate, many soft drinks, and many OTC drugs	Low	Low	Alertness, sleeplessness, specific blood vessel constriction, increase in heart rate and contraction, rapid heartbeat, psychomotor agitation, diuresis, insomnia, nervousness, gastrointestinal complaints	Anxiety, sleep disturbances, mood changes, psychophysiological complaints, respiratory failure, death	

TABLE 2.3 *Continued*

| Classification | Trade or Other Names | Dependence | | Possible Effects | Effects of Overdose | Withdrawal Syndrome |
		Physical	Psychological			
Amphetamines	Speed, crystal (meth), crank, batu, slate, glass, ice	Possible	High	Tolerance, intense CNS arousal; rapid heartbeat, excitation, insomnia, loss of appetite	Rapid heartbeat, hypertension, headache, profuse sweating, severe chest pain, delirium, panic, paranoia, hallucinations	Depression, fatigue, increased appetite, prolonged sleep with REM; death due to extreme heat elevation, convulsions, circulatory collapse
Cannabis	Indian hemp, marijuana, hashish (hash), pot, grass, dope, Mary Jane	Unknown	Moderate	Psychological: euphoria, grandiosity, impairment of short-term memory, impaired judgment, distorted sensory perceptions, impaired motor performance, impaired perception of time Physiological: increased appetite, conjunctival injection, dry mouth, rapid heartbeat	Intoxication, delirium, hallucinations, delusions, anxiety, psychosis	
Hallucinogens	LSD, ecstasy, mescaline, psilocybin, psilocyn, PCP, angel dust, TCP, peyote	LSD, mescaline, peyote, psilocybin, psilocyn: none. Others: unknown	PCP, angel dust, TCP: high. Others: unknown	Dizziness, weakness, tremor, intensified hearing, visual distortions, dreamlike imagery, synesthesia, sleeplessness, poor perception of time and distance, marked anxiety or depression, pupillary dilation, rapid heartbeat, palpitations, sweating, blurred vision, tremors, incoordination	Dissociative anesthesia, coma, psychosis, possible death	Not reported

72

| Volatile Substances or Inhalants | Solvents, glue, gasoline, thinners, aerosols, correction fluid, cleaning fluids, refrigerant gases (fluorocarbons), anesthetics, whipped cream propellants, organic nitrites, cooking or lighter gases | None Neurotoxicity is related to type and dose of inhalant. Neurotoxicity of short-term high dosage appears to be reversible; chronic, high dose use produces irreversible neurological syndromes | Unknown | Excitation, drowsiness, disinhibition, agitation, lightheadedness, dizziness, disorientation, slurred speech, unsteady gait, tremor, depressed reflexes, blurred vision. Chronic use: weight loss, muscle weakness, general disorientation, inattentiveness, incoordination | Sleeplessness, general muscle weakness, headaches, joint pain, nystagmus, hallucinations, disruptive behavior; damage to kidneys, liver, lungs, heart, and blood | Lethargy, sleep, headaches |
| Anabolic-Androgenic Steroids | Andro | Low | Low | Increased muscular strength, aggression, self-confidence, euphoria | Cardiovascular conditions, masculinizing effects on women, depression, psychotic conditions | Depression, appetite and sleep disturbances |

REFERENCES

American Psychiatric Association. (1994). *Diagnostic and statistical manual of mental disorders* (4th ed.). Washington, DC: Author.

Andreasen, N. (1984). *The broken brain: The biological revolution in psychiatry.* New York: Harper & Row.

Blum, K., & Payne, J. E. (1991). *Alcohol and the addictive brain.* New York: Free Press.

Blume, S. B. (1997). Women: Clinical aspects. In J. H. Lowinson, P. Ruiz, R. B. Millman, & J. G. Langrod (Eds.), *Substance abuse: A comprehensive textbook* (3rd ed., pp. 645–654). Baltimore: Williams & Williams.

Bozarth, M. A. (1987). Opiate reward mechanisms mapped by intracranial self-administration. In J. E. Smith & J. D. Lane (Eds.), *Neurobiology of opiate reward processes* (pp. 331–359). Amsterdam: Elsevier North Holland Biomedical Press.

Bradbury, A. F., Smyth, D. G., Snell, C. R., Birdsall, N. J. M., & Hulme, E. C. (1976). C fragment of lipotropin has a high affinity for brain opiate receptors. *Nature, 260,* 793–795.

Broekkamp, C. L. E. (1987). Combined microinjection and brain stimulation reward methodology for the localization of reinforcing drug effects. In M. A. Bozarth (Ed.), *Methods of assessing the reinforcing properties of abused drugs* (pp. 479–488). New York: Springer.

Cabaj, R. P. (1997). Gays, lesbians, and bisexuals. In J. H. Lowinson, P. Ruiz, R. B. Millman, & J. G. Langrod (Eds.), *Substance abuse: A comprehensive textbook* (3rd ed., pp. 725–733). Baltimore: Williams & Wilkins.

Cohen, S. (1988). *The chemical brain: The neurochemistry of addictive disorders.* Irvine, CA: CareInstitute.

Doweiko, H. E. (1999). *Concepts of chemical dependency* (4th ed.). Pacific Grove, CA: Brooks/Cole.

Dressler, F. A. (1990). Quantitative analysis of amounts of coronary arterial narrowing in cocaine addicts. *Journal of the American Medical Association, 263,* 31–97.

Esposito, R. U., Porrino, L. J., & Seeger, T. F. (1987). Brain stimulation reward: Measurement and mapping by psychophysical techniques and quantitative 2-(14c) deoxyglucose autoradiography. In M. A. Bozarth (Ed.), *Methods of assessing the reinforcing properties of abused drugs* (pp. 421–445). New York: Springer.

Finnegan, L. P., & Kandall, S. R. (1997). Maternal and neonatal effects of alcohol and drugs. In J. H. Lowinson, P. Ruiz, R. B. Millman, & J. G. Langrod (Eds.), *Substance abuse: A comprehensive textbook* (3rd ed., pp. 513–534). Baltimore: Williams & Wilkins.

Fischbach, G. D. (1992). Mind and brain. *Scientific American (Special issue), 267*(3), 48–57.

Forman, R., Klein, J., & Barks, J. (1994). Prevalence of fetal exposure to cocaine in Toronto, 1990–1991. *Clinical Investigations in Medicine, 17*(3), 206–211.

Galloway, G. P. (1997). Anabolic-androgenic steroids. In J. H. Lowinson, P. Ruiz, R. B. Millman, & J. G. Langrod (Eds.), *Substance abuse: A comprehensive textbook* (3rd ed., pp. 308–318). Baltimore: Williams & Wilkins.

Ganapathy, V., & Leibach, F. (1994). Current topic: Human placenta, a direct target for cocaine action. *Placenta, 15,* 785–795.

Gardner, E. L. (1997). Brain reward mechanisms. In J. H. Lowinson, P. Ruiz, R. B. Millman, & J. G. Langrod (Eds.), *Substance abuse: A comprehensive textbook* (3rd ed., pp. 51–84). Baltimore: Williams & Wilkins.

Gilbert, P. E., & Martin, W. R. (1978). The effects of morphine and nalorphine-like drugs in the nondependent, morphine dependent and cyclazocine-dependent chronic spinal dog. *Journal of Pharmacology and Experimental Therapy, 198,* 66–82.

Gitlin, M. J. (1996). *The therapist's guide to psychopharmacology* (2nd ed.). New York: Free Press.

Gold, M. S. (1997). Cocaine (and crack): Clinical aspects. In J. H. Lowinson, P. Ruiz, R. B. Millman, & J. G. Langrod (Eds.), *Substance abuse: A comprehensive textbook* (3rd ed., pp. 181–199). Baltimore: Williams & Wilkins.

Goldstein, A., Tachiban, S., Lowney, L. I., Hunkapiller, M. & Hood, I. (1979). Dynorphin (1-13), an extraordinarily potent opioid peptide. *Proceedings of the National Academy of Science, USA, 76,* 6666–6670.

Goodwin, D. W., & Gabrielli, W. F., Jr. (1997). Alcohol: Clinical aspects. In J. H. Lowinson, P. Ruiz, R. B. Millman, & J. G. Langrod (Eds.), *Substance abuse: A comprehensive textbook* (3rd ed., pp. 142–148). Baltimore: Williams & Wilkins.

Greden, J. F., & Walters, A. (1997). Caffeine. In J. H. Lowinson, P. Ruiz, R. B. Millman, & J. G. Langrod (Eds.), *Substance abuse: A comprehensive textbook* (3rd ed., pp. 294–307). Baltimore: Williams & Wilkins.

Grinspoon, L., & Bakalar, J. B. (1997). Marihuana. In J. H. Lowinson, P. Ruiz, R. B. Millman, & J. G. Langrod (Eds.), *Substance abuse: A comprehensive textbook* (3rd ed., pp. 199–206). Baltimore: Williams & Wilkins.

Grob, G. S., & Poland, R. E. (1997). Designer drugs. In J. H. Lowinson, P. Ruiz, R. B. Millman, & J. G. Langrod (Eds.), *Substance abuse: A comprehensive textbook* (3rd ed., pp. 269–275). Baltimore: Williams & Wilkins.

Hooper, J. & Teresi, D. (1986). *The three pound universe: The brain*. New York: Dell.

Hughes, J., Smith, T. W., Kosterlitz, H. W., Fothergill, L. A., Morgan, B. A, & Morris, H. R. (1975). Identification of two related pentapeptides from the brain with potent opiate agonist activity. *Nature, 285,* 577–579.

Jaffe, J. (1990). Tobacco smoking and nicotine dependence. In S. Wonnacott, M. A. H. Russell, & I. P. Stolerman (Eds.), *Nicotine psychopharmacology: Molecular, cellular and behavioral aspects* (pp. 1–37). New York: Oxford University Press.

Jaffe, J. H. (1992). Drug addiction and drug abuse. In A. G. Gilman, T. W. Rall, A. S. Niew, & P. Taylor (Eds.), *Goodman and Gilman's the pharmacological basis of therapeutics* (8th ed., pp. 522–573). New York: Pergamon.

Jaffe, J. H., Knapp, C. M., & Ciraulo, D. A. (1997). Opiates: Clinical aspects. In J. H. Lowinson, P. Ruiz, R. B. Millman, & J. G. Langrod (Eds.), *Substance abuse: A comprehensive textbook* (3rd ed., pp. 158–166). Baltimore: Williams & Wilkins.

Jones, K. L., & Smith, D. W. & Ulleland, C. M. (1973). Pattern of malformation in offspring of chronic alcoholic mothers. *Lancet, 1,* 1267–1271.

Karch, S. B. (1996). *The pathology of drug abuse* (2nd ed.). Boca Raton, FL: CRC.

Khachaturian, H., Lewis, C., & Schafer, M. K. H. (1985). Anatomy of the CNS opioid systems. *Trends in Neuroscience, 8,* 111–119.

King, G. R., & Ellinwood, E. H. (1997). Amphetamines and other stimulants. In J. H. Lowinson, P. Ruiz, R. B. Millman, & J. G. Langrod (Eds.), *Substance abuse: A comprehensive textbook* (3rd ed., pp. 207–223). Baltimore: Williams & Wilkins.

Liska, K. (1994). *Drugs and the human body* (4th ed.). Upper Saddle River, NJ: Prentice Hall.

Mansour, A., Khachaturian, H., Lewis, M., Akil, H., & Watson, S. (1988). Anatomy of CNS opioid receptors. *Trends in Neuroscience, 11,* 308-314.

Milkman, H., & Sunderwirth, S. (1986). *Craving for ecstasy: The consciousness & chemistry of craving*. Lexington, Mass: Lexington Books.

Moir, A., & Jessel, D. (1991). *Brain sex: The real difference between men and women*. New York: Carol.

Morgan, J. P. (1997). Designer drugs. In J. H. Lowinson, P. Ruiz, R. B. Millman, & J. G. Langrod (Eds.), *Substance abuse: A comprehensive textbook* (3rd ed., pp. 264–269). Baltimore: Williams & Wilkins.

National Institute on Alcohol Abuse and Alcoholism. (1990). *Alcohol Alert, 16,* 1-3.

National Institute on Drug Abuse. (1989). *National Household Survey on Drug Abuse*. Washington, DC: U.S. Government Printing Office.

National Institute on Drug Abuse. (1999a). Cigarettes and other nicotine products [On-line]. Available: *www.nida.nih.gov/Infofax/tobacco*.

National Institute on Drug Abuse. (1999b). Chronic marijuana users become aggressive during withdrawal [On-line]. Available: *www.nida.nih.gov/Med/adv/99/NR-420.html*.

National Institute on Drug Abuse. (1999c). Cocaine use and addiction [On-line]. Available: *www.nida.nih.gov/researchreports/cocaine*.

National Institute on Drug Abuse. (1999d). The economic costs of alcohol and drug abuse in the United States [On-line]. Available: *www.nida.nih.gov/EconomicCosts*.

National Institute on Drug Abuse. (1999e). Heroin: Abuse and addiction [On-line]. Available: *www.nida.nih.gov/ResearchReports/heroin*.

National Institute on Drug Abuse. (1999f). Inhalant abuse [On-line]. Available: *www.nida.nih.gov/ResearchReports/Inhalants*.

National Institute on Drug Abuse. (1999g). Long-term brain injury from use of "Ecstasy" [On-line]. Available: *www.nida.nih.gov/MedAdv/99/NT-6146.html*.

National Institute on Drug Abuse. (1999h). Marijuana [On-line]. Available: *www.nida.nih.gov/ResearchReports/Marijuana*.

National Institute on Drug Abuse. (1999i). Methamphetamine: Abuse and addiction [On-line]. Available: *www.nida.nih.gov/ResearchReports/Methamph*.

National Institutes of Health. (1996). *Chronic morphine use produces visible changes in brain cells* [On-line]. Available: *www.nih.gov/news/pr/oct96/nida-07.htm*

Nightingale, S. L. (1990). New indication for Alprazolam. *Journal of the American Medical Association, 264(22)*, 28-63.

Pechnick, R. & Ungerleider, J. T. (1997). Hallucinogens. In J. H. Lowinson, P. Ruiz, R. B. Millman, & J. G. Langrod (Eds.). *Substance abuse: A comprehensive textbook* (3rd ed., pp. 230–237). Baltimore: Williams & Wilkins.

Preston, J. D., O'Neal, J. H., & Talaga, M. C. (1997). *Handbook of clinical psychopharmacology for therapists* (2nd ed.). Oakland, CA: New Harbinger.

Radcliffe, A., Rush, P., Sites, C. F., & Cruse, J. (1985). *The pharmacological basis of therapeutics* (6th ed., pp. 592–607). Upper Saddle River, NJ: Prentice Hall.

Ray, O., & Ksir, C. (1993). *Drugs, society, & human behavior*. St. Louis, MO: Mosby–Year Book.

Saraf, H., Dombrowski, M., & Leach, K. (1995). Characterization of the effect of cocaine on catecholamine uptake by pregnant myometrium. *Obstetrics and Gynecology, 85(1)*, 93–95.

Schmitz, J. M., Jarvik, M. E., & Schneider, N. G. (1997). Nicotine. In J. H. Lowinson, P. Ruiz, R. B. Millman, & J. G. Langrod (Eds.), *Substance abuse: A comprehensive textbook* (3rd ed., pp. 276–293). Baltimore: Williams & Wilkins.

Sharp, C. W., & Rosenberg, N. L. (1997). Inhalants. In J. H. Lowinson, P. Ruiz, R. B. Millman, & J. G. Langrod (Eds.), *Substance abuse: A comprehensive textbook* (3rd ed., pp. 246–264). Baltimore: Williams & Wilkins.

Shatz, J. (1992). Mind and brain. *Scientific American: Special Issue, 267*, 39–48.

Siegel, R. K. (1989). *Intoxication*. New York: Plenum.

Simon, E. J. (1997). Opiates: Neurobiology. In J. H. Lowinson, P. Ruiz, R. B. Millman, & J. G. Langrod (Eds.), *Substance abuse: A comprehensive textbook* (3rd ed., pp. 725–733). Baltimore: Williams & Wilkins.

Substance Abuse and Mental Health Services Administration. (1995). *National Household Survey on Substance Abuse*. Rockville, MD: Department of Health and Human Services.

U.S. Department of Health and Human Services. (1990). *The health benefits of smoking cessation: A report of the surgeon general*. Washington DC: U.S. Government Printing Office.

Valenzuela, C. F., & Harris, R. A. (1997). Alcohol: Neurobiology. In J. H. Lowinson, P. Ruiz, R. B. Millman, & J. G. Langrod (Eds.), *Substance abuse: A comprehensive textbook* (3rd ed., pp. 119–142). Baltimore: Williams & Wilkins.

Wesson, D. R., Smith, D. E., Ling, W., & Seymour, R. B. (1997). Sedative-hypnotics and tricyclics. In J. H. Lowinson, P. Ruiz, R. B. Millman & J. G. Langrod (Eds.), *Substance abuse: A comprehensive textbook* (3rd ed., pp. 223–230). Baltimore: Williams & Wilkins.

Winick, C. (1997). Epidemiology of alcohol and drug abuse. In J. H. Lowinson, P. Ruiz, R. B. Millman, & J. G. Langrod (Eds.), *Substance abuse: A comprehensive textbook* (3rd ed., pp. 10–16). Baltimore: Williams & Wilkins.

Wise, R. A. (1988). The neurobiology of craving: Implication for the understanding and treatment of addiction. *Journal of Abnormal Psychology, 2*, 118–132.

Wise, R. A. (1991). The neurobiology of craving: Implication for the understanding and treatment of addiction. *Journal of Abnormal Psychology, 2*, 118–132.

Zukin, S. R., Sloboda, Z., & Javitt, D. C. (1997). Phencyclidine. In J. H. Lowinson, P. Ruiz, R. B. Millman, & J. G. Langrod (Eds.), *Substance abuse: A comprehensive textbook* (3rd ed., pp. 238–245). Baltimore: Williams & Wilkins.

Etiological Theories of Substance Abuse

SHARON H. ERICKSON, PH.D., R.N.

This chapter explores the theories that attempt to explain substance abuse and discusses the implications for use of these theories in counseling. It will, at times, appear ambiguous, reflecting the controversy and contradictory findings of current research. No single model fully explains why substance abuse occurs. However, progress is being made in sorting out the factors that contribute to this multifaceted condition. Schools of thought in this process are discussed in the following chapter.

The etiology of a disease is the cause of that disease. In the study of substance abuse and addiction, it can more accurately be said that the etiology is the sum of knowledge regarding its causes, as much remains to be learned. Determination of the cause of addictions and substance abuse has historically been a complex and developing issue. Many theories have been offered, but substantive research has been scarce. Multiple factors are often cited, but to date, there is no clear consensus by researchers and clinicians as to why people engage in substance use and why some people become addicted. Moreover, alcoholism and other drug addictions appear to be similar in many respects, yet different in others. In spite of the lack of consensus, it is important to have a conceptual framework of the etiology on which therapeutic assumptions can be based, even while that framework is still evolving. Knowing the cause of any disease or condition is essential in five areas: (a) general understanding of the condition, (b) selection and implementation of appropriate treatment, (c) prediction of possible outcomes of treatment, (d) construction of appropriate research, and (e) prevention of the condition.

Viewed from the moral theory, substance abuse is the result of willful overindulgence and moral degradation and can be cured with willpower and a desire to abstain. The disease theory treats addictions, particularly alcoholism, from a medical viewpoint and looks for biomedical reasons for vulnerability to, and the development of, substance abuse. Genetic theories look for biologically inherited reasons for the development of substance abuse. Systems theorists consider interactions with others, notably the family of origin, as a basis for intergenerational transmission of substance abuse. Behavioralists look to faulty learning patterns and attempts at stress reduction as major components in the establishment and continuation of substance abuse. Sociocultural theory examines cultural factors, social pressures, and environmental conditions that foster the development of substance abuse and addictions. And, increasingly, biopsychosocial theory views substance abuse as a complex, interactional condition, to which all of the aforementioned theories may contribute.

MORAL THEORY

Until the middle of the 19th century, alcohol consumption was considered a part of everyday life. It was assumed that most people would drink, and public drunkenness seldom occurred. Alcohol was commonly used as a table beverage in many cultures and was a featured part of parties and revelry. As America began to move from a largely rural society to the more formal structure of towns in the early 1800s, social control mechanisms began to be felt (Siegal & Inciardi, 1995). Although alcohol consumption was common and condoned, people were supposed to be able to "hold" their liquor, and drunkenness and dependence on alcohol was considered sinful and a shameful example of lack of willpower. Drunkenness was seen as an individual weakness and a threat to society. The resulting moral theory gained impetus during the Civil War, when concern over heavy drinking supported the temperance movement (Nace, 1987). Church and conservative elements of the community made it clear that such moral degradation was inexcusable and was not to be tolerated. Imbibing of alcohol was considered sinful and the imbiber morally corrupt. It was assumed that alcohol intake was under one's control and that willpower and desire alone could prevent overindulgence.

The temperance movement reached its pinnacle in 1919 with the passage of the 18th Amendment to the U.S. Constitution (prohibition amendment), which prohibited the manufacture, sale, and transportation of intoxicating liquors. Prohibition was deemed successful, at first, as alcohol consumption decreased. However, some continued to drink heavily, and a whole new industry of bootlegging developed. This illegal activity developed into organized crime in the United States (Siegal & Inciardi, 1995). By the 1930s, abstinence was no longer the social norm, and the 18th Amendment was repealed in 1933 (Siegal & Inciardi, 1995).

A shift in thinking away from the moral model was accompanied by the development in 1935 of a unique self-help organization for the treatment of alcoholism—Alcoholics Anonymous (AA). AA retained some elements of the moral model in believing that the help of a Higher Power is needed to achieve and maintain sobriety (Blum, 1991) and that individuals are responsible for seeking their own recovery. However, AA was a shift in philosophy from the moral model in that the individual was no longer held responsible for "having the disease" of alcoholism, only for seeking help to overcome it. This shift toward the disease model gained validity when the American Medical Association recognized alcoholism as a disease in 1956, followed by the American College of Physicians in 1969 (Nace, 1987). It is this shift in paradigms that has allowed alcoholism and other substance abuse to be scientifically studied, precipitating the development of new theoretical models to explain their causes.

DISEASE THEORY

E. M. Jellinek, in his work in the 1950s, defined alcoholism as a disease, developing the theory that alcoholism is caused by a physiological deficit in an individual making the person unable to tolerate the effects of alcohol. The disease theory implies that regardless of their history in becoming alcoholic, all alcoholics have the same disease (e.g., the lawyer who is alcoholic has the same disease as the homeless alcoholic), and treatment for all is essentially the same.

In 1950, Jellinek published a description of the disease of alcoholism, based on a survey of 98 male AA members (Pratsinek & Alexander, 1992). He described five types of drinking behaviors numbered by the first five letters of the Greek alphabet: alpha, beta, gamma, delta, and epsilon (George, 1990; Light, 1985) and suggested that there are distinct signs and symptoms of alcoholism, a criterion important if it is to be termed a disease (Light, 1985). These symptoms are clustered into stages of alcoholism: early, middle, and late. According to Jellinek's stages, an individual uses alcohol early in the disease to relieve pain, whether physical pain, emotional pain, tension from job or family, or other stress. Driving while intoxicated and memory blackouts can occur during this stage. As the disease progresses to the middle stages, more visible changes occur, such as job or family problems, absenteeism, financial problems, or changes in moral behavior. Physical changes are also taking place during the middle phases, and treatment is important. If allowed to progress into the late stages, deterioration of the body or brain may make effective treatment impossible. For in-depth reference to Jellinek's theories, see George (1990) or Light (1985).

Generalities from Jellinek's theories should be used with caution because of limitations in the sample population that he used for his study. The sample was small (98) and homogeneous, being male, late-stage, gamma alcoholics (George, 1990). Females were included only as the control group. Further, Jellinek's theory did not explain emerging evidence of a genetic vulnerability to alcoholism (Anthenelli & Schuckit, 1997). Nevertheless, Jellinek's contribution in conceptualizing alcoholism as other than a moral problem is the important foundation for other theories.

CASE DISCUSSIONS

Case 1 (Sandy and Pam).   Both Sandy and her daughter, Pam, would be considered to have the disease of alcoholism. Although Sandy is not currently drinking, she is still "recovering" and will never be considered "cured." When drinking,

Sandy exhibits symptoms of midstage alcoholism: problems with relationships, family, and moral changes. Pam is still in the early stages, using alcohol to deal with stress, anxiety, and social problems. Unless she seeks treatment, Pam's dependence on alcohol will increase and the disease will progress to more serious physical and emotional symptoms.

Case 2 (Joe and Jane).   Both Joe and Jane are addicted to alcohol and cocaine. Neither is able abstain for long, and once they ingest cocaine or alcohol, they use the substance compulsively. The addiction and its effects will worsen if intervention does not take place, and physical, emotional, and social changes will continue. Treatment must include abstinence. Jane continues to deny that her cocaine use is having any untoward effects on anyone, enabling her to continue with its use.

Strengths and Limitations of Disease Theory

Strengths

1. Acceptance of an addictive disorder as a disease means that the substance abuser does not live as a social outcast. Employers and family members are empowered to support efforts of treatment and rehabilitation.

2. Relieving the guilt and shame felt by addicts for having the disease might make them more amenable to treatment.

3. Viewing addiction as a disease opens it to research on its etiology, symptomology, progression, and treatment.

Limitations

1. In claiming to have a disease, some addicts may deny responsibility for change, especially since denial is a main symptom of substance abuse. Some may attempt to deny responsibility for entering treatment programs with the attitude of "What do you expect from a person with a disease?"

2. Alcoholism and other substance abuse are treated in the same way, without recognition of the complex factors that accompany polydrug use.

3. Some authors suggest that a key factor in the maintenance of the myth of the disease concept is that "recovering" alcoholics and addicts commonly work as paraprofessional staff members in treatment and educational programs on substance abuse. The concern is that this group, most without scientific or professional training, uses their personal experiences and anecdotal stories as evidence that substance abuse is a disease, rather than referring to scientific evidence (George, 1990).

Summary

The concept that alcoholism is a disease gained in popularity in the mid-20th century, lifting substance abuse forever from the realm of corrupt morals and lack of willpower to a more acceptable and treatable form. The founders of Alcoholics Anonymous followed this theme in 1935 when they began a self-help movement that does not blame the alcoholic for having the condition, but only for not seeking help. Jellinek, in 1960, defined signs and symptoms, as well as progression of the disease. These form the basis of 12-step or Anon-type treatment programs for substance abuse today. Although not universally accepted, the disease concept has allowed research to be conducted on substance abuse, treatment programs to be developed and evaluated, and public and private monies to be applied to the research and treatment of the problem.

GENETIC THEORY

Is substance abuse of result of heredity or environment? Research involving intergenerational studies, twin studies, adoption studies, and a search for trait markers of alcoholism have all been used to attempt to answer this question.

Several caveats must be observed when reviewing current genetic research. Most of the studies have focused on alcoholism and have used males as subjects. Current researchers, such as Anthenelli and Schuckit (1997), believe that the family, twin, and adoption studies, taken as a whole, suggest that genetics plays an important part in the etiology of alcoholism in both men and women. However, because of limitations in their sample populations, generalizations of many of the studies to chemical dependency and to women may or may not be accurate. Further, genetic studies for alcoholism and other substance abuse differ in several important ways. Thus, studies on alcoholism and other substance abuse will be discussed separately.

Genetic Studies on Alcoholism

Relatives of alcoholics have been found to be at substantially greater risk for alcoholism when compared to nonalcoholics, and evidence of genetic predisposition to alcoholism is growing (Anthenelli & Schuckit, 1997). Stanton (1999) states that genetic influence is identifiable in 35% to 40% of alcoholic-dependent people. Current research has pointed to several genes associated with alcoholism, but none has been identified as the "smoking gun" or factor that triggers the development of alcoholism. Numerous studies have found children of alcoholics to have a three- to four-fold greater chance of developing alcoholism than children of nonalcoholic parents (Anthenelli & Schuckit, 1997). However, the fact that only 15% to 36% of children of alcoholics actually develop problems with alcohol (Stanton, 1999) indicates that other factors also play a role its development. Discerning actual causality of alcoholism is complex because of the multifactorial origins. One possibility being pursued by several researchers is that there are several types of alcoholism, each with different amounts of heritability.

Several studies suggest the presence of many distinct types of alcoholism, differing in both characteristics and heritability (Anthenelli & Schuckit, 1997; Sigvardsson, Bohman, & Cloninger, 1996). Type 1 alcoholism is associated mostly with women and their male offspring, has an onset after age 25, with rapid onset of dependency, passive-dependent personality traits, and minimal criminal behavior. In contrast, type 2 alcoholism is characterized by onset in adolescence, with resulting recurrent social and legal problems. However, findings are preliminary. Anthenelli and Schuckit (1997) have found an overlap between type 2 alcoholics and those with antisocial personality disorder, for whom alcoholism is just one of the symptoms of the personality disorder. Although the presence of several distinct types of alcoholism would help explain some of the complexity of the condition, more research is needed to verify and refine the findings.

Twin Studies

Twin studies compare the similarities or concordance rates for alcoholism or substance abuse of monozygotic twins (those developing from one ovum and sperm) with those of dizygotic twins (those developing from two sets of ovum and sperm). If a disorder is genetically influenced or predetermined, monozygotic twins, who share all of the same genes, should have a higher concordance rate than dizygotic twins, who develop from two separate fertilized ova. Environmentally determined disorders, on the other hand, would show no significant difference between the two types of sets of twins, provided the environments were very similar (Anthenelli & Schuckit, 1997). Current twin studies on males support the theory that genetics influences the transmission of alcoholism, suggesting that inherited factors might affect the quantity and frequency of alcohol consumption (Anthenelli & Schuckit, 1997; Pickens & Svikis, 1991), although not all studies agree. Results on twin studies on females are less consistent. The issues of drug abuse other than alcohol, unfortunately, are more complicated, and the results of twin studies on them are less clear (Anthenelli & Schuckit, 1997).

Adoption Studies

Adoption studies are particularly effective in separating effects of inherited traits and the effects of the environment. If alcoholism were influenced by genetic factors, a high rate of incidence of alcoholism would be found in children of alcoholics, regardless of whether they were raised by their alcoholic parent or by nonalcoholic foster or adoptive parents. Conversely, if the condition were more influenced by the environment, one would expect to find a higher rate of occurrence of alcoholism in children of alcoholics raised by their alcoholic parent when compared to children of alcoholics raised by nonalcoholic foster or adoptive parents.

Recent adoptive studies support the theory that heredity affects development of alcoholism (Anthenelli & Schuckit, 1997). Those who had a biological parent with severe alcohol problems were significantly more likely to have severe alcohol problems themselves than those raised by alcoholic surrogate parents. In Denmark, researchers found that sons of alcoholics were about four times as likely to be alcoholic than those of nonalcoholic parents. Furthermore, being raised by nonalcoholic adoptive parents or by biological parents did not affect this risk (Anthenelli & Schuckit, 1997).

Sigvardsson and colleagues (1996), in another study, found a fourfold increased lifetime risk of severe alcoholism in adopted men when both genetic factors characteristic of type 1 alcoholism and environmental risk factors were present. They also found that if either the genetic history or history of dysfunctional adoptive family were not present, there was no significant increase of type 1 alcoholism in these men. In contrast, adopted men with a genetic history of type 2 alcoholism exhibited a six-fold risk of developing type 2 alcoholism, regardless of their adoptive environment. Neither the group with genetic history of type 1 nor type 2 alcoholism was found to be at risk for the other type. Thus, each type of alcoholism seems to have separate characteristics and factors for heritability.

Generalities on conclusions drawn from the adoptive and twin studies should be reviewed with some caution. The population studied has been northern European, and the studies have not been replicated on other populations. Moreover, heritability of alcoholism has been found in males, but has not been seen to the same degree in women (Anthenelli & Schuckit, 1997). Genetic effects of alcoholism, then, may hold true for northern Europeans and men, but not universally to other populations (Kumpfer & Hopkins, 1993). Studies on daughters of alcoholics and children of alcoholic mothers are less conclusive than those on sons of alcoholics or children of alcoholic fathers, as most of the research has been done on father-son samples (Anthenelli & Schuckit, 1997; Searles, 1991).

Research for Genetic Markers for Alcoholism

Results of intergenerational, twin, and adoptive studies have led researchers to look for specific genetic markers for the condition. In 1990, Blum, with a group of other researchers, identified a gene, an allele of dopamine receptor D2 (DRD2), that appeared to be associated with severe cases of alcoholism (Anthenelli & Schuckit, 1997). There may also be linkage between DRD2 and other substance abuse, leading some theorists to dub it the "reward gene" (Anthenelli & Schuckit, 1997). Any cause-and-effect linkage bas been hotly debated, but its discovery precipitated the study of molecular genetics as a possible factor in the etiology of alcoholism. If a linkage were found, such markers could indicate physical differences between alcoholics and nonalcoholics, such as physiological predispositions for alcohol abuse, differing rates of alcohol metabolism, or varying chemical breakdowns in the metabolism of alcohol, creating differing reactions to the chemical. It would help explain why, when living in similar circumstances, some people will develop alcoholism and some will not.

Several possibilities as to how the genetic components of alcoholism work have been raised:

1. *Altered metabolism of ethanol or acetaldehyde.*   Several studies have found that alcoholics break down acetaldehyde into acetate at about half the speed of the metabolism in nonalcoholic individuals (George, 1990). Indications are that the metabolic abnormality exists even prior to heavy drinking. Like their alcoholic parents, children of alcoholics studied who had never drunk alcohol were unable to convert acetaldehyde to acetate at normal speeds. This may be partially due to liver enzyme malfunction, causing a buildup of acetaldehyde throughout the body. These large amounts of acetaldehyde interact with the brain amines to form active compounds with morphinelike properties. These, in turn, trigger the alcoholic's need to drink more and more alcohol to counter the painful effects of the high levels of acetaldehyde (George, 1990).

2. *Atypical reaction to ethanol ingestion.*   Another finding relating to the metabolism of ethanol is the lack of aldehyde dehydrogenase (ALDH) in some who do not drink much alcohol. ALDH is the major enzyme that degrades the first metabolite of ethanol, acetaldehyde, in the liver (Anthenelli & Schuckit, 1997). A lack of isoenzyme forms of ALDH causes affected individuals, after consuming alcohol, to develop higher acetaldehyde levels, resulting in the unpleasant symptoms of facial flushing, tachycardia, and a burning sensation in the stomach (Anthenelli & Schuckit, 1997; Doweiko, 1999). Half of Asians lack this enzyme, which may at least partially explain their lower rate of alcoholism and lower consumption of alcohol (Anthenelli & Schuckit, 1997). The genetically predicted enzyme system may affect their societal attitudes and habits with regard to alcohol consumption.

3. *Monoamine oxidase.*   Monoamine (MAO), a major degradative enzyme system for many neurotransmitters, has also come under recent study as a possible deciding variable in the development of alcoholism. Some studies have found a decreased level of MAO in alcohol abusers, which may precipitate a preference for alcohol, development of tolerance to its rewarding effects, and personality characteristics, such as impulsivity (Anthenelli & Schuckit, 1997).

Other factors being considered by researchers in the genetic transmission of alcoholism include a search for a link with alcoholism and biochemical markers, electrophysiological markers of brain activity, antisocial personality disorder, personality variables, or an increased risk as a result of other psychiatric disorders (Anthenelli & Schuckit, 1997).

From a genetic perspective, alcoholism is seen as a condition that arises from an imbalance in the brain's production of neurotransmitters responsible for our sense of well-being (Blum, 1991) or in the metabolism of ethanol. Physiological studies hold promise for unraveling the mystery of why some people develop alcoholism and others do not. Genetic predispositions could make some people susceptible to development of alcohol abuse and addiction. Recent studies demonstrating differences in characteristics and heritability between types of alcoholism support that reasoning.

Some theorists (Devor, 1994; Tarter & Vanyukov, 1994) feel that a search for a genetic basis for alcoholism is simplistic and not reflective of the complex nature of the disease. They believe alcoholism to be a complex developmental disorder based on genetic tendencies that are activated by environmental conditions or interactions. Genetic differences in temperament and developing personality traits allow individuals to react differently to environmental factors, leading some to develop alcoholism and others to not have problems with alcohol. This viewpoint greatly complicates research into the causes of alcoholism, as individual factors are extremely difficult to isolate, but it may be more realistic. It also is reflective of the developing biopsychosocial theories, discussed later in this chapter, which include all factors that might affect an individual and the development of substance abuse.

CASE DISCUSSION

Case 1 (Sandy and Pam).   Pam comes from a family with a pattern of alcohol abuse. Geneticists would note the alcoholism of her mother, Sandy, and would be interested in looking at aunts, uncles, and previous generations for similar patterns of alcohol abuse. A family genogram might be utilized to examine substance abuse history over several generations, pointing to a genetic (as well as learned) basis for the abuse (see Figure 3.1).

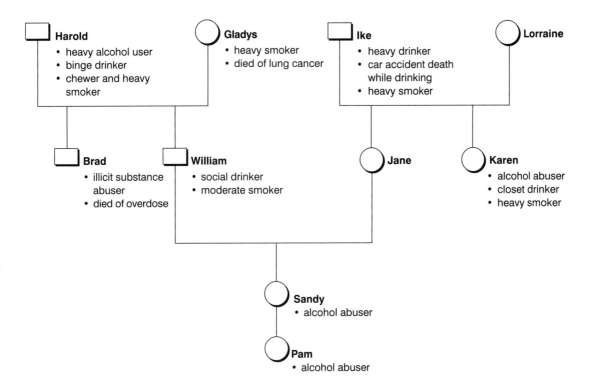

As indicated above, the genogram of Pam and Sandy reveals that alcohol and other substances have been abused for four generations, causing family problems and death throughout the family's history.

FIGURE 3.1   Genogram: Pam and Sandy

The strong family history of alcohol and other substance abuse could indicate a hereditary component to Pam and Sandy's alcohol abuse. Geneticists would also be interested in the way in which Pam and Sandy react to alcohol consumption for clues in metabolism of the substances. For example, if they "feel good" only after drinking, disturbances in liver enzyme function would be suspected, since the morphinelike qualities of the high blood levels of acetaldehyde could cause elevated mood and increased desire to drink more.

Genetic Studies on Other Substance Abuse

It has been more difficult, for many reasons, to conduct research on genetic factors in substance abuse other than alcoholism:

1. While alcoholics comprise a substantial proportion of the population, the numbers of substance abusers fluctuate over the generations, following fads and trends.
2. Alcoholism has been the subject of study for many years, allowing for intergenerational studies to take place. Study of other substance abuse has been done more recently.
3. While the study of alcoholism consists of examination of the effects of only one substance, ethanol, other substance abuse includes a wide range of chemicals, each affecting the body differently.
4. Drug abuse comes in "fads," one chemical becoming popular among a certain population for a time, only to be replaced by another.
5. Polydrug use is common, with one chemical compounding the actions of others.
6. Abusers of substances frequently have dual diagnoses—a diagnosis of both substance abuse and other psychiatric or personality disorders, making it difficult to distinguish markers for predisposition for drug abuse from the preexisting mental disorder.

Research on substance abuse other than alcoholism is limited and preliminary, at best. There does appear to be a general feeling that some hereditary risk factor exists, but identification of any marker and the complicated mechanisms that may convert this predisposition into actual substance abuse lie in the future.

Strengths and Limitations of Genetic Theory

Strengths

1. Research findings on biological differences between those who abuse substances and those who do not abuse substances lay the foundation for further research and a foundation for theories of treatment.

2. Intergenerational studies are useful in detecting the patterns of occurrence in substance abuse. Viewing a family of an individual abusing alcohol or drugs for several generations can provide clues as to the long-term and intergenerational transmission of the condition.

3. Intergenerational studies give a broad overview of the condition, indicating trends and frequency of substance abuse. Such an overview can suggest areas in which further research might be fruitful.

Limitations

1. Intergenerational studies are ineffective in discerning the effects of genetics versus environment and can only imply genetic transmission.

2. Some authors, such as Fingarette (1988) and Searles (1991), have disputed conclusions on genetic studies. Flaws in the design and results of the studies are cited (Searles, 1991). Furthermore, it is argued that the statistics that indicate a genetic tendency in the intergenerational transmission of alcoholism can be turned around, offering the opposite conclusion. For example, if the findings indicate that one-third of the biological children became alcoholics themselves, it can also be said that two-thirds of the children of alcoholics did not become alcoholic (Fingarette, 1988; Searles, 1991; Stanton, 1999).

Summary

Alcoholism runs in families. A review of the literature reveals a consensus that children of alcoholics run a higher risk of developing alcoholism than children in the general population. Recent studies indicate that the genetic influence is one of degree, rather than solely determinant, with environmental influences playing an important role (Stanton, 1999). The results of several studies suggest a genetic predisposition to alcoholism. Others point to dysfunctional dynamics of the alcoholic family in predicting the intergenerational transmission of alcoholism. Recent studies point to the possibility that there may be several distinct types of alcoholism, each with its own pattern of heritability and susceptibility to the influence of environment. Regardless, the child of the alcoholic and adult child of the alcoholic appear to be at risk for emotional maladjustment, alcoholism, and multiple life problems. This does not discount the fact that most children of alcoholics do not become alcoholic or reveal why some children seem to be more resilient to the intergenerational effects of alcohol than others. Genetic components of other substance abuse and addiction are less clear, and research in this area is in its infancy.

SYSTEMS THEORY

There is no evidence that elements within a family can be the sole causal factor in substance abuse and addiction. Yet, it has long been observed that dysfunctional patterns are present in most families that include an alcoholic or an abuser of other substances. Moreover, these dysfunctional patterns often pass from generation to generation. Whether the substance abuse is a cause or effect of the dysfunction, or whether the dysfunction is merely descriptive of the circular pattern of adaptive responses by family members to an abnormal situation, is hotly debated. Nevertheless, because of the presence of these elements in many families with substance abusers, it is useful to observe the patterns that are descriptive of the process and may act as precipitating or contributing causes or may foster the maintenance of substance abuse within the family.

The intergenerational transmission of alcoholism has been observed for centuries, while the debate continues as to whether it is genetically or environmentally transmitted, or both. Systems theorists would note the replication of family structure and dynamics from generation to generation and seek causative factors in substance abuse from these patterns (Doweiko, 1999). Stanton and Todd (cited in Daw, 1995) suggest that intergenerational patterns of alcohol abuse are like scripts that are passed from one generation to another.

In adapting to the presence of substance abuse, roles and power distribution change in the family. In other words, the system changes to accommodate the substance abuser, with family members adapting to keep the family functioning. Thus, they may assume roles and act in ways they may not otherwise act to fulfill the needs of the family. For example, in a home with an alcoholic wife, the husband may assume more of the responsibility for and household chores formerly done by the wife, thereby assuring that the children are cared for, shopping is done, and so forth. Once the system has found stability, great pressure is applied within the system for individuals not to change too much or too fast, for to do so would threaten the integrity of the system and require uncomfortable reciprocal change in other family members (Doweiko, 1999).

In homes where substance abuse is present, individual needs, particularly during times of transition during the family life cycle, may not be met (Berenson, 1986). Chronic alcoholism can also distort the normative life cycle, interfering with the normal emotional growth and development of individuals within the family (Steinglass, 1987). For example, a teenager who has assumed parenting chores because his mother is frequently drunk may meet with resistance from parents when attempting to leave home, as his absence will require a shift in the responsibilities and roles of the parents and children remaining in the home.

Malfunctions in the Family System

Substance abuse can be seen as being both systems maintained and systems maintaining (Lewis, 1992; Lewis, Dana, & Blevins, 1994). Reactive changes in family dynamics usually occur when substance abuse is introduced into the family. Once the family assimilates these changes and reorganizes around the substance abuse, these changes actually support the addiction or substance abuse. For example, if a 10-year-old child begins to watch over a 3-year-old sibling because their mother is high on crack, family function is preserved, if imperfectly. However, this assumption of parental roles by the child also makes it easier for the mother to continue with her crack use, causing a circular pattern of reinforcement.

There is no one prototype for the substance-abusing family. The function that alcohol or drug abuse serves for the family may vary and the response of the family may serve to either isolate or magnify its effect. We can note, however, common stresses on the system of the family with a member who is a substance abuser that can, and frequently do, cause certain alterations of functioning and symptoms in the members.

Families with an alcoholic or other substance-abusing member experience high anxiety levels. It is stressful for anyone living close to an alcoholic (Kaufman, 1986). Other family members of an alcoholic must assume more of the household tasks and responsibilities as the substance abuser assumes an underfunctioning position in the family. Spouses are affected by the characteristics of their substance-abusing partners, as well as the negative consequences of substance-abusing behavior (e.g., financial problems, increased social isolation, family conflicts). Increased depression, anxiety, and physical symptoms have been found in spouses of alcoholics (Kaufman, 1986).

Because substantial differences appear between families in which a member abuses alcohol and those in which a member abuses another substance, families with alcohol and those with other substances will be discussed separately.

Alcoholic Families

Children of alcoholics comprise one of the most prevalent high-risk groups in this country for a wide variety of emotional and behavioral problems, frequently reflecting some of the dysfunction of the home in which they are raised (Velleman, 1992; Werner, 1986). Parental abuse and neglect is common in homes of substance-abusing adolescents (Nowinski, 1990). Researchers have found a significant proportion of these children exhibit problems associated with prolonged stress: low self-esteem, external locus of control, conduct disorders, learning disabilities, repeated delinquencies, alcohol and drug use, and suicidal tendencies (Russell, Henderson, & Blume, 1983). Additionally, some researchers have found that children of alcoholics were more likely to report drug use than children of depressives or children of "normal" parents (Johnson, Leonard, & Jacob, 1989), have a higher risk of alcohol abuse (Kubicka, Kozeny, & Roth, 1990), and tend to drink at a younger age. Other studies have found more social and personal drinking-related problems at an earlier age than do alcoholics having no history of alcoholism in the family. However, a growing number of researchers point out that not all children from alcoholic homes emerge with major problems and focus instead on those who survive. Finding protective factors and factors that create resiliency in children would be important in interrupting the intergenerational transmission of alcoholism. Doweiko (1999) names several factors that affect the impact of parental alcoholism on offspring: (a) gender of the substance abusing parent, (b) gender of the child, (c) length of time of active substance abuse, (d) family constellation and birth position of the child, and (e) whether the child has a surrogate parent that assumes some of the parental role of the alcoholic parent.

When a family attempts to reorganize itself in the face of a prolonged crisis such as alcoholism, changes in roles, rules, and boundaries of the family occur in an effort to stabilize the system. Behavior of family members within the dysfunctional system, observed from the outside, can appear strange or abnormal while, when viewed within the context of the dysfunctional family, they can be seen as being adaptive or an integral part of maintenance of family homeostasis. In other words, dysfunctional behavior can actually be an attempt to preserve the family system (Lewis et al., 1994).

Structural Characteristics of Alcoholic Families

Boundaries   One of the features that allows one family to identify itself, and to identified by others, is its external boundaries. Families with healthy boundaries are well defined yet flexible enough to allow for appropriate exit of family members. Alcoholic families tend to have overly rigid boundaries, restricting contact with others outside the system. The family uses secrecy to protect the family from shame, and concealment of the problem and silence protect the alcoholic from outsiders (Blum, 1991; Lewis, 1992). However, secrecy also makes the family structure rigid and unable to cope with change.

Coalitions   The family also has internal boundaries. One of the functions of the family is delegation of power, usually along generational lines, forming a hierarchy in which the parents hold the most power. Boundaries normally exist between generations, with the parents clearly separate from the children in terms of rules, roles, and power and in charge of the caretaking of young children. In couples who abuse substances, this coalition between parents may become strained or damaged (Lewis, 1992; Preli & Protinsky, 1988). Hierarchical reversals in the family, in which mothers and children are placed in lateral positions of power, may be found. These intergenerational coalitions, either higher or lower than the alcoholic father in terms of power, suggest that children are enlisted into hierarchically inappropriate caretaking positions in alcoholic families, most often with the nonalcoholic spouse. This blurring of the generational boundaries frequently results in the child being placed in the position of "parenting" the parent or meeting intimacy needs that are inappropriate in the parent-child relationship (Lewis, 1992).

Roles   Roles within the family are delegated by the family, and interactions among family members and between the family and the larger social structure are monitored and regulated by the family (Goldenberg & Goldenberg, 1985). Thus, problems of any family member change the dynamics and interactions both within the family and with the larger community social structure.

Several authors (Black, 1979; Wegscheider, 1981; Woititz, 1983) have described roles that are commonly assumed by children living in alcoholic homes. It is currently acknowledged that these roles are frequently present in many dysfunctional families of all types. This anecdotal-based theory has not yet been substantiated in research, but its general concepts are frequently used to treat family members of recovering alcoholics.

Black (1979) describes several roles that children of alcoholics frequently assume: (a) the *responsible child*, who provides structure and stability to an otherwise chaotic family; (b) the *adjuster*, who adapts by withdrawing and detaching from the family; and (c) the *placater*, who smoothes over family conflicts to reduce the family pain. These roles reflect Alfred Adler's birth order theory in which sibling position affects roles adopted within the family. The oldest child is most likely to adopt a responsible child role, the middle child the role of adjuster, and the youngest child that of the placater.

Woititz (1983) adds the roles of the *scapegoat*, who absorbs the blame for the family's dysfunction, and the *clown*, who distracts the family from its pain. The scapegoat, frequently the second child or one who is "different" for some reason, feeling hurt, may engage in delinquency or acting-out behavior. This gives the scapegoat attention, albeit negative attention, and preserves the family system by shifting focus away from the alcoholic.

Wegscheider (1981) describes similar roles. The *hero*, often the oldest child, overachieves out of feelings of inadequacy and guilt, providing self with attention and the family with a sense of self-worth. Enduring feelings of loneliness, a middle child may assume a *lost child* role, appearing shy and choosing solitariness. In this way family pain may be escaped and the family given some relief. The *mascot*, often the fourth or youngest child, may deal with fear through clowning or hyperactive behavior. This gives the alcoholic family some comic relief and the mascot attention.

Although these roles allow for survival in an unbalanced family, the cost to the child may be great. And when carried into adulthood, these roles become dysfunctional. Using Black's (1979) role classifications, responsible or parental children, as adults, take control and continue the pattern of being very serious and unable to enjoy themselves. Moreover, they may be unable to receive help from others. Adjusters may stay in unhealthy situations in adulthood, not having mastered the skill of disengagement and decision making. This may be partly accountable for the large number of adult children of alcoholics who marry alcoholics. Placaters are not likely to ask others for help in meeting their personal needs and spend time caring for others (Black, 1979). Ackerman (1989) and Pilat and Jones (1984–1985) report that a high percentage of professionals in the helping professions are adult children of alcoholics. The interest of many therapists in the field of alcoholism may be related to early exposure to parental alcoholism. It is theorized that they may have been responsible, hardworking, sensitive members of the alcoholic family system and carry this role into adulthood.

Scapegoats (Woititz's classification) may continue to see themselves as the cause of problems as adults, with resulting low self-esteem and a self-fulfilling prophesy to continue to place themselves in situations in which they will be seen as the cause for others' troubles. They may perpetuate self-destructive tendencies and may be prone to addiction. Clowns may continue to be the life of the party as adults but not take themselves seriously (Woititz, 1983). Overuse of humor by clowns aids them in avoiding underlying emotional conflict.

Similarly, using Wegscheider's classifications (1981), the hero, in adulthood, may continue to control and have a compulsive drive. The lost child may experience social isolation in adulthood, and the mascot may be at risk for immaturity and emotional illness.

A home with inconsistent and confusing parental messages and expectations can be fertile ground for the development of dysfunctional personal attributes. These conflicting expectations create double-bind situations and paradoxes in which the child cannot succeed. Attributes that are frequently reported in studies of adult children of alcoholics are low self-esteem, lack of trust, shame, and no real sense of self, which puts the adult child of an alcoholic parent at risk for alcoholism and other emotional dysfunctions (Doweiko, 1999).

Researchers disagree as to whether growing up in a home where there is alcoholism or other substance abuse causes the children growing up there to abuse alcohol or other substances. Some researchers and theorists allege that an unstable childhood does not predict later alcoholism, although it does predict later regular usage of prescribed medication and mind-altering drugs (Vaillant, 1983). Velleman (1992), in his review of the literature, concludes that although there is ample evidence that children of problem drinkers are at a higher risk for developing a number of childhood problems and disorders, these differences between children of alcoholics and children of nonalcoholic parents may not carry through into adulthood. Some recent research has supported this conclusion, not finding a significant difference in emotional adjustment of adult children of alcoholics and other individuals (Harman, Armsworth, Hwang, Vincent, & Preston, 1995). Others suggest that the emotional differences found are not caused specifically by the presence of alcohol in the family but by the presence of any family dysfunction.

Some writers are beginning to talk about those that do survive with psychological health within dysfunctional families, pointing out that many of those growing up in a family in which substance abuse is present become well-adjusted adults. Doweiko (1999) raises the point that there are differences in the depth of psychological trauma within alcoholic families; for example, members of the family in which the father is a "happy drunk" will probably suffer less than those in which the father is violent when drunk. Individual resiliency to psychological trauma may also play a part in the adult health of the person who grew up in a substance-abusing or other dysfunctional family. Some individuals seem to use the challenge of the dysfunctional situation to learn more adaptive skills, becoming more resilient to psychological stress. Nowinski (1990) emphasizes the presence of spirituality as a source of protection against the onset of use of substances in adolescents and in providing psychological resiliency in the presence of substance abuse. Family rituals also seem to affect the transmission of alcoholism intergenerationally. Rituals in which heavy use of alcohol plays an important role are often re-created from one generation to another. Several studies have also suggested that meeting the needs of the alcoholic family member, rather than continuing with the ritual, is frequently associated with the development of alcoholism in the children. Conversely, ignoring the behavior of the alcoholic member and continuing with the family rituals appears to interfere with the replication of the alcoholic behavior. In other words, "deliberateness" in choosing the structure of rituals and in ignoring certain behavior of the alcoholic become protective factors. Thus, children of a family who continued with plans to go on a Sunday picnic, leaving Dad home drunk, would have less likelihood of developing alcoholism than those in the family that would cancel the picnic to stay home to care for Dad.

CASE DISCUSSION

Case 2 (Joe and Jane Smith).   Both Joe and Jane came from alcohol-centered homes, in which emotional and physical abuse were also present. In their present home, alcohol and cocaine use seem to regulate interactions. Sarah may be seen to be acting as the family scapegoat, distracting from both her mother and Joe's drug and alcohol abuse by calling attention to her acting-out behavior. Sarah is also reflecting the replication of the abusive and conflictual homes of her mother and stepfather and is making movements to leave home at an early age. Karen acts as the "lost child," doing her part to stabilize the home by staying out of the way and being quiet.

Substance-Abusing Families

Substance abuse typically begins in adolescence, when tendencies toward risk-taking behaviors occur and movement toward independence increases reliance on the peer group. Such a quest for independence and separation from the family is appropriate for the adolescent stage of psychosocial development (Nowinski, 1990). As in other stages of transition in family life, the changes of one family member precipitate an imbalance in the family system, thereby initiating reciprocal allowance of some independence by the parents. Ideally, the parents will find a balance between maintaining complete authority over the adolescent and abdicating authority altogether.

Most substance abusers are enmeshed (Kaminer, 1991; Ranew & Serrit, 1992)—that is, closely tied to the families that raised them. Multiple studies, replicated in England, Italy, Puerto Rico, and Thailand (Stanton & Heath, 1997), have found that adult addicts and substance abusers are much more likely to live with their parents than their nonabusing cohorts. Differentiation of the child during adolescence causes a crisis in the enmeshed family, and an interactive pattern involving drugs may ensue. Rebelling against inappropriately rigid family boundaries, the adolescent may experiment with drugs, which, in turn, unites the family in an attempt to "help" the drug user. Clinicians have noted, however, that when the substance abuser stops using, a familial crisis often erupts, such as marital problems or the acting out of a sibling (Stanton et al., 1982). This brings the former substance abuser, finally capable of leaving home, back into the nest where the drug abuse is resumed. Thus, the substance abuse provides a dependency in the user that maintains the rigid family boundaries and preserves the enmeshment of the family, and the substance abuser becomes the symptom-bearer for the family. The addict, in effect, provides the family with a solution of pseudoindividuation, a paradoxical resolution to their dilemma of maintaining or dissolving the family by seeming to be independent but, in reality, remaining dependent on the family to meet the addict's, and the family's, needs.

Children who grow up in homes with substance abuse are at risk for becoming substance abusers themselves (Ranew & Serrit, 1992). The quality of parenting suffers, and the child may experience parental neglect and emotional and physical abuse. Contact with neighbors and others may deteriorate, and the family becomes more socially isolated. And the child is more reluctant to bring others into the home, where they might see the abusive behavior of the parent (Ranew & Serrit, 1992). Thus, in the presence of deteriorating parenting, the family system becomes more closed, exacerbating the effects of the neglect and abuse for the child.

CASE DISCUSSION

Case 3 (Leigh).   Leigh can be viewed as the scapegoat of the family. Her rebellion serves to distract her mother and father from their fighting and to unite them as they attempt to control her behavior. It also serves to help solve the dilemma of whether she should leave home, leaving her mother alone. She distances herself by using drugs and alcohol but cannot really leave home and her mother because of her irresponsible behavior. Her brother has the role of the hero of the family, doing well and being responsible while the parents are in conflict. Through the use of their roles, the estranged family continues to function, albeit less than satisfactorily.

Strengths and Limitations of Systems Theory

Strengths

1. Systems theories identify relationships that act as underlying factors in maintaining maladaptive behavior, making it more amenable to change.
2. Sociological forces and relationships that influence the development and maintenance of addiction are considered.
3. The dysfunctional parenting that may precipitate the intergenerational transmission of alcoholism and other substance abuse can be assessed and addressed in treatment.

Limitations

1. Although descriptive of the interactions of individuals within a home with a substance abuser, systems theory does not provide an empirically based cause for substance abuse.
2. There is conflicting research concerning the intergenerational transmission of substance abuse.

3. In those studies finding intergenerational transmission of substance abuse, it is difficult to separate the effects of living in a dysfunctional home from the effects of living in the presence of substance abuse.

Summary

The intergenerational transmission of alcoholism and substance abuse has long been observed. Whether this effect is due to the presence of substance abuse in the family or results from living in a dysfunctional family with inadequate parenting remains controversial. Systems theory describes the structure and interactions of the substance-abusing family, observing the effect of the presence of alcohol or substances on each member. Finding family environment patterns that predispose children for alcoholism and other substance abuse may enable counselors to prevent these conditions in children considered to be at risk. Dysfunctional family patterns can be changed through family therapy and parent training. With more nurturing and functional parenting, children in such families have a better chance of becoming well-rounded, resilient adults.

BEHAVIORAL THEORY

The behavioral theories, including social learning theory, have their theoretical roots in experimental psychology and learning theory (Bennett & Woolf, 1990). Addictions are viewed as learned, socially acquired behaviors with multiple causes (MacKay, Donovan, & Marlatt, 1991). Substance abuse, like other behaviors, is seen as being influenced by biological makeup, cognitive processes, past learning, situational antecedents, and reinforcement contingencies. An assumption is made that all substance abuse, from incidental social use through abuse of alcohol and other substances to addiction, is governed by similar principles of learning and cognition. Current behavioral theories have added cognitive factors as mediating variables to the learning patterns believed to be responsible for development of addictions. Other etiological factors, such as genetic elements, sociocultural influences, and physiological factors, are not rejected. Thus, while most behavioralists believe that learning plays an important part in addiction in some individuals, other etiological factors may also play an important role (George, 1990).

Researchers are beginning to look at the chemical rewards of abusable substances themselves as reinforcers to continue using the substance (Gardner, 1997). Action of the chemical on the brain, causing availability of more dopamine to be present, appears to be highly reinforcing. Circularity of the pattern of use is established when the brain reward circuits, sensitized during the development of substance dependence, create an aversive stimulus during substance withdrawal, acting as a negative reinforcer for the continuation of use (Gardner, 1997).

Social learning theory, developed by Albert Bandura, also forms a part of the behavioral theory about substance abuse (Abrams & Niaura, 1987; George, 1990).

Cognitive, genetic, and sociocultural factors are thought to predispose or influence the experimentation with alcohol or drugs as well as subsequent usage. It is suggested that abuse of substance occurs when an individual's coping abilities, through the interaction of personality sets, learned responses, and current circumstances, are overwhelmed; thus, substance abuse can be seen as one coping mechanism in response to severe stressors. The consequences of substance abuse then become, in themselves, stressors, leading to further substance abuse. A circular behavioral pattern of stress and attempts at stress relief develops. Abrams and Niaura (1987) point out that the immediate tension-reducing properties of alcohol must be measured against the longer-term negative consequences of drinking in deciding to control or stop drinking.

Situational antecedents, such as time of day of drinking, place of drinking, and association with certain people or emotional states, are all important when analyzing the cause of the behavior (Snow & Wells-Parker, 1986). For example, drinking with friends at the local bar three to four times a week to blow off steam, snorting cocaine at parties with friends once a week, and shooting heroin alone would be evaluated for behavioral and situational antecedents, associations, and situational settings. Each of these factors is analyzed so that the maladaptive behavioral sequences can be restructured and changed.

Cognitive processes involved in the behavior are also considered. Anticipating the desired effects of the drug, remembering past pleasant associations with the behavior, and modeling the behavior by others are all important as reinforcements of substance use (Abrams & Niaura, 1987; MacKay et al., 1991). A current trend in behavioral approaches to substance abuse is to address both behavioral excesses (excessive consumption of psychoactive drugs) and a lack of social or behavioral skills.

Addictive behavior is maintained by reinforcement (i.e., the rewarding aspects of drug consumption and the social setting). Several principles of reinforcement are active in behavior formation and maintenance, including addictive behavior:

1. The more rewarding or positive an experience is, the greater the likelihood that the behavior leading to that experience will be repeated (Gardner, 1997; MacKay et al., 1991). Thus, a normally shy individual who becomes "the life of the party" after drinking will want to re-create that experience by drinking again.

2. The greater the frequency of obtaining positive experiences through drug consumption, the more likely that drugs will be consumed again (MacKay et al., 1991).

3. The more closely in time that the behavior (drug consumption) and consequences of the behavior are experienced, the more likely the behavior will be repeated (Childress, Ehrman, Rohsenow, Robbins, & O'Brien, 1992; MacKay et al., 1991). Conversely, the further in time a consequence of the behavior is experienced, the less the likelihood that the consequence will affect future behavior. For example, a lonely man who finds companionship in the bar drinking with others is likely to remember the camaraderie associated with the drinking, and the hangover the next day is more easily attributed to "overdrinking" than to drinking with certain friends. It is this reinforcing association of the two events that increase the likelihood of his drinking when feeling lonely or isolated.

The rapid onset of the effects of substance that are inhaled (e.g., cocaine, tobacco) or injected directly into the bloodstream (e.g., heroin) becomes extremely psychologically reinforcing (Ray & Ksir, 1993). Furthermore, a major problem in the rehabilitation of opioid addicts is the long-lasting effects of the chemical—long after detoxification (Thomason & Dilts, 1991). Results of heroin-induced brain changes, such as disturbances and problems with bladder control, require months to reverse themselves, whereas it only takes a few minutes to get a "high." Unable to feel good without drugs for months during withdrawal, an individual gets immediate reinforcement for drug-taking behavior when feeling good only after drug ingestion.

Alcohol and other substance usage can also be viewed as an attempt to relieve stress. Stress response dampening is one theory that attempts to explain substance usage based on anxiety or stress relief (George, 1990). Alcohol is frequently used as a self-prescribed agent to reduce stress. Stress response dampening, although useful, is generally viewed as only a partial explanation for the abuse of alcohol and other drugs under stress. For example, the stress response dampening theory does not predict that alcohol consumption will reduce stress or which stressful events will initiate usage, nor does it take into consideration individual differences. In situations in which drug use is punished or prohibited, the stress-dampening theory may not be predictive of drug use.

Concurrent use of alcohol and other substances is commonly found. Doweiko (1999) cites correlations to be 74% between tobacco and alcohol-dependent persons, 77% with cocaine-dependent persons, and 85% with those dependent on heroin. The high incidence of concurrent multiple drug usage may be due to a common motivation (e.g., reaching for a cigarette and/or an alcoholic drink when under stress) or may be the result of the effects of one drug on another (Sher, 1987).

CASE DISCUSSIONS

Case 1 (Sandy and Pam).   Sandy appears to be right: Pam has learned how to cope with life and how to relate to others from her mother and is clearly following her example. Both have learned that closeness in a relationship hurts and use alcohol to approach men. Behavior patterns are learned, established, and continuous.

Pam has begun to experience anxiety attacks when fearful of being alone. Feeling abandoned as a child, she is afraid of being deserted. At the same time, she distrusts men. Alcohol acts as a stress dampener, relieving, at least temporarily, the anxiety felt when facing this paradox. The pattern of behavior is replicated.

Cases 2 and 3 (Jane and Leigh).   Both Jane and Leigh use cocaine when with friends. They have learned that using helps them fit in—to be "one of the gang." Jane is even supplied by customers at the bar. It would be difficult to stop using without changing friends and, in Jane's case, her job as well. Being a bartender is also a risky job if sincere about abstaining from alcohol use. Both Jane and Leigh would have to change their behavior and the settings in which those behaviors take place to stay clean. The use of substances has sociobehavioral roots. From a behavioral perspective, both Jane's and Leigh's use is reinforced by the social environment.

Strengths and Limitations of Behavioral Theory

Strengths

1. Behaviors are easily observed.
2. Behaviors are easily measured, as are the results of interventions attempted.
3. Treatment goals for changing the behavior or antecedent reinforcements are easily formulated.

Limitations

1. The individual is treated in isolation from family and family of origin. Reinforcing or maladaptive behaviors within the social system of the identified patient will remain, putting pressure on the recovering addict not to change, so as to "fit" into the maladaptive family or social group.
2. Biological aspects of addiction are only beginning to be addressed.
3. Genetic predispositions to addiction are largely ignored.

Summary

The behaviorist approaches substance abuse, as with all behavior, as the product of learning. Recent theories add cognitive factors and brain reward mechanisms as mediating variables to the learning patterns believed responsible for addictions. Addiction and substance abuse are seen as the result of learning patterns, and antecedent actions and situational factors are analyzed to determine the sequence of these patterns. Stress response dampening may be one reason that people learn to rely on the effects of substances of abuse.

A major disadvantage of the behavioral approach is that the intergenerational, family, and biological factors are not directly addressed. Critics would claim that, although present behavior of the individual might be changed, long-lasting change requires a change in family patterns and attention to the biological changes involved in addiction, as well as to genetic differences in addicts. Behavioral approaches may not have the total answer to causal factors in abuse of alcohol and other substance, but they do have certain advantages. Relationships between antecedent actions and addictive behavior can be clearly viewed and measured, as can social conditions associated with that behavior. Treatment plans, designed to change these patterns of behavior, can then be planned.

SOCIOCULTURAL THEORY

Social and cultural influences on substance abuse cannot be ignored. However, most theorists, while recognizing the importance of sociological factors in the initiation and continuation of substance abuse, view them as part of a complex mechanism that supports the whole.

Alcohol Abuse

Environmental support for heavy drinking is an important sociological variable contributing to alcoholism (Smith-Peterson, 1983; Snow & Wells-Parker, 1986). Attitudes toward alcohol consumption and abuse vary from culture to culture and greatly affect the amount and context of alcohol consumption. In general, solitary, addictive, pathological drinking is more associated with urbanized, industrial societies than with societies that remain largely rural and traditional. Additionally, socially disruptive use of alcohol tends to occur almost exclusively in social settings; drunken behavior is seldom seen when alcohol is used in a religious context. Nonmoralistic attitudes toward alcohol generally appear to accompany nonpathological use in a culture (Smith-Peterson, 1983). For example, in many European countries, such as France and Italy, wine is the beverage of choice with meals, and watered wine is served to children as a table beverage. Conversely, cultures with a recent history with alcoholic beverages, which have yet to completely develop a set of values regarding their use, generally experience more alcohol abuse. American Indian tribes are an example (Smith-Peterson, 1983).

Pressure can be great to conform and to "fit in." Peers and parents show how and where to drink. In conditions of poverty, boredom, and hopelessness, often found in inner cities and Indian reservations, excessive alcohol consumption, as well as other substance abuse, is common and even expected (Smith-Peterson, 1983). To refuse to comply with societal expectations to drink heavily or to seek treatment for alcoholism may mean turning away from previous friends and changing relationships with one's family. Issues raised by cultural and societal norms and expectations must be addressed by the clinician if effective intervention is to take place.

Women are beginning to be included in alcohol studies, some researchers suggest that risk factors for women may differ from those of men. Subgroups of women with elevated rates of heavy drinking include younger women, those lacking social roles or occupying unwanted social status, women in nontraditional jobs, cohabiting women, and ethnic minority women experiencing rapid acculturation (Wilsnack, 1993). Interestingly, most of these factors are associated with the rapidly changing societal conditions for women in this country. Other risk factors for women include living with a heavy-drinking husband or partner, depression, sexual dysfunction, or violent victimization in childhood or adulthood (Wilsnack, 1993).

Substance Abuse

Several components of the environment affect the likelihood that an individual will become involved with substance abuse. On a national scale, multiple social crises in recent decades have encouraged expansion of drug use, abuse, and sale of illicit drugs (Johnson & Muffler, 1997). The expansion of the urban ghetto has encouraged the growth of substance abuse as an industry. A decline in labor-intensive jobs has caused unskilled laborers to sink further into poverty. At the same time, the increased cost of adequate housing has created a sizable population who has inadequate, or no, housing. The proportion of families headed by single mothers, particularly among minorities, has increased dramatically. Black children living in mother-only households increased from 30% to 51% between 1970 and 1985. Moreover, nearly 90% of black families headed by a single woman under 30 will live below the poverty line (Johnson & Muffler, 1997). Such families are also likely to have inadequate housing or live with relatives in crowded conditions. Inner-city youths are less likely to finish high school or to have marketable skills. Child abuse and neglect have increased, and homicide has become a leading killer of young black men. As households experience several of the crises concurrently, which inner-city families do, many are socialized into deviant behavior, such as antisocial acts, child abuse or neglect, or criminal activity (Johnson & Muffler, 1997). In such settings, inner-city families may also experience learned helplessness and feel disenfranchised from society as a whole (Johnson & Muffler, 1997). Within this realm of hopelessness, opportunity for abuse and sale of drugs becomes attractive. Moreover, use of substances may be a way of emotional self-regulation for socioeconomically disadvantaged adolescents, relieving daily stress (Ruiz & Langrod, 1997).

Use and abuse of particular drugs follow faddish patterns of popularity and changes over time. The popularity of marijuana, psychedelic drugs, opiates, and "designer drugs" as drug of choice have waxed and waned (Ray & Ksir, 1993). In the 1960s and 1970s, use of marijuana became popular, peaking in 1979, when 36% of high school seniors were current users. This declined to 15% in 1980 (Inciardi & McElrath, 1995; Johnson & Muffler, 1997). A substantial proportion of the present population has at least experimented with marijuana and may continue to use it as a recreational drug. Marijuana is not only the most commonly used illegal drug in this country but also currently a common secondary drug used by most drug abusers (Inciardi & McElrath, 1995; Johnson & Muffler, 1997). While approximately half of marijuana users do not use other drugs, virtually all of the users of other drugs use marijuana. For this reason, it is sometimes known as a "gateway drug" (Johnson & Muffler, 1997; Ray & Ksir, 1993). Moreover, the heavier the usage of marijuana, the greater the likelihood of using cocaine, heroin, or other drugs or of becoming involved with the sale of illegal drugs (Ray & Ksir, 1993).

Johnson and Muffler (1997) report that the popularity of heroin increased from 1965 to 1973, primarily among inner-city youth in large cities. Usage of heroin typically involved injection on a near daily, or even multiple-daily, basis. In Manhattan, heroin use of young males increased from 3% in 1963 to a peak of 20% in 1972, followed by a decline to 13% in 1974. Johnson and Muffler (1997) state that those born from 1970 to 1975 seem to have developed a strong norm against the use of heroin, particularly in injectable form.

Cocaine usage, primarily snorting (nasal inhalation) and freebasing (inhaling fumes from freebase cocaine), gained in popularity from 1979 to 1984 (Johnson &

Muffler, 1997). Freebasing caused a rapid increase in frequency of usage, as the rapid euphoria felt after inhaling lasts only about 20 minutes and is followed by rapid dysphoria, in which the user feels worse than usual. Relief of the dysphoria is experienced with repeated freebasing, and the cycle of psychological reinforcement continues.

The time period from 1985 to 1990 can be called the "crack era" for the rock or crystalline form of freebase cocaine sold in vials or bags. During this period, a major expansion of existing drug abuse and sales of drugs in inner cities was seen accompanying the use of crack cocaine. New users of crack began to decline in 1990, a trend that continued into the mid-1990s (Johnson & Muffler, 1997).

Developmental and Family Factors of Socialization

A variety of family and social factors affect an individual's decision to start and to continue the use of substances, including alcohol. Family factors, such as attitudes and customs of the family involving alcohol and other substances, tolerance toward public intoxication and drug use, and childhood exposure to alcohol and drug use models, form a background for adolescent attitudes toward substance usage. Additionally, several types of parenting have been associated with an increase in substance abuse in offspring: the alcoholic parent, the teetotaling parent, the overdemanding parent, and the overprotective parent (Lawson, 1992). Social rewards or punishment for substance usage, coupled with this background, can then influence an individual's decision to begin or continue to use substances.

Parental substance use and abuse, particularly when viewed by the young child, provides models for later behavior by offspring. This modeling is also one component of the social learning theory (see the earlier section on behavioral theories of substance abuse). Parental attitudes toward substance usage and parent-child interactions are also strongly predictive of future substance use by offspring (Kaminer, 1991). Young people who perceive their family as caring and against drug usage are more likely to choose peer groups with similar standards. They are also more likely to get better grades, which is also a predictor in abstaining from drug use. In addition to providing role models for future behavior and influencing formation of attitudes toward substance use and abuse, family factors such as high stress, poor and inconsistent family management skills, neglect, and lack of interaction among family members are predictive of later substance use and abuse.

The socialization of the adolescent creates factors that influence drug and alcohol experimentation and abuse that may differ from those of adults. The predominant American culture of the 1990s did not tolerate dysphoria well, and adolescents learn such attitudes quickly. The peer group grows increasingly important in the actions and beliefs of the adolescent, and risk-taking action, common in adolescents, can be an attempt to fit in with peer groups. Groups of peers, or peer clusters (Ray & Ksir, 1993), have great influence on whether an adolescent within that group will or will not use drugs. It may be "cool" to experiment with or abuse drugs, or it may considered "in" to abstain. Moreover, the peer group can facilitate substance use by providing the social structure within which use is part of the culture, as well as providing the substances to use (Nowinski, 1990). The adolescent developmentally is in a group that not only feels omnipotent and invulnerable to life's tragedies but also is attracted to risk-taking behavior and may feel a rise in self-esteem when accepted by a group who approves of drug usage.

Antisocial behavior is also linked with substance abuse, although the causality is unclear. They may share risk factors, antisocial behavior may be caused by substance abuse, or substance abuse may result from antisocial behavior disorder (Robins, 1998). Further research is needed to determine any link to cause and effect or association by risk factors.

CASE DISCUSSIONS

Case 1 (Sandy and Pam).   Sociocultural influences are apparent in their family. Sandy was raised in a home in which alcohol was abused and family relationships were distant and abusive. This scenario has continued into Pam's generation. Not only were the nurturing and positive teaching of life skills absent in their homes, but missing also was the modeling of meaningful relationships with others. There was also a great deal of stress and inconsistency in their families, predictors of future substance abuse. Teaching people how to have nurturing relationships is difficult when they have neither experienced one nor seen one. This effect is reflected in Sandy's and Pam's attraction to relationships with abusive men.

Case 3 (Leigh).   Leigh found acceptance in a counterculture when she felt rejection at home. With divorced parents, a distant father, overly stressed mother, and parents arguing over the kids, Leigh has poor self-esteem and feels that she is the cause of some of the problems. She finds that using drugs with other kids relieves boredom, fear, and loneliness. She feels accepted and acceptable when she is using with them.

Strengths and Limitations of Sociocultural Theory

Strengths

1. Substance abusers are viewed within the larger context of their environment.
2. The importance of social pressure in the development of substance abuse, particularly among adolescents, is recognized.
3. The use of alcohol and drugs is viewed within the cultural context of the individual using them.

Limitations

1. Genetic factors are ignored.

2. Family dynamics are not directly addressed.

3. Individual development and personality factors are not addressed.

Summary

Sociological and cultural factors in substance use and abuse cannot be ignored. The early socialization of the child forms the basis for attitudes toward substance use that are acted upon in adulthood. Adolescence—with its striving toward individuation, reliance on the peer group, and tendency toward risk-taking behavior—creates an environment conducive to the development of abuse of alcohol and other drugs, and the culture of the inner city can encourage its continuance. However, sociocultural influences cannot, alone, fully explain the development of substance abuse behavior. Genetic, family, and behavioral/learning factors work together in forming attitudes and probabilities toward substance abuse behavior.

BIOPSYCHOSOCIAL THEORY

Current research cites many factors contributing to, or having an effect on, substance abuse: genetics, family environment and structure, and brain changes from addiction expressed in behavioral ways and within a social context (Leshner, 1997). The biopsychosocial theory, which takes all of these factors into consideration, conceptualizes behavior as a function of mutual determination and reciprocal effects of an individual, the environment, and behavior. It assumes that many influences combine to create the conditions under which an individual will abuse, or not abuse, alcohol or other substances. It is an integrated theory, rather than an eclectic one, in that it weaves all of the influences and components into holistic concepts with contributing parts, rather than being a collection of ideas and concepts. The research on type 1 and type 2 alcoholism with distinct characteristics and differing amounts of heritability and response to the environment (Sigvardsson et al., 1996) would fit well within this framework. This theory also accounts for differences in substance use and abuse, based on differences in the biopsychosocial structure of an individual. For example, identical twins, raised in the same family, have identical predispositions toward alcohol abuse based on their liver enzyme production. One of the twins begins drinking at an early age, experiencing a heightened sense of reinforcement. The other twin becomes successfully engaged in sports and school activities, avoiding the use of alcohol. Thus, they have identical genes, but have a different addiction profile.

Research in the area of predisposing factors, such as biological and genetic factors, appears particularly promising. Genetic makeup may predispose an individual to alcoholism, allowing the disorder to be triggered by other factors. Kumpfer and

Hopkins (1993) suggest that addictions are multicausal, involving a complex interaction of genetic, physiological, and environmental precursors. They include such factors as individual differences in pleasurable reactions to alcohol, psychophysiological differences, neurochemical differences, cognitive functioning differences, temperament or personality differences, and environmental differences within the family, school, community, and peer group. Research on genetic antecedents for other substance abuse is in its infancy and is much more difficult to quantify because of the variety of drugs, often used together, and the faddish nature of their use (Anthenelli & Schuckit, 1997).

Sociocultural influences, too, appear to offer mitigating factors in the development of alcohol abuse. For example, blacks and Hispanics have more legal and medical reports for opiate use, white teens have higher incidences of alcohol use and abuse than blacks, and Native Americans are at high risk for substance dependence (Winick, 1997). It is uncertain whether these sociocultural differences are due to genetic predispositions, socioeconomic conditions, or cultural attitudes toward drinking, but the overall effect remains clear: some ethnic groups have more problems concerning alcohol consumption than others.

Psychological factors that may interact with a genetic or biological predisposition and sociocultural factors include the effects of growing up in an alcoholic home, learned or conditioned drinking and behavior, and cognitive deficiencies. All of the preceding factors—genetic predisposition, sociocultural factors, and psychological factors—may be present, yet an individual may not abuse alcohol or other substances. Researchers are still looking for reasons that a portion of the population seems to be invulnerable or resilient in response to these effects (Harman et al., 1995). Some theorize that a trigger, or precipitating factor, must also be present to set off the cycle of substance abuse (George, 1990). Several theories have been presented: that cumulative trauma, a severe loss, or sudden success can initiate a downward progression into substance abuse. For example, an individual made vulnerable by other factors may turn to drink or chemicals as a way of coping when threatened by severe loss of health or problems with work, school, or family. Other individuals, such as those with masochistic neuroses and neurotic character structures, when faced with sudden success, may turn to alcohol or other chemicals. Unconsciously feeling unworthy of success, they may become depressed and turn to substances as a palliative measure. This behavior can be observed in some entertainers following sudden and overwhelming fame. Interest and research in these areas are growing and may shed light on the interaction of factors in substance abuse in the future.

CASE DISCUSSIONS

Case 1 (Sandy and Pam). From a biopsychosocial perspective, Sandy and Pam would be seen coming from a family in which many members abused alcohol. Genetic components to a predisposition to alcohol abuse would be suspected. The intergenerational transmission of alcoholism would also be looked at from a systems and learning theory perspective, in which roles and ways to interact with others are learned within the home.

Case 2 (The Smiths).   The family has at least several generations of substance abuse in its history. A predisposition to alcohol and possibly drug abuse would be suspected. The intergenerational effects of living in the highly dysfunctional homes would also be considered, as would the modeling of the family in how to relate to others. The family is substance centered, and drastic reorganization would need to occur to stop the intergenerational transmission of substance abuse.

Strengths and Limitations of Biopsychosocial Theory

Strengths
1. All contributing factors for the development of substance abuse are considered.
2. Treatment can be multifaceted, dealing with many interacting underlying issues.

Limitations
1. It may be too encompassing and too broad to describe precisely the origins of substance abuse.
2. As a combination of other theories, it is difficult to state its basic assumptions and beliefs concisely.

Summary

Biopsychosocial theories of substance abuse are experiencing growing support for their integrated approach. By accepting the influence of many different factors on the individual—namely, genetic, biological, sociocultural, and family—a multifaceted approach can be used for treatment, and comprehensive solutions can be sought. It is increasingly accepted that an individual does not live in a vacuum, and behavior has many influences, both from within and from without. This integrated theory allows for the exploration of all influencing factors in attempting to explain and to change undesirable behavior, such as substance abuse.

CONCLUSION

The concept of etiology of substance abuse, summarized in Table 3.1, has changed dramatically in this century. Initially, substance abuse was considered from a moral model and was thought to be caused by corrupt morals and a weak will. Society began to soften this critical attitude in the 1930s. Jellinek refined the disease concept in the 1950s, defining signs and symptoms of alcoholism, stages of the illness, the course of the disease, and delineating types of alcoholics. Later models of substance abuse have included the genetic concept, behavioral models, sociocultural models, systems theory, and biopsychosocial models. Each model has strengths in explaining certain aspects of substance abuse.

The behavioral and sociocultural models appear particularly useful in the explanation of drug use, while the genetic model shows particular promise for identifying predisposing factors in alcoholism. Systems theories are useful in examining the intergenerational aspects of substance abuse and the forces in the family that seem to help perpetuate its transmission. The biopsychosocial theory is rapidly growing in popularity for explaining substance abuse, as the issues involved are exceedingly complex and not easily explained.

Each of the theories has strengths in explaining the origins of substance abuse, yet none is complete in its explanation. Research is particularly difficult because the factors involved in the abusive behavior are so numerous and complex. Recent trends in treatment of substance abuse reflect this complexity and lean toward the use of combined theories, addressing the interactive aspects of the causative factors.

TABLE 3.1 Comparisons of etiological theories of substance abuse

	Moral Model	Disease Model	Genetic Model
Characteristics	Alcoholism and drug abuse caused by lack of willpower or moral degradation. Willpower and determination are sufficient to overcome addictions. The predominant theory of alcoholism and substance abuse through history until the 1930s.	Substance abuse is a disease, with signs, symptoms, and disease progression. As a disease, substance abuse can be treated. Afflicted individual has sole responsibility for the solution.	Looks for biological reasons for occurrence of substance abuse through intergenerational studies, twin studies, adoption studies, and a search for genetic markers. Suggests a predisposition for substance abuse can be inherited.
Strengths		Removes societal stigma from substance abuser. Relieves feelings of guilt and shame from abuser, facilitating treatment. Allows for research on the disease. Gives hope for a favorable prognosis. Lays the foundation for treatment programs and self-help groups.	Research on biological explanations for substance abuse forms a foundation for further research and treatment theories. Intergenerational studies can reveal patterns of occurrence of substance abuse. Intergenerational studies give an overview of trends in type and frequency of substance abuse.
Limitations	Does not take into account recent research on families, culture, and genetic transmission of substance abuse. Creates a tendency to blame and belittle the substance abuser.	Can be misused by substance abuser to avoid responsibility for seeking treatment. No differentiation between alcoholism and substance abuse is made in treatment. Critics argue that it is an unscientific concept propagated by recovering substance abusers.	Intergenerational studies can only imply genetic transmission. There is some dispute over research methods and conclusions of some intergenerational research.
Advocates	Aristotle Temperance movement advocates (predominant theory until 1930s)	Jellinek Alcoholics Anonymous and other Anon groups Light	Goodwin Schuckit Cloninger Pickens

TABLE 3.1 *Continued*

	Systems Theory	Behavioral Theory	Sociocultural Theory	Biopsychosocial Theory
Characteristics	Considers the family and larger social system for clues to the development of substance abuse.	Addictions are learned, socially acquired behaviors with multiple causes.	Environmental and social pressures contribute to the development of substance abuse.	Substance abuse results from the interaction of predisposing factors, sociological factors, and psychological factors.
	Treats the family system as the patient, changing its structure or interactions as part of the recovery process.	Substance abuse is influenced by biological makeup, cognitive processes, past learning, situational antecedents, and reinforcement contingencies.	Multiple social pressures such as unemployment, single-parent families, and poverty foster the development of substance abuse.	Substance abusers are seen within the larger context encompassing all known influences for development of substance abuse.
	Assumes that families change in the presence of a substance abuser. These changes can actually support the substance abuse.	Behavioral and learning factors are applied in both determining the cause of substance abuse and its treatment.	Societal attitudes toward alcohol and drugs contribute to their use or nonuse.	
	Substance abuse can be a symptom of a larger malfunction within the family.	Social learning theory and stress response dampening are behavioral explanations for development of substance abuse.	Family and peer attitudes toward substances influence their usage.	
	Considers family characteristics such as family member roles, boundaries, and developmental stages when evaluating malfunctions of the family system.	Behavioral factors such as behavioral sequences, situational contingencies, and stressors are analyzed to ascertain the cause of substance abuse.	Peer clusters have great influence over adolescent attitudes toward substance usage.	
Strengths	More elements of the substance abuser's life are used in treating the condition.	Behaviors are easily observed.	Views substance abusers within the larger context of their environment.	All contributing factors for the development of substance abuse are considered.
	Family members are treated, as well as the substance abuser.	Behaviors are easily measured.		

	Family members can support change in the substance abuser.	Treatment goals are easily formulated for changing the behavioral or antecedent reinforcements.	Acknowledges the importance of social pressure in the development of substance abuse, particularly among adolescents. Views use of alcohol and drugs within the cultural context of the individual using them.	Treatment is multifaceted, dealing with many interacting underlying issues.
Limitations	Some critics challenge research that claims an association between children of substance abusers and later development of substance abuse in those children.	The individual is treated in isolation from the family and larger social system. Pressures not to change by the family or to conform to peer norms are not addressed directly. Biological aspects of substance abuse are not addressed. Genetic predispositions to alcohol are ignored.	Genetic factors are largely ignored. Family dynamics are not directly addressed.	Is really a combination of theories, which may weaken its applicability. May be so broad and encompassing that too much can be included.
Advocates	Haley Stanton Todd Bowen Goldenberg Berenson Steinglass Black Woititz	Bandura Woolf Sher	Lawson Kaminer Johnson Muffler Smith-Peterson	George Nace Blane Leonard

REFERENCES

Abrams, D. B., & Niaura, R. S. (1987). Social learning theory. In H. T. Blane & K. E. Leonard (Eds.), *Psychological theories of drinking and alcoholism* (pp. 131–178). New York: Guilford.

Ackerman, R. J. (1989). *Perfect daughters: Adult daughters of alcoholics.* Deerfield Beach, FL: Health Communications.

Anthenelli, R. M., & Schuckit, M. A. (1997). Genetics. In J. H. Lowinson, P. Ruiz, R. B. Millman, & J. G. Langrod (Eds.), *Substance abuse: A comprehensive textbook* (3rd ed., pp. 41–51). Baltimore: Williams & Wilkins.

Bennett, G., & Woolf, D. S. (1990). Current approaches to substance abuse therapy. In G. Bennett, C. Vourakis, & D. S. Woolf (Eds.), *Substance abuse* (pp. 341-369). New York: Wiley.

Berenson, D. (1986). The family treatment of alcoholism. *Family Therapy Today, 1*(6), 1–2, 6–7.

Black, C. (1979). Children of alcoholics. *Alcohol Health and Research World, 4,* 23–27.

Blum, K. (1991). *Alcohol and the addictive brain.* New York: Free Press.

Childress, A. R., Ehrman, R., Rohsenow, D. J., Robbins, S. J., & O'Brien, C. P. (1992). Classically conditioned factors in drug dependence. In J. H. Lowinson, P. Ruiz, R. B. Millman, & J. G. Langrod (Eds.), *Substance abuse: A comprehensive textbook* (2nd ed., pp. 56–69). Baltimore: Williams & Wilkins.

Daw, J. L. (1995, December). Alcohol problems across the generations. *Family Therapy News, 19.*

Devor, E. J. (1994). A developmental-genetic model of alcoholism: Implications for genetic research. *Journal of Consulting and Clinical Psychology, 62*(6), 1108–1115.

Doweiko, H. E. (1999). *Concepts of chemical dependency* (4th ed.). Pacific Grove, CA: Brooks/Cole.

Fingarette, H. (1988). *Heavy drinking: The myth of alcoholism as a disease.* Los Angeles: University of California Press.

Gardner, E. L. (1997). Brain reward mechanisms. In J. H. Lowinson, P. Ruiz, R. B. Millman, & J. G. Langrod (Eds.), *Substance abuse: A comprehensive textbook* (3rd ed., pp. 51–84). Baltimore: Williams & Wilkins.

George, R. L. (1990). Etiology of chemical dependency. In *Counseling the chemically dependent: Theory and practice* (pp. 22–46). Upper Saddle River, NJ: Prentice Hall.

Goldenberg, I., & Goldenberg, H. (1985). *Family therapy: An overview* (2nd ed.). Monterey, CA: Brooks/Cole.

Harman, M. J., Armsworth, M. W., Hwang, C., Vincent, K., & Preston, M. (1995). Personality adjustment in college students with a parent perceived as alcoholic or nonalcoholic. *Journal of Counseling & Development, 73,* 459–462.

Inciardi, J. A., & McElrath, K. (1995). Marijuana. In J. A. Inciardi & K. McElrath (Eds.), *The American drug scene: An anthology* (pp. 85–87). Los Angeles: Roxbury.

Johnson, B. D., & Muffler, J. (1997). Sociocultural. In J. H. Lowinson, P. Ruiz, R. B. Millman, & R. G. Langrod (Eds.), *Substance abuse: A comprehensive textbook* (3rd ed., pp. 107–117). Baltimore: Williams and Wilkins.

Johnson, S., Leonard, K. E., & Jacob, T. (1989). Drinking, drinking styles and drug use in children of alcoholics, depressives, and controls. *Journal of Studies on Alcohol, 50,* 427–431.

Kaminer, Y. (1991). Adolescent substance abuse. In R. J. Frances & S. I. Miller (Eds.), *Clinical textbook of addictive disorders* (pp. 310–346). New York: Guilford.

Kaufman, E. (1986). The family of the alcoholic patient. *Psychosomatics, 27*(5), 347–358.

Kubicka, L., Kozeny, J., & Roth, Z. (1990). Alcohol abuse and its psychosocial correlates in sons of alcoholics as young men and in the general population of young men in Prague. *Journal of Studies on Alcohol, 51,* 49–58.

Kumpfer, K. L., & Hopkins, R. (1993, March). Prevention: Current research and trends. *Psychiatric Clinics of North America, 16*(1), 11–20.

Lawson, G. W. (1992). A biopsychosocial model of adolescent substance abuse. In G. W. Lawson

& A. W. Lawson (Eds.), *Adolescent substance abuse: Etiology, treatment, and prevention* (pp. 3–10). Gaithersburg, MD: Aspen.

Leshner, A. I. (1997). Foreword. In J. H. Lowinson, P. Ruiz, R. B. Millman, & J. G. Langrod (Eds.), *Substance abuse: A comprehensive textbook* (3rd ed., p. ix). Baltimore: Williams & Wilkins.

Lewis, J. A. (1992). Treating the alcohol-affected family. In L. L'Abate, J. E. Farrar, & D. A. Serritella (Eds.), *Handbook of differential treatments for addictions*. Needham Heights, MA: Allyn & Bacon.

Lewis, J. A., Dana, R. Q., & Blevins, G. A. (1994). *Substance abuse counseling: An individualized approach*. Pacific Grove, CA: Brooks/Cole.

Light, W. J. (1985). *Alcoholism: Its natural history, chemistry, and general metabolism*. Springfield, IL: Thomas.

MacKay, P. W., Donovan, D. M., & Marlatt, G. A. (1991). Cognitive and behavioral approaches to alcohol abuse. In R. J. Frances & S. I. Miller (Eds.), *Clinical textbook of addictive disorders* (pp. 452–481). New York: Guilford.

Nace, E. P. (1987). *The treatment of alcoholism*. New York: Brunner/Mazel.

Nowinski, J. (1990). *Substance abuse in adolescents and young adults*. New York: Norton.

Pickens, R. W., & Svikis, D. S. (1991). Genetic contributions to alcoholism diagnosis. *Alcohol Health & Research World, 15*(4), 272–277.

Pilat, J. M., & Jones, J. W. (1984–1985). Identification of children of alcoholics: Two empirical studies. *Alcohol, Health & Research World, 9*(2), 27–33.

Pratsinek, G., & Alexander, R. (1992). *Understanding substance abuse and treatment*. Springfield, VA: Goodway Graphics.

Preli, R., & Protinsky, H. (1988). Aspects of family structures in alcoholic, recovered, and nonalcoholic families. *Journal of Marital and Family Therapy, 14*(3), 311–314.

Ranew, L. F., & Serrit, D. A. (1992). Substance abuse and addiction. In L. L'Abate, J. E. Farrar, & D. A. Serritella (Eds.), *Handbook of differential treatments for addictions* (pp. 84–86). Needham Heights, MA: Allyn & Bacon.

Ray, O., & Ksir, C. (1993). *Drugs, society, & human behavior* (6th ed.). St. Louis, MO: Mosby.

Robins, L. N. (1998). The intimate connection between antisocial personality and substance abuse. *Social Psychiatry and Psychiatric Epidemiology, 33*(8), 393–399.

Ruiz, P., & Langrod, J. G. (1997). Hispanic Americans. In J. H. Lowinson, P. Ruiz, R. B. Millman, & J. G. Langrod (Eds.), *Substance abuse: A comprehensive textbook* (3rd ed., pp. 705–711). Baltimore: Williams & Wilkins.

Russell, M., Henderson, C., & Blume, S. B. (1983). *Children of alcoholics: A review of the literature*. New York: Children of Alcoholics Foundation.

Schuckit, M. (1983). Alcoholic men with no alcoholic first-degree relative. *American Journal of Psychiatry, 140*, 439–443.

Searles, J. S. (1991). The genetics of alcoholism: Impact on family and sociological models of addiction. *Family Dynamics of Addictions Quarterly, 1*(1), 3–21.

Sher, K. J. (1987). Stress response dampening. In H. T. Blane & K. E. Leonard (Eds.), *Psychological theories of drinking and alcoholism* (pp. 227–271). New York: Guilford.

Siegal, H. A., & Inciardi, J. A. (1995). A brief history of alcohol. In J. A. Inciardi & K. McElrath (Eds.), *The American drug scene: An anthology* (pp. 45–49). Los Angeles: Roxbury.

Sigvardsson, S., Bohman, M., & Cloninger, C. R. (1996). Replication of the Stockholm Adoption Study of alcoholism. *Archives of General Psychiatry, 33*(8), 681–687.

Smith-Peterson, C. (1983). Substance abuse treatment and cultural diversity. In G. Bennett, C. Vourakis, & D. Woolf (Eds.), *Substance abuse: Pharmacologic, developmental, & clinical perspectives* (pp. 370–383). New York: Wiley.

Snow, R. W., & Wells-Parker, E. (1986). Drinking reasons, alcohol consumption levels, and drinking locations among drunken drivers. *International Journal of the Addictions, 21*, 671–689.

Stanton, M. D. (1999). Alcohol use disorders. *Clinical Update, 1*(3).

Stanton, M. D., & Heath, A. W. (1997). Family and marital therapy. In J. H. Lowinson, P. Ruiz, R. B. Millman, & J. G. Langrod (Eds.), *Substance abuse: A comprehensive textbook* (3rd ed., pp. 448–454). Baltimore: Williams & Wilkins.

Stanton, M. D., Todd, T. C., Heard, D. B., Kirschner, D., Kleiman, J. I;, Mowatt, D. T., Riley, P., Scott, S. M., & Van Deusen, M. M. (1982). A conceptional model. In M. D. Stanton, T. C. Todd, & Associates, *The family therapy of drug abuse and addiction* (pp. 7–30). New York: Guilford.

Steinglass, P. (1987). *The alcoholic family*. New York: Basic Books.

Tarter, R. E., & Vanyukov, M. (1994). Alcoholism: A developmental disorder. *Journal of Consulting and Clinical Psychology, 62*(6), 1096–1107.

Thomason, J. H. H., & Dilts, S. L. (1991). Opioids. In R. J. Frances & S. I. Miller (Eds.), *Clinical textbook of addictive disorders* (pp. 103–120). New York: Guilford.

Vaillant, G. E. (1983). *The natural history of alcoholism*. Cambridge, MA: Harvard University Press.

Velleman, R. (1992). Intergenerational effects: A review of environmentally oriented studies concerning the relationship between parental alcohol problems and family disharmony in the genesis of alcohol and other problems. I: The intergenerational effects of alcohol problems. *International Journal of the Addictions, 27*(3), 36–39.

Wegscheider, S. (1981). From the family trap to family freedom. *Alcoholism, 1*(3), 36–39.

Werner, E. E. (1986). Resilient offspring of alcoholics: A longitudinal study from birth to age 18. *Journal of Studies on Alcohol, 47*, 4–40.

Wilsnack, S. C. (1993). Drinking and problem drinking in U.S. women: Patterns and recent trends. *Recent Developments in Alcoholism, 12*, 29–50.

Winick, C. (1997). Epidemiology. In J. H. Lowinson, P. Ruiz, R. B. Millman, & J. G. Langrod (Eds.), *Substance abuse: A comprehensive textbook* (3rd ed., pp. 10–16). Baltimore: Williams & Wilkins.

Woititz, J. G. (1983). *Adult children of alcoholics*. Deerfield Beach, FL: Health Communications.

Assessment and Diagnosis | 4

LINDA L. CHAMBERLAIN, PSY.D., AND CYNTHIA L. JEW, PH.D.

Accurate assessment and diagnosis in treating substance abuse are crucial for adequate treatment planning and delivery of services. Improper assessment and faulty diagnosis can lead counselors to create ineffective treatment plans, have inappropriate expectations for therapy, and instill an overall sense of frustration in both the client and the therapist. You cannot treat what you do not recognize or understand. As with other diseases and disorders, the earlier a therapist diagnoses a substance abuse problem, the better the prognosis for the client.

This chapter will present a theoretical and practical framework for assessment and acquaint clinicians with several methods and tools that can aid in diagnosing substance abuse or dependence. Guidelines for conducting an assessment interview and obtaining a reliable history are provided. Several major assessment instruments generally available to clinicians will be reviewed. The issue of diagnosis and the problems related to differential and dual diagnosis will be explored. Counselors thereby should receive a pragmatic orientation to making an accurate diagnosis of a substance abuse problem.

ASSESSMENT METHODS AND ISSUES

It may be helpful to note at the onset that the assessment and diagnosis of substance abuse is not an exact science. At the present time, there is no single medical or psychological test that can determine with absolute certainty that a person is drug- or alcohol-dependent. Also, the inconsistency in social attitudes about alcohol and drug use, and the imprecise standards that define what constitutes a drinking or drug problem, often complicate a clinician's awareness and attitudes about a client's substance use. The stigma associated with alcoholism or drug addiction often leads to denial by the user, their family, and many health professionals.

Gallant (1987, p. 47) notes that the beginning therapist must be aware of several other problems that may interfere with the diagnostic process. First, the therapist may have developed some biases about substance abuse clients. Beliefs that substance abusers are uncaring, irresponsible, untrustworthy, dangerous, or untreatable are certain to interfere with a clinician's ability to conduct an accurate and sensitive diagnostic interview. Second, the client's attitude about alcohol or drugs and his or her sense of shame in seeking help from a mental health professional may create a barrier to accurate assessment. It is not unusual for clients to seek help from clinicians for problems such as depression or anxiety that may be secondary to their drug use or drinking. The stigma of being labeled a "drunk" or "addict" is still a powerful deterrent to disclosing their pattern of substance use for many people, especially women.

In large part, a clinician's awareness of common factors and problems related to substance abuse is of great importance. An understanding of the dynamics of denial, tolerance, loss of control, and the diverse medical consequences associated with different drugs of abuse is an essential prerequisite for accurate diagnosis. A familiarity with Jellinek's (1960) symptom chart for alcoholism and other similar charts that delineate the progression of symptoms for other drugs of abuse can help guide the clinician in the assessment process. Later in this chapter, the behavioral and social characteristics associated with substance abuse will be described in greater detail. Previous chapters have described some of the symptoms, effects, and dynamics that should serve as "red flags" for pursuing more formal diagnostic procedures. However, assessment still is somewhat a process of "skunk identification," meaning if it looks, smells, and walks like a skunk, it's probably a skunk.

The process of diagnosing substance abuse is perhaps most relentlessly complicated by the phenomenon of denial. Denial and minimization of the severity of a drug abuse problem are often an essential part of how substance abusers learn to function in their world. Without the mechanism of denial, users could not continue their pattern of substance abuse. Although not all substance abusers exhibit patterns of denial, most minimize or avoid facing the consequences of their use on both themselves and others. Denial or minimization serves to keep reality at arm's length and allows the dependent person to believe that no one is aware of the excessive drug use and the negative impact it is having on his or her life. The use of denial to delude both the user and others tremendously complicates the assessment process. Therefore, establishing some standardized format for assessment and diagnosis is essential in helping clinicians maintain consistency in providing appropriate detection and treatment for their clients.

THE DIAGNOSTIC INTERVIEW

The most important aspect of any assessment of substance abuse is the diagnostic interview. A carefully planned and conducted interview is the cornerstone of the diagnostic process. The initial contact with someone for the assessment of substance abuse may occur within the context of individual, family, group, or marital counseling. The clinician may be aware of the possible problem by the nature of the referral or may discover it within the context of a family or marital problem. Referrals from physicians, other clinicians, or the legal system may be clearly defined as a referral for the purpose of assessing a drug or alcohol problem. Most assessments, however, will initially be undertaken as a part of the clinician's normal interviewing procedure. It is striking how many mental health professionals do not include at least some questions about a client's drug and alcohol use history in their standard interview format. Clinical training programs are often lacking in course work or opportunities for practical experience that expose medical and mental health professionals to the dynamics and treatment of addictions.

Given the prevalence of denial on the part of substance abusers, if there is any suspicion about a possible substance use problem, it is important in the first interview to request permission to involve family members, friends, coworkers, and others who may be able to provide more objective information about the client's pattern of substance use and related behaviors.

Initially, it is still important to ask the client directly about his or her use of drugs or alcohol. A useful question is "Do you believe that your use of alcohol or other drugs has caused problems in your life?" Many clinicians find it helpful to assure the client that they are not asking questions about substance use to make judgments. Often, people will respond less defensively if they are reassured that "I'm not here to tell you that you are or aren't an addict. I simply need to understand as much about the problem as I can and to help you (and your family) determine whether your drug and/or alcohol use may be playing a role in the current situation." Also ask significant others in the client's life about his or her use to obtain information on whether they view the client's problems as related to substance abuse.

An interview format that gathers information specific to substance abuse should be a standard part of the assessment process. An example of a structured interview format is the Substance Use History Questionnaire. It may be given to the client to complete, or the questions can be asked during the interview. (See Questionnaire 1, Substance Use History Questionnaire, in the appendix to this chapter.) The information from this procedure will help in determining what additional assessment instruments to use. Information regarding work habits, social and professional relationships, medical history, and previous psychiatric history are also necessary for the assessment. Questions related to each of these areas should be included as a part of the standard intake interview.

Family members and significant others may be unaware of or reluctant to divulge information about the client's substance use patterns. Like the client, they are often experiencing denial or avoiding a confrontation with the user. Common misinformation about substance abuse may divert the focus of the problem to other factors that are then presented as the primary problem. For example, a wife may describe her husband as using alcohol to relieve feelings of depression rather than identifying the substance use as a causal or maintaining factor in her partner's emotional turmoil. Because of the shame and embarrassment that frequently accompany the admission of substance abuse, the clinician may need to reassure everyone involved in the assessment that appropriate help can only be made available if an understanding of the problem is accurate and complete.

DSM-IV Diagnosis

One of the primary difficulties encountered in diagnosing alcohol and drug problems may lie in the inadequate definitions commonly used. In an attempt to provide more comprehensive, specific, symptom-related criteria for diagnosis, the American Psychiatric Association (1994) developed categories for "Substance-Related Disorders" in the *Diagnostic and Statistic Manual IV* (DSM-IV). The term *substance* is used to refer to a drug of abuse, a medication, or a toxin. Substances are grouped into 11 classes: alcohol; amphetamines; caffeine; cannabis; cocaine; hallucinogens; inhalants; nicotine; opioids; phencyclidine (PCP); and sedatives, hypnotics, or anxiolytics (antianxiety drugs). The Substance-Related Disorders are divided into two basic groups: the Substance Use Disorders (Substance Dependence and Substance Abuse) and the Substance-Induced Disorders (including Substance Intoxication and Substance Withdrawal). The essential features of the Substance Use Disorders are as follows:

Criteria for Substance Dependence

A maladaptive pattern of substance use, leading to clinically significant impairment or distress, as manifested by three (or more) of the following, occurring at any time in the same 12-month period:

1. tolerance, as defined by either of the following:
   a. a need for markedly increased amounts of the substance to achieve intoxication or desired effect
   b. markedly diminished effect with continued use of the same amount of the substance
2. withdrawal, as manifested by either of the following:
   a. the characteristic withdrawal syndrome for the substance
   b. the same (or a closely related) substance is taken to relieve or avoid withdrawal symptoms
3. the substance is often taken in larger amounts or over a longer period than was intended
4. there is a persistent desire or unsuccessful efforts to cut down or control substance use
5. a great deal of time is spent in activities necessary to obtain the substance (e.g., visiting multiple doctors or driving long distances), use the substance (e.g., chain smoking), or recover from its effects
6. important social, occupational, or recreational activities are given up or reduced because of substance use
7. the substance use is continued despite knowledge of having a persistent or recurrent physical or psychological problem that is likely to have been caused or exacerbated by the substance (e.g., current cocaine use despite recognition of cocaine-induced depression, or continued drinking despite recognition that an ulcer was made worse by alcohol consumption) (p. 181)

Criteria for Substance Abuse

A. A maladaptive pattern of substance use leading to clinically significant impairment or distress, as manifested by one (or more) of the following, occurring within a 12-month period:

1. recurrent substance use resulting in a failure to fulfill major role obligations at work, school, or home (e.g., repeated absences or poor work performance

related to substance use; substance-related absences, suspensions, or expulsions from school; neglect of children or household)

2. recurrent substance use in situations in which it is physically hazardous (e.g., driving an automobile or operating a machine when impaired by substance use)
3. recurrent substance-related legal problems (e.g., arrests for substance-related disorderly conduct)
4. continued substance use despite having persistent or recurrent social or interpersonal problems caused or exacerbated by the effects of the substance (e.g., arguments with spouse about consequences of intoxication, physical fights)

B. The symptoms have never met the criteria for Substance Dependence for this class of substance. The category of Substance Dependence is the more severe diagnosis and is the DSM-IV description of what may otherwise be defined as addiction. The DSM-IV also lists several criteria for rating the severity of the dependence. Clinicians should be acquainted with the physiological and psychological manifestations of both acute drug or alcohol intoxication and withdrawal symptoms as outlined in the DSM-IV. Certain drugs, such as barbiturates, can have serious medical complications associated with withdrawal and clients must be under a physician's care in order to assure they will safely complete the detoxification period. (pp. 182–183)

Behavioral Characteristics

Substance abuse almost always occurs within the context of other problems. Common presenting problems that are related to substance abuse are marital and family conflict, child abuse, unemployment, financial problems, multiple medical problems, depression, suicide, and problems with aggression and violence. In assessing the role of substance abuse within the context of other problems, the clinician needs to understand the dynamics of other behavioral problems and how they may be exacerbated by substance abuse. For example, it is estimated that most domestic violence occurs during periods when one or both parties are abusing some substance and that as many as two-thirds of homicides and serious assaults involve alcohol. Criminal behavior such as child abuse or sexual molestation may be committed when the perpetrator is under the influence of a drug or alcohol. In one study, Chasnoff (1988) found that 64% of all child abuse cases in New York City involved a perpetrator who was under the influence of drugs and/or alcohol. Although there is some disagreement about the exact nature of the relationship between substance abuse and violence, clearly a strong correlation exists between the two.

An important question for the clinician during a first interview is "Did all or any of these problems [the presenting problems] occur while you were drinking or using any other type of drug?" If the answer is yes, one can then begin to gather information to determine whether a pattern of use is causing or contributing to the client's behavioral symptoms. Again, given the nature of denial, this query should also be made with significant others who are participating in the assessment.

As a general rule, a drug or alcohol problem exists and requires treatment if the use of the substance continues despite significant interference in any one of the six major areas of a person's life:

1. Job or school
2. Relationships with family
3. Social relationships
4. Legal problems
5. Financial problems
6. Medical problems

Behaviorally, addiction can be considered any use of a psychoactive substance that causes damage to the individual or society or both.

Becoming dependent on any substance is a process that occurs over differing periods of time for different individuals and varies with the use of different substances. A dependence on alcohol may take several decades to develop, whereas an addiction to cocaine, especially "crack" cocaine, may occur almost immediately. Individuals are likely, however, to pass through certain phases as their dependence on a substance increases. An old proverb regarding alcoholism outlines the progression of addiction: "The person takes a drink, the drink takes a drink, and the drink takes the person." The journey from controlled use to being controlled by the use is the nature of addiction. No one begins using alcohol or other drugs with the goal of becoming addicted. A more in-depth, definitive review of the behavioral symptoms will provide a basis for recognizing the path that substance abusers travel.

Phase 1: The Prodromal Phase

The first phase of chemical addiction can be labeled the prodomal phase. In this phase, casual or social use of a substance begins to change, and the first signs of dependence can be charted. In this early phase, the following behavioral changes generally occur:

1. Developing increased tolerance
2. Experiencing the first blackout or loss of significant time to drug use
3. Sneaking drinks or drugs
4. Becoming preoccupied with drinking or drug use
5. Gulping drinks or hurried ingestion of chemicals
6. Avoiding reference to drinking or drug use

The first symptom noted in the prodromal phase is an increase in tolerance. Tolerance can be defined as "[t]he adaptation of an organism to a drug, so that the same dose repeated produces less and less of an effect" (Palfai & Jankiewicz, 1991, p. 500). Physiologically, the brain and central nervous system adapt over time to the effects of any psychoactive substance. Therefore, the user must increase over time the amount of the substance or the frequency of use to achieve the sought-after effect. Counselors should ask about any changes in the amount or frequency of drug use to establish the symptom of tolerance.

The second symptom in this phase is the onset of blackouts. A blackout is not unconsciousness; the user remains awake and active but later does not remember what was said or done while he was using. It is an indication that the user was able to ingest enough of the substance to "anesthetize" the part of the brain that processes short-term memory. Blackouts do not occur with all categories of substances but are a prominent feature of alcohol abuse.

The third behavioral symptom is sneaking drinks or drugs. This often means that the user will "preuse" by drinking or using before a social gathering to assure that she has enough. The user also begins "stockpiling" her drugs or hiding them from others who might share them. The user typically experiences discomfort or irritability with others who are not keeping up with her rate of drinking or using drugs.

The fourth symptom involves a cognitive change in which the user becomes more preoccupied with time spent using. Behaviorally, it is manifested by making social plans that increasingly focus on the opportunity to drink or use, leaving work early to have extra time to drink, becoming irritable if there is any interruption in the time set aside to get high, and spending an increased amount of time and effort in assuring that the user has plenty of alcohol or drugs available.

The fifth symptom, a more hurried ingestion of drugs or alcohol, is an extension of the development of tolerance. Users become concerned that they will not have enough of the substance to relax or "get a buzz" and thus use more quickly to get a higher level in their system. Nearly all of the behaviors in the first stage can be summarized by describing the user who might develop a serious problem as the one who must "have a drink (or drug), and have it fast" (Blue Cross and Blue Shield Associations, 1979).

The final symptom in the prodromal phase sets the stage for denial. The user begins to feel uncomfortable with others' comments or questions about the changes in her pattern of drug or alcohol use and avoids confrontation. She begins to estrange herself from others who might express concern about her use and avoids questioning herself about the change in her relationship with the substance.

Phase 2: The Crucial Phase

In the middle or crucial phase, the substance abuser experiences some of the more obvious and pronounced behavioral changes associated with addiction. This phase is considered "crucial" because it offers the most hope for an intervention in the growing physical and psychological dependence before some of the more severe medical and social consequences enter the picture. It is also during this phase that family and significant others usually become more aware of the user's growing dependence on drugs or alcohol. In this second phase, the following behavioral symptoms usually occur:

1. Loss of control of substance use
2. Denial and minimization of use
3. Confrontation by others
4. Behavioral loss of control
5. Guilt and remorse

6. Periodic abstinence or change in patterns of use

7. Losses

8. Medical and psychological interventions

9. Growing alienation and resentment

10. More frequent substance use

The first symptom, loss of control of the substance, is often misunderstood and poorly defined. In the dynamics of addiction, loss of control means loss of predictability. For example, an individual who is abusing alcohol begins to experience times when he drinks more than he intends. On one night, he may have only the three beers he planned to drink after work. On the following night, his same plan falls apart and he drinks until he passes out. The user cannot predict with any certainty when he will be able to stick to his plan and when he will use more than he intended.

The next set of behavioral symptoms (numbers 2 through 6) will be considered together since they usually occur as part of a pattern of confrontation and denial. At this point, changes in the user's behavior related to drugs or alcohol is generally more obvious. While intoxicated or recovering from a binge, the user is more likely to become aggressive, impulsive, extravagant, or otherwise unpredictable in her behavior. If confronted, the user is likely to insist that she can control it and stop any time. In fact, the user may quit for a brief period of time to "prove" she has control. Guilty feelings may begin when the user is confronted with the result of some harmful behavior that occurred while she was intoxicated (e.g., missing a child's birthday because she was drinking with buddies at the bar instead of picking up the birthday cake and going home as she had promised). Fear sets in, followed by flashes of remorse and sometimes aggressiveness or isolation to keep others at a distance. The consequences of her actions while using are increasingly difficult to minimize, rationalize, or deny.

The final group of symptoms in the crucial phase (numbers 7 through 10) outline some of the more overt consequences that users experience as the addiction progresses. The more overt losses include loss of friends, divorce, loss of a job or financial setbacks, loss of other interests such as hobbies or leisure pursuits, and loss of a normal, daily routine that does not revolve around substance use. Other, less clearly observable losses include a loss of ordinary willpower, loss of self-respect, and an abandonment of moral or spiritual values. Often during this phase, the user experiences some acute medical consequences related to the use and will seek medical intervention for secondary symptoms (problems that are secondary to their drug or alcohol use). For example, a cocaine user may experience periodic heart arrhythmias (irregular heartbeat) and seek a doctor's advice for the heart problem but not for the cocaine use that is causing the difficulty (the primary problem). Denial creates and perpetuates a vicious circle. Since the user denies that he has a problem, he cannot go to others to talk about it. Therefore, he may use more to overcome the guilt or anxiety that results from the loss of control of his behavior. As the user becomes further trapped in the cycle of remorse, his resentment and blame externalize the fears and lead to increased alienation.

Phase 3: The Chronic Phase

The final, or chronic, phase of addiction is typified by a complete loss of behavioral control and by the physical manifestations that accompany chronic drug or alcohol abuse. The following general symptoms appear and often continue in a vicious circle until the user either dies or finds help:

1. Continuous use of the substance for longer periods
2. Indefinable fears and vague spiritual desires
3. Impaired judgment and irrational thinking
4. Tremors, malnutrition, overdoses, decreased tolerance, and/or other physiological problems associated with the drug
5. Obsessive use of the substance until recovery or death

Binges, benders, daily use, and the inability to stop without help are characteristic of this phase. The user engages in prolonged, continuous use and is unable to function without using her drug of choice on some regular basis. The addict neglects her daily needs to the point of not eating or caring for herself. Attempts to control her usage are abandoned as the periods of intoxication and recovery encompass most of her time.

Symptoms 2 and 3 reflect the loss of ability to function that accompanies brain deterioration associated with prolonged use of psychoactive drugs and alcohol. He cannot think clearly and will make outlandish claims that are obviously irrational. The addict, for example, will claim and believe that someone broke into the house and took all his cocaine while he was asleep. As the fears increase, the addict may experience a vague yearning for some miracle or "divine intervention" to stop him from continuing in the downward spiral that is the course of addiction.

The final two symptoms comprise the absolute deterioration of the addict prior to death. Especially with alcohol dependence, the addict may experience a "reverse tolerance" in which she once again becomes very intoxicated by a smaller dose of alcohol. This is an indication that the user's system has essentially been saturated with alcohol and cannot process the alcohol quickly enough to remove it from the body. Obsessive use, if unbroken, ultimately leads to death, by suicide, homicide, accident, or medical complications. Here, the drug truly "takes the person" by becoming the solitary focus of her life. She becomes obsessed with using not to get high but to feel normal and avoid the consequences of withdrawal.

Assessing the Behavioral Symptoms

The questions in Figure 4.1 are suggested to help the clinician evaluate the behavioral symptoms of addiction. They are classified under the headings Preoccupation, Increased Tolerance, Rapid Intake, Using Alone, Use as a Panacea (Cure-All), Protecting Supply, Nonpremeditated Use, and Blackout (for alcohol).

---

1. Preoccupation

Yes   No

_____ _____ Do you find yourself looking forward to the end of a day's work so you can have a couple of drinks or your drug of choice and relax?

_____ _____ Do you look forward to the end of the week so you can have some fun getting high?

_____ _____ Does the thought of using sometimes enter your mind when you should be thinking of something else?

_____ _____ Do you sometimes feel the need to have a drink or "hit" at a particular time of the day?

2. Increased Tolerance

Yes   No

_____ _____ Do you find that you can sometimes use more than others and not show it too much?

_____ _____ Have friends ever commented on your ability to "hold your alcohol or drugs"?

_____ _____ Have you ever experienced an increased capacity to drink or use drugs and felt proud of this ability?

3. Rapid Intake

Yes   No

_____ _____ Do you usually order a double or like to drink your first two or three drinks fairly fast, or use your drug of choice in a way it works the fastest to get you high?

_____ _____ Do you usually have a couple of drinks before going to a party or out to dinner or use a drug before going out to "get a head start"?

4. Using Alone

Yes   No

_____ _____ Do you routinely stop in a bar alone and have a couple of drinks or go home and get high by yourself?

_____ _____ Do you sometimes use alone or when no one else with you is using?

_____ _____ Do you usually have an extra drink by yourself when mixing drinks for others or have extra drugs of your own when using with others?

FIGURE 4.1   Questions for assessing behavioral symptoms

The more yes answers a client gives, the more indications there are of serious abuse or dependence on substances. In assessing the behavioral components of a client's substance use, it is important to remember that each individual will experience some diversity in the pattern of addiction. Some individuals who are addicted to cocaine will experience periods of profound depression following a binge and

5. Use as a Panacea (Cure-all)

Yes	No	
___	___	Do you fairly routinely drink or get high to calm your nerves or reduce tension or stress?
___	___	Do you find it difficult to enjoy a party or social gathering if there is nothing to drink or use?
___	___	Do you often think of relief or escape as associated with your use?
___	___	When encountering any physical or emotional problems, is your first thought to use?
___	___	Does life seem easier knowing your drug of choice will help you out?

6. Protecting the Supply

Yes	No	
___	___	Do you sometimes store a bottle or drug away around the house in the event you may "need" to use, or do you fear you may run out?
___	___	Do you ever keep a bottle or substance in the trunk of your car or office desk or stashed in the house in case you might need it?

7. Nonpremeditated Use

Yes	No	
___	___	Do you sometimes start to have a drink or two or use just a little and have several more drinks or hits than you had planned?
___	___	Do you sometimes find yourself starting to use when you had planned to go straight home or do something else?
___	___	Do you sometimes use more than you think you should?
___	___	Is your use sometimes different from what you would like it to be?

8. Blackouts (for Alcohol)

Yes	No	
___	___	In the morning after an evening of drinking, have you ever not been able to remember everything that happened the night before?
___	___	The morning after a night of drinking, have you ever had difficulty recalling how you got home or who you were with and what you did?

FIGURE 4.1   *Continued*

some will not. Not all alcoholics will experience a reverse tolerance even in the chronic stage of the addiction. The symptoms certainly overlap and occur in a variety of different orders depending on the individual situation. The description of the behavioral characteristics and questions about behavioral changes are meant to serve as guidelines and directions for further exploration with the client.

Social Characteristics

It is through the investigation of a client's social and family life that evidence of substance abuse is often initially detected. As users continue to become more heavily involved in abuse or dependence on a drug, their primary relationship in life eventually becomes the relationship with the substance. As their use becomes increasingly important and central to their lives, it is inevitable that other social relationships will suffer.

Abusers develop clear patterns over time of focusing their life on social activities that afford them opportunities to indulge in substance use. Especially with the use of illegal substances, to protect herself from detection, the user becomes increasingly involved in socializing with others who also use. Drinkers prefer to drink with others who drink like them. Family members or friends who are "straight" become excluded from a significant part of the user's life. As a person's "affair" with a substance grows and the barrier of denial is fortified, the chasm in her relationships with family and friends deepens. Increasing family conflict related to the substance use, a very constricted social life, lack of involvement in activities that do not afford an opportunity to use, and general withdrawal from "straight" friends are signals that the "affair" with a substance is well under way. The more advanced the dependence on the substance, the more alienated the user becomes from others who do not indulge with her.

Patterns of behaviors that are found in families of abusers are well established (Treadway, 1989). The strength of the dependence on the substance is easily evidenced when users fail to make attempts to prevent family breakups or isolation from significant others to maintain their substance use. Intimate relationships that endure a user's increasing dependence on a substance become distorted through the denial or "enabling" behaviors exhibited by the user's family.

Family Characteristics

Family members, like the user, progress through different phases in their journey with the addict. Addiction is often classified as a "family illness" because those who are in a close relationship with the abuser also experience effects of addiction that, while different, are frequently as serious as those suffered by the addict. Essentially, everyone in the addict's family and social system suffers.

Four Stages in the Family System of the Addict

The dynamics often seen in families with substance-dependent members can be delineated by stages or phases (Washousky, Levy-Stern, & Muchowski, 1993). Although these stages represent common patterns of family interaction with substance users, not all families can be defined or described using these criteria. These are not discrete stages; it is likely that they will overlap somewhat or that several stages will be in evidence simultaneously. Also, not every family will experience the same intensity or exact set of responses in each stage.

Some families may stay in a prolonged state of denial, even to the point of the addict's death. The description of the stages, however, can provide some guidelines for assessing the dynamics in the user's family and provide a basis for treatment planning with both the addict and other family members.

Denial   In this stage, family members deny that there is a substance abuse problem. They try to hide the substance abuse both from each other and from those outside the family. Excuses are made, members "cover" and make excuses for the addict's behavior, other explanations are offered, and the family begins to isolate from others who might suspect "something is wrong."

Home Treatment   Family members try to get the addict to stop using. Hiding drugs or bottles, nagging, threatening, persuasion, and sympathy are attempted. Home treatment, or the family's effort to stop the addict from using without seeking outside help, may fail because the focus is on controlling the behavior of someone else. The roles in the family often change significantly, usually with deleterious effects. Children may try to care for a parent, coalitions among family members are formed, and family members ignore or minimize their own problems by keeping the focus on the addict.

Chaos   The problem becomes so critical that it can no longer be denied or kept secret from those outside the family. Neighbors and friends become aware of the addiction. Conflicts and confrontations escalate without resolution. The consequences for family members become more pronounced, and a child or partner of the addict may experience serious emotional or physical problems. Threats of divorce, separation, or withdrawal of family support are often made but not acted upon.

Control   A spouse or family member attempts to take complete control of and complete responsibility for the user. If still living within the family, the addict becomes an emotional invalid who exists as a type of parasite on the family. Control is often exercised through divorce, separation, or a total emotional alienation from the family. The family, like the addict, exists in a state of suspended animation, trapped in a cycle of helplessness and futile attempts to control the addict's behavior.

Assessing the Social and Family-Related Symptoms

As previously noted, it is important to have access to family members, friends, and/or important others in the addict's life to assess a substance abuse problem adequately. If an addict has somehow entered the mental health system, through a doctor's referral or employer's recommendation, it is highly likely that the situation has become unmanageable enough for significant others in the addict's life to break the barrier of denial. As with the addict, it is critically important to undertake the assessment in a supportive, caring, nonjudgmental manner. Many family members experience a high degree of guilt or shame about the addict's behavior and feel that the continuation of the addiction is somehow their fault. They may feel that they have not been a good enough spouse, child, or parent or that they have created so much stress in the addict's life that they have promoted the addiction.

The questionnaire in Figure 4.2 can be given to family members or friends to gain important information about the user's pattern of substance use. Information gathered from others can be compared to the responses given by the client to assess the degree of minimization or denial that may be present. A yes response to any of the questions indicates some possibility of substance abuse; a yes response to four or more indicates a substance abuse problem.

Questionnaire: Do You Have a Spouse, Friend, or Loved One Who Has a Drinking or Drug Abuse Problem?

1. Do you worry about how much they drink or use drugs?
2. Do you complain about how often they drink or use?
3. Do you criticize them for the amount they spend on drugs or alcohol?
4. Have you ever been hurt or embarrassed by their behavior when they are drinking or using?
5. Are holidays in your home unpleasant because of their drinking or drugging?
6. Do they ever lie about their drinking or drug use?
7. Do they deny that drinking or drugs affect their behavior?
8. Do they say or do things and later deny having said or done them?
9. Do you sometimes think that drinking or drug use is more important to them than you are?
10. Do they get angry if you criticize their substance use or their drinking or drug-using companions?
11. Is drinking or drug use involved in almost all of your social activities?
12. Does your family spend almost as much on alcohol or drugs as it does on food or other necessities?
13. Are you having any financial difficulties because of their use?
14. Does their substance use keep them away from home a good deal?
15. Have you ever threatened to end your relationship because of their drinking or drug use?
16. Have you ever lied for them because of their drug use or drinking?
17. Do you find yourself urging them to eat instead of drink or use drugs at parties?
18. Have they ever stopped drinking or using drugs completely for a period of time and then started using again?
19. Have you ever thought about calling the police because of their behavior while drunk or high?
20. Do you think that alcohol or drugs creates problems for them?

FIGURE 4.2   Questions to determine patterns of substance abuse

In addition to gathering information from others who are familiar with the addict, counselors must be alert to some of the common social consequences that frequently appear in an addict's life. Frequent job loss, a driving under the influence (DUI) arrest or other legal problem (particularly domestic violence), the breakup of important relationships, a series of moves (also called "the geographic cure"), a history of psychological or medical problems that are unresolved, and a lack of interest in activities that were once important to the individual are all indicators of an addiction. Several of the assessment devices discussed in the next segment of the chapter will assist the clinician in gathering information related to the social characteristics of substance abuse.

MAJOR ASSESSMENT DEVICES

To assist in the diagnosis and assessment of substance abuse, psychometric instruments are often very helpful. A variety of specific psychometric instruments are generally available to counselors. Material from the initial interview should help the clinician select appropriate measures that will enhance their understanding of the exact nature, dynamics, severity, and effects of the client's substance use. For example, several tools are focused on alcohol abuse only; others include abuse of additional or other substances.

The measures reviewed here are only a sample of those available to counselors. They were chosen based on their widespread use and availability, ease of administration and scoring, and reliability and validity. The assessment devices that are included in this segment include the Michigan Alcoholism Screening Test (MAST) and the Short Michigan Alcoholism Screening Test (SMAST), the Drug Abuse Screening Test (DAST-20), the CAGE Questionnaire, the Alcohol Use Inventory (AUI), the Substance Abuse Subtle Screening Inventory-2 (SASSI-2), and the Addiction Severity Index (ASI). In addition, those who are trained to use the Millon Clinical Multiaxial Inventory (MCMI-II) and/or the Minnesota Multiphasic Personality Inventory (MMPI-2) may use information from those tests to help with diagnostic and treatment considerations. Some information on using these tests in the assessment of substance abuse will also be reviewed.

The Michigan Alcoholism Screening Test (MAST)

The most researched diagnostic instrument is the self-administered Michigan Alcoholism Screening Test (MAST), which was created in 1971 by M. L. Selzer (1971; see Questionnaire 2 in this chapter's appendix). The 25-item MAST correctly identifies up to 95% of alcoholics, and the SMAST, an even shorter 10-question form of the MAST, has also been shown to identify over 90% of the alcoholics entering general psychiatric hospitals (Mendelson & Mello, 1985, p. 304). The MAST was originally validated with treatment-seeking alcoholics. Numerous studies have used the MAST to assess both adolescent and adult populations in a variety of settings. It may realistically and effectively be used with virtually any population.

The MAST is simple to administer; it is given to the client with the instruction that they answer all questions either yes or no. After the client completes the test, the points assigned to each question are totaled. The MAST sample test form (see Questionnaire 2) indicates the number of points assigned for each question. It should be noted that questions 2, 5, 7, and 8 are assigned points for a no answer; all other questions are scored for a yes answer. A total of 4 points is presumptive evidence of alcoholism; a total of 5 or more points makes it extremely unlikely that the individual is not alcoholic. In addition, given the scoring values, a positive (yes) response to items 10, 23b, or 24b would be enough to diagnose alcohol addiction. Three questions abstracted from the MAST can also quickly diagnose potential alcohol problems:

1. Has your family ever objected to your drinking?
2. Did you ever think you drank too much in general?
3. Have others said you drink too much for your own good?

These three questions can be easily incorporated into the interview process to serve as indicators for a more thorough evaluation. They may also be adapted to use with clients who are abusing other substances by substituting using their drug of choice instead of "drinking."

Short Michigan Alcoholism Screening Test (SMAST)

The Short Michigan Alcoholism Test (SMAST) is administered in the same manner as the MAST or can be given verbally. It consists of the following 13 of 25 questions taken from the MAST:

1. Do you feel you feel you are a normal drinker?
2. Does your wife/husband, a parent, or other near relative ever worry or complain about your drinking?
3. Do you ever feel guilty about your drinking?
4. Do friends or relatives think you are a normal drinker?
5. Are you able to stop drinking when you want?
6. Have you ever attended a meeting of Alcoholics Anonymous?
7. Has drinking ever created problems between you and your wife/husband, a parent or other near relative?
8. Have you ever gotten into trouble at work because of drinking?
9. Have you ever neglected your obligations, your family, or your work for 2 or more days in a row because you were drinking?
10. Have you ever gone to anyone for help about your drinking?
11. Have you ever been in a hospital because of drinking?

12. Have you ever been arrested for drunken driving, driving while intoxicated, or driving under the influence of alcoholic beverages?

13. Have you ever been arrested, even for a few hours, because of other drunken behavior?

The SMAST is very easy to score. One point is given for each of the following answers: no on questions 1, 4, and 5; yes on all other questions (2, 3, and 6 through 13). A score of 0 to 1 indicates a low probability of alcoholism, a score of 2 points suggests the client is possibly alcoholic, and a score of 3 or more points indicates a strong probability of alcoholism.

The Drug Abuse Screening Test (DAST-20)

The DAST-20 (Skinner, 1982; see Questionnaire 3 in the appendix) is a 20-item self-report inventory designed to measure aspects of drug use behavior, not including alcohol. It was derived from the Michigan Alcoholism Screening Test (MAST) and reflects similar content. DAST-20 scores are computed by summing all items positively endorsed for drug use. Higher scores indicate a greater likelihood of drug dependency. The DAST-20 is designed for use with adult male and female drug users.

The DAST-20 is a useful tool for helping to differentiate among several categories of drug users. In clinical trials, the DAST-20 scores demonstrated significant differences among the alcohol, drug, and polysubstance abuse groups. DAST-20 scores were also found to correlate highly with other drug use indices.

The CAGE Questionnaire

The CAGE (Ewing, 1984) is a four-item questionnaire that includes questions related to a history of attempting to cut down on alcohol intake (C), annoyance over criticism about alcohol (A), guilt about drinking behavior (G), and drinking in the morning to relieve withdrawal anxiety, sometimes known as an "eye-opener" (E) (Gallant, 1987, p. 50). Most questionnaires duplicate information by using different phrases or words to detect similar patterns of behavior. The authors of the CAGE found that they could eliminate many questions and still have a powerful tool for assessing alcohol dependency. This is also an extremely useful questionnaire to use with family members or others that are participating in the assessment.

The CAGE was originally developed and used with adult alcoholics presenting for treatment. Like the MAST, the CAGE may be used to screen for alcoholism in a variety of health care settings. Use of the CAGE questions effectively discriminates alcoholics from nonalcoholics at or above the 90% range.

The CAGE is generally administered verbally as part of the diagnostic interview. Instructions for administering the CAGE include observing the client's attitude in responding to the questions. The counselor should ask them to explain any yes answer and watch for signs of rationalization, denial, projection of blame, and minimization. The first question deals with the alcoholic's common problem of repeatedly trying to get the drinking under control only to lose control again and again once she resumes drinking. The next question detects sensitivity to criticism of her drinking behavior. The third question taps into the personal sense of guilt, and the fourth looks at the tendency to use morning drinking as a remedy for excessive drinking the night before.

To administer the CAGE, the client is asked to answer yes or no to the following questions:

1. Have you ever tried to cut down on your drinking?
2. Are you annoyed when people ask you about your drinking?
3. Do you ever feel guilty about your drinking?
4. Do you ever take a morning eye-opener?

Only affirmative responses are scored on the CAGE. One yes response indicates a possibility of alcoholism, two or three yes responses indicate a high alcoholism suspicion index, and four yes responses suggest an alcoholism diagnosis is highly likely. As with the SMAST, the CAGE questions can be adapted as an assessment tool for other substances.

A variation of the CAGE Questionnaire that offers alternative questions to assess abuse of substances other than or in addition to alcohol is also available (see Questionnaire 4). Several follow-up inquiries are noted on this form that can assist the clinician in getting more detailed information if the client answers yes to any of the four questions. Also, a version of the CAGE for Youth and Adolescents (see Questionnaire 5) is helpful in assessing substance abuse problems with clients in this age range.

The Substance Abuse Subtle Screening Inventory-2 (SASSI-2)

The Substance Abuse Subtle Screening Inventory-2 (SASSI-2) (Miller, 1985) is a single-page, paper-and-pencil questionnaire. On one side are 52 true/false questions that generally appear unrelated to chemical abuse; on the other side are 26 items that allow clients to self-report the negative effects of any alcohol and drug use. Clients can complete the SASSI-2 in approximately 10 to 15 minutes, it is easily scored, and training is available in interpretation and use of the SASSI-2 as a screening tool for identifying substance abuse.

The primary strength of the SASSI-2 is in identifying abuse patterns that are hidden by the more subtle forms of denial common to substance abusers. Items on the SASSI-2 touch on a broad spectrum of topics seemingly unrelated to chemical abuse (e.g., "I think there is something wrong with my memory" and "I am often resentful"). The questions are designed to be nonthreatening to abusers to avoid triggering the clients' defenses and denial. The SASSI-2 is resistant to faking and defeats efforts to "second-guess" the "right" answer. As a result, the SASSI-2 is effective in identifying clients who are minimizing or in denial about their substance abuse. It is also effective in identifying substance abuse regardless of the drug of choice. There is both an adult and adolescent inventory that is adapted for either male or female clients.

The data from research with the SASSI-2 indicate approximately a 90% accuracy in identifying substance abuse patterns in clients. Thousands of test items were designed or considered and then given to samples of alcoholics, other drug abusers, and controls (non-substance-abusing people). The inventory was tested over 16 years and is still being adapted and updated. In 1994, the Adult SASSI-2 replaced the adult SASSI. Two scales from the original test were dropped, and three new scales were added. Counselors have used the SASSI-2 as a screening tool for court-ordered substance abuse programs, employee assistance programs, and in general mental health settings. Information, training, and materials are available through the SASSI Institute, P.O. Box 5069, Bloomington, IN 47407.

The Alcohol Use Inventory (AUI)

The Alcohol Use Inventory (AUI) (Horn, Wanberg & Foster, 1986; Wanberg & Horn, 1983) is a hierarchically organized set of self-report scales that provides a basis for diagnosing different problems associated with the use of alcohol. The AUI is based on the hypothesis that alcoholism should be diagnosed from a multiple-syndrome model, and the AUI scales are designed to provide an operational definition of the multiple manifestations of alcohol related problems. It should be used to provide a more thorough diagnostic picture if there are clear indications from the MAST or CAGE that an alcohol problem is probable. Like the SASSI, the AUI is a protected test. More information and materials are available by contacting PsychSystems.

The AUI consists of 228 multiple-choice items (expanded from 147 in the original test). The specific areas of assessment that are the focus of the AUI are motivation for treatment, physical health, anger/aggression management, risk-taking behavior, social relationships, employment and/or educational situation, family situation, leisure-time activities, religious/spiritual activities, and legal status. The AUI is a very simple test to administer and can generally be given to the client with little additional instruction. The client should be told that it is important to respond as honestly as possible to all questions and not to skip questions or give more than one response per question. Both hand- and computer-scored versions of the AUI are available (Horn, Wanberg, & Foster, 1983). A Substance Use Inventory (SUI) is a similar test for assessment of dependence on substances other than alcohol.

The Addiction Severity Index (ASI)

The Addiction Severity Index (ASI) (Fureman, Parikh, Bragg, & McLellan, 1990) provides basic information that is useful both for the clinician and the clients. The ASI manual provides clear instructions for administration, scoring, and use of the data in planning treatment strategies. The current ASI is designed for use with adults, but variations for adolescent use are being developed. A particular strength of the ASI is its utility with dual-diagnosis populations. For treatment planning purposes, the ASI is especially helpful in determining the severity of the client's drug use and the need for additional or extended treatment.

The ASI is administered as a structured interview with specific questions that cover several basic areas of treatment needs, including medical, employment/support, drug/alcohol use, legal, family/social relationships, and psychiatric. The drug/alcohol subscale includes an extensive history of all drug and alcohol abuse, the longest period of abstinence, and previous drug treatment history. Administration of the ASI relies on fairly basic clinical interviewing skills. Counselors can adjust questions to use terms that are familiar to the client and fit with the client's level of education and sophistication. In some treatment settings, the ASI questions can also be given as writing projects for the client to further examine his history of drug/alcohol use and the impact it has had on his situation.

The client uses a 0- to 4-point scale to rate how "bothered" she has been in the past 30 days by problems in the different areas of assessment. This provides a clearer picture from the client's perspective of how she rates the severity of her problem and some indication of her desire for treatment. These ratings are then compared with the counselor's ratings on the same scales. With the influence of denial or minimization on the client's perceptions, it is common for the interviewer to perceive a higher severity of problems than the client.

A final benefit of the ASI is its usefulness as a training tool for counselors. It can greatly facilitate training in substance abuse and dual-diagnosis work, particularly when clients are somewhat resistant or evasive. The structured format of the ASI gives the counselor someplace to go when clients are not forthcoming. As Richards (1993) notes, "Becoming familiar with and understanding the rationale for the items on each scale [of the ASI] is in itself a kind of primer course on reciprocal causal connections between substance use and other aspects of the individual's existence" (p. 128).

The Millon Clinical Multiaxial Inventory (MCMI-II) and Minnesota Multiphasic Personality Inventory (MMPI-2)

Although both the MCMI-II and the MMPI-2 are primarily designed for the assessment of personality, they are often used to assess a full range of psychopathology, including substance abuse. Both are copyrighted, protected evaluation instruments that require additional training to administer, score, and interpret. Both have elaborate computer-scoring programs available through the resources that sell the tests. Incorporated into both the MMPI-2 and MCMI-II are validity scales that may help identify clients who are "attempting to look good" or answering randomly.

It is not in the scope of this text to provide an in-depth understanding of either of these instruments. As noted, additional training is required to use these tests. Some information, however, can be used in a basic assessment.

The MCMI-II is useful in identifying several aspects of personality functioning: clinical syndromes (e.g., depression, anxiety), changing symptoms, and personality styles or disorders. It is certainly a useful addition to any evaluation in which there is a question of dual diagnosis. It is a simple, true/false, 173-question self-report regarding the client's behavior and experience. Given the difficulty of hand scoring, it is generally scored by a computer program.

The symptom scales on the MCMI-II are useful in corroborating a clinical impression of the types or patterns of symptoms experienced by the client. The personality scales may help a clinician understand the relationship between the client's substance use and his typical pattern of managing his experience and relationships. For example, someone with a score indicating a Narcissistic Personality style may use drugs to establish or maintain a particular image. Understanding a client's basic personality can be very useful in planning treatment to address specific character traits that may either support or undermine his recovery.

Like the MCMI-II, the MMPI-2 is useful in identifying behavioral and personality patterns and clinical symptoms. These tests are generally used as part of a comprehensive personality or behavioral assessment. The MMPI-2 is a self-report questionnaire that consists of 567 true/false questions. There is also a version of the MMPI-2 for adolescent populations, the Minnesota Multiphasic Personality Inventory-Adolescent (MMPI-A).

The MMPI has been used extensively for over 20 years in the evaluation of alcoholics. Gilberstadt and Drucker's (1965) research indicates a common pattern in MMPI scores among alcoholics. Elevations on scales 2, 7, and 4 represent a combination of personality characteristics commonly found in male alcoholics. These scores reflect depressive, obsessive-compulsive, and sociopathic features. These researchers also reported symptoms of anxiety, marital discord, financial problems, insomnia, and tension that were reflected in the MMPI profiles of alcoholics.

In addition to the basic clinical scales, both the MMPI-2 and MMPI-A contain items that indicate the possibility of substance abuse problems. A subscale of both tests, the MacAndrew Alcoholism Scale-Revised (MAC-R), was developed using items from the original MMPI and became widely used as a method of screening for substance abuse problems. The revised MAC (MAC-R) deleted several questions and added others to further refine the content of the scale. The MAC-R has been an effective tool for identifying substance abuse problems in both adults and adolescents (Graham, 1990).

Two other subscales on both MMPIs are the Addiction Acknowledgement Scale (AAS) and the Addiction Potential Scale (APS). Persons who obtain a high score on the AAS are usually acknowledging a substance abuse problem, and additional assessment of the nature of their substance use is indicated. The APS may help discriminate between persons who abuse substances and those who do not. Both the APS and AAS are still in the process of being validated and evaluated for their reliability in assessing substance abuse problems. Particularly with the APS, high scores on this scale should be corroborated with other data and information.

DIAGNOSIS

Professionals who have to make decisions about the presence or absence of addiction for their clients must make a series of complex judgments. An adequate conceptualization of substance abuse and addiction emphasizes the interaction among the individual user, the physiological effects, and the social context in which the user functions. Establishing a standard set of rigid diagnostic criteria for addiction is not only improbable but is also not likely to be beneficial to clients. The simple diagnostic definition that "addiction exists when drug or alcohol use is associated with impairment of health and social functioning is a useful general thesis" (Mendelson & Mello, 1985, p. 18).

The diagnosis of substance abuse has always been complicated by inconsistent attitudes and imprecise standards for what constitutes an "addiction." Inadequate definitions of chemical dependence have often been cited as the primary reason for a lack of success in developing adequate epidemiological, diagnostic, and prognostic assessment tools. As Gallant (1987) notes, "With many medical illnesses . . . the etiology or pathologic abnormality, prognosis, and treatment are known, and no preexisting public or medical concepts interfere with the scientific identification of the illness" (p. 1). This is certainly not the case with the diagnosis of substance abuse. Here, much of the information needed to establish a diagnosis is based on self-reports from an often unreliable population given the preponderance of denial. Making an adequate diagnosis is further complicated by long-standing prejudices and moral attitudes.

Differential Diagnosis

Frequently, one of the most challenging aspects of diagnosing substance abuse is the interplay of addiction and other mental disorders. Counselors who effectively treat individuals with a primary diagnosis of substance abuse may be faced with treating additional psychological disorders. Other DSM-IV diagnostic categories such as personality disorders, posttraumatic stress disorder, mood disorders, and thought disorders are common differential or coexisting diagnoses. Symptoms related to other disorders may be accentuated or mollified by a client's substance abuse.

Clinicians working with substance abusers should be trained in diagnosing other mental disorders as well as substance abuse. Many symptoms of intoxication or withdrawal from certain substances mimic the behaviors seen in psychiatric disorders. Clinicians who are untrained in the recognition of such problems as depression, mania, psychosis, and dementias may risk misdiagnosing a client. For example, if a client arrives in the counselor's office with symptoms of slurred speech, difficulty with coordination, and difficulty focusing his attention, the counselor might assume this behavior is evidence of a substance abuse problem. These symptoms, however, are also associated with certain neurological diseases such as multiple sclerosis. In addition, differentiating between a bipolar or manic-depressive disorder and the highs and lows experienced by substance abusers is often a complicated diagnostic process.

Generally, a longitudinal approach is useful in differentiating between psychiatric and substance abuse–related symptoms (Schuckit, 1988). Many symptoms of substance intoxication and withdrawal improve or are alleviated within days or weeks. It is not unusual for a substance abuser to appear far more disturbed when initially assessed than she will after a period of abstinence. Family or others who can be consulted regarding the client's behavioral history prior to the onset of abusing substances can also be invaluable in accurately diagnosing and planning for treatment.

A standard rule of practice for counselors working with substance abusers is to refer clients for a thorough physical as an early part of the assessment process. Establishing a good working relationship with a physician who is familiar with drug and alcohol abuse is a mandatory step in providing appropriate and adequate services. Also, a psychologist who is trained in differential diagnostic techniques for assessing addiction and other psychological and neuropsychological problems should be a part of the counselor's assessment referral network. Licensed psychologists have a broader range of standardized evaluation techniques that they can administer to help differentiate between emotional, characterological, or psychological disorders and alcohol- or drug-related problems.

Dual Diagnosis

Many individuals diagnosed with substance abuse problems also meet the criteria for other psychological disorders. It is important to discover whether symptoms of a psychological problem either preceded the onset of the abuse problems or persisted after the substance abuse had been treated and a period of abstinence had been maintained for several months. For example, alcoholics typically exhibit a high rate of depressive symptomology owing to the depressant effects of their chronic use of alcohol. Sleep and appetite disturbances, feelings of helplessness and hopelessness, and loss of pleasure and motivation are symptoms of depression and also part of the pattern of addiction to alcohol. The deterioration of an alcoholic's lifestyle and health, the loss of significant relationships, and other problems related to excessive drinking along with the basic chemical effects of alcohol make it nearly inevitable that an alcohol-addicted client will appear depressed while they are actively drinking. However, this depression is usually reactive and should decrease significantly with abstinence and efforts to resolve life problems that accumulated during the period of addiction. In alcoholics with a primary depression, the symptoms either preceded the onset of alcohol abuse or became more pronounced during periods of abstinence (Mayfield, 1985).

Some clients may have begun using drugs to alleviate symptoms of anxiety or depression. Psychoactive drugs may initially offer some relief to individuals who suffer from mood disorders. Clinicians should question clients carefully about their psychological history prior to using drugs or alcohol, seeking information regarding a family history of psychological problems. The learning theory of chemical dependency in fact proposes that the concept of anxiety reduction related to drug or alcohol use is the basis for many addictions.

Research addressing the question of whether substance abusers are more likely to exhibit personality and other psychiatric disorders has produced mixed results. In some of the research studies, the link between substance abuse and passive-dependent, antisocial, or narcissistic personality types have not been confirmed (Westermeyer, 1976). One obvious difficulty is that if a person is involved in using an illegal substance such as cocaine, some aspects of his lifestyle necessarily engender the symptoms of an antisocial or paranoid personality. It is a matter of self-preservation for the user to become suspicious, secretive, alienated from others who do not use, and, by definition of his cocaine use, involved in illegal pursuits. However, these behaviors may be secondary to the dependence on cocaine and should diminish when the person maintains abstinence.

In other research, approximately one-third of the substance-abusing population sampled met the criteria for one of the DSM-IV psychiatric diagnoses (Helzer & Pryzbeck, 1988). Among those with the diagnosis of alcoholism, almost half (47%) had a second psychiatric diagnosis. Phobias were particularly common among males, followed by depression, schizophrenia, panic, and mania. For alcoholic women in this study, phobias and depression, followed by antisocial personality, panic, schizophrenia, and mania, were the most prevalent.

Other social and familial factors appear more frequently in substance-abusing groups. Also, genetic factors have been clearly related as a predisposing factor for the development of alcohol addiction (Goodwin, 1985). A "lack of family cohesiveness" involving such factors as an early death or divorce or separation of parents appears to be associated with an increase in alcohol-related problems for offspring of these families. Burnside, Baer, McLaughlin, and Pokorny (1986) found that compared with control groups, adolescents who later became substance abusers were more likely to

- identify with groups who shared alcohol and drugs during adolescence,
- be more impulsive, and
- display greater evidence of rebelliousness and/or nonconformity.

Other researchers (Goldstein & Sappington, 1977) obtained a similar profile of behavioral traits with the inclusion of a tendency for substance abusers to be less likely to learn from experience and less conservative or reserved behaviorally than their peers.

There is also a frequent relationship between substance abuse and suicide. Most surveys report that approximately 25% of substance abusers entering treatment have made a suicide attempt at some point in the past (Frances & Miller, 1991). The incidence of completed suicide is probably three to four times higher than that found in the general population (Murphy, 1988). As previously noted, these clients may be using alcohol or other drugs to treat the symptoms of depression. In these clients, it is essential to provide an accurate diagnosis and initiate treatment for the depression as soon as possible. Involvement of a qualified psychologist and physician to assist in diagnosing and providing treatment for these clients is critical at an early stage. Schuckit (1980) summarizes the therapeutic importance of assessing depression that is dually diagnosed with substance abuse.

CASE DISCUSSIONS

Case 1 (Sandy and Pam).   Effective assessment and diagnosis in the case of Sandy and Pam would begin with the diagnostic interview. Using the Substance

Use History Questionnaire (see Questionnaire 1 in the appendix), information would be gathered regarding each of their histories of substance use and abuse. Significant factors to consider about Sandy's substance use are as follows:

- She has a history of alcohol use dating back to junior high.
- By self-report, she has admitted to continuing to abuse alcohol into adulthood.

In assessing Sandy's substance use, it is apparent that her alcohol use has affected her family life and social relationships. She reports that she had married Joe, a violent alcoholic, and that during her drinking days, she left the children at home so she could go to bars and pick up numerous men. This behavior would clearly indicate that Sandy's alcohol abuse affected her judgment and ability to care for herself and her children.

With the information from the Substance Use History Questionnaire, it is possible to assess the phase of abuse/dependence that Sandy is experiencing. The crucial phase (see p. 119) is characterized by obvious and pronounced behavioral changes. Sandy has reported behavioral loss of control coupled with guilt and remorse about her actions while using alcohol.

In diagnosing Sandy's substance abuse, additional information is needed. The CAGE Questionnaire (see p. 129) and the MAST (see p. 127) would be useful in differentiating whether Sandy meets the criteria for substance abuse or substance dependence in the DSM-IV. Sandy's childhood history indicates the potential for a personality or mood disorder. Her marriage to Joe may indicate that she has suffered some type of physical or emotional abuse. Posttraumatic stress disorder is also a diagnostic possibility. Differential or dual diagnoses must be considered when evaluating Sandy's substance abuse. After a period of sobriety, additional psychological testing would be indicated to assess whether Sandy needs treatment for other disorders.

Pam's history of substance use includes cocaine and alcohol. In assessing Pam's substance use, the significant factors are

- her employment history,
- her unstable relationships, and
- report of anxiety symptoms.

In addition to the diagnostic interview using the Substance Use History Questionnaire, use of the Substance Abuse Subtle Screening Inventory-2 (SASSI-2; see p. 130) would be useful in identifying treatment issues and potential diagnoses. Clearly, Pam's substance abuse has also affected her judgment regarding relationships. The history with her live-in boyfriend seems to indicate intense conflict resulting in potential negative outcomes.

Pam's history of unsuccessful employment indicates that she may be in the crucial phase (see p. 119) of the progression of substance abuse/dependence. This pattern of substance abuse after a loss is a clear indicator of the overt consequences of the progression. Other factors that need to be explored are the periodic abstinence or changes in Pam's pattern of substance use.

The information from the SASSI-2 may be helpful in distinguishing between the DSM-IV diagnosis of substance abuse or substance dependence with a focus on polydrug use. Pam's childhood and recent conflicts with her boyfriend may indicate a possible personality disorder or mood disorder. Her statement regarding her boyfriend, that she "feels drawn to him" and wants to "make it work," may indicate a dependent personality style. Pam's increasing anxiety could indicate either periodic withdrawal from the substances or an underlying anxiety disorder.

In summary, additional information gathered through an assessment is needed in both cases to make accurate diagnoses and assist in planning treatment. Contacting other family members or significant others to gather information would be useful. Once each woman had established abstinence of at least 2 months, further assessment would help with answering questions about dual diagnoses.

Case 2 (Joe and Jane Smith).   In the case of the Smith family, Joe and Jane's substance abuse is of primary importance and must be addressed. It is important to note that Jane and Joe admit to abusing alcohol for 23 years and to recent use of cocaine. Both continue to have ample access to both substances through contacts at work.

In assessing substance abuse/dependence, some psychometric instruments may be valuable in gaining more information. Using the Substance Use History Questionnaire (see Questionnaire 1 in the appendix) and the Drug Abuse Screening Test (DAST-20; see Questionnaire 2) would help in evaluating the degree of substance abuse. It is extremely useful to distinguish between substance abuse and substance dependence to plan appropriate treatment. In addition, the questionnaire for families should be given to Sarah and Karen, and the girls should also be interviewed on an age-appropriate level. This approach would provide further information regarding the parents' substance use and its impact on the family.

In assessing Jane's substance use, some significant factors are

- her attempt to stop drinking for health reasons;
- her reluctance to give up drugs completely; and
- her traumatic childhood history with an alcohol-abusive mother, sexual abuse by a brother, and foster home placement.

Jane's substance use indicates that she is in the crucial to chronic phase (see pp. 119–121) of substance abuse/dependence evidenced by her denial and minimization of her cocaine use and her 5-year periodic attempts at abstinence from alcohol.

Jane's traumatic childhood history needs to be evaluated as to the impact that these factors have in her substance use. Diagnostically, Jane would meet the criteria for substance dependence in the DSM-IV (see p. 116). Her history may indicate that other diagnoses such as a personality disorder, depression, and post-traumatic stress disorder are likely.

In assessing Joe's substance use, the significant factors are

- his frequent substance use,
- his family history, and
- Joe and Sarah's increasing conflict over Joe's drinking.

Joe's history of alcohol use everyday, marijuana use on the weekend, and behavioral changes when drinking are indicative of the crucial phase of substance abuse/dependence. It is clear that when Joe drinks, he loses control and acts inappropriately toward Sarah. In addition, Joe's longest period of abstinence was 9 days; after that, he drank to the point of intoxication. This pattern indicates a tolerance for alcohol, as well as minimization and denial.

Diagnostically, Joe would meet the criteria for substance dependence in the DSM-IV (see p. 116). In addition, diagnoses of depression and personality disorder need to be investigated. Additional information about Joe's childhood experiences should be gathered.

In summary, it is clear that Jane and Joe's substance use is a major factor to be considered in treatment of the Smith family. Sarah's escalating behavioral problems may be indicative of her response to her parents' drinking and drug use. Sarah may also be at risk for abusing substances. The patterns of both children should be evaluated using information about typical coping styles or roles adopted by children in response to substance abuse problems in the parents (see p. 124).

Case 3 (Leigh).   Leigh's substance use needs to be evaluated in the context of her developmental stage. Coupled with her reported substance use, other factors such as problems at school, shoplifting, parental conflict, parental divorce, and relocation to a new area are issues that need to be examined.

During the diagnostic interview, the adolescent version of the Substance Abuse Subtle Screening Inventory-2 (SASSI-2; see p. 130) can be administered along with other instruments to determine a general level of functioning. In assessing Leigh's substance use, the significant factors include

- her development stage (adolescence),
- loss of parental support,
- increased conflict with her mother, and
- ambivalent feelings toward the conflict between her mother and father.

Leigh's acting-out behavior may indicate substance abuse, or the substance use may be an outlet for her problems. This distinction needs to be evaluated before treatment interventions can be implemented. It is clear that Leigh's behavior at school and in the community needs to be addressed. Her appearance of being "overly thin" must be investigated so that a possible eating disorder can be assessed. Referral to a physician for a thorough physical is indicated.

To diagnose substance abuse/dependence with Leigh, more information needs to be gathered from relatives and school personnel. Family members should be interviewed to address family conflict and Leigh's feelings of isolation. Parent-child conflict, adjustment disorder, and eating disorder are potential dual diagnoses.

In summary, Leigh may be experiencing some prodromal phase (see p. 118) symptoms related to her substance abuse. It will be important, however, to more carefully evaluate her previous functioning to determine whether her substance use is a temporary, reactive response to conflict and changes in the family.

REFERENCES

American Psychiatric Association. (1994). *Diagnostic and statistical manual of mental disorders* (4th ed.). Washington, DC: Author.

Blue Cross and Blue Shield Associations. (1979). *Alcoholism*. Chicago: Author.

Burnside, M. A., Baer, P. E., McLaughlin, R. J., & Pokorny, A. D. (1986). Alcohol use by adolescents in disrupted families. *Alcoholism: Clinical and Experimental Research, 10,* 274–278.

Chasnoff, I. J. (1988). Drug use in pregnancy: Parameters of risk. *Pediatric Clinics of North America, 35*(6), 1403–1412.

Ewing, J. A. (1984). Detecting alcoholism: The CAGE questionnaire. *Journal of the American Medical Association, 252,* 1905–1907.

Frances, R. J. & Miller, S. I. (Eds.). (1991). *Clinical textbook of addictive disorders.* New York: Guilford.

Fureman, B., Parikh, G., Bragg, A., & McLellan, A. (1990). *Addiction severity index (5th edition): A guide to training and supervising ASI interviews based on the past ten years.* Philadelphia: University of Pennsylvania/VA Center for Studies of Addiction.

Gallant, D. (1987). *Alcoholism: A guide to diagnosis, intervention, and treatment.* New York: Norton.

Gilberstadt, H., & Drucker, J. (1965). *A handbook for clinical and actuarial MMPI interpretation.* Philadelphia: Saunders.

Goldstein, J. N., & Sappington, J. T. (1977). Personality characteristics of students who become heavy drug users: An MMPI study of an avant-garde. *American Journal of Alcohol and Drug Abuse, 4,* 401–412.

Goodwin, D. G. (1985). Alcoholism and genetics: The sins of the fathers. *Archives of General Psychiatry, 42,* 171-174.

Graham, J. R. (1990). *MMPI-2: Assessing personality and psychopathology.* New York: Oxford University Press.

Helzer, J. I., & Pryzbeck, T. R. (1988). The co-occurrence of alcoholism with other psychiatric disorders in the general population and its impact on treatment. *Journal of Studies on Alcohol, 49*(3), 219–224.

Horn, J. L., Wanberg, K. W., & Foster, F. M. (1983). *The alcohol use inventory (AUI): Computerized and paper-pencil forms.* Baltimore: PsychSystems.

Horn, J. L., Wanberg, K. W., & Foster, F. M. (1986). *The alcohol use inventory: Test booklet.* Minneapolis, MN: National Computer Systems.

Jellinek, E. M. (1960). *The disease concept of alcoholism.* New Haven, CT: Hillhouse.

Mayfield, D. (1985). Substance abuse in the affective disorders. In A. I. Alterman (Ed.), *Substance abuse and psychopathology.* New York: Plenum.

Mendelson, J., & Mello, N. (Eds.). (1985). *The diagnosis and treatment of alcoholism.* New York: McGraw-Hill.

Miller, G. (1985). *The substance abuse subtle screening inventory.* Bloomington, IN: SASSI Institute.

Murphy, G. E. (1988). Suicide and substance abuse. *Archives of General Psychiatry, 45,* 593–594.

Palfai, T., & Jankiewicz, H. (1991). *Drugs and human behavior*. Dubuque, IA: Brown.

Richards, H. J. (1993). *Therapy of the substance abuse syndromes*. Northvale, NJ: Aronson.

Schuckit, M. A. (1980). Alcohol and depression. *Advances in Alcohol, 1,* 1–3.

Schuckit, M. A. (1988). Evaluating the dual diagnosis patient. *Drug Abuse and Alcoholism Newsletter, 17,* 1–4.

Selzer, M. L. (1971). The Michigan alcoholism screening test: The quest for a new diagnostic instrument. *American Journal of Psychiatry, 127,* 1653–1658.

Skinner, H. A. (1982). Statistical approaches to the classification of alcohol and drug addiction. *Alcoholism: Clinical and Experimental Research, 77,* 259–273.

Treadway, D. (1989). *Before it's too late: Working with substance abuse in the family.* New York: Norton.

Wanberg, K. W., & Horn, J. L. (1983). Assessment of alcohol use with multidimensional concepts and measures. *American Psychologist, 38* (10), 1055-1069.

Washousky, R., Levy-Stern, D., & Muchowski, P. (1993, January/February). The stages of family alcoholism. *EAP Digest,* 38–42.

Westermeyer, J. (1976). *Primer on chemical dependency.* Baltimore: Williams & Wilkins.

Appendix: Substance Use Questionnaires

Substance Use History Questionnaire

1. What substances do you currently use? (check all that apply)

   _____ alcohol   _____ amphetamines (uppers)
   _____ cocaine   _____ barbiturates (downers)
   _____ marijuana   _____ nicotine (cigarettes)
   _____ other (specify) _____

2. What are your current substance use habits?

   _____ daily use   _____ social use (with friends or at parties)
   _____ weekend use only   _____ occasional heavy use (to point of intoxication)
   _____ occasional light use
         (not to point of intoxication)

3. How many days ago did you last take a drug or drink? _____ days

4. Have you used daily in the past 2 months? _____ yes _____ no

5. Do you find it almost impossible to live without your drugs or alcohol? _____ yes _____ no

6. Are you always able to stop using when you want to? _____ yes _____ no

7. Where do you do most of your drinking or drug use? (check all that apply)

   _____ home
   _____ with friends
   _____ bars, restaurants, or other public places
   _____ parties or social gatherings
   _____ other

8. Do you drink or use during your workday? _____ yes _____ no

9. Do most of your friends use like you do? _____ yes _____ no

10 With whom do you use or drink? (check all that apply)

   _____ alone   _____ neighbors
   _____ family   _____ co-workers
   _____ friends   _____ strangers

11. Do you consider yourself to be a

   _____ very light user   _____ fairly heavy user
   _____ moderate user   _____ heavy user
   _____ nonuser

12. Do friends or family think you use more than other people? _____ yes _____ no

13. Have any family or friends complained to you about your drug or alcohol use?
    _____ yes _____ no

QUESTIONNAIRE 1   Substance use history questionnaire for general use

14. Do you think you use more than other people who use? _____ yes _____ no

15. Were your drug use or drinking habits ever different from what they are now?
_____ yes _____ no
If yes, please explain why the habits changed.
_____
_____
_____

16. Has your drinking or drug use ever caused you to (check all that apply):
_____ lose a job or have job or academic problems
_____ have legal problems (DUI, arrest for possession)
_____ have medical problems related to your use
_____ have family problems or relationship problems
_____ be aggressive or violent

17. Have you ever neglected your obligations, family, or work for 2 or more days in a row because you were drinking or using drugs? _____ yes _____ no

18. Because of your alcohol or drug use, have you felt (check all that apply):

	often	sometimes	seldom	never
tense or nervous?	_____	_____	_____	_____
suspicious or jealous?	_____	_____	_____	_____
worried?	_____	_____	_____	_____
lonely?	_____	_____	_____	_____
angry or violent?	_____	_____	_____	_____
depressed?	_____	_____	_____	_____
suicidal?	_____	_____	_____	_____

19. Do you ever feel bad about things you have done while using? _____ yes _____ no
If yes, please specify: _____
_____

20. People use alcohol and/or drugs for different reasons. How important would you say that each of the following is to you?

	very important	somewhat important	not at all
It helps me relax.	_____	_____	_____
It helps me be more sociable.	_____	_____	_____
I like the effect.	_____	_____	_____
People I know use dugs or drink.	_____	_____	_____
I use when I get upset or angry.	_____	_____	_____
I want to forget or escape.	_____	_____	_____

QUESTIONNAIRE 1 *Continued*

	very important	somewhat important	not at all
It helps cheer me up.	_____	_____	_____
It makes me less tense or nervous.	_____	_____	_____
It makes me less sad or depressed.	_____	_____	_____
It helps me function better.	_____	_____	_____
I use to celebrate special occasions.	_____	_____	_____

Other (please specify): _____

_____

_____

21. Have you tried to stop using drugs or alcohol in the past 2 months? _____ yes _____ no

If yes, did you experience any medical or physical problems when you stopped? (please explain)

_____

_____

_____

22. Have you ever gone to anyone for help about your drinking or drug use? _____ yes _____ no

If yes, please explain:_____

_____

_____

23. Have you ever attended a meeting of Alcoholics Anonymous (AA) or any other self-help group because of your drug or alcohol use? _____ yes _____ no

24. Do you think you have an addiction to alcohol or drugs? _____ yes _____ no

25. Do you want help with a drug or alcohol problem at this time? _____ yes _____ no

QUESTIONNAIRE 1   *Continued*

MAST Test

Yes	No		
____	____	1.	Do you enjoy a drink now and then?
____	____	2.	Do you think you are a normal drinker? (By normal, we mean you drink less than or as much as most other people.)
____	____	3.	Have you ever awakened the morning after drinking the night before and found that you could not remember part of the evening?
____	____	4.	Does your wife, husband, a parent, or other near relative ever worry or complain about your drinking?
____	____	5.	Can you stop drinking without a struggle after one or two drinks?
____	____	6.	Do you ever feel guilty about your drinking?
____	____	7.	Do friends or relatives think you are a normal drinker?
____	____	8.	Are you able to stop drinking when you want to?
____	____	9.	*Have you ever attended a meeting of Alcoholics Anonymous (AA)?
____	____	10.	Have you gotten into physical fights when drinking?
____	____	11.	Has your drinking ever created problems between you and your wife, husband, a parent, or other near relative?
____	____	12.	Has you wife, husband (or other family member), ever gone to anyone for help about your drinking?
____	____	13.	Have you ever lost friends because of your drinking?
____	____	14.	Have you ever gotten into trouble at work because of drinking?
____	____	15.	Have you ever lost a job because of drinking?
____	____	16.	Have you ever neglected your obligations, your family, or your work for 2 or more days in a row because you were drinking?
____	____	17.	Do you drink before noon fairly often?
____	____	18.	Have you ever been told you have liver trouble? Cirrhosis?
____	____	19.	After heavy drinking have you ever had delirium tremens (DTs) or severe shaking, or heard voices or seen things that weren't there?
____	____	20.	Have you ever gone to anyone for help about your drinking?
____	____	21.	Have you ever been in a hospital because of drinking?
____	____	22.	Have you ever been a patient in a psychiatric hospital or on a psychiatric ward of a general hospital where drinking was part of the problem that resulted in hospitalization?
____	____	23.	Have you ever been seen at a psychiatric or mental health clinic or gone to any doctor, social worker, or clergyman for help with any emotional problem, where drinking was part of the problem?
____	____	24.	Have you ever been arrested for drunken driving, driving while intoxicated, or driving under the influence of alcoholic beverages? (If yes, how many times? _____)
____	____	25.	Have you ever been arrested, taken into custody, even for a few hours, because of other drunken behavior? (If yes, how many times _____)

*If you went to an AA meeting because you were concerned about your drinking, answer the question yes; if not, answer no.

QUESTIONNAIRE 2   The Michigan Alcohol Screening Test (MAST)

Source: "The Michigan Alcohol Screening Test: The Quest for a New Diagnostic Instrument" by M. L. Selzer, 1971, *American Journal of Psychiatry, 127,* pp. 1653–1658. Used by permission.

Name_____ Date _____

Drug Use Questionnaire (DAST-20)

The following questions concern information about your potential involvement with drugs, *not including alcoholic beverages,* during the past 12 months. Carefully read each statement and decide if your answer is "yes" or "no." Then circle the appropriate response beside the question.

In the statements, *drug abuse* refers to (1) the use of prescribed or over-the-counter drugs in excess of the directions, and (2) any nonmedical use of drugs. The various classes of drugs may include cannabis (marijuana, hash), solvents, tranquilizers (such as Valium), barbiturates, cocaine, stimulants (such as speed), hallucinogens (such as LSD), or narcotics (such as heroin). Remember that the questions *do not* include alcoholic beverages.

Please answer every question. If you have difficulty with a statement, choose the response that is mostly right.

These questions refer to the past 12 months.   **Circle Your Response**

1. Have you used drugs other than those required for medical reasons? ....Yes   No
2. Have you abused prescription drugs? ....Yes   No
3. Do you abuse more than one drug at a time?..Yes   No
4. Can you get through the week without using drugs? ....Yes   No
5. Are you always able to stop using drugs when you want to?.....................................Yes   No
6. Have you had "blackouts" or "flashbacks" as a result of drug use? ....Yes   No
7. Do you ever feel bad or guilty about your drug use? ....Yes   No
8. Does your spouse (or parents) ever complain about your involvement with drugs?..Yes   No
9. Has drug abuse created problems between you and your spouse or your parents? Yes   No
10. Have you lost friends because of your use of drugs?...Yes   No
11. Have you neglected your family because of your use of drugs? ....Yes   No
12. Have you been in trouble at work because of drug abuse? ....Yes   No
13. Have you lost a job because of drug abuse? ....Yes   No
14. Have you gotten into fights when under the influence of drugs? ....Yes   No
15. Have you engaged in illegal activities in order to obtain drugs? ....Yes   No
16. Have you been arrested for possession of illegal drugs?...Yes   No
17. Have you ever experienced withdrawal symptoms (felt sick) when you stopped taking drugs? ....Yes   No
18. Have you had medical problems as a result of your drug use (e.g., memory loss, hepatitis, convulsions, bleeding, etc.)?...Yes   No
19. Have you ever gone to anyone for help for a drug problem?......................................Yes   No
20. Have you been involved in a treatment program specifically related to drug use? ....Yes   No

QUESTIONNAIRE 3   Drug Use Questionnaire (DAST-20)

Source: © 1992 by the Addiction Research Foundation. Author: Harvey A. Skinner, Ph.D. For information on the DAST, contact Dr. Harvey Skinner at the Addiction Research Foundation, 33 Russell St., Toronto, Canada, M5S 2S1.

The CAGE Questionnaire

C Have you ever felt a need to CUT DOWN on your drinking/drug use?

Alternative questions—Have you ever tried to cut down on your usage? Were you successful? What was it like? Why did you decide to cut down or go on the wagon? Are you able to drink as much now as you could a year ago? Five or ten years ago? How do you feel about your drinking or use of drugs now? Has anyone ever commented on how much you are able to consume?

A Have you ever been ANNOYED at criticism of your drinking/drug use?

Alternative questions—Have you ever been concerned about your usage? Has anyone else been concerned about your drinking or use of drugs? What caused the concern or worry? Do you get irritated by their concern? Have you ever limited how much you use in order to please someone?

G Have you ever felt GUILTY about something you've done when you've been drinking/high from drugs?

Alternative questions—Do you feel that you are a different person when you are high? How would you compare yourself when you're using and when you're not? Have you ever been bothered by anything you have said or done while you have been high/drunk? Has anyone else been bothered by your usage?

E Have you ever had a morning EYE OPENER—taken drink/drugs to get going or treat withdrawal symptoms?

Alternative questions—Do you ever get a hangover? How often? Have you ever felt shaky after a night of heavy drinking? Have you ever had a drink to relieve the hangover or the shakiness? Have you ever had trouble sleeping after a heavy night of drinking or getting high? Do you ever have difficulty remembering what happened while you were high? How many times has this occurred?

QUESTIONNAIRE 4 The CAGE Questionnaire for Adults

Source: "Detecting Alcoholism: The CAGE Questionnaire" by J. A. Ewing, 1984, *Journal of the American Medical Association, 252*, pp. 1905–1907. Used by permission.

CAGE for Youth and Adolescents

1. Have you ever used before or during school?

2. Have you ever missed school (or been truant) because of use or just to use?

3. Have you ever lied in order to use?

4. Have you ever avoided nonusers?

5. About how often do you get intoxicated?

6. About how often do you use more than one drug when you get intoxicated?

QUESTIONNAIRE 5   The CAGE Questionnaire for Youth and Adolescents

Treatment Setting and Treatment Planning

PHILIP J. PEREZ, PH.D.

5

And the frame is but a means to hold the picture up so that it can be seen. A frame that hides the picture has no purpose. Without the picture is the frame without meaning. (*A Course in Miracles*, p. 521)

In Chapter 4 the authors describe various methods for developing accurate assessments and diagnoses for substance abusers and dependents. This essential first step provides the theoretical and practical base for making future decisions about how to develop and organize an effective treatment experience for clients.

We continue our study of substance abuse by presenting the next step in organizing treatment. By building on the concepts of accurate assessment and diagnosis, this chapter will introduce the reader to the basic terms and processes of treatment settings and treatment planning. Each element will be defined, described, and illustrated, providing a strong base by which to understand topics from subsequent chapters, including treatment modalities, working with special populations, and relapse prevention. In this chapter, it is assumed that case examples received adequate and reliable assessment and diagnosis, which paved the way for the treatment considerations of setting and planning.

WHAT IS A TREATMENT SETTING?

Treatment setting is the place or environment where substance abuse treatment services are provided. These environments may look very different to the outside observer and range from most restrictive to least restrictive. *Restrictive* refers to the degree of physical and social structure provided by the professional staff for the recovering substance abuser. For example, a highly restrictive environment would be considered a locked, inpatient hospital setting where clients are encouraged to live and receive their treatment. In contrast, a weekly voluntary outpatient substance abuse treatment program would be considered a setting of less restriction where clients generally reside in their homes and attend scheduled meetings with professionals at designated agencies, offices, churches, and/or treatment facilities.

As mentioned in the previous chapter, clients fall within a range of diagnoses and severity of illness. In general, the more severe the substance abuse diagnosis (abuse vs. dependence), the more restricted the environment or setting that is recommended. This rationale suggests that clients need settings that match their diagnosis and degree of severity for treatment to be effective. Selection of treatment settings is similar to the way physicians prescribe different medications, medication strengths, and dosing schedules for patients. Settings, like medications, should fit the diagnosis, meeting the needs of the client and presenting problems.

Clients can move between settings depending on their progress in treatment and the recommendation of treatment staff. The goal is always to provide the least restrictive environment that offers the optimal types of services that match client needs. This approach ensures a respect for the client's autonomy and ability to move away from unhealthy dependency. It embraces the client's self-determination skills, which are essential in initiating and maintaining substance abuse/dependency recovery.

This chapter provides examples of seven of the most common treatment settings. It is not an exhaustive list but will provide a working knowledge of traditional treatment settings, ranging from most restrictive to least restrictive:

- Medical detoxification and stabilization
- Dual-diagnosis hospital inpatient
- Free-standing rehabilitation and residential programs
- Partial hospitalization
- Temporary recovery or halfway homes
- Intensive outpatient
- Outpatient DUI/DWAI/DUID programs

Important distinctions among the settings exist even though similar services may be offered within each setting, such as prevention, counseling, education, and/or self-help. Clients involved in any one setting can be either voluntary or involuntary participants. This means that within any one setting, some of the participants may be court ordered or mandated while others enter treatment without legal requirement.

Most settings do not consistently reflect the client's voluntary or involuntary status. An exception to this rule would be prison-based drug treatment facilities and DUI diversion programs. Otherwise, many substance abuse treatment professionals argue that most "voluntary" clients entering treatment have an "involuntary" element to their decision to enter treatment. These "voluntary" clients can often feel very pressured from coworkers, family members, and/or physicians. Studies (e.g.,

Collins & Alison, 1983; Lawental et al., 1996; Matuschka, 1985) have suggested that voluntary/involuntary status has little predictive value in determining treatment success of the program participants. Other considerations may determine the client's success or failure, such as the quality and effectiveness of the treatment program.

CASE DISCUSSION

Case 3 (Leigh). To illustrate the concept of treatment settings, let us extend case 3 and imagine Leigh, a 17-year-old marijuana and alcohol user who has run into trouble with her substance use. Her problems intensified one evening when she and her friends were brought into custody for questioning by police. Leigh was partying with some new friends in a wooded area close to the middle school she attends. Police, responding to a complaint initiated by neighbors in the area, confronted the adolescents and found alcohol and marijuana. Officials were concerned about the underage drinking, illegal use of marijuana, and in particular Leigh's emotional state, which was hostile, disoriented, and apparently intoxicated.

Police contacted Leigh's mother and discussed the possibility of charging Leigh with possession of marijuana and disorderly conduct. After several unsuccessful attempts by police to persuade Leigh to seek immediate medical care, she was evaluated to be at risk to herself and was involuntarily admitted to medical detoxification. After several days of detoxification and getting "clear headed," she voluntarily agreed to attend a rehabilitation program. After 28 days of successful treatment, her counselors recommended an intensive outpatient program to continue her recovery.

This scenario illustrates that treatment settings are not stagnant environments but integrative opportunities to move clients toward recovery and health. The reverse is also possible. Leigh might have a relapse (or slip) and need a temporary, more restrictive setting to regain her hard-won progress.

Moving up and down this continuum of care provides a multitude of treatment services designed to fit the client's unique needs. The effectiveness of treatment settings comes from their flexibility, adaptability, and responsiveness to the client's current recovery needs.

TYPES OF TREATMENT SETTINGS

Medical Detoxification and Stabilization

Detoxification is the safe and complete withdrawal of incapacitating substances such as alcohol, barbiturates, hallucinogens, and heroin. Detoxification units can be within hospitals or freestanding units.

Medical necessity is established before admission and refers to the risk of medical problems (e.g., seizures) or psychiatric difficulties (e.g., suicidal ideation) the client exhibits. These medical units usually employ pharmacological detoxification protocols that are based on the type of drugs abused and the patient's concomitant medical conditions (Jaffe et al., 1995). These protocols include gradual tapering of the drug(s) over a period of several days or weeks. For example, heroin can be weaned from an individual and substituted with a longer-acting opioid such as methadone. Other medications may be administered to lessen physical and psychological symptoms associated with withdrawal.

The length of stay is usually less than 2 weeks. Detoxification should be considered only the beginning of treatment. Many patients mistakenly believe that after detoxification no further intervention is necessary (Jaffe et al., 1995). Transition plans (discharge planning) should begin soon after admission (Weiner, 1991). The next treatment placement should be based on the patient's needs. However, follow-up treatment often depends on other factors such as community resources, ability to pay, and insurance coverage.

Detoxification settings provide:

- screening for presence of withdrawal symptoms and/or psychiatric conditions;
- on-site medical and psychiatric care that promotes safe and complete withdrawal;
- staff who structure and nurture the environment;
- staff who protect clients from self-harm or harm to others; and
- staff who educate and counsel clients about substance abuse and dependency.

Dual-Diagnosis Hospital Inpatient

Dual-diagnosis programs are usually based in psychiatric hospitals and are designed to treat clients with the presence of both serious psychiatric illness and substance abuse/dependency. Services are provided to diagnose and treat substance dependency as well as symptoms attributable to psychiatric illness. Each condition must be assessed independently and in relation to the other presenting conditions or symptoms. This is done to withdraw the affected client safely from substances, stabilize the client emotionally and physically, and identify and treat the concomitant disorders.

The personnel's expertise is helping dually diagnosed clients stop abusing substances and maintain their psychiatric treatment regimens, which may include prescribed psychotropic medication (e.g., antidepressants, antipsychotics, antianxiety drugs). Specialized training in dual diagnosis requires staff and counselors to understand how concomitant disorders can interact and manifest in the clients' lives. Individuals may reside in these hospital units from several days to several weeks. Programs are designed for either adult or youth treatment.

Dual-diagnosis hospital inpatient settings provide:

- on-site medical and psychiatric care that includes 24-hour nursing and milieu supervision and locked units with limited access to family and friends;

- personnel with specialized knowledge in dual diagnosis;
- 7-, 14-, or 28-day stays in a protective, restricted environment;
- psychiatric and substance abuse crisis stabilization;
- more intensive assessment and diagnostic services; and
- daily intensive group contact with other clients and staff.

Figure 5.1 defines some common staffing patterns for inpatient and partial hospital treatment settings.

Free-Standing Rehabilitation and Residential Programs

Rehabilitation Programs

Rehabilitation programs are usually freestanding, nonhospital-based facilities that are often oriented to the well-recognized Minnesota Model of addiction treatment (Straussner, 1993). Hazelden, an inpatient and outpatient treatment facility dedicated to treating alcoholics, is considered to be one of the major contributors to the Minnesota Model. Founded in 1949, Hazelden pioneered the 28-day rehabilitation program for alcoholics. McElrath (1997) suggests that the early years of Hazelden contributed to the Minnesota Model: (a) the grace of a beautiful environment that promoted respect, understanding, and acceptance of the dignity of each client; (b) a treatment based essentially on the program and process of AA; (c) the belief that time away and association with other alcoholics was central to recovery; and (d) a very simple program whose expectations were for all clients to make their beds, comport themselves politely, attend the daily lectures on the 12 steps, and talk with one another while sitting around. Since 1949, over 100,000 men and women have gone through treatment in one of Hazelden's facilities (McElrath, 1997).

Today the Minnesota Model denotes an effective and frequently used philosophy and methodology of delivering treatment. It has elements of medical (disease), social (psychological), and self-help approaches (McElrath, 1997). The medical elements emphasize a professional staff who direct and control the planning process and its implementation (e.g., enforce and maintain facility rules, provide treatment recommendations and evaluations, educate clients about substance abuse). The social/self-help elements encourage clients to be responsible for developing their own recovery within a context of help from peers and recovering staff (Borkman, 1998). (See this chapter's appendix for a listing of self-help groups.)

The medical elements of treatment suggest that:

- chemical dependency is a disease, and all clients have the same disease;
- the disease is primary, pervasive, and progressive;
- loss of control and denial are primary characteristics;
- recovering and nonrecovering clinical staff are valued;
- education and therapy are central to program effectiveness;

Attending Physician or Provider

In a medical/hospital setting, the physician, psychologist, or other approved mental health professional who "attends" the patient's stay is responsible for approving the course and methods of treatment and will assume dispensing or monitoring of correct medications; credentialed by the hospital medical staff.

Medical Director

Typically, an addictions-trained physician who oversees the delivery of services in the unit; not necessarily a direct provider of patient care; assumes general supervision of the nursing staff; occasionally directly involved with addictions counselors directly assigned to patient care.

Nursing Staff

Generally responsible for day-to-day patient care; often 24 hours per day on site or directly supervising nonmedical unit staff members; will help determine program procedures, patient care, treatment, and discharge planning.

Social Worker

Will provide required transition, discharge, or placement planning; will assure all record documentation meets standards; often has a portion of his or her time allocated from the social services department to the chemical dependency (CD) unit; not required to be addictions certified. Will conduct assessments and make treatment recommendations. Often not the primary counselor or assigned therapist.

Mental Health Workers

Mental health professionals trained in the delivery of general mental health and counseling services; not typically the primary provider or attending practitioner; assist in treatment planning, conducting education portions of the IP milieu, cofacilitating, activity, therapy, or skill-building groups; on dual diagnosis units, need not be certified in addictions treatment.

Certified Substance Abuse or Addictions Specialists; or, Primary Care Counselors

In a medical facility, a member of the treatment team under the direction of the attending practitioner; certified by the state as a trained counselor in the field of addictive disorders. In residential, nonmedical setting, often the primary counselor/therapist directly responsible for clinical care, treatment planning, education sessions, group treatment, and after-care planning. In residential, free-standing units, may be a recovering individual with no primary or advanced degrees, but with technical, approved training in the field of substance abuse treatment.

Clinical Director

Generally a trained, advanced-degree mental health professional who is a certified or licensed addictions specialist; oversees the delivery of clinical care to patient and significant others; may directly provide group and specialty services, such as CD education, couples' group therapy, multifamily therapy, and so on; supervises primary counseling staff; if advanced in training, may supervise all medical and clinical functions.

FIGURE 5.1   Inpatient and partial hospital modalities: common staffing patterns

- families should be included in treatment; and
- self-help groups enhance treatment (Straussner, 1993).

The social and self-help elements of treatment suggest that:

- planning for recovery is a skill acquired by clients;
- experiential education is emphasized and encouraged;
- self-governing peer support is stressed and encouraged; and
- developing sober/clean support networks in the community prepares clients for leaving the rehabilitation program (Borkman, 1998).

The Minnesota Model consists of three phases of integrated care: detoxification, rehabilitation, and aftercare (Straussner, 1993; Wallace, 1992).

Detoxification   The detoxification phase is the process of safely and thoroughly relieving symptoms of intoxication in either a hospital or nonhospital (community-based) setting. Patients may already be detoxified at entry, though many programs have their own detoxification facilities. Withdrawal from alcohol and/or drugs can be accomplished from several days to 1 week depending on the substances abused and the client's unique physiology. Once a client is detoxified and given medical clearance, he or she is then enrolled into the rehabilitation phase of treatment.

Rehabilitation   The rehabilitation phase can occur in either inpatient or outpatient settings. Clients range in "drug of choice" and mental health conditions. Daily routines for structured inpatient settings (e.g., group therapy, 12-step support groups, recreation, community meetings) are the same for all clients. Peer interaction and confrontation are encouraged to develop a recovering, supportive community atmosphere. The social milieu is an essential element of treatment and attended to by professional staff just as vigorously as any other services provided (Jaffe et al., 1995).

Individualized treatment plans (which will be described in detail later in this chapter) are used to guide treatment. These plans identify behavioral problems and develop goals and strategies for their resolution. Common problem areas are maintaining abstinence, family relations, career decisions, and social interactions. Often a "level system" for privileges and benefits is used to encourage clients to participate successfully in the program. Inpatient stays are typically 21 to 28 days.

Outpatient rehabilitation, a less restrictive environment, typically includes group therapy meetings three times per week. Homework is given to extend learning into home and work environments. Clients maintain their place of residence and employment while committing to a program of recovery that includes abstinence. If a client is unable to maintain sobriety and/or is not making sufficient progress, a more restrictive environment such as inpatient rehabilitation might be recommended.

Aftercare   Aftercare is the least restrictive phase of the Minnesota Model and considered to be a continuation of the rehabilitation process based on the notion that recovery from alcohol and drugs is a lifelong endeavor. Aftercare helps clients transition into a sober/clean lifestyle that is lasting and integrated into their everyday lives. It is provided by the program for approximately 1 year and may take the form of weekly or biweekly individual, family, or group therapy. Consistent attendance of 12-step meetings is encouraged to help clients maintain their sobriety by deepening their connections with other recovering individuals.

For most rehabilitation programs, psychiatric evaluations are usually done off site, but some may staff their own psychiatrists.

Residential Programs

Residential programs are often used as a bridge between the more restrictive dual-diagnosis inpatient and rehabilitation programs and the less restrictive outpatient programs. Many use a level system similar to the Minnesota Model but are designed for long-term treatment stays. Sometimes, with lower-income clients, residential programs are used as an alternative to outpatient programs because of their housing resources.

Residential programs are intermediate-care facilities that allow individuals to live within a residential setting, be employed during the day, and receive comprehensive treatment, including individual, group, and family therapy as well as education and relapse prevention services. Average stays can range from 4 months up to a year (Jaffe et al., 1995). Rehabilitation and residential programs are designed for either adult or adolescent/youth treatment.

Youth services offer rehabilitative and residential programs specially designed to meet the needs of children and adolescents. Such programs recognize that drug use and abuse in youth is multidetermined, with contributing factors pertaining to youth cognitive structures (way of thinking), family relations, peer associations, school performance, and neighborhood context (Henggeler, 1997). Henggeler argues that because of the debatable impact of broad-based prevention strategies (e.g., DARE programs) for high-risk youth, drug abuse rehabilitation and residential youth programs have to attempt to address the multiple, entrenched determinants of youth substance abuse. This is a difficult task that has required reliance on expensive and restrictive treatments and highly integrated services, such as on-site schooling and other youth specific services.

Research reviews (e.g., Hawkins, Catalano, & Miller 1992; Kumpfer, 1989; Office of Technology Assessment, 1991) suggest the following youth problem areas:

- Individual: other antisocial behaviors, low self-esteem, low social conformity, positive expectancies for drug effects
- Family: ineffective discipline, low warmth, high conflict, parental drug abuse, poor family management
- Peer: association with drug-using peers, low association with prosocial peers
- School: low intelligence, achievement and commitment to achievement
- Neighborhood: disorganized, high crime

Henggeler (1997) suggests that rehabilitation and residential youth substance abuse treatment should adopt Stroul and Friedman's (1994) guidelines. These advocate the development of integrated service systems that are family centered, community based, youth focused, individualized, comprehensive, less restrictive, and accountable for client outcome and satisfaction.

Rehabilitation and residential programs provide:

- varied treatment stays ranging from 14 days to 1 year;
- comprehensive, structured, and intensive treatment services to transition clients to sober/clean independent living;
- development of communal recovering environment;
- ancillary services such as social workers, discharge planners, and job placement specialists to support continued recovery; and
- adolescent/youth and adult treatment options.

Partial Hospitalization

Partial hospitalization, occasionally referred to as day treatment, offers comprehensive substance abuse treatment in a semirestrictive program where clients live at home and attend treatment during the day. Similar to other more restrictive treatment settings, partial hospital programs require completion of a detoxification program. Only clients *without* medical or psychiatric complications requiring inpatient care are admitted. These settings are for clients who need a level of restrictiveness between hospital inpatient/rehabilitation/residential and intensive outpatient. It is considered that the client should attend a daily, intensive, structured treatment program or otherwise be at high risk for relapse.

The setting includes a 5-day-a-week, 6-hour-a-day, structured daily schedule, including a combination of cognitive-behavioral therapy (lectures, life skills groups), individual therapy weekly or as needed, family education, self-help, and medical monitoring as necessary. The daily schedule begins at 9:00 A.M. and ends at 4:00 P.M.; clients usually stay an average of 3 to 4 weeks (Frances, Wilson, & Wiegand, 1997).

Partial hospitalization provides:

- a cost-effective level of care between full hospitalization/rehabilitation and intensive outpatient; and
- a professionally staffed structured environment providing treatment services.

Temporary Recovery or Halfway Homes

A recovery/halfway house is usually a community-based home or a building near a rehabilitation or residential facility. Resident clients rely on the safe and supportive group social structure of a transitional living arrangement with less monitoring than a more restrictive environment. Requirements for residence typically are abstinence, employment, attendance of 12-step recovery meetings, and possible urine testing to evaluate recovery progress and maintain a safe, sober house. Staff are usually considered "paraprofessional," and most often are self-identified recovering alcoholics or addicts. Stays can vary ranging from several weeks to several months.

Recovery or halfway homes provide:

- a minimum structured transitional living in a recovering environment;
- an opportunity to save money to live independently; and
- help maintaining a connection with a recovering community while dealing with day-to-day trials.

Intensive Outpatient

Intensive outpatient treatment consists of substance-free treatment that can range from daily all-day activities to once-a-week meetings. In traditional comprehensive "intensive outpatient" programs, clients are initially enrolled to attend three evenings of 3-hour group therapy with 1 hour of family therapy per week. In addition, clients are expected to attend a certain number of AA/NA 12-step meetings established by treatment personnel.

Group therapy meetings can range in theme from managing stress to handling dysfunctional family patterns. Random urine testing is usually an integral part of these programs. Continued participation is based on abstinence as evidenced by self-report and/or urine testing. Completion is usually determined by documented behaviors such as length of abstinence, attendance in groups, and keeping scheduled individual and family counseling appointments. Intensive outpatient programs are typically 90- to 120-day commitments.

Weekly or biweekly outpatient settings are often for those clients who have successfully completed the intensive portion of treatment and demonstrated sustained abstinence, employment, and a sober/clean lifestyle (e.g., staying away from high-risk substance-using friends).

Intensive outpatient provides:

- comprehensive treatment with off-site living arrangements while establishing or maintaining employment;
- graduated treatment services; and
- possibly longer-term, intensive treatment than hospitals and rehabilitation settings.

Sample of a Three-Phase Intensive Outpatient Program

Phase 1

Schedule

Three to five evenings per week, 2 to 4 hours each night for an average of 6 weeks

Initial Tasks

Client completes medical evaluation

Assessment and diagnosis completed

Treatment plans developed and signed

Meetings with significant others of client

General Goals

Address denial

Share extent of substance abuse with treatment group

Demonstrate compliance with program

Outcomes

Completion of personal and family history

Assigned readings

Participation in self-help groups

Verification of abstinence (drug/alcohol screening)

Compliance with program expectations

Phase 2

Schedule

Two nights per week, 1.5- to 3-hour group sessions for 6 weeks. Family/significant others attend "family group" and possibly individual family sessions.

General Goals

Uninterrupted abstinence

Replacement of substance abuse behaviors with recovery or routine activities and/or responsibilities

Outcomes

Sustained demonstrated willingness to change

Evidence of use of peer groups as support

Achievement and maintenance of treatment plans

Demonstration of nurturing self-care and respect of others

Assumption of consequences of own actions and ability to identify and engage in corrective actions

Phase 3

Schedule

Introduction to weekly aftercare group sessions

One and a half to 3 hours in length for 4 weeks

General Goals

Both an external and internal commitment to a substance-free lifestyle

Identification of ongoing recovery issues

Development of a posttreatment lifestyle plan that includes maintaining changes and expanding life changes in social, psychological, and spiritual realms

Outcomes

Active use of community-based self-help groups

Consistent demonstration of appropriate response to life stressors

Completion of a relapse prevention education series

Consistent ability to serve family, community, and self in a substance-free manner

Outpatient DUI/DWAI/DUID Programs

Driving under the influence (DUI), driving while ability impaired (DWAI), and driving under the influence of drugs (DUID) are some of the titles used by state legislatures to address the problem of driving intoxicated or drug impaired. Most states have well-defined penalties and treatments for the impaired driver that vary from state to state.

Beginning in the mid-1970s, large institutions such as the National Institute on Alcohol Abuse and Alcoholism began funding pilot projects known as alcohol-driving countermeasures (ADC) programs. These were most often administratively placed under motor vehicle divisions or highway safety departments. In the early 1980s and with the onset of action groups such as Mothers Against Drunk Driving (MADD) and Students Against Drunk Driving (SADD), treatment programs and citizen advocacy groups collaborated to influence the development of more formalized and strictly mandated programs targeting impaired drivers (Manfrin, 1998).

Despite the involuntary nature of the clients attending these programs (the majority are court ordered), they are considered the least restrictive treatment setting. Typical alcohol/drug education track programs are for 12 weeks with 90-minute group meetings, the basics of which are:

- describing the physiological effects of alcohol and drugs;
- describing the possible psychological consequences of use/abuse of drugs;

- defining the legal limits of blood alcohol levels;
- presenting current theories of alcohol and drug abuse and addiction; and
- developing alternatives to impaired driving.

The Importance of Matching Treatment to Client Needs

Thus, far we have described a broad range of treatment settings available to the drug abuser. In practice, various treatment programs often offer very similar services. None of the settings can claim general treatment efficacy over any other. Any one of them may be the most appropriate treatment choice for a particular client under particular circumstances. Circumstances that may affect treatment setting choices may include but are not limited to:

- ability to pay;
- method of payment;
- geographic availability of specific services;
- current employment, housing, and family conditions;
- previous treatment experiences;
- reliability of assessment information;
- availability of space in existing settings;
- level of self-care; and
- current emotional and behavioral state.

The most effective matching method creates a comprehensive and reliable assessment and diagnosis that fully takes into account the client's unique wishes, needs, and capabilities (Jaffe et al., 1995).

Helpful Hints for Clinicians: Know Your Facility Setting
- Know what organization accredits your facility (e.g., Joint Commission on Accreditation of Health-care Organizations) and all its documentation requirements and procedures.
- Develop relationships with facility administrators.
- Study your orientation manual.
- Know your job description.
- Know how your facility gets reimbursed for services (e.g., insurance, private pays, state/national funds, HMOs).
- Know the expertise of the setting (e.g., detoxification, comprehensive treatment).
- Know the referral sources of the facility: how do clients enter your facility?
- Know how clients are assessed and diagnosed: who is responsible for such tasks?

This section provided an overview of the major treatment settings encountered in the field of substance abuse. (Table 5.1 summarizes the various treatment settings.) It was designed to prepare clinicians to make informed decisions about treatment options. The following section introduces the more specific clinical skill of treatment planning. Planning for treatment is an essential element of all treatment settings. It offers clear and concise expectations and guidelines for the client and clinician within

TABLE 5.1   Summary of treatment settings

Type of Setting	Characteristics
Medical detoxification and stabilization	Short-term, specialized medical care to screen for the presence of withdrawal symptoms and/or psychiatric conditions
	Promotion of safe withdrawal of substances and psychiatric stabilization
	Protection from self-harm and harm to others
	Referrals made for further substance abuse treatment
Dual-diagnosis hospital inpatient	On-site medical and psychiatric care
	24-hour nursing, milieu supervision, restricted environment
	Specialized assessment, evaluation, and treatment of dual-diagnosis disorders
	Individual and group counseling
Free-standing rehabilitation and residential programs	Short- and long-term on-site treatment stays
	Comprehensive, intensive, structured services
	Ancillary services
Partial hospitalization	Full-day treatment, 5 days per week
	Comprehensive, intensive, structured services
	Hospitalization and outpatient alternative
Temporary recovery or halfway homes	Transitional living supporting sober/clean lifestyle
	Recovering social environment
	Flexible stays
Intensive outpatient	Comprehensive, intensive structured services with off-site living arrangements
	Lower cost and less restrictive than inpatient treatment settings
Outpatient DUI/DWAI/DUID programs	Specific treatment protocols
	Court-referred clients
	Weekly 90-minute group meetings

their particular context or setting. Planning addresses the specific problems of the client and answers the who, what, when, where, and how of treatment.

WHAT IS TREATMENT PLANNING?

Treatment plans are written documents that detail how problems are defined and treatments are formulated for the substance abuser. Each plan is specific and individualized to meet the client's needs and goals and must be measurable in terms of setting milestones that can be used to chart the client's progress (Stout & Jongsma, 1998).

Treatment planning, which began in the medical sector during the 1960s, was created to provide an analytical and critical way of thinking for counselors, clients, substance abuse treatment administrators, insurance companies, and government agencies. Treatment plans are for the benefit of all participants in treatment, including the substance-abusing client. It is very easy for the counselor and client to lose sight of the issues that initially brought the patient into treatment. The treatment plan serves to structure the focus of the therapeutic relationship and contract. However, treatment plans are designed to evolve and change and should be used as a dynamic document. They must be updated to reflect any changes occurring during substance abuse treatment such as:

- addressing additional problems;
- resolving problems;
- redefining problems;
- adding goals;
- defining new or redefining objectives; and
- incorporating new or redefined interventions (Stout & Jongsma, 1998).

Treatment plans are also very helpful when many service providers (e.g., psychiatrist, social worker, activities counselor, family therapist, milieu therapist) are working with one substance-abusing client, encouraging effective and efficient information exchange. Treatment plans not only help clarify objectives but also serve to delineate who does what, when, and why (Stout & Jongsma, 1998).

How to Develop a Treatment Plan

The foundation of any treatment plan is the data or information gathered in a thorough assessment interview and testing. (Refer to Chapter 4 for a full discussion of how to obtain a complete biopsychosocial assessment and diagnosis.) Once the assessment and diagnosis is complete, the counselor can then begin formulating the treatment plan.

This chapter describes a method developed and designed by Richard J. Laban (1997) to address the needs of the substance-dependent client. Theoretically Laban draws from medical, psychological, and social models of substance abuse treatment. He suggests that substance abuse/dependency treatment plans can be categorized into nine common problem domains that reflect the three major models of substance abuse:

- Initial treatment (first 24 hours)
- Medical/health
- Emotional barriers
- Interpersonal
- Recognition versus resistance
- Reuse (relapse)
- Social milieu
- Recovery environment
- Home environment

These domains are viewed as possibilities for potential problems often seen in chemical dependency treatment settings. Laban (1997) cautions that identifying a problem and matching it with the applicable domain may not be a cut-and-dried process. There can be overlap and diffusion into other problem domains. He attributes this to the very nature of the domains' interrelatedness. "It is difficult to identify any one problem that exists in a vacuum, unaffected by (or not affecting) other life areas" (Laban, 1997, p. ix).

Let us return to the case of our 17-year-old, polysubstance-abusing client Leigh. After her arrest and detoxification, she was admitted to a 30-day chemical dependency rehabilitation program. Her biopsychosocial assessment revealed a history of using alcohol and marijuana at parties and sometimes during school hours.

She has had some moderate school-related problems (e.g., lateness) and a shoplifting charge. She described a new, well-defined group of peers who "I like to hang out with and party with." Some potential problem domains related to Leigh's situation might be as follows:

Social milieu: gravitates toward unhealthy, drug-using peers

Home environment: disengaged relationship with father, financial stressors, and feelings of having to choose between parents

Medical/health: potential dietary problems, disheveled appearance, and poor hygiene

It is important to have an accurate, reliable, and detailed assessment to identify problem areas and match them to the most fitting problem domain. Each problem domain should have a separate, written treatment plan.

The Elements of a Substance Abuse/Dependency Treatment Plan

Laban (1997) identifies nine elements necessary for an effective chemical dependency treatment plan:

- Type of plan (initial, master, update)
- Problem
- Indicators
- Long-term goals
- Short-term goals
- Objectives
- Methods
- Frequency of services provided
- Signatures

The following sections describe each element in more detail, and Figures 5.2 through 5.4 are examples of treatment plans.

Type of plan—There are three types of plans: initial (usually developed within the first 24 hours of admission), master (may be several treatment plans fitting the client's unique problem domains), and update (plans that revise or review changes in master treatment plans).

Problem—A statement of the problem should consider assessment data and client's perception of presenting problem.

Indicators—Indicators refer to tangible evidence or supporting data confirming the problem.

Long-term goal—The long-term goal is the patient's condition reflecting a desired outcome 6 months to 1 year after discharge.

Short-term goal—This goal reflects a desired consequence realized during the treatment stay. It is assumed that the short-term goal will facilitate attainment of the long-term goal.

Objective—The objective is a realistic, measurable, and mostly behavioral statement of a desired state or condition. More than one objective is possible but all should have target dates or due dates (dates when objective will be successfully completed).

Method—The method entails specific behavioral interventions and tasks assigned to the client to fulfill the desired objective and short- and long-term goals.

Frequency of services provided—Particular therapy services are described that will be used to implement the treatment plan.

Initial: _____   Master: _____   Update: _____

Client Name:

Problem #: You are at risk for having difficulties getting used to being in a drug-free and structured living situation here at [facility].

Indicators: New patient in treatment here at [facility] and first time in treatment.

Long-Term Goal: You will have a satisfactory and rewarding treatment experience at [facility].

Short-Term Goal: You will understand the reason and importance for following all directions and treatment plan instructions.

Objective #: You will display the ability to follow all directions and instructions to help you settle into treatment.

Due Date: _____   Date Completed: _____

Methods:

1. You will need to perform your daily assigned house chore posted in the _____ area on the bulletin board.

2. You will need to be at all scheduled group activities as indicated on your daily schedule 5 minutes before the group starts.

3. You will have an assigned buddy for your first week. After this, you will be assigned a new person to whom you will be a buddy. Learn all you can from your buddy this week.

4. You will report to the nurses' station for vital signs for first _____ days in treatment at 7:30 A.M., after lunch, and again at dinner time. The nurse will inform you of any changes in times.

5. You will need to review your Patient Handbook to familiarize yourself with the routine and expectations of _____. Bring any questions to your assigned counselor or any staff on duty.

Services and Frequency Provided: Group therapy ___ × 's weekly; Individual therapy ___ × 's weekly; activities group ___ × 's weekly; therapeutic work assignment daily as assigned; daily attendance at AA and NA meetings; peer feedback group ___ × 's weekly; family therapy ___ × 's weekly; family program ___ × 's weekly; medication lecture 1 × ; ___ lecture series daily (indicate)

Client Signature: _____   Date: _____

Staff Signature: _____   Date: _____

FIGURE 5.2   Initial admission plan

Source: Adapted from *Chemical Dependency Treatment Planning Handbook,* by R. J. Laban, 1997, Springfield, IL: Thomas.

Initial: Master: Update:

Client Name:

Problem #: You are preoccupied with legal matters and situations outside treatment that could interfere with your need to stay focused on recovery.

Indicators: Self-disclosure during admission; repeated requests to call probation officer; comments to peers that your probation officer "pushed" you into treatment.

Long-Term Goal: Stable and self-directed involvement in a recovery program.

Short-Term Goal: You will understand the need to focus your full attention and energies to the treatment program in order to get well for you.

Objective #: You will demonstrate an ability to maintain a 70% or greater focus in the treatment program over a 48- to 72-hour period.

Due Date: _____ **Date Completed:** _____

Methods:

1. You will write down, and prioritize, the five things in your life that continue to cause you the most pain. Discuss with your group these five situations and ask for feedback, specifically if they believe these issues are interfering with your ability to commit to a recovery program.

2. Write about your fears and preoccupations—that is, exactly what kinds of thoughts you have, how they affect your behavior (negatively), and how you have dealt with these in the past. Share with your group and ask them for feedback re positive alternatives.

3. Make a list of all those things you are focused on or worried about that are outside treatment. Next to each item, describe in detail the impact your addiction and behaviors have had on each area. Read this to your group and let them critique your level of honesty into the assignment. What does this tell you about your use and need for treatment?

4. You will be given [_____ days] to get settled into treatment, but will be expected to present a convincing appeal to your counselor and group at the end of this time telling them why you should be allowed to remain in treatment. This appeal needs to be convincing. When done, your group will respond as to how convincing you were, and the treatment team will make a decision.

Services and Frequency Provided: Group therapy ___ ×'s weekly; individual therapy ___ ×'s weekly; activities group ___ ×'s weekly; therapeutic work assignment daily as assigned; daily attendance at AA and NA meetings; peer feedback group ___ ×'s weekly; family therapy ___ ×'s weekly; family program ___ ×'s weekly; medication lecture 1×; ___ lecture series daily (indicate)

Client Signature: _____ **Date:** _____

Staff Signature: _____ **Date:** _____

FIGURE 5.3   Sample treatment plan 1

Initial: Master: Update:

Client Name:

Problem #: Your difficulty accepting the severity of your alcoholism and not engaging in a recovery program will put you at risk for future drinking.

Indicators: [client] compares her drinking against others and states "I was never that bad."

Long-Term Goal: [client] will acknowledge the truth of her chemical dependency as evidenced by active participation in a recovery program.

Short-Term Goal: [client] will recognize that she needs treatment for herself and that she is chemically dependent.

Objective #: [client] will verbalize her pledge to follow all treatment recommendations that will help her stay sober.

Due Date: _____   **Date Completed:** _____

Methods:

1. You will fill in answers for every question in the workbook on "Step 1," including 20 areas that ask for examples of powerlessness and unmanageability. You should answer all areas and share your results with your group. Read the explanation of these terms and ask any staff for assistance. You need to present 20 examples of powerlessness and unmanageability relating to your addiction. Share in therapy group and ask for honest and critical feedback.

2. You will review the progression chart for the Disease of Alcoholism and place a checkmark next to every item that you can identify with. Write down several personal examples for each as well on a separate sheet of paper. Identify the stage of your disease process (early, middle, late). Explain in therapy group in what stage of addiction you see yourself and personal examples of items checked.

3. Give examples of how your denial system causes you to minimize what and how much you use and to blame external factors for your use. Discuss in the group and ask the group for examples of how they see you minimizing and blaming. When finished, talk about the feelings associated with this assignment.

Services and Frequency Provided: Group therapy ___ ×'s weekly; individual therapy ___ ×'s weekly; activities group ___ ×'s weekly; therapeutic work assignment daily as assigned; daily attendance at AA and NA meetings; peer feedback group ___ ×'s weekly; family therapy ___ ×'s weekly; family program ___ ×'s weekly; medication lecture 1 ×; ___ lecture series daily (indicate)

Client Signature: _____   **Date:** _____

Staff Signature: _____   **Date:** _____

FIGURE 5.4   Sample treatment plan 2

Signatures—This refers to the development of the client's active involvement and commitment. Signatures should represent consent and understanding of the entire treatment plan. They also serve to meet regulatory and licensing standards.

Sample Substance Abuse/Dependency Treatment Plan: Social Milieu

Facility: Shady Pines Rehabilitation Center

Client name: Leigh

Problem: Client states that all friends drink and use drugs/she will find it difficult to change friends and remain sober/clean.

Indicators: Client cannot identify sober friends and is reluctant about giving up current group.

Long-term goal: Client will develop a healthy, sober/clean network of friends.

Short-term goal: Client will identify peer changes necessary to avoid drugs and alcohol.

Objective: Client will devise a written plan addressing changes she needs to realize to remain sober/clean

*Due date:*_____

*Date completed:*_____

Methods:

1. Client will relate in therapy group 10 examples of high-risk situations and/or encounters. Client will describe how she will handle such situations. Role-play and group feedback will be elicited.

2. Client will write a plan stating how she plans to develop new sober friends. This plan will be developed with individual counselor and group feedback.

3. Client will meet with two outside AA members (selected by staff) and talk with them about their recovery and changes they made with friends who used drugs. Results will be presented in group.

Frequency of services provided: Group therapy five times weekly; individual therapy twice weekly; therapeutic work assignment daily as assigned; daily attendance of NA or AA meetings; family therapy once weekly; daily house meetings; daily lecture series

Client signature:_____ Date:_____

Staff signature:_____ Date:_____

External Reviewers of Treatment Planning: Health Care Accreditation Organizations and Managed Care

Clinics, hospitals, and free-standing treatment agencies seeking to qualify for third-party reimbursement must attain and maintain accreditation from entities such as the

Joint Commission on Accreditation of Health-care Organizations (JCAHO). The JCAHO's main purpose is to give its stamp of approval to substance abuse treatment programs (SATPs) and facilities that are providing respectful, ethical assessment, care, and education to clients and their families.

Acceptable care consists of a continuum of services that can provide a range of services extending from pretreatment to treatment to follow-up. To evaluate the adequacy of a program's continuum of care, Joint Commission surveyors (evaluators who site-visit settings to ensure compliance) expect evidence that the program affords access to an integrated system of treatment environments, interventions, and care levels. They also expect patients' needs to be considered wherever possible in the treatment system process (Brown, O'Farrell, Maisto, Boies-Hickman, & Suchinsky, 1997).

When evaluating SATP functions, accreditation visitors/surveyors examine the structures and processes that are used in six areas of performance:

1. Do structures and processes improve the SATP system and care provision?
2. Are leaders providing the structure and program administrative activities that are critical to developing, delivering, and evaluating good health care?
3. Are there safe and supportive environments for clients and staff?
4. Is the atmosphere conducive to staff self-development for the purpose of improving care?
5. What is the quality of the processes by which health care providers communicate and document?
6. Are there appropriate and effective surveillance and infection prevention and control (Brown et al., 1997)?

SATPs that are accredited and those considering accreditation consider accreditation visits very important. They are taken very seriously and can determine the viability of the organization and its ability to provide care to substance abusers. The JCAHO requires care standards that are divided into five major areas: treatment planning, medication use, nutrition care, rehabilitation care and services, and special treatment services.

JCAHO *requires* that SATP clinical staff write treatment plans. Its guidelines for treatment planning are the following:

• Use diagnostic summaries (DSM) to identify complex treatment needs of each client.
• Design a program intervention tailored to meet those needs.
• Develop treatment objectives that are reasonable, attainable, and written in measurable and objective terms.
• Determine patient goals for treatment and involve patients in developing their own treatment plans (Brown et al., 1997).

It is important to remember that JCAHO is only one of several accrediting bodies and each has its own set of treatment planning standards. Clinicians should know the accrediting body that guides and monitors their facility and understand all aspects of this increasingly important element of delivering substance abuse treatment.

Insurance companies and managed care companies are insisting that counselors move quickly through assessing the problem, formulating treatment plans, and implementing interventions. Managed care companies function as health care "gate-keepers of services" for the people participating under their particular plans. The "gate" is the point at which insured individuals can begin to access their mental health and/or substance abuse treatment benefits. It is common today for counselors to interact with managed care professionals such as preauthorization specialists, care reviewers, primary care physicians, and employee assistance professionals.

"The demand for accountability from third party payers and health maintenance organizations (HMOs) is partially satisfied by a written treatment plan and complete progress notes" (Stout & Jongsma, 1998). The plan's uniformity, detail, and written/signed nature is valued by lawyers, administrators, regulatory agency workers, and managed care case reviewers. These important nonclinical professionals are very much involved in the treatment of substance abuse/dependency. They often rely on the written word, whereas chemical dependency treatment counselors are trained to rely on the spoken word and nonverbal communication. For nonclinical support professionals, without whom treatment would be impossible, "if it isn't documented, it didn't happen."

Substance abuse counseling by its very nature often relies on the interpersonal, emotional, nonverbal, intuitive and the intangible. These are necessary clinical skills brought to any effective and efficient treatment experience. But equally important are the skills of team building and communication that are demanded by the emerging needs of managed care and accreditation organizations.

Treatment plans offer a language to bridge the sometimes seemingly divergent cultures of clinical and nonclinical professionals. If providers work together in establishing and maintaining a clear and coherent communication system, the delivery of substance abuse treatment services is greatly enhanced and improved. The big winner in this quest for quality is the client, one of the central reasons we decide to enter a career in substance abuse counseling.

Helpful Hints for the Substance Abuse Counselor and Managed Care

- Know the various problem domains for substance abuse.
- Know the behavioral symptoms of addictive disorders.
- Know DSM diagnostic criteria and terminology.
- Know the limits and strengths of your treatment setting.
- Develop strong treatment planning skills.
- Know the language of managed care.
- Know the procedural requirements of each managed care company your facility interfaces with.
- Document, document, document.
- Use detailed standardized forms when possible.
- Communicate using behavioral language.

CASE DISCUSSIONS

Case 1 (Sandy and Pam).   The appropriate treatment setting for Sandy and Pam should be determined by evaluating the assessment and diagnosis information suggested in Chapter 4. Setting selection will depend on the answers to such questions as these: What is the severity of chemical dependency or phase of abuse for Sandy and Pam? What psychiatric symptoms or disorders might be present? Is Pam in need of detoxification? What DSM diagnoses might be appropriate? What previous substance abuse and/or psychiatric treatment have the mother and daughter had? If Pam's substance use is considered abusive or dependent, would she be willing to attend treatment? If not, would involuntary procedures be necessary?

Both clients volunteered for family counseling and do not seem to be a danger to themselves or others. The extent of Pam's alcohol and drug use is uncertain, but if she attempts to stop using substances, she might be at risk medically and psychologically. A detoxification program might be necessary to ensure her safety. If Pam is diagnosed as an alcohol/drug abuser/dependent and is willing to attend treatment, the type of setting will depend on the severity of dependency. If psychiatric problems also exist for Pam, a dual-diagnosis program may be appropriate.

Treatment planning would identify several important problem areas for each family member such as substance abuse/dependency, enabling, and transgenerational patterns of coping. Modalities might include individual, family, and group counseling. Methods emphasizing solution-oriented approaches might incorporate "the miracle question," scaling questions, and discussions of previous attempts at abstinence. Pam and Sandy might also benefit from 12-step meetings and the development of a sober peer network.

Case 2 (The Smith Family).   Joe and Jane Smith reportedly have a long history of substance abuse (alcohol, cocaine, and marijuana). Such long-standing polysubstance abuse can be difficult to treat. Abstaining from all mind- and mood-altering substances might be overwhelming for such dependent individuals. Intensive, simultaneous inpatient or outpatient treatment would be recommended for both partners.

The logistics for arranging treatment for both partners could be complex. What if their diagnosis suggested that they *both* needed separate freestanding rehabilitation programs? Would the spouses enter treatment voluntarily? What if one partner was willing and the other was not? Who would care for their daughters Sarah and Karen if both attended rehabilitation programs? Does the family have health insurance that would cover such extensive treatment?

Depending on their diagnoses, this couple may benefit from intensive outpatient programs that would enable them to live at home and attend treatment. Family therapy should be reconsidered in light of both parents' possibly being diagnosed with substance dependency. Should family therapy continue while Joe and Jane attend their treatment programs? What would be the benefits or concerns of continuing family therapy? Is it effective to continue family therapy while both parents may be abusing substances? How would the children be involved in their parents' substance abuse treatment?

Treatment planning would be very important for such a complex counseling scenario. Coordinating two separate treatments and possibly family therapy while maintaining individual confidentiality would require considerable planning and ongoing assessment and evaluation. The potential for confusion among treatment providers and family members is high when many individual and family services are used at once. Providers would need to decide who gets what kind of information. Written documentation would be critical for providing clear, responsive, and effective substance abuse treatment. Getting everyone "on the same page" while respecting individual differences in treatment progression would be a focus for the treatment providers of this family.

CONCLUSION

The substance abuse/dependency treatment industry is a vastly diverse collection of team members who have organized themselves to provide ways (e.g., research, clinical, administrative, financial) to help those who struggle with substance abuse and dependency. The treatment settings described in this chapter give only an overview of the diversity of how substance abuse treatment is currently delivered. One can be sure that new and innovative settings will emerge to better meet the needs of the substance-abusing client and their care providers. Treatment planning and its place in accreditation organizations and managed care companies are an increasingly important element of this changing health care system—a system that will only expand in significance and sophistication.

This chapter has presented guidelines to condense information and promote analytic/rational thinking. Study these suggestions with a critical eye, and use them as a springboard for your own professional development. The substance abuse treatment field is rapidly changing, requiring constant vigilance to changing expectations and laws. Continuing education and professional development workshops and seminars are highly recommended to continue to provide current, effective, and ethical health care for substance-abusing clients.

REFERENCES

Borkman, T. J. (1998). Is recovery planning any different from treatment planning? *Journal of Substance Abuse Treatment, 15*(1), 37–42.

Brown, E. D., O'Farrell, T. J., Maisto, S. A., Boies-Hickman, K., & Suchinsky, R. (1997). *Substance abuse program accreditation guide.* Thousand Oaks, CA: Sage.

Collins, J. J., & Alison, M. (1983). Legal coercion and retention in drug abuse treatment. *Hospital & Community Psychiatry, 34,* 1145–1150.

Frances, R. J., Wilson, E., & Wiegand, J. H. (1997). Hospital-based alcohol and drug treatment. In R. K. Schreter, S. S. Sharfstein, & C. A. Schreter (Eds.), *Managing care not dollars* (pp. 91–108). Washington, DC: American Psychiatric Press.

Hawkins, J. D., Catalano, R. F., & Miller, J. Y. (1992). Risk and protective factors for alcohol and other drug problems in adolescence and early adulthood: Implications for substance abuse prevention. *Psychological Bulletin, 112,* 64–105.

Henggeler, S. W. (1997). Effective drug-abuse services for youth. In J. A. Egertson, D. M. Fox, & A. I. Leshner (Eds.), *Treating drug abusers effectively* (pp. 253–279). Malden, MA: Blackwell.

Jaffe, J. H., et al. (Eds.). (1995). *Encyclopedia of drugs and alcohol* (1st ed., vols. 1–4). London: Macmillan.

Kumpfer, K. L. (1989). Prevention of alcohol and drug abuse: A critical review of risk factors and prevention strategies. In D. Shaffer, I. Philips, & N. B. Enzer (Eds.), *Prevention of mental disorder, alcohol and other drug use in children and adolescents* (OSAP Prevention Monograph 2). Rockville, MD: Office for Substance Abuse Prevention, Department of Health and Human Services.

Laban, R. L. (1997). *Chemical dependency treatment planning handbook.* Springfield, IL: Thomas.

Lawental, E., et al. (1996). Coerced treatment for substance abuse problems, detected through workplace urine surveillance: Is it effective? *Journal of Substance Abuse*, *8*(1), 115–128.

Manfrin, C. (1998). Treatment settings. In P. Stevens-Smith & R. L. Smith (Eds.), *Substance abuse counseling: Theory and practice* (pp. 135–167). Upper Saddle River, NJ: Merrill/Prentice Hall.

Matuschka, P. R. (1985). The psychopharmacology of addiction. In T. E. Bratter & G. G. Forrest (Eds.), *Alcoholism and substance abuse: Strategies for clinical intervention* (pp. 85–106). New York: Free Press.

McElrath, K. (1997). The Minnesota model. *Journal of Psychoactive Drugs*, *29*(2), 141–144.

Office of Technology Assessment, U.S. Congress (1991). *Background and the effectiveness of selected prevention and treatment services.* (Adolescent Health-Volume II: OTA-H-466, pp. 499–578). Washington, DC: U.S. Government Printing Office.

Stout, C. E., & Jongsma, A. E., Jr. (1998). *The continuum of care treatment planner.* New York: Wiley.

Straussner, S. L. A. (Ed.). (1993). *Clinical work with substance abusing clients.* New York: Guilford.

Stroul, B. A., & Friedman, R. M. (1994). *A system of care for children and youth with severe emotional disturbance.* Washington: Georgetown University Child Development Center.

Wallace, B. C. (Ed.). (1992). *The chemically dependent: Phases of treatment and recovery.* New York: Brunner/Mazel.

Weiner, N. (1991). *Handbook for detoxification and stabilization.* Denver, CO: Author.

Appendix:
12-Step, 12-Tradition Groups

Adult Children of Alcoholics (ACoA)
P.O. Box 3216, Torrance, CA 90510;
(213) 534-1815

Alcoholics Anonymous (AA)
Central office: Box 459, Grand Central Station,
New York, NY 10163
*Directories available for the United States,
Canada, and international*

Al-Anon and Alateen
Central office: Al-Anon Family Groups,
P.O. Box 182, Madison Square Station,
New York, NY 10010
*Directories available for the United States,
Canada, and international*

Cocaine Anonymous (CA)
Central office: P.O. Box 1367,
Culver City, CA 90239
Also listed: 6125 Washington Blvd, No. 202,
Los Angeles, CA 90230; (213) 559-5833

Codependents Anonymous (CoDA)
P.O. Box 33577, Phoenix, AZ 85067-3577;
(602) 277-7991

Codependents of Sex Addicts (CoSA)
Central office: P.O. Box 14537, Minneapolis,
MN 55414; (612) 537-6904

**Co-Dependents of Sex/Love Addicts
Anonymous (Co-SLAA)**
P.O. Box 614, Brookline, MA 02146-9998

Debtors Anonymous (DA)
P.O. Box 20322, New York, NY 10025-9992;
(212) 642-8222

Drugs Anonymous (DA)
P.O. Box 473, Ansonia Station, New York, NY
10023; (212) 874-0700

Emotional Health Anonymous (EHA)
P.O. Box 429, Glendale, CA 91209;
(818) 240-3215

Emotions Anonymous
P.O. Box 4245, St. Paul, MN 55104;
(612) 647-9712

Gamblers Anonymous (GA)
Central office: P.O. Box 17173, Los Angeles,
CA 90017; (213) 386-8789
*Directories available for the United States, Europe,
and Australia*

Gam-Anon Family Groups
P.O. Box 157, Whitestone, NY 11358

Incest Survivors Anonymous (ISA)
P.O. Box 5613,
Long Beach, CA 90805-0613; (213) 428-5599
National organization: (213) 422-1632

Narcotics Anonymous (NA)
P.O. Box 9999, Van Nuys, CA 91409;
(818) 780-3951

Nar-Anon Family Group
P.O. Box 2562, Palos Verdes, CA 90274-0119;
(213) 547-5800

Nicotine Anonymous (formerly Smokers
Anonymous)
2118 Greenwich Street,
San Francisco, CA 94123; (415) 922-8575

O-Anon Family Group (Family Group for OA)
P.O. Box 4305, San Pedro, CA 90731

Overeaters Anonymous (OA)
Central office: 2190 190th Street,
Torrance, CA 90504
Also listed: P.O. Box 92870,
Los Angeles, CA 90009; (800) 743-8703

Parents Anonymous (use volunteer professionals
as resources)
6733 S. Sepulveda Blvd., No. 270,
Los Angeles, CA 90045; (800) 421-0353

Pill Addicts Anonymous
P.O. Box 278, Reading, PA 19603;
(215) 372-1128

S-Anon (patterned after Al-Anon)
P.O. Box 5117, Sherman Oaks, CA 91913;
(818) 990-6910

Sex Addicts Anonymous (SAA)
Central office: P.O. Box 3038, Minneapolis,
MN 55403; (612) 339-0217

Sex and Love Addicts Anonymous (SLAA)
Central office: P.O. Box 529, Newton, MA 02258
Also listed: P.O. Box 119, New Town Branch,
Boston, MA 02258; (617) 332-1845

SexAholics Anonymous (SAA)
Central office: P.O. Box 300, Simi Valley, CA
93062; (818) 704-9854

Sexual Compulsives Anonymous (SCA)
P.O. Box 1585, Old Chelsea Station, New
York, NY 10011; (212) 439-1123

Survivors of Incest Anonymous (SIA)
World service: P.O. Box 21817,
Baltimore, MD 21222

Workaholics Anonymous
P.O. Box 661501, Los Angeles, CA 90066;
(310) 859-5804

Note: *Central office* and *World service* are terms used to identify central locations for national and international information.

Individual and Group Treatment | 6

Patricia Stevens, Ph.D.

This chapter presents an overview of individual and group modalities used to provide treatment to individuals who are either substance abusers or dependent on substances. As a counselor in training, you complete a variety of courses that contribute to a knowledge base in the areas of individual counseling theory, group counseling theory, and systems counseling theories. It is beyond the scope of this chapter to provide a thorough review of each theory or model presented; rather, a collaborative framework will be presented that integrates individual and group work. The next chapter will consider in detail the dynamics involved in substance-abusing families and their treatment. Such a framework appears to result in the highest rate of success in a treatment program for substance abusers.

The use of treatment modalities is affected by a variety of factors that vary from program to program. If a setting is basically an alcohol treatment facility, then the use of methadone maintenance will not be of interest to these program administrators or participants. Some programs have detox centers or areas; others do not. Also, as in every aspect of the mental health field, the theoretical basis on which the program is grounded will in many ways determine the components used in treatment.

The etiological-biopsychosociofamilial model of substance use also represents an effective model for treatment. Anecdotal as well as empirical research substantiates that the use of substances interferes with every aspect of a person's life. It seems reasonable, therefore, that a treatment program needs to incorporate every aspect of the individual's life. The previous chapters in this book integrate this concept into assessment, diagnosis, and treatment planning. Before treatment can begin, however, the individual must be engaged in the therapeutic process.

GETTING THE INDIVIDUAL INTO TREATMENT

For any type of treatment to be successful, the individual must stop the use of any chemicals. Therefore, the first order of business in treatment is to interrupt the substance-using behaviors (Lewis, Dana, & Blevins, 1994). The process whereby the individual has reached the point in her life that change is necessary may initiate this. This voluntary admission of the need for treatment is sometimes called "hitting bottom." In the early treatment literature, it was believed that an individual had to reach this point in order for treatment to be successful. Today, the profession recognizes that there are many ways for people to enter treatment and to be successful—through self-recognition or the concern of an employer, a spouse, or significant other.

Coercive versus Voluntary Treatment

Much has been said about the influence of motivation in recovery. Is motivation present when individuals are coerced to begin treatment rather than voluntarily choosing to stop their substance use? The term *voluntary* may, however, be a misnomer. Individuals who are substance abusers or are substance-dependent will often continue to use in spite of the consequences. In fact, this is one of the criteria for diagnosis in the DSM-IV. Only when intense external pressure occurs to address the issue of use—in the form of family intervention, legal intervention, employment intervention, or medical intervention—may treatment be considered.

Legal intervention, or court-ordered treatment, usually involves the individual being arrested for a drug-related charge, such as driving under the influence, public drunkenness, or possession of an illegal chemical substance. The judge may offer treatment as an alternative to incarceration. Court-ordered intervention can be a powerful motivation for treatment (Moylan, 1990). Studies indicate that individuals who are court ordered into treatment do as well or better than those who are motivated to come to treatment "voluntarily" if the staff does not see this as a hindrance and when court-mandated clients are involved in their treatment planning and goals (Collins & Alison, 1983; Howard & McCaughrin, 1996; Matuschka, 1985; Ouimette, Finney, & Moos, 1997).

Another form of coercive intervention is through employers. Many times the substance abuser's job will be in jeopardy if the substance use is not discontinued. The widespread use of urine toxicology testing and the increasing awareness of the economic cost of substance use on the job have made employer-mandated treatment more common (Doweiko, 1999). Employees with alcohol/drug problems are shown to be absent 16 times as often as nonabusing employees (Lawental, McLellan, Grisson, Brill, & O'Brien, 1996). When an either/or ultimatum is given (i.e., "Either you go to treatment or lose your job"), treatment results appear to be as beneficial, if not more so, than non-employer-mandated treatment. However, employers should seek legal advice before giving such an ultimatum, as employees do have certain rights in this process (Adelman & Weiss, 1989; Lawental et al., 1996).

Other forms of coercive intervention may come from significant others or the medical profession. The family may indicate an either/or situation in which either the individual enters treatment, or the relationship with the family ends. This may "motivate" the individual to seek treatment (see "The Process of Intervention").

Medical professionals may influence the individual to seek treatment due to physical problems that result from prolonged substance use. Or, in some states, substance abusers can be voluntarily committed for treatment by a medical professional. For involuntary commitment, there must be sufficient evidence of *imminent* harm to self or others. However, harm to self may be defined as (a) neglect of self, (b) when the chemical use may be defined as neglect of self, or (c) when the chemical use puts the client or others at high risk. However, reluctance to seek treatment is usually not considered sufficient reason for involuntary commitment.

The Process of Intervention

One method of confronting an individual about substance abuse problems is called *intervention,* which is the process of stopping someone who is experiencing the harmful effects of alcohol or other drugs (Anderson, 1993). As such, intervention can happen on a variety of levels. Individuals who stop smoking because of the educational materials they have read and teenagers who are caught and punished for drinking and subsequently stop have experienced successful interventions (Doweiko, 1999).

In the professional field, however, this term refers to a more formal process. V. E. Johnson of the Johnson Institute, who pioneered this process, defines intervention as a

> process by which the harmful, progressive and destructive effects of chemical dependency are interrupted and the chemically dependent person is helped to stop using mood-altering chemicals, and to develop new, healthier ways of coping with his or her needs and problems. (Johnson Institute, 1987, p. 61)

This process involves all the significant people in the substance abuser's life: the partner, children, siblings, parents, friends, supervisors and coworkers, minister, medical professionals, and any other support people in the person's world. Although it is possible to complete an intervention successfully without professional assistance, because of the emotionally charged situation, it is highly recommended that the planning and completion be performed under the supervision of a substance abuse counselor who is trained in the process of intervention.

The purpose of an intervention is to get the abuser to look at the rationalization, denial, and externalization of blame he is using to justify the substance use. The result of an intervention is, ideally, the individual's agreement to seek immediate treatment (Doweiko, 1999). Interventions should be structured to let the abuser know that he is cared for but that there are limits to and consequences of continued substance use.

Individuals involved in an intervention "break the silence" concerning the individual's substance-abusing behaviors. It is important to have many significant people involved in the intervention. Anyone who has ever tried to challenge a substance abuser one on one knows the frustration and power of the abuser's excuses, rationalizations, projection, and denial. Each individual should bring specific situations or incidents involving the abuser to the intervention, with a focus on facts or firsthand observations of behaviors. Again, owing to the emotion involved, participants may need to write down what they want to express. With a large and well-prepared group of people present at the intervention, it becomes very difficult for the abuser to manipulate the facts of any situation or to discount the seriousness of the situation.

Remember that the purpose of the intervention is not just to confront the person with the effects of his behavior. It is an act of caring for the individual substance abuser and for the people involved with the abuser (Johnson Institute, 1987). This is a time when significant others can address their feelings about the person's chemical use and its effect on them (Twerski, 1983). The purpose of the intervention is to break through the substance abuser's denial and to have the person accept the need for immediate treatment (Doweiko, 1999; Johnson Institute, 1987; Williams, 1989).

Substance abuse counselors who are trained in this treatment technique should supervise interventions. They should be planned and rehearsed before the actual intervention. Individuals participating in the intervention should be clear as to the purpose of the intervention. Additionally, these individuals should be certain as to their response if the substance abuser refuses treatment. This response may include detaching from the person when treatment is not forthcoming. Detachment may take many forms: excluding the person from family functions, refusing to give the individual money, or filing for divorce. For the employer, it may mean putting the person on leave or actually firing the individual. The medical professional may choose to seek involuntary commitment.

Any of these actions should be well thought out before the intervention begins. Any consequence will be difficult and should not be thought of as punishment for the substance abuser or as a manipulation to force the person to seek treatment. It is, rather, an alternative behavior for significant others when the abuser denies treatment and "an opportunity for healing" (Meyer, 1988, p. 7). The abuser obviously has the option to seek treatment or not; similarly, significant others have the option to continue to engage with the individual or not if chemical use continues.

To sum up the process, Daley and Raskin (1991) suggest four steps for a successful intervention:

1. *Gather the team.*   At least two significant people should be involved; three to five seem to be a most effective team. The professional involved may be responsible for gathering appropriate individuals together.

2. *Gather the data.*   This includes facts about use and behaviors well as information about available treatment alternatives.

3. *Rehearse the intervention.*   The intervention should be practiced at least once. A "chairperson" should be chosen. Sequence of speakers needs to be determined as well as a rehearsal of exactly what will be said.

4. *Finalize the details.*   Meet once more before the actual intervention to clarify such facts as when and where the intervention will take place and whether treatment options are finalized.

Ethical and Legal Concerns of Intervention: A Word of Caution

In today's litigious society, it behooves the substance abuse counselor to move carefully. Rothenberg (1988) addresses the concern for a thorough diagnosis of substance dependency before an intervention begins. Should this be an independent diagnosis? Are there any legal sanctions for a substance abuse counselor who supervises an intervention without this diagnosis (Doweiko, 1999)? Some families may use intervention as a tool to control behavior, which raises ethical concerns also (Claunch, 1991). As there are no precedent cases, these concerns have not been answered in a court of law.

The question of the individual's right to leave at any time may also be a legal as well as ethical question. Does the substance abuser need to be informed that she has the right to leave at any time? What might be the legal difficulties if this information is not provided?

In this and other situations, simply be aware of the ethical and legal implications of practice. Since interventions are by their very nature high-stress activities, clear rules or action should be established and agreed on beforehand. All participants should be made aware of their rights and responsibilities.

Summary

No matter what path the person takes to reach treatment, once the decision is made, effective treatment needs to take a holistic approach. All aspects of the individual's life—physical, emotional, behavioral, familial, and social—should be considered in the path toward recovery. To facilitate this, a variety of methods should be incorporated in the treatment planning. Individual therapy, group therapy, and family therapy, as well as a physical exercise and nutritional plan for the client, can combine for an effective framework to counsel substance abusers.

INDIVIDUAL THERAPY

An assortment of treatment approaches is used in individual therapy with substance abusers: cognitive-behavioral therapy (Ellis & Velten, 1992; Emick & Aarons, 1990), reality therapy (Schuster, 1978-1979), Gestalt therapy (Buelow & Buelow,

1998), aversion therapy (Miller, 1990), and social skills training (Emick & Aarons, 1990; Lewis et al., 1994), among others. No empirical research indicates that one theory or model is more effective than any other or under what conditions one theory or model may be more effective than another (Schilit & Gomberg, 1991).

It appears, however, that in the early stages of treatment, the tasks that need to be accomplished seem to respond best to the cognitive-behavioral schools of thought. With prolonged treatment and recovery, many of the other insight-oriented models work as well as a continuation of the cognitive-behavioral models. The therapist's job in early treatment is to act as a coach in these behavioral strategies for abstinence. Another important responsibility is to assist in the establishment of structure. Since recovering individuals are usually not as intact as they appear on the surface, establishing structure is vital to continued recovery (Yalom, 1995).

Miller and Hester (1986b) reviewed controlled studies and found that strategies or models that were most effective fell into two categories: direct-effect strategies and broad-spectrum strategies.

Direct-Effect Strategies

The first category has a direct effect on the discontinuation of chemical use. Three therapies that appear to be effective are aversion therapy, behavioral self-control training, and medication.

Aversion Therapy

Aversion therapy or conditioning is designed to reduce or eliminate an individual's desire for alcohol "[by] pairing unpleasant stimuli or images with alcohol consumption" (Rimmele, Howard, & Hilfrink, 1995, p. 134). Although not used frequently today, this therapy has the longest history of use in the field and was most frequently used with alcoholics. Several different aversion approaches were common, including electric shock, nausea-producing drugs, and covert sensitization. Neither electric shock aversion nor nausea-producing drugs have shown consistent positive outcome results (Cannon, Baker, Gino, & Nathan, 1986). Early reported outcome results with alcoholics appear modestly positive, but the results are unclear because of the lack of controlled studies (Baker & Cannon, 1979; Blake, 1965). There are also no substantiated studies with drug abusers showing positive results using either electrical or chemical aversion therapy (Lesser, 1976; Lieberman, 1969; Wolpe, 1965). However, covert sensitization using imagery appears to produce positive effects (Miller, 1985; Rimmele, Miller, & Dougher, 1990).

Covert sensitization has advantages over aversion therapy because of the lack of medical concerns. This technique is based on the desensitization techniques developed by Wolpe (1965). Counselors train individuals in relaxation and then have them imagine aversive scenes that include the use of chemicals. Scenes of nausea, vomiting, sweats, cramps, and so forth, are paired with the smell, sight, and taste of the drug. Repetition of this pairing results in conditioned aversion to the chemical.

Some studies using covert sensitization suggest that conditioned nausea responses can occur and that subjects (about 69% of those treated) who develop these responses maintain significant periods of abstinence (Elkins, 1975, 1980). Again, there are no controlled studies using covert sensitization with drug abusers, but positive outcomes have been shown in single-subject studies with drug-free periods of up to 18 months (Palakow, 1975; Wisocki, 1973).

Covert sensitization and imagery are easy for the client to learn and use when the client feels a craving for the drug. Used in conjunction with other interventions, this technique can also be tailored to the individual's drug use, particular patterns of behaviors, and environment (Lewis et al., 1994).

Behavioral Self-Control Training

Behavioral-self control training teaches clients a variety of self-regulating techniques to modify their own chemical use patterns (Miller, 1990). Recognizing, analyzing, and monitoring situations that the individual associates with chemical use are imperative in recovery. As these situations are identified, individuals can develop coping strategies that maintain recovery. Coping strategies need to be both cognitive and behavioral. Cognitive strategies include self-statements and alternative planning. Behavioral techniques include relaxation training, assertiveness training, covert sensitization, and the use of alternative behaviors such as exercise.

Medication

The third technique in this category is the use of medication. The most commonly used drug in the treatment of alcoholism is disulfiram (Antabuse). If this drug is taken regularly, the individual will become violently ill when drinking alcohol. Significant physical effects are possible from the combination of disulfiram and alcohol that should be communicated to the individual when the drug is prescribed, such as skin rash, fatigue, halitosis, peripheral neuropathies, severe depression, psychosis, and possible death (Schuckit, 1996). Disulfiram is also not recommended for persons with a history of cardiovascular or cerebrovascular disease, kidney failure, depression, seizure disorders, women who might be pregnant, or the elderly. Because of these side effects, initial monitoring by medical personnel is recommended. Despite these cautions, studies show compliance when the drug is taken regularly and indicate that the drug is effective in working with couples (involving the partner as a monitor) and that persons on disulfiram have a lower relapse rate (Adelman & Weiss, 1989).

The use of methadone in the treatment of heroin addicts is another example of medication as treatment. The number of individuals on methadone maintenance varies greatly, with an upper estimate of 120,000. In New York City alone, it is estimated that there are 35,000 maintenance patients (Levy & Rutter, 1992; O'Brien, 1996).

Methadone mimics the production of endorphins in the body, producing a feeling of satisfaction without the high of heroin. Once methadone has occupied these receptor sites, subsequent heroin or morphine produces no psychoactive effects. It also occupies these receptor sites much longer than heroin or morphine. Methadone must be administered under the supervision of a professional. Therefore, the individual is required to come to a treatment facility to receive a daily dose of methadone. Tolerance does develop and withdrawal symptoms will appear if the drug is stopped acutely.

For these reasons, methadone use has been criticized as simply trading one addiction for another (Cornish, McNicholas, & O'Brien, 1995), and many methadone users also use other drugs recreationally. One particular drug is propoxyphene (Darvon, Darvocet-N) as this drug enhances the effect of the methadone to produce a euphoric feeling akin to the heroin rush (DeMaria & Weinstein, 1995). Methadone is, however, a medication that was designed to be used as an adjunct to other treatment modalities. When used in conjunction with psychosocial support systems, it allows a significant increase in abstinence time (McLellan, Arndt, Metzger, Woody, & O'Brien, 1993).

Broad-Spectrum Strategies

The second category of strategies falls under what Miller and Hester (1986b) term *broad-spectrum strategies*. These include social skills training, stress management, community reinforcement, and solution-focused therapy (Holder, Longabaugh, Miller, & Rubonis, 1991). These approaches focus on life problems and circumstances rather than on the discontinuation of the chemical use. Their purpose is to help the individual learn to cope with situations and circumstances that elicit the chemical use. The discontinuation of the substance is a secondary goal.

Social Skills Training

Social skills training, or assertiveness training, is well established as a successful strategy in the treatment of substance abuse (Ferrell & Galassi, 1981; Holder et al., 1991; Monti, Abrams, Kadden, & Cooney, 1989). Many substance-abusing individuals failed to learn social skills and may report that the use of the substance "eases the way" in social situations. Still others may have lost their social skills through many years of substance use. In both cases, relearning assertiveness and social skill behaviors is an important concept in learning coping mechanisms to avoid substance use. Monti et al. (1989) list a variety of social skills to be taught in treatment, beginning with starting conversations to forming close and intimate relationships.

Social learning skills can be taught through modeling, role play, and demonstration. Various forms of these techniques are available in treatment. For example, other clients can be used as appropriate role models for specific behaviors. Audio- and videotapes are also available for demonstration purposes and learning. Role play and role taking help the client increase skills (George, 1990).

Refusal skills and assertiveness training are closely related. "Assertion is the behavior or trait that allows people to appropriately express their personal rights and feelings" (Lewis et al., 1994, p. 115). Assertiveness training is most often practiced in the group setting. Being assertive means that you can express thoughts and feelings in direct, honest, and appropriate ways; defend yourself when necessary; and express your needs and wants. It also means, particularly for the substance abuser, that you identify situations in which you will need to be assertive in order not to resume substance use. Examining the illogical beliefs related to these situations, developing new strategies to cope with the situation, and practicing these strategies lead to a new strength for the abuser (George, 1990).

Assertive behavior can be contrasted with other behavioral responses: aggression, passive/aggressive behavior, and passive behavior. Assisting the client to recognize assertive behavior as well as practice assertive responses is an important part of treatment. Assertive behavior increases self-esteem and the feeling or personal power while decreasing feelings of self-pity, thereby decreasing the cues for substance use (Lewis et al., 1994).

Another skill that is necessary for clients to develop is the skill to refuse drugs and alcohol. Goldstein, Reagles, and Amann (1990) list core skills that they believe to be essential in the recovery process. These include but are not limited to asking for help, knowing your feelings, dealing with fear, dealing with being left out, responding to persuasion, and making a decision. Their teaching model includes role playing, performance feedback, modeling, and transfer of this learning into real-life situations.

Stress Management

Anxiety is often a precursor to substance use. Anxiety occurs through a combination of factors including social, environmental, cognitive, and affective components. Substance abusers usually manage anxiety through the use of their "drug of choice." Learning to manage this anxiety through other means is an important individual consideration in treatment. Relaxation training is one mechanism for anxiety or stress management. Although relaxation does not facilitate resolution of the underlying problems, it is a way the client can deal with the outward aspects of stress (George, 1990). Relaxation is incompatible with anxiety; in other words, one cannot be anxious and relaxed at the same time. Therefore, it is an easy-to-use, positively reinforcing technique for clients that appears to yield long-term results of decreased substance use (Chaney, O'Leary, & Marlatt, 1978; Ferrell & Galassi, 1981; Lewis et al., 1994).

Progressive relaxation training methods have been developed that teach individuals to tense and relax a particular set of muscles, then another and another, until the entire body is relaxed (Jacobsen, 1968). Audiotapes of relaxation techniques are also available that the client can use individually. Imagery may also be used as part of the relaxation training. Relaxation and imagery are two strategies that the client can use easily after leaving treatment.

Community Reinforcement

Community reinforcement approaches combine an assortment of strategies such as medication, couple therapy, and assistance with job searches. A program using a variety of methods appears to be the most effective (Miller & Hester, 1986b), while traditional treatment approaches (educational films and lectures, medication, confrontational therapy) appear to be the least effective (Annis & Chan, 1983; Miller & Hester, 1986a; Powell, Penick, Read, & Ludwig, 1985). In spite of the availability of this outcome information, many treatment programs continue to use this traditional treatment model. The reasons for this continuation remain a mystery. Perhaps it is associated with the plethora of recovering individuals in counseling positions in the field or rooted in the financial structure of the facilities.

Another individual treatment strategy is involvement in a self-help group, such as Alcoholics Anonymous, Narcotics Anonymous, or Cocaine Anonymous. These groups are easy to find, accessible, and cost-effective. As a supplement to treatment, they are invaluable if the individual is motivated to participate. On the down side, participation in these groups is controversial and difficult to assess. The empirical outcome studies examining AA attendance efficacy are inconclusive due to methodological flaws (Brandsma, Maultsby, & Welsh, 1980; Stimmel et al., 1983). In addition, when individuals are forced to attend (as in some treatment programs), the result can be resistance and treatment failure (Lewis et al., 1994).

None of these self-help groups profess to be treatment groups. They were established as and remain support groups for recovering substance users. The need for support is a central issue in recovery. Self-help groups provide peer support in which members understand the feelings and problems faced by a recovering person. They confront when necessary and offer encouragement when it is needed (George, 1990). As such, they are an invaluable tool in treatment and recovery.

Solution-Focused Therapy

The last individual strategy to be discussed is solution-focused, brief therapy. Much of our treatment planning today has become economically driven by health care systems. Managed care, insurance companies, employers, and other third-party providers have placed limitations on the number of sessions available and/or amount of financial compensation for care.

Additionally, there is an increased competitive treatment marketplace. It is wise for treatment facilities to investigate techniques that are cost-efficient and effective. Numerous studies have shown no appreciable difference between short- and long-term treatment outcome. In fact, this research shows that alcohol-abusing clients respond positively and rapidly to only minimal or brief intervention when treatment is "targeted, individualized, and focused." The mean number of sessions attended by clients in these studies was five and six (Berg & Gallagher, 1991; Berg & Miller, 1992; Hester & Miller, 1989).

Berg and Miller (1992) outline the steps in solution-focused, brief therapy for substance abuse as follows:

1. Developing a cooperative client-therapist relationship
2. Developing "well-formed" treatment goals: negotiation and cooperation between the client and therapist

3. Interviewing for change
4. Delivering treatment interventions
5. Developing strategies for maintaining progress

These five steps are, of course, built on the framework of solution-focused therapy. The emphasis is on the exception to the problem—in other words, how to strengthen and maintain those times when the individual was not using drugs. Client strengths, resources, and abilities are emphasized. This therapy also maintains that change is inevitable and that the therapist need only "tip the first domino" (Rossi, 1973, p. 14) to create the beginning of that change.

Solution-focused therapy is atheoretical and client determined. This means that time in session is not devoted to figuring out why a problem exists. A client's view is accepted, and the task of finding solutions begins immediately (Berg & Miller, 1992, p. 8). Goals are measurable and attainable—which also suits managed care requirements.

The central philosophy of solution-focused therapy is stated in three simple rules:

1. If it ain't broke, DON'T FIX IT!
2. Once you know what works, DO MORE OF IT!
3. If it doesn't work, then don't do it again, DO SOMETHING DIFFERENT! (Berg & Miller, 1992, p. 17)

Obviously, the criticism of solution-focused, brief therapy with substance abusers is the same as with other populations. Many believe it to be only a "Band-Aid" for the problems that clients bring to therapy. While some professionals believe that it discounts the immense pain that clients may have, others praise the embrace of strength and wellness that it offers. Solution-focused therapy is an alternative to the traditional means to this end.

Summary

In summary, individual therapy may take many forms. As with all therapy, it is based on the unique problems and situations presented by the client. The underlying goal of therapy with this population, however, is the minimization of, or at best the discontinuation of, the use of chemical substances to cope with life. Whether one believes in the moral model, the disease model, or the biopsychosocial model, increasing the individual's healthy coping skills will assist the individual toward this goal.

GROUP THERAPY

Group therapy traditionally has been the most popular form of treatment for substance abusers. Whether this popularity rests on the efficacy of group therapy or on the fact that group treatment is less expensive is an issue yet to be determined since measurable benefits are inconsistent (Galanter, Castaneda, & Franco, 1991; Miller & Hester, 1985). In fact, it *is* less expensive than individual or family therapy, and it also *appears to work*. Anecdotally the literature is enthusiastic regarding the effectiveness of group therapy. Early literature touted group therapy as "the treatment of choice for the psychological problems of the alcoholic" (Stein & Friedman, 1971, p. 652) and more recently as "the treatment of choice for chemical dependency" (Matano & Yalom, 1991, p. 269) as well as "the definitive treatment for producing character change" (Alonso, 1989, p. 1).

Some explanation of why group therapy works may lie in the basic nature of humankind—the ongoing and constant participation in groups of all kinds throughout our lives—and on the characteristics of substance-abusing clients themselves (George, 1990). Matano and Yalom (1991) attribute this to the power of the group—"the power to counter prevailing cultural pressures to drink, to provide effective support to those suffering from the alienation of addiction, to offer role modeling, and to harness the power of peer pressure, an important force against denial and resistance" (pp. 269–270).

Despite these positive descriptions, research on efficacy in group therapy is sparse. Bowers and al-Redha (1990) found that group therapy with couples was more effective than individual therapy in both lowering alcohol consumption and reported increasing relationship adjustment. Another study of schizophrenic substance abusers in group therapy found that over 1 year, they had a marked decrease in hospitalization days (Hellerstein & Meehan, 1987). Some types of substance-abusing patients appear to respond more positively to group therapy than do others. One such study determined that group therapy is more useful for alcoholic clients with dependent personality disorder than with those clients who have antisocial disorders (Poldrugo & Forti, 1988).

Therapeutic Factors in Group Therapy

There appears to be more consistency in the research that addresses the factors that influence the group experience as well as agreement on the types of skills that are important in the group process. Yalom's (1975) early work provides the foundation for today's group therapy. He developed a Q-sort technique that he used to study basic curative factors in psychotherapy groups. Using this process, Yalom constructed a ranking of interpersonal input, catharsis, group cohesiveness, and insight. These four curative factors were ranked highest in the assortment. A replication of this Q-sort with inpatient alcoholics resulted in an identical outcome for the first four curative factors (Feeney & Dranger, 1976).

George and Dustin developed another model of therapeutic factors in 1988. Although titled differently, these factors seem to coincide with Yalom's factors with the addition of one, vicarious learning. They include the following:

1. Instillation of hope
2. Sense of safety and support

3. Cohesiveness

4. Universality

5. Vicarious learning

6. Interpersonal learning

As previously stated, interpersonal relationships are an area in which substance abusers have great difficulty, whether it is from a deficit in early learning or in the paucity of intimacy resulting from years of chemical use. Clients frequently come into therapy feeling isolated and distrustful of others. Because of their consistent substance use, clients may have a distorted perception of themselves and the world (Lewis et al., 1994). Group therapy reduces the sense of isolation via what Yalom calls interpersonal input, or feedback received from other group members and the counselor as to the client's personal interactions. As a result, clients gain knowledge and learn new behaviors. This type of therapy is also beneficial in altering the client's distorted worldview through the interactions and reinforcement in the group setting (Vannicelli, 1992).

Cohesiveness, or the feeling of being accepted by other group members, increases the feeling of safety for the client. While individual therapy may increase anxiety, group therapy may permit the client to be more open and less anxious in treatment. It may also enable the client, in this supportive atmosphere, to admit and explore the abuse problem.

Catharsis, or the release of strong feelings, can be therapeutic by virtue of releasing previously repressed feelings. The knowledge that others in the group now are aware of these intense feelings and the situations that brought them about can be a step toward self-acceptance (George, 1990). However, catharsis alone has limited merit. Insight into the individuals' participation and responsibility in these situations as well as their ability to make personal choices and changes are imperative in the recovery process.

The factors isolated by George and Dustin (1988) incorporate many of the same characteristics as Yalom's factors. Installation of hope, safety and support, cohesiveness, and universality are related to group acceptance. Hope is instilled by the fact that others share the same concerns as the client, accept the client as an individual, and continue to be supportive. Safety also comes from acceptance. As group members continue to interact in a mutually supportive manner, trust builds. As trust grows, sharing of issues, problems, and concerns increases. Clients learn that they are not unique in their problems and feel a sense of relief. Interpersonal learning is the process of input or feedback and output, or developing more effective models of interaction with others (Bloch, 1986). As the group continues, members become more aware of the effect of their behavior on others, both positive and negative. This learning can then be used in the world outside the group to facilitate change in interpersonal relationships. The circle is completed as this knowledge brings more hope.

Group therapy provides a fertile ground for vicarious learning. It is an optimum experience for molding appropriate behavior. As group members try new behaviors in the process of recovery, modeling and feedback by the group can reinforce the desirability of these behaviors. Individuals learn through observation of others what works and does not work for them (George, 1990; Gladding, 1999).

Group Dynamics

Group therapy with substance abusers has many of the same components as does group therapy with any individuals. As the process unfolds, many of the tasks and accomplishments are consistent. Groups "supply a mixture of therapeutic forces not available in any other single modality of treatment" (Washton, 1992, p. 508). Also, groups share an awareness of the appreciation of the healing power of the connection with others that begins with the discovery that you are not alone in your problems. Features of a group that are imperative to success in any setting include structure or ground rules, goal setting, a sense of trust/safety, cohesiveness, confrontation, immediacy, and role playing (Gladding, 1999).

Structure or Ground Rules

Establishing the structure, purpose, and rules in group therapy is an important task in the first phase of the group setting, particularly when working with substance abusers. Two areas in which substance-abusing clients frequently need change are their sense of personal responsibility and clear boundary setting. Establishing rules of attendance, conduct, and participation early in the process allows the client to begin the change process immediately.

Allowing the group members to participate in this decision-making process is an empowering exercise. Many of these groups are time limited because of treatment mandates and are closed, so that the same members will participate throughout the entire group therapy process. When the group members negotiate, compromise, and set limits about the group, they develop a higher investment in the process. Also, a group-set rule carries more intrinsic weight than does a leader-set or therapist-set rule.

Goal Setting

Goal setting for the group can also be an experiential learning process. Many of these individuals have no experience in setting goals for the day or for their lives. In the beginning sessions, group members should be asked to discuss their expectations for the group as well as their individual recovery goals. During this period of discussion, common themes and goals will emerge (Lewis et al., 1994) that will foster feelings of commonality and trust among the group members.

Self-disclosure by the group leader can be used as a therapeutic tool during the goal-setting stage. Self-disclosure is when the group leader "expresses his or her feelings, values, opinions and beliefs to the group" (George, 1990, p. 155). It is used to express feelings about what is happening in the here-and-now experience of the group, including reactions to the interactions within the group. Self-disclosure also serves as a way to "personalize the leader within the group" (George, 1990, p. 155), allowing group members to see the leader as genuine and human and thus facilitating trust between the leader and the group members.

Trust, Safety, and Cohesiveness

Again, the process of mutual goal setting increases trust and cohesion within the group. Trust is difficult for a substance-abusing client, as is cohesiveness. As members develop a sense of each other as well as the commonality of their problems and concerns, a feeling of belonging occurs. This sense of belonging, or cohesiveness, may be the first time the client has felt accepted and protected.

Obviously, these behaviors lead to a more beneficial group experience for the members. As the group becomes more cohesive, intimacy develops. Members become aware of the ways they have created barriers to intimacy and trust. Within the group experience, they learn new relational skills that can be useful in the outside world.

Confrontation

As the group process moves into the working stage, the activities within the group also change. Confrontation of conflictual behaviors or talk and behavior is important. Substance abusers are often unaware of the inconsistencies in their lives. Presenting an individual with this awareness can be an effective therapeutic tool. Inconsistency may result from a person saying one thing and doing another, saying one thing and nonverbally contradicting the verbal statement (e.g., smiling when saying "I am angry"), or making contradictory statements on two different occasions.

The primary purpose of confrontation is to provide insight and allow the individual to grow. Confrontation should never be used in a hurtful or negative manner but rather in a caring, supportive, and thoughtful way. Leaders should be the model of appropriate confrontation for the group members. Group leaders should always be aware of managing the anxiety that confrontation stimulates within the group (Golden, Khantzian, & McAuliffe, 1994). An essential component of confrontation is assertiveness. In appropriate use of confrontation, the group leader will be modeling assertive behavior and caring, two important aspects of recovery.

Immediacy

Immediacy, or the awareness of one's emotional experiences in the present, is an essential component of recovery. Substance abusers often have difficulty feeling and identifying their emotions. When they do feel, a learned coping mechanism is to cover the feeling by using a chemical. In a cohesive group setting, members learn to recognize a feeling, name it, and appropriately manage the feeling. They are supported and encouraged in the group setting as they struggle with this new skill.

Role Playing

Many of the behaviors mentioned thus far can be developed and strengthened in the group experience through role playing. Bandura (1989) emphasizes the importance of role play in his steps for changing high-risk behaviors. He believes that practicing new behaviors is fundamental for change. He adds that practicing these new behaviors within a safe environment will reinforce the ability to attempt them in a less-than-safe environment.

Group members can role-play a variety of situations. They can practice new behaviors for high-risk relapse situations. Members can act out the roles they currently play in different situations and the roles that they would like to play in these same situations. Learning new assertiveness and intimacy skills as a means of relating to others is useful for group members. The group leader may use role playing to illustrate alternative behavioral responses to the same situation and the consequences of each of these responses.

As group members role-play new behaviors within the group, they experience success, which further empowers them to experiment with the behaviors in other settings. Repeated role playing also lends a level of comfort to the new behavior that encourages repetition outside the group.

Psychoeducational Groups

The preceding sections have described modified psychotherapeutic groups used in many treatment settings, but psychoeducational groups are also commonly used in this field. These groups are used with the general public, individuals who engage in high-risk behaviors such as driving under the influence of alcohol or other drugs (DUI classes), and individuals in treatment settings (Schilit & Gomberg, 1991). The primary purpose of these groups is to provide information. They are usually time-limited and closed-ended groups. A lecture/discussion format is common. Members may be either voluntary or court mandated. In many situations (e.g., DUI classes), follow-up treatment is recommended. These groups do not have a high level of effective outcome, but sometimes they are the only treatment modality available or mandated.

Summary

Group therapy is a powerful adjunct to individual and family therapy in treatment planning. The value of group members as confrontational and supportive factors is significant. Many times, clients will "hear" information from their peers with less defensiveness than from the therapist, and the value of common experience as a supportive mechanism is beneficial to clients as they begin to reconstruct their lives.

OTHER TYPES OF TREATMENT

Other modalities of individual and group therapy should be at least briefly mentioned. One such technique is videotaping/self-confrontation. This involves videotaping people while they are using chemicals and then showing them the videotape at a later time. The goal is to allow individuals to determine their own need for treatment (Holder et al., 1991).

Acupuncture has recently been studied in the treatment of cocaine addiction but with no significant results (Avants, Margolin, Chang, & Birch, 1995). The harm reduction (HR) model of treatment focuses on limiting the damage done by the use of chemicals until the individual is able to be completely chemical-free. Nicotine patches and gum exemplify this approach (Marlatt, 1994).

The needle exchange program (NEP) is active in many U.S. cities and abroad. These programs allow addicts to exchange dirty needles for clean ones in an effort to slow the spread of the HIV virus in this population. Although controversial, this model offers an alternative to zero tolerance (Doweiko, 1999). In Boston, Berkeley, Boulder, New Haven, San Francisco, Portland, Santa Cruz, and Seattle, these programs operate with varying degrees of success. Programs to promote the sale, distribution, or exchange of syringes in pharmacies have been a central element of the response to the HIV epidemic in Canada, Great Britain, Australia, New Zealand, Switzerland, Spain, France, and Germany. The only pharmacy-based NEP in the United States is in Tacoma, Washington, and operates on a one-for-one exchange basis out of a health department agency. Finally, Germany, Italy, Denmark, and the Netherlands have taken the lead in developing vending machines that either sell or exchange syringes (School of Public Health, 1999).

COUNSELOR CHARACTERISTICS

No matter what treatment method is chosen, research consistently shows that the characteristics of the counselor provide the most powerful condition of therapy for the client (Bell, Montoya, & Atkinson, 1997). Clinical skills are essential but so are personal characteristics that may be genetically and environmentally developed (Perkinson, 1997). In 1961, Rogers suggested a number of characteristics that stand today as the model of necessary counselor characteristics:

- Warmth
- Dependability
- Consistency
- The ability to care for and respect the client
- The ability to be separate from the client, which is to say the ability not to try and "live through" a client
- The ability not to be perceived as a threat by the client
- The ability to free one's self from the urge to judge or evaluate the client
- The ability to see the client as a person capable of growth (as cited in Doweiko, 1999, p. 175)

Perkinson (1997) elaborates on desirable counselor qualities as follows:

- Being loving—These counselors love their work and love themselves. They care about clients without becoming overinvolved or overemotional.
- Being sensitive—These counselors have a "sixth sense" that allows them to understand client feelings and motivations.
- Being an active listener
- Having good boundaries
- Being patient (pp. 211–215)

In a 1989 study, Adelman and Weiss concluded that counselors with the highest level of interpersonal skills were the best equipped to help their clients. Other essential characteristics are the ability to instill trust, to be dependable, and to be open (Doweiko, 1999). Doweiko also emphasizes the necessity of the counselor being chemical-free and having no "pressing personal issues" (p. 174).

We would be remiss not to also discuss the basic skills that are necessary specifically for chemical dependency counselors. This list was developed by the Curriculum Review Committee of the addiction Technology Transfer Centers, funded by the National Center for Substance Abuse Treatment. These include:

> clinical evaluation skills such as screening and assessment, treatment planning, referral skills, case management including implementing the treatment plan, consulting, and continuing assessment and treatment planning, individual counseling skills, documentation, supervision, and client and community education. (Lawson & Lawson, 1998, p. 22)

To this extensive list, we would add group therapy skills and family counseling skills. As you can see, this is an impressive list of clinical skills necessary for effective treatment of substance abuse.

CONCLUSION

In summary, to be most effective treatment should be addressed at both the individual and group level. Individual therapy addresses the person's intrapsychic conflict and issues, whereas group therapy allows a platform for change and support on the interactional level. An overriding factor in all types of therapy is the characteristics of the counselor. The last component to effective recovery treatment planning is family therapy, which will be discussed in the following chapter.

REFERENCES

Adelman, S. A., & Weiss, R. D. (1989). What is therapeutic about inpatient alcoholism treatment? *Hospital and Community Psychiatry, 40(5),* 515–519.

Alonso, A. (1989, September). *Character change in group therapy.* Paper presented at Psychiatric Grand Rounds, Cambridge Hospital, Cambridge, MA.

Anderson, G. L. (1993). *When chemicals come to school.* Greenfield, WI: Community Recovery Press.

Annis, H. M., & Chan, D. (1983). The differential treatment model: Empirical evidence from a personality topology of adult offenders. *Criminal Justice and Behavior, 10,* 159–173.

Avants, S. K., Margolin, P., Chang, T. R., & Birch, S. (1995). Acupuncture for the treatment of cocaine addiction: Investigation of a needle puncture control. *Journal of Substance Abuse, 12,* 195–205.

Baker, T., & Cannon, D. S. (1979). Taste aversion therapy with alcoholics: Techniques and evidence of a conditioned response. *Behavior Research and Therapy, 17,* 229–242.

Bandura, A. (1989). Perceived self-efficacy in the exercise of control over AIDS infection. In V. M. Mays (Ed.), *Primary prevention of AIDS: Psychological approaches* (pp. 128–141). Newbury Park, CA: Sage.

Bell, D. C., Montoya, I. D., & Atkinson, J. S. (1997). Therapeutic connection and client progress in drug abuse treatment. *Journal of Clinical Psychology, 53,* 215–224.

Berg, I. K., & Gallagher, D. (1991). Solution focused brief treatment with adolescent substance abusers. In T. Todd & M. Selekman (Eds.), *Family therapy approaches with adolescent substance abusers.* Boston: Allyn & Bacon.

Berg, I. K. & Miller, S. D. (1992). *Working with the problem drinker: A solution-focused approach.* New York: Norton.

Blake, G. B. (1965). The application of behavior therapy to the treatment of alcoholism. *Behavior Research and Therapy, 3,* 75–85.

Bloch, S. (1986). Therapeutic factors in group psychotherapy. In A. J. Frances & R. E. Hales (Eds.), *Annual review* (Vol. 5, pp. 678–698). Washington, DC: American Psychiatric Press.

Bowers, T. G., & al-Redha, R. (1990). A comparison of outcome with group/marital and standard/individual therapies with alcoholics. *Journal of the Study of Alcoholism, 51,* 301–309.

Brandsma, J. M., Maultsby, M. C., & Welsh, R. J. (1980). *The outcome treatment of alcoholism: A review and comparative study.* Baltimore: University Park Press.

Buelow, G. D., & Buelow, S. A. (1998). *Psychotherapy in chemical dependency treatment.* Pacific Grove, CA: Brooks/Cole.

Cannon, D. S., Baker, T., Gino, A., & Nathan, P. E. (1986). Emetic and electric shock alcohol aversion therapy: Assessment of conditioning. *Journal of Consulting and Clinical Psychology, 49,* 2–33.

Chaney, E. F., O'Leary, M., & Marlatt, G. A. (1978). Skill training with alcoholics. *Journal of Consulting and Clinical Psychiatry, 46,* 1092–1104.

Claunch, L. (1991). Intervention can be used as a tool or as a weapon against clients. *The Addiction Letter, 10(4),* 1–2.

Collins, J. J., & Alison, M. (1983). Legal coercion and retention in drug abuse treatment. *Hospital & Community Psychiatry, 34,* 1145–1150.

Cornish, J. W., McNicholas, L. F., & O'Brien, C. P. (1995). Treatment of substance-related disorders. In A. F. Schatzberg & C. B. Nemeroff (Eds.), *Textbook of psychopharmacology.* Washington, DC: American Psychiatric Press.

Daley, D. C., & Raskin, M. (1991). *Treating the chemically dependent and their families.* Newbury Park, CA: Sage.

DeMaria, P. A., & Weinstein, S. P. (1995). Methadone maintenance treatment. *Postgraduate Medicine, 97(3),* 83–92.

Doweiko, H. F. (1999). *Concepts of chemical dependency* (4th ed.). Pacific Grove, CA: Brooks/Cole.

Elkins, R. L. (1975). Aversion therapy for alcoholism: Chemical, electric, or verbal imagery. *International Journal of the Addictions, 10,* 157–209.

Elkins, R. L. (1980). Covert sensitization treatment for alcoholism: Contribution of successful conditioning to subsequent abstinence maintenance. *Addictive Behavior, 5,* 67–89.

Ellis, A., & Velten, E. (1992). *Rational steps to quitting alcohol: When AA doesn't work for you.* Fort Lee, NJ: Barricade.

Emick, C. D., & Aarons, G. A. (1990). Cognitive-behavioral treatment of problem drinking. In H. B. Milkman & L. I. Sederer (Eds.), *Treatment choices for alcoholism and substance abuse* (pp. 265–286). New York: Lexington.

Feeney, D. J., & Dranger, P. (1976). Alcoholics view group therapy: Process and goals. *Journal of Studies on Alcohol, 38(5),* 611–618.

Ferrell, W. L., & Galassi, J. P. (1981). Assertion training and human relations training in the treatment of chronic alcoholics. *International Journal of the Addictions, 16(3),* 959–968.

Galanter, M., Castaneda, R., & Franco, H. (1991). Group therapy and self-help groups. In R. J. Franco & S. I. Miller (Eds.), *Clinical textbook of addictive disorders.* New York: Guilford.

George, R. L. (1990). *Counseling the chemically dependent: Theory and practice.* Upper Saddle River, NJ: Prentice Hall.

George, R. L., & Dustin, D. (1988). *Group counseling: Theory and practice.* Upper Saddle River, NJ: Prentice Hall.

Gladding, S. T. (1999). *Group work: A counseling specialty* (3rd ed.). Upper Saddle River, NJ: Merrill/Prentice Hall.

Golden, S. J., Khantzian, E. J., & McAuliffe, W. E., (1994). Group therapy. In M. Galanter & H. D. Kleber (Eds.), *The American Psychiatric Press textbook of substance abuse treatment* (pp. 303-314). Washington, DC: American Psychiatric Press.

Goldstein, A. P., Reagles, K. W., & Amann, L. L. (1990). *Refusal skills: Preventing drug use in adolescents.* Champaign, IL: Research Press.

Hellerstein, D. J., & Meehan, B. (1987). Outpatient group therapy with schizophrenic substance abusers. *American Journal of Psychiatry, 144,* 1337–1339.

Hester, R., & Miller, W. (1989). *Handbook of alcoholism treatment approaches: Effective alternatives.* New York: Pergamon.

Holder, H., Longabaugh, R., Miller, W. R., & Rubonis, A. V. (1991). The cost effectiveness of treatment for alcoholism: A first approximation. *Journal of Studies on Alcohol, 52,* 517–540.

Howard, D. L., & McCaughrin, W. C. (1996). The treatment effectiveness of outpatient substance misuse treatment organizations between court-mandated and voluntary clients. *Substance Use and Misuse, 31,* 895–925.

Jacobsen, E. (1968). *Progressive relaxation.* Chicago: University of Chicago Press.

Johnson Institute. (1987). *The family enablers.* Minneapolis, MN: Author.

Lawental, E., McLellan, A. T., Grissom, G. R., Brill, R., & O'Brien, C. (1996). Coerced treatment for substance abuse problems detected through workplace urine surveillance: Is it effective? *Journal of Substance Abuse, 8,* 115–118.

Lawson, A., & Lawson, G. (1998). *Alcoholism and the family: A guide to treatment and prevention.* Gaithersburg, MD: Aspen.

Lesser, E. (1976). Behavior therapy with a narcotics user: A case report: Ten-year follow-up. *Behavior Research and Therapy, 14(5),* 381.

Levy, S. J., & Rutter, E. (1992). *Children of drug abusers.* New York: Lexington.

Lewis, J. A., Dana, R. Q., & Blevins, G. A. (1994). *Substance abuse counseling: An individualized approach.* Pacific Grove, CA: Brooks/Cole.

Lieberman, R. (1969). Aversive conditioning of drug addicts: A pilot study. *Behavior Research and Therapy, 6,* 229–231.

Marlatt, G. A. (1994). Harm reduction: A public health approach to addictive behavior. *Division of Addictions Newsletter, 2*(1), 1, 3.

Matano, R. A., & Yalom, I. D. (1991). Approaches to chemical dependency: Chemical dependency and interactive group therapy—A synthesis. *International Journal of Group Psychotherapy, 41,* 269–293.

Matuschka, P. R. (1985). The psychopharmacology of addiction. In T. E. Bratter & G. G. Forrest (Eds.), *Alcoholism and substance abuse: Strategies for clinical intervention* (pp. 49–75). New York: Free Press.

McLellan, A. T., Arndt, I. O., Metzger, D. S., Woody, G. E., & O'Brien, C. P. (1993). The effects of psychosocial services in substance abuse treatment. *Journal of the American Medical Association, 269,* 1953–1959.

Meyer, R. (1988). Intervention: Opportunity for healing. *Alcoholism & Addiction, 9(1),* 7.

Miller, W. R. (1985). Motivation for treatment: A review of special emphasis on alcoholism. *Psychological Bulletin, 98,* 84–107.

Miller, W. R. (1990). Alcohol treatment alternatives: What works? In H. B. Milkman & L. I.

Sederer (Eds.), *Treatment choices for alcoholism and substance abuse* (pp. 253–264). New York: Lexington.

Miller, W. R., & Hester, R. K. (1985). The effectiveness of treatment techniques: What works and what doesn't. In W. R. Miller (Ed.), *Alcoholism: Theory, research and treatment* (pp. 526–534). Lexington, MA: Ginn.

Miller, W. R., & Hester, R. K. (1986a). The effectiveness of alcoholism treatment: What research reveals. In W. R. Miller & N. Heather (Eds.), *The addictive behaviors: Processes of change* (pp. 121–174). New York: Plenum.

Miller, W. R., & Hester, R. K. (1986b). Inpatient alcoholism treatment: Who benefits? *American Psychologist, 41,* 794–805.

Monti, P. M., Abrams, D. B., Kadden, R. M., & Cooney, N. L. (1989). *Treating alcohol dependence: A coping skills training guide*. New York: Guilford.

Moylan, D. W. (1990). Court intervention. *Adolescent Counselor, 2(5),* 23–27.

O'Brien, C. P. (1996). Recent developments in the pharmacotherapy of addiction. *Journal of Consulting and Clinical Psychology, 64,* 677–686.

Ouimette, P. C., Finney, J. W., & Moos, R. H. (1997). Twelve-step and cognitive behavioral treatment for substance abuse: A comparison of treatment effectiveness. *Journal of Consulting and Clinical Psychology, 65,* 230–240.

Palakow, R. L. (1975). Covert sensitization treatment of a probationed barbiturate addict. *Journal of Behavior Therapy and Experimental Psychiatry, 6,* 53–54.

Perkinson, R. R. (1997). *Chemical dependency counseling: A practical guide*. Thousand Oaks, CA: Sage.

Plomin, R. (1990). The role of inheritance in behavior. *Science, 248,* 183–188.

Poldrugo, F., & Forti, B. (1988). Personality disorders and alcoholism treatment outcome. *Drug and Alcohol Dependency, 21,* 171–176.

Powell, B. J., Penick, E. C., Read, M. R., & Ludwig, A. M. (1985). Comparison of three outpatient treatment interventions: A twelve-month follow-up of men alcoholics. *Journal of Studies on Alcohol, 46,* 309–312.

Rimmele, C. T., Howard, M. O., & Hilfrink, M. L. (1995). Aversion therapies. In R. K. Hester & W. R. Miller (Eds.), *Handbook of alcoholism treatment approaches: Effective alternatives* (pp. 134–147). New York: Pergamon.

Rimmele, C., Miller, W. R., & Dougher, M. (1990). Aversion therapies. In R. K. Hester & W. R. Miller (Eds.), *Handbook of alcoholism treatment approaches: Effective alternatives* (pp. 215–235). New York: Pergamon.

Rossi, E. L. (1973). Psychological shocks and creative moments in psychotherapy. *American Journal of Clinical Hypnosis, 16(1),* 9–22.

Rothenberg, L. (1988). The ethics of intervention. *Alcoholism & Addiction, 9(1),* 22–24.

Schilit, R., & Gomberg E. S. L. (1991). *Drugs and behavior: A sourcebook for the helping professions*. Newbury Park, CA: Sage.

School of Public Health, University of California, Berkeley, and Institute for Health Policy Studies, University of California, San Francisco. (1999). *The public health impact of needle exchange programs in the United States and abroad: Summary conclusions and recommendations* [On-line]. Available: http://www.caps.ucsf.edu.publications/needlereport.html#J

Schuckit, M. A. (1996). Alcohol, anxiety, and depression. *Alcohol Health & Research World, 20,* 81–86.

Schuster, R. (1978–1979). Evaluation of a reality therapy stratification system in a residential drug rehabilitation center. *Drug Forum, (7)1,* 59–67.

Stein, A., & Friedman, E. (1971). Group therapy with alcoholics. In H. I. Kaplan & B. J. Sadock (Eds.), *Comprehensive group psychotherapy*. Baltimore: Williams & Wilkins.

Stimmel, B., Cohen, M., Sturiano, V., Hanbury, D., Forts, D., & Jackson, G. (1983). Is treatment of alcoholism effective in persons on methadone maintenance? *American Journal of Psychiatry, 140,* 862–866.

Twerski, A. J. (1983). Early interventions in alcoholism: Confrontational techniques. *Hospital & Community Psychiatry, 34,* 1027–1030.

Vannicelli, M. (1992). *Removing the roadblocks: Group psychotherapy with substance abusers and family members*. New York: Guilford.

Washton, A. M. (1992). Structured outpatient group therapy with alcohol and substance abusers. In J. H. Lowenson, P. Ruiz, B. Millman, & J. G. Langrod (Eds.), *Substance abuse: A comprehensive textbook* (pp. 508–519). Baltimore: Williams & Wilkins.

Williams, E. (1989). Strategies for intervention. *Nursing Clinics of North America, 24(1),* 95–107.

Wisocki, P. A. (1973). The successful treatment of a heroin addict by covert conditioning techniques. *Journal of Behavior Therapy and Experimental Psychiatry, 4,* 55–61.

Wolpe, J. (1965). Conditioned inhibition of craving in drug addiction: A pilot experiment. *Behavior Research and Therapy, 2,* 285–287.

Yalom, I. D. (1975). *The theory and practice of group psychotherapy* (2nd ed.). New York: Basic Books.

Yalom, I. D. (1985). *The theory and practice of group psychotherapy* (3rd ed.). New York: Basic Books.

Yalom, I. D. (1995). *Treating alcoholism.* San Francisco: Jossey-Bass.

Family Therapy in Substance Abuse Treatment

PATRICIA STEVENS, PH.D.

Systems theory and the addiction field have often been at odds with one another. Much of this disagreement has focused on whether addiction is an individual or a family problem. Is the addiction secondary to the dysfunction in the family (i.e., a result of it) or the primary cause of the dysfunction? Although how the clinician views the problem determines the door through which that person enters treatment, both conceptualizations are probably true. The power of the family system to impact behavior of its members cannot be denied. On the cause/result debate, this author takes the position, like Bateson (1971), that it is not an either/or proposition but a "both/and" problem. Basing this position on the already stated philosophy that the etiology of abuse/dependency is biopsychosociofamilial, it makes sense to incorporate family therapy into the treatment model. Furthermore, it is less important for the family therapist to determine the etiology of the problem than it is for the therapist to determine how the problem is maintained (Lawson & Lawson, 1998).

Over the years, research in the use of family therapy in the substance abuse field has been delineated into two separate tracks: working with the "alcoholic family" and working with the "substance abuse family." Research in the area of alcoholism has tended to focus on families of white middle-class males in their mid-40s. Research on families of substance abusers (individuals whose primary drug is not alcohol) has tended to focus on adolescents or young adults. Unknowingly, researchers might have been studying the same family from two different perspectives (Schilit & Gomberg, 1991). Many young adults who are polydrug users have alcoholic parents, further substantiating the need to address multigenerational patterns of transmission with families along with individual issues in the treatment plan.

During the past two decades, it has become increasing apparent that family structure and dynamics play an important role in the continuation of substance use within a family (Bennett, Wolin, & Reiss, 1987; Jacob & Seilhammer, 1987; Moos, Fenn, & Billings, 1989; Steinglass, 1994; Wolin, Bennett, & Noonan, 1980) and, conversely, that substance use increases other dysfunctional patterns of behavior in families such as domestic violence (Gondolf & Foster, 1991), child abuse, and incest (Sheinberg, 1991) as well as increased criminal behavior (Buelow, 1994). It has also been shown that biomedical models account for "less than half of the expressed variance in incidence and course of the condition" (Plomin, cited in Steinglass, 1994, p. 246).

Dramatic statistics have been gathered about substance-abusing families. Kaufman and Kaufman's (1992) study determined that approximately 90% of the mothers were pathologically enmeshed with their substance-abusing child. This was true across ethnic groups involved in the study. Additionally, this coalition between mother and child tended to create a father-child brutality, particularly with male children, and to negatively effect the spousal dyad. Men's relationships in these families tended to be the opposite of the females'—disengaged and distant. In addition, 70% of alcoholic males were still living with their mothers at age 23 and 50% at age 30. The U.S. Department of Health and Human Services (1995) study indicates that 50% of all addicted people had parents who were addicted, 50% of all adult children of alcoholics (ACOA) become alcoholics (as opposed to 10% of non-ACOAs), and abut 50% marry a chemically dependent partner (vs. 13% of non-ACOAs). This study also concluded that a third of all American families have an immediate family member with an alcohol- and drug-related problem, that drugs are implicated in 50% to 90% of cases of domestic violence, and that drugs play a significant part in the violent or sexually inappropriate behavior between siblings. These data support the fact that not only does the family influence the substance abuser but that the substance abuser influences the family.

Family therapy with addicted families strives to stop the present, active abuse and to mitigate the multigenerational transmission process noted in these statistics. No matter what your belief about the etiology of addiction—biological, sociological, psychological—it does run through generations in some families and does not appear in others. Stanton (as cited in Daw, 1995), in searching for the "first alcoholic" across family generations, found that the generation preceding the "first" had suffered an immense loss from which it was unable to recover. This view of the beginning of the abuse depathologizes the family patterns and allows the family to choose to keep, update, or replace these multigenerational patterns of coping (Daw, 1995; Lawson & Lawson, 1998).

This chapter will not detail the numerous and diverse theories available to the systems practitioner but will discuss the general concepts underlying all systemic theories. The theory that one might choose to work with clients varies with the individual's beliefs, values, philosophy, and personality. To choose a particular systemic theory, the reader is referred to the vast literature available on these theories, which include but are not limited to experiential/symbolic family therapy (Nichols & Schwartz, 1995; Satir, 1967), structural family therapy (Minuchen, 1974), strategic family therapy (Bateson, Jackson, Haley, & Weakland, 1956; Jackson, 1960), Adlerian family therapy (Lowe, 1982), and transgenerational/Bowenian family therapy (Bowen, 1974). Goldenberg and Goldenberg (1999) and Gladding (1998) present excellent overviews of these systemic theories.

DEFINING FAMILY

It is important to recognize that the definition of family varies from culture to culture. Much of the research in the family therapy field, as well as in the addiction field, is focused on the white Anglo-Saxon Protestant definition of family as an intact nuclear family in which lineage is important in tracing one's ancestry (McGoldrick, 1989). However, we know that ethnicity is no prerequisite for abuse or addiction—that this is a universal problem. It therefore behooves us to pay attention to the different cultural definitions, expectations, and structures of families as we begin to work in this field (see Chapter 9).

Another definition of family would be the nuclear family with whom the person is currently living. Individuals in relationships come together from their respective families of origin to create this nuclear family. However, it is impossible to explain the nuclear family without examining its interrelatedness with the family of origin. The present nuclear family becomes the family of origin for the next generation, shaping the multigenerational transmission process of behavioral patterns (Lawson & Lawson, 1998).

GENERAL SYSTEMS CONCEPTS

A *system,* as defined by *Webster's Collegiate Dictionary,* is "a regularly interacting or interdependent group of items forming a unified whole." To understand family functioning adequately, the individual behavior must be examined within the context of the family interactions. Virginia Satir (1967) first described this interaction using the example of a mobile. All pieces are connected yet independent to the extent that the mobile hangs in balance with pieces not touching. However, if moved, for example, by a breeze, the parts are shown to be interdependent because when one piece moves, it causes the other pieces to move as well. As the breeze diminishes and finally ceases, the pieces also stop moving and return to balance.

The foundation of all family therapy work comes from the literature on systems functioning (Bertalanffy, 1968; O'Connor & McDermott, 1997). Some general systemic concepts of functioning need to be discussed to understand this idea of interdependence that is systems or, for our purposes, families. The family therapy/system theory framework is based on several underlying concepts:

1. All systems seek *homeostasis.*
2. All systems incorporate *feedback loops* to function.
3. *Hierarchy* is an integral part of systemic functioning, including all the *roles, rules,* and *subsystems* necessary. *Boundaries* are necessary to facilitate the existence of roles, rules, and subsystems.
4. The system cannot be understood by reductionism but must be examined as an entity, synthesizing the component parts into a *whole.*
5. *Change* in one part of the system creates change in all parts of the system.
6. *Family values* encompass some of these concepts and are passed down from one generation to another, affecting the dynamics of the family system.

A closer look at each of these concepts is presented in the following sections.

Homeostasis

The term *family homeostasis* is used to define the "natural tendency of families to behave in such a manner as to maintain a sense of balance, structure, and stability in the face of change" (Jackson, cited in Fisher & Harrison, 1997, p. 193). Inherent in this definition is the assumption that change in one family member will create change in all other family members. Buelow and Buelow (1998) argue that the family, unlike our bodies, which have a set temperature or balance point at which they operate optimally, does not have an optimal or normal balance point. They believe that homeostasis is always changing in response to the family endeavoring to meet its members' needs. They also state that each person in the system may be affected to "greater or lesser degrees and with vastly different consequences" (p. 183).

There will be times when change requires the family to adjust. Families (systems) have a natural resistance to change, which serves as a mechanism to avoid complete chaos during the change process. During these times families will need to renegotiate their roles, rules, and boundaries to fashion a new, more functionally balanced structure to manage these changes. If families are too resistant to change, they become rigid and decline into entropy. Conversely, too much flexibility produces chaos.

Feedback Loops

The essence of systems is feedback loops. Feedback loops provide the communication that enables the system to continue functioning and to maintain homeostasis, to promote or resist change. They are the systems method of self-regulation and self-maintenance or, in simple terms, the communication between parts of the system or members of the family. Feedback serves two purposes: to move the system toward change and to bring the system back into balance.

Reinforcing feedback moves the system toward change. Sometimes called *positive feedback,* this interaction can be thought of as "heating up" the system. As feedback continues, it increases, sometimes exponentially, the system's move from the original balance. Just as a snowball gains size as it rolls downhill, so reinforcing feedback moves the system rapidly away from its first point of balance. Balancing feedback (sometimes called *negative feedback*), on the other hand, brings the system back to balance. This represents the "cooling down" of the system. Balancing feedback brings the system back to its goal. How dissonant the system is from its goal determines how much feedback is necessary to regain homeostasis. A good example of balancing feedback is being thirsty. Your body begins in fluid balance then loses that balance as you exercise or sit in the hot sun. As a result, you experience the sensation of thirst, drink water, and your body then regains fluid balance. How thirsty (or out of balance) you are determines the amount of water you drink, which in turn determines your return to fluid balance (O'Connor & McDermott, 1997).

Hierarchy, Roles, Rules, Subsystems, and Boundaries

These systemic concepts are so interrelated that is impossible to discuss one without discussing all of them. *Hierarchy* refers to the structure of the family, how the members are classified according to ability or rules and role definition within their cultural perspective. Roles may be determined by the individual's behaviors in performing rights and obligations associated with a certain position within the family and are usually related to complementary expected roles of others with whom the person is involved (Shertzer & Stone, 1980). It is through these roles, and their interaction, that families act out the covert and overt family rules.

Although roles vary across cultures, there appear to be some generic rules that define the roles of being male, female, mother, father, husband, wife, and child within a familial structure. As children grow, they will experience childhood, adolescence, and young adulthood. Additionally, throughout the individual's life cycle, a person takes on a variety of roles: child, student, worker, spouse, partner, parent, retiree, grandparent, and so on (Super, 1990). Marital and parental roles, in particular, are often derived from the family of origin. These old roles may or may not be suitable for the present family. This situation may create unbalance and conflict as the new family endeavors to shift and change roles. Therefore, as family members move in and out of these roles and as rules change, the family becomes unbalanced and attempts to reestablish homeostasis through the creation of a new structure.

Rules are the mutual assumptions of the family as to how members should behave toward each other and the outside world. Fisher and Harrison (1997) state that rules within families may govern:

> 1) what, when, and how family members can communicate their experiences about what they see, hear, feel, and think, 2) who has permission to speak to whom about what, 3) the extent and manner in which a family member can be different, 4) the manner in which sexuality can be expressed, 5) what it means to be a male or female, and 6) how family members acquire self worth and how much self worth a member can experience. (p. 196)

Culture may not change how the family is governed but may well change the consequences of breaking the family rules. For example, a Euro-American family might punish a child who "talks back," while an Asian family might use shame to correct the child who breaks the family rule.

Subsystems are the smaller systems within each system—systems within systems. Families are composed of multiple subsystems that assist the family in carrying out its day-to-day functions. Each subsystem contributes to the entire system's maintenance. Subsystems may be established by a variety of means: along generational lines (grandparents, parents, siblings), by mutual interest (who likes to read, play ball, shop), by gender (female-female or male-male), or by task (who cleans the house, who washes the car). Within each subsystem, a family member plays a particular role that has rules and expectations accompanying it. Family members, of course, can be in more than one subsystem, requiring the person to use the appropriate role and rules for that subsystem.

The clarity of the subsystem boundaries is more important than the constitution of the subsystem. For example, the marital (or partner) dyad is a primary subsystem. It is a closed system in the sense that there are certain duties and primary functions that are performed only by this marital subsystem (e.g., earning money, managing the home). With the birth of a child, this partnership changes and expands to become a parental subsystem with added duties and functions. In effect, we now have two subsystems, the marital subsystem with responsibilities toward the relationship itself and the parental subsystem with parenting duties of caretaking, discipline, scheduling of activities, and so forth.

Boundaries, as already implied, define the subsystems. They are like fences: they keep things out and they keep things in. Boundaries exist between family members, between subsystems, and between the family and society. The best boundary can be compared to a picket fence. It is strong enough to keep the dogs out of the garden but open enough to see the flowers across the street and to visit with friends who walk by your yard. In family systems, boundaries are on a continuum from clear and overly rigid, to clear but flexible, to unclear and diffuse. In families with overly rigid boundaries, communication is constricted and family members are disengaged or isolated. There is a lack of expressed love, a low sense of belonging, and a lack of family loyalty. Clear boundaries are the most functional. They allow separateness but closeness, freedom and flexibility, and are based on mutual respect.

Again, the clinician must be aware of cultural norms when evaluating families' boundaries. In Asian families, for example, the cultural expectation would be that the father is more disengaged (i.e., has more rigid boundaries). The opposite of disengagement, enmeshment, occurs when the boundaries are unclear and diffuse. Enmeshed families leave little room for difference; unity is stressed, and emotions are shared (if the mother cries, so does the child). Again, culture colors the perspective of terms such as *disengagement* and *enmeshment*. In the Latino/Hispanic culture, for example, an "enmeshed" mother is not only expected but highly valued (Erekson & Perkins, 1989; Lawson & Lawson, 1998; Minuchen, 1992).

Olson and Killorin (1987) completed a study that compared chemically dependent families and nonchemically dependent families on the measure of cohesion, which is a function of boundaries. In their model, cohesion is the continuum of closeness and distance that a family engages in. They found that 44% of the chemically dependent adolescents rated their families as disengaged as compared to 8% of the nonchemically dependent adolescents. Fifty-two percent of these adolescents rated their families as chaotic as compared to 20% of the nonchemically dependent adolescents. The paradox of this information is that to the outside world, these families may appear enmeshed, therefore tempting the therapist to ask the family to disengage. The result would be adolescents who feel even more disenfranchised from their family system (Lawson & Lawson, 1998).

Wholeness

Another systems concept is that of wholeness. System theorists believe that the system cannot be understood by dissecting it into its individual parts but only by observing the whole system. This concept of wholeness carries with it the idea of "emergent properties" (O'Connor & McDermott, 1997). These are the properties of the system that only exist when the system is whole and functioning; conversely, if you take the system apart, the emergent properties no longer exist. For example, H_2O is the chemical equation for water. When you dissect water into its component parts, you have hydrogen and oxygen, but when you combine these elements, you have water. Nothing in the individual elements or even in the idea of combining the elements prepares you for the wetness of water (the emergent property). Also, the picture on a television is the emergent property of that system. Take a TV apart and you will not find the picture anywhere in the parts.

In families, emergent properties are the behaviors that when operating as a system the family members exhibit but when separated into individuals do not exist. All of us have had the experience of talking with a friend about someone with whom they are involved. The dynamics of the relationship are explained through the eyes of the individual (or the part of the system). Then, when we see these two people together, the experience is very different than what has been explained. This different experience of the functioning couples system is the emergent property of that system.

Change

We have already discussed the concept of how change in one part of the system, or individual, changes the other parts of the system. An important aside to this concept, especially for counseling, is always to expect side effects. Remember: with a family system, you can never change just one interaction or behavior because of this systemic effect.

Family Values

One last concept that is important in working with family systems is that of family values. *Family values* are the composite of the rules, roles, boundaries, and subsystems in both the nuclear family and the family of origin. Values may be shared or more strongly valued by one partner than another. Examples of values are receiving an education, engaging in athletics, having musical ability, becoming wealthy, being a good wife and mother, and being the good male provider. Conflict occurs in families when mutually exclusive values are embraced or in families with a female child who value males. Cultural values are also superimposed on the family values, impacting the family values as well as individual members and their accomplishments and behaviors.

Not only is it important for therapists to understand the family value system, it is imperative for therapists also to be aware of their own values, beliefs, and prejudices. Counselors do not leave their family values at the door of the therapy room. These values are apparent in each intervention, question, or comment in therapy. The therapist's values can impact the client family system in both positive and negative ways. Therefore, it is necessary for the ethical therapist to recognize that there is no value-free therapy.

THE ADDICTIVE FAMILY SYSTEM

Many of these families share common characteristics. Secrecy, for example, is extremely important. Denial of the problem is also paramount. Family members will go to extreme measures to keep the secret and to avoid dealing with the issue of alcohol/drug use. The family will readjust itself and redistribute responsibilities to accommodate the user. In fact, Ackerman (1983) states that the "key to surviving in an alcoholic home is adaptation" (p. 16).

Hypervigilance is also a characteristic of individuals in these families. Never knowing when or where the abuser will act out creates a constant state of fear for other family members. Lack of trust is a byproduct of this unstable and uncertain atmosphere. Another feature of addictive families is the inability to express feelings. Since the user/abuser is the feeling carrier and the only one allowed to express feelings in the family, other family members lose the ability to identify and express appropriate feelings.

The Marital Dyad and Substance Abuse

Little research has delved into the dynamics of the marital dyad of substance-abusing couples. However, research has examined the alcoholic marital dyad, in which one partner is abusing alcohol and the other is not. From this research, we may be able to extrapolate interactions within substance-abusing couples.

One interesting study shows that individuals tend to moderate their drinking patterns to a more acceptable level at marriage. Too many external factors were present at this point in the person's life (e.g., independence, employment) to determine whether the act of marriage itself instituted the change or whether a combination of life events created the shift in drinking behavior (Leonard & Roberts, 1996). It is thought that marriage provides the individual with a drinking partner and that the two will adjust their drinking behavior until it matches. In the cases where this match does not happen, the alcohol will have a negative impact on the couple. Over time, a role reversal may happen, with the alcohol-dependent person giving up power to the nondependent person (Ackerman, 1983).

Issues of control are central to the alcohol-abusing marriage. Both partners are endeavoring to maintain control and to decrease the chaos in the relationship, but for their own purpose. The alcohol-abusing partner does not want the other person to leave, and the non-alcohol-abusing person is also often afraid of abandonment. Conditional love becomes a daily part of their lives. Behaviors are centered around "If you love me, you will (or will not). . . . "

Communication in these marriages is often angry, hostile, and critical. They appear to have an extensive use of projection, display poor psychological boundaries, and use blame frequently. These marriages also have a "borderline personality" involving either intense love or hate, being totally in control or totally out of control, or being enmeshed or disengaged. These relationships tend to be highly symbiotic or, in the current jargon, codependent. These partners are so interrelated that they are inseparable emotionally, psychologically, and sometimes physically (Beavers, 1985; Jacob, Ritchey, Cvitkovic, & Blane, 1981).

The codependent is usually the person closest to the alcohol abuser and the first person to react dysfunctionally. As the codependent becomes more vulnerable and reactive to the dependent (user), the user increases the drinking. Therefore, the codependent must become more reactive and protective, which does not allow the drinker to experience the consequences of the behavior. The drinker's rationalizations support the misunderstanding of the problem. However, this cycle engages both partners in self-deception, which allows the problem to remain hidden and progress (Curtis, 1999).

Gorski (1992) defines *codependency* as a "cluster of symptoms or maladaptive behavior changes associated with living in a committed relationship with either a chemically dependent person or a chronically dysfunctional person either as children or adults" (p. 15). Common elements are that the codependent person is overinvolved, obsesses over attempting to control the other's behavior, gains self-worth from the approval of others (many times primarily the chemically dependent person), and makes great sacrifices for others.

The multigenerational transmission pattern of behavior is readily seen in codependency. No matter how abusive or unsatisfactory children see their parents' relationship to be, they will likely repeat the pattern in their own relationships (Curtis, 1999).

Codependency is a controversial topic in this field. Many believe that it does not exist and/or that the definition itself tends to blame the victim (Collins, 1993; Kasl, 1992). Both Doweiko (1999) and Zelvin (1993) view codependency as a continuum from totally dependent to totally disregarding the feedback of others. Zelvin states that there are three aspects to the codependent individual: focusing too much on the opinions of others, not knowing what he or she wants or likes, and being drawn into relationships with needy individuals.

The nondrinking partner will shield the drinking partner as much as possible in an effort to maintain the couple homeostasis. This pattern of preserving balance soon becomes a common coping mechanism within the marriage. This form of protection is sometimes called *enabling*. Enabling is anything done to protect the chemically dependent person from the consequences of his or her behavior (Curtis, 1999). It comes from attempts to adapt to the chemical use rather than confront it. Enabling may come from sources outside the marriage, as it does not require a committed relationship. Codependence and enabling can be mutually exclusive. In other words, someone might enable the drinker and not be codependent—for example, a coworker or an employer.

These marriages also use alcohol to triangulate their relationship. Bowen (1976) says that the smallest stable relationship is a triangle. In alcoholic marriages, when the tension reaches an unbearable level, instead of bringing in a child or another family member, these couples triangulate in the alcohol. Alcohol then becomes the third "person" in the relationship and one that is as loved (or more so) as the other partner for the alcohol abuser.

Boundaries in these couples are not well defined, vacillating from overly rigid to overly diffuse. Communication is usually strained and incongruent with feelings. Subsystems may be cross-generational, with each partner seeking advice, consolation, or love from the mothers, fathers, sisters, or brothers.

Given these couple dynamics, it is not surprising that alcohol is involved in many domestic violence incidents. Studies (Pernanen, 1991; Sonkin, Martin, & Walker, 1985) indicate that alcohol plays a part in as high as 80% of domestic violence cases. In one study, 62% of the male batterers were under the influence at the time of the incident (Collins & Messerschmidt, 1993). The counselor who works with individuals who abuse alcohol and other drugs needs to understand how the dynamics of violence interacts with alcohol/drug abuse (Miller, 1999).

THE FAMILY AND SUBSTANCE ABUSE

From the overview of marital dynamics, it is apparent how such a family is impacted when children enter the system. Family homeostasis and growth are organized around the chemically dependent person's behavior. In many of these families, alcohol-related behavior is a part of daily functioning.

Kaufman (1985) describes four different structures of alcoholic families: functional, neurotic enmeshed, disintegrated, and absent. The *functional* family is usually one in the early stages of abuse, and the abuse is connected to social or personal problems. Family members might talk about the chemical problem but are more concerned about other issues. The *neurotic enmeshed* family is the stereotypical alcoholic family. This family encompasses the all the characteristics listed earlier for the alcoholic couple. Clues to the chemical use are apparent from the parental role reversal, the history of using in the family of origin, and the protection of the abusing parent by the child. The *disintegrated* family is the family in which temporary separation occurs between the abuser and other family members. This is usually the neurotic enmeshed family at a later stage. These families may present for therapy after the abuser has completed an inpatient or intensive outpatient program. Kaufman and Kaufman (1992) further separated the disintegrated family into two stages: the first stage involves the temporary separation, and the second stage is where chemicals are the focus of the family and conflict is open and apparent. The *absent* family is one with a permanent separation between the chemically dependent person and the other members. This is usually seen in chronic abusers or chemically dependent people.

Steinglass (1980) has developed a Family Life History Model that evaluates the alcoholic family system using a developmental model. The author describes three developmental phases: early, middle, and late. In the early phase, the family is in the process of developing a solid family identity. They may over- or underreact to problems related to the alcoholism. In the middle phase, the family has already established identity. This family usually presents with a nonalcoholic problem and a vague history of abuse. They will develop short-term, rigid methods for maintaining homeostasis that incorporates the chemical use behavior in the system. Late-phase families focus on the intergenerational issues regarding chemical use. The wife might ask the husband to resolve issues about his father's alcoholism before they have children, or the wife might need to "do something" about her alcoholic mother (Fisher & Harrison, 1997, p. 208).

It is important to understand that the family with an alcoholic member "has alcoholism" in that alcoholism regulates all behaviors in the family life. If the primary relationship in the family is with alcohol or drugs, then other relationships in the family will suffer. Since denial is an integral component of the family homeostasis mechanism, the family will blame factors outside the family for their problems. This externalization of blame reflects the powerlessness felt throughout the family system. The chemically dependent member functions to bring the family together through the crises that are caused by the same abuse (Fisher & Harrison, 1997).

Criticism, anger, blame, guilt, and judgment characterize communication in the family, as in the couple. Parenting is inconsistent, and the boundaries are unclear and constantly changing. Rules and limits are also in flux depending on whether the member is actively using.

Black (1981) states three rules that govern the alcoholic family: don't talk, don't trust, and don't feel. These three rules sum up the interactions seen within the alcoholic family. Family members develop survival roles to cope with the increasing dysfunction in the family. These roles build a wall of defenses around the individual members that allow each person to deny feelings and to fit into the family. The continuing action/reaction to the chemically dependent person is self-deluding. As the protective barriers increase, family members become more out of touch with themselves and with each other (Curtis, 1999).

Steinglass (1976) makes an interesting point about the dysfunction in alcoholic families. In most dysfunctional families, the identified patients or symptom bearers are the children. In alcoholic families, the parents are the symptom bearers. He further notes that the adult chemically dependent person may have developed the problem in adolescence, thereby being the symptom bearer in his family of origin where parents were also using. It is important for the counselor working with these families to understand the process that the symptom serves in the family. It is also imperative to remember that "[n]o matter how sick it may appear to the outside observer, the established equilibrium represents that family's attempt to minimize the threats and disruption" in the family system (Meeks & Kelly, 1970, p. 400).

Children in the Addictive Family

Parental alcoholism appears to create the same type of dysfunction that exists in families with sexual, physical, or emotional abuse. This makes the children in these families at high risk for the development of a variety of stress-related disorders (Kelly & Myers, 1996; Owings-West & Prinz, 1987; Treadway, 1990), including conduct disorders, poor academic performance, and inattentiveness. Furthermore, since these children live in chronic chaos and trauma, they might develop long-lasting emotional disturbances, antisocial personality disorders, or chemical dependence in later life (Brown & Lewis, 1995; Silverman, 1989). Other studies indicate that these children may become addicted to excitement or chaos and may develop inappropriate behaviors such as fire setting or, conversely, may become the "superresponsible" child in the family, taking on parental roles (Webb, 1989).

A number of factors affect the impact of the parental chemical dependence on children. One is the sex of the abusing parent: the impact of a chemically dependent mother is far different than that of an abusing father. Because mothers commonly have the primary care position in the family, this dynamic often creates a greater sense of loss and responsibility (parentified child) than does paternal chemical use. The second factor is the sex of the child. Again, males and females may respond differently. The sex of the parent in conjunction with the sex of the child is also a complicating factor, with mother-daughter, mother-son, father-daughter, and father-son pairings all having different dynamics. The third factor is the length of time the parent has been actively abusing. A fourth factor is the age of the child during the period of active abuse. Finally, the extent of the abuse/dependence on the chemical influences the effects on children. Ackerman (1983) believes that children can avoid the worst of the impact if they are able to find a parental surrogate. The impact that one stable, caring adult—whether a family member or not—can have in a child's life has since been researched and proven. The presence of such a person is one of the major factors in children who are resilient—who survive dysfunctional families and environments with healthy attitudes and behaviors (Wolin & Wolin, 1993). Factors that distinguish these children from less resilient children are not well defined in the literature but may include the child's personal characteristics or "constitutional moderators" (Seilhammer & Jacob, 1990). Other factors that seem to impact a child's resilience are environmental factors and the support from the larger social system, such as religious influence, peer influences, and community or educational influences (Seilhammer, 1991).

"Children in families with alcohol and drug abuse may leave their families in many ways but they usually feel that although they never really belonged to the family they can never really leave" (Lawson & Lawson, 1998, p. 64). This comment addresses the pseudomutuality that is a sustaining dynamic in the addictive family. It also expresses the problems experienced by these children as they move out into the world. This connectedness to the family of origin creates the highest probability for the child to re-create that family's dynamics in their present family.

Siblings in the Addictive Family

There has been minimal research on the impact of sibling on sibling in the addictive family. This research (like much of the research in this field) focuses on the Euro-American family and on the male children in these families. Although these studies are based on male siblings, we may assume that the same relationships exist between female siblings. Research concerning mixed-sex influence (male to female and female to male) on relationships does not exist at this time.

Kaufman and Kaufman (1992) present three ways in which siblings affect other siblings within these systems. The first is through the *personality influence* mechanism. Through this mechanism the older brother's personality influences the younger brother through identification and leads to similar values, goals, and behaviors. The second mechanism is *genetic temperamental* connection. This biological link may strengthen the personality influence. The third pathway is the *environmental reactive* mechanism, or the environmental link between the two brothers. Tension between the two seems to increase intrapsychic distress in the younger brother. In this case, the younger brother may disengage from the relationship and any responsibilities regarding the relationship.

Male siblings can, therefore, have positive or negative influences on each other. Siblings can influence other siblings' drug use by modeling the drug use behavior or by providing the drug. Conversely, the sibling can support the drug-using sibling when the need for help is apparent.

Children's Roles

Black (1981) and Wegscheider (1981) both discuss a set of roles for children in alcoholic families. Both authors state that children take roles that are related to their sibling position in the family: the family hero, the scapegoat, the lost child, and the mascot. Respectively, they are the oldest child, the middle children, and the youngest, or the baby of the family. Black believes that once set, children rigidly adhere to these roles throughout their lives even after leaving the chemically dependent family of origin.

The Hero

The family hero is usually the oldest child and is the confidant of the codependent. Children playing this role know much of what is happening in the system and feel the most responsible for the family's pain. They learn to anticipate the needs and wants of others. They also learn that achievement is a means to gain recognition not only in the outside world but also in the family. Achievement brings compliments to heroes.

These children are an example to the outside world of how well the family is functioning. Sadly, no amount of achievement make "it" (the family dysfunction) go away. Hero children feel inadequate because they cannot "fix" the family. They are also the caretakers of the family. As they try to manage the family situation, they fulfill the self-worth needs of both the dependent and the codependent but not their own.

Heroes are most likely to marry an abuser and become the enabler in the relationship. As children and as adults, these individuals are perfectionistic, superresponsible, and an overachiever. As adults, heroes may become workaholics. These adults many times enter the helping professions to continue their caretaking role. Personally, they are locked in a cycle of feeling unworthy and inadequate no matter how much they perform, thereby leading to exhaustion and burnout. Their personal search is for approval and appreciation.

The Scapegoat

The scapegoat is the problem child. Children in this role reflect the stress in the family, but only to a minute degree. They are the disruptive, "acting-out" children in the family. This disruptive behavior takes the attention away from the family dysfunction and demands immediate attention. Scapegoats are aware of both the enabler's and the hero's efforts to manage the dependent person, seeing how manipulative they are in their communication and behavior. Also, they see that their efforts are not working.

Scapegoats feel apart from the hero and the enabler. In an effort to feel connected, they have further reason to be disruptive and then are reprimanded and also criticized and belittled. Although negative, this direct communications give scapegoats the message that they are responsible for the family chaos. Any criticism of the system is labeled as disloyalty to the family, causing further rejection.

Scapegoats are also jealous of the relationship that the hero has with the parental dyad. Unable to express this feeling, these children turn it inward as self-pity, defiance, and hostility. They also look outside the family for self-worth and overvalue the peer group. Scapegoat children are at the greatest risk for substance abuse at the earliest age. As adults, these individuals may have problems controlling anger, accepting authority, keeping employment, and forming meaningful relationships.

The Lost Child

The lost child is the "flip side" of the scapegoat. Both have many of the same feelings of disconnectedness and unimportance; the difference is how they decide to react to these feelings. Children in the lost child role are aware of the time and energy spent in protecting the chemically dependent person. They are loners who never "need" attention, never create a problem, and never get into trouble. This behavior is a relief to the already stressed system and reinforces the behavior by complementing the withdrawal.

Loners are often excluded from information about the family functioning and so lack necessary information. Communication with others is a problem. These children also leave the system to seek self-worth but many times enter a fantasy world to replace the family (e.g., television, music, reading, the Internet). The created fantasy world allows loners to survive but blurs the boundary between reality and fantasy. These children are never quite sure what is really true. In this fantasy world, however, they are in control.

As an adult, these children have problems with developing relationships, as they feel inadequate in their ability to communicate. They are confused, and this confusion leads to mistakes in judgement about circumstances such as friendship versus intimacy, emotional closeness/distance, and disagreements. These individuals in adulthood are still usually loners and superindependent. They may also be overly attached to possessions, becoming materialistic. Loners are also at risk for sexual identity problems.

The Mascot

The mascot is usually the youngest child or the baby of the family. Such children have the most protected position in the system and many times have no idea what is actually happening in the family. They are the cute one, bringing humor and fun to the system. These children learn early and quickly that the best way to break up a heated argument is by doing something funny. This behavior also works to get attention from the parents. As the hero and the scapegoat both vie for attention from the family, the mascot also enters the game but through a different door. The mascot commands center stage with humor and fun. This is rewarded by the family and gives the mascot attention, control, and creates internal good feelings. As a result, mascots may be hyperactive and do anything to get a laugh. The price for this attention is loneliness since no one knows the real person, only the "clown."

In adulthood, mascots may remain immature and unable to express honest feelings. They may not be taken seriously by coworkers or others. They also have a great amount of self-anger at their inability to express true feelings.

Summary

All of these roles represent a dysfunctional and rigid method for these children to survive in the addictive family. Certainly, as mentioned earlier, many factors affect how resolutely these roles are enacted. It should also be noted that these roles within the system are complementary and thereby serve to maintain the family balance both separately and in interaction with each other.

Jenkins, Fisher, and Harrison (1993) studied these roles in relationship to their rigidity and came up with a different conclusion than Black and Wegscheider. They state that in 75% of the alcoholic families and in 60% of the other dysfunctional families, the children took on more than one role. The most frequent combination of roles was the hero and the lost child. Jenkins et al. suggest that the hero may well try to deflect the family dysfunction through achievement but may adopt the lost child role to avoid disclosing the family pain in social situations.

It is apparent, whether or not one believes in the rigidity of the role assumption, that the dysfunctional pattern of behavior and communication in the marital/parental dyad filters down to the children. It is not a great leap to assume that these children, in their adult relationships, will continue the behaviors that worked well for them in their dysfunctional family of origin, thereby creating another generation of dysfunctional families.

TREATMENT WITH ADDICTIVE FAMILIES

With compelling evidence of the family's impact in the etiology and maintenance of abuse and dependency, it seems appropriate to incorporate family systems therapy in the treatment process. Some outcome research supports the efficacy of family therapy in working with substance abusers. Studies (Collins, 1990; Oxford, 1984; Steinglass & Robertson, 1983) show that family therapy consistently has a better outcome than individual therapy. Other studies have shown that family involvement increases client engagement in both detoxification and treatment stages (Jacobson, Holtzworth-Munroe, & Schmaling, 1989; Liepman, Nirenberg, & Begin, 1989; Sisson & Azrin, 1986). Still other research shows that family therapy was more effective than individual therapy alone (Alexander & Guyther, 1995; Edwards & Steinglass, 1995).

However, many treatment programs do no more than pay lip service to family therapy. Partially, this may be due to the politics and available monies through managed care for substance abuse treatment today. Treatment programs tend to compartmentalize individual and family therapy, offering a time-limited family component to augment ongoing individual treatment. This artificial compartmentalization itself denies a systems approach to treatment.

Additionally, many treatment facilities do not have clinicians trained in family systems theory. Therefore, counselors who are minimally trained in the theory and techniques of family theory are offering the "family therapy" component. In spite of these problems, family therapy can still be a powerful adjunct in the treatment of substance abusers, from assessment, to detoxification, and through treatment and aftercare.

As already discussed, an underlying principle of systems theory, no matter which school of family theory that one adheres to, is that systems (in this case, families) are self-regulating and self-maintaining. This one sentence speaks volumes for the inclusion of family members in treatment. The identified patient (IP) or substance abuser would be unable to continue the behavior without a system (family or other significant support system) to maintain the behavior. This in no way implies that the system prefers the individual's continued use of drugs but that the system accommodates and adjusts itself to the individual's use. The family may be traumatized by the consequences of the abuse but at the same time finds it essential that the individual continue using to maintain the system's homeostasis. Therefore, when the individual decides to stop abusing, the family balance is disrupted. Based on systems theory, without intervention, the system will seek to return to its previous homeostasis or balance, which in this case includes a substance-abusing family member.

The value of including the family in assessment lies in the multiple perspectives that become available when family members are included. No longer does the clinician have to rely on the individual abuser's information about drug use but has access to a variety of information about the individual's patterns of behavior. Additionally, the clinician has information concerning the effects on the family's problem-solving skills, daily routines, and rituals (Steinglass, 1994) or, more specifically, how the family maintains itself in the face of the dysfunctionality.

It may also be important for the counselor to address the difference in the family's behavior patterns when an individual is using and when the individual is not using ("wet" and "dry" conditions). Developing a clear understanding of these behavior patterns can be essential in assisting the family in change.

The author shares with many other practitioners in the field the belief that meaningful psychotherapy can only begin after an individual stops using mind-altering drugs. Therefore, detoxification is a fundamental beginning for treatment. The family therapy approach to detoxification includes a contract with the entire family for detoxification that involves not only the abstinence of the individual but also a shift in the self-regulating patterns of behavior that have developed around the use of drugs in the family (Steinglass, 1994).

When an individual stops using alcohol or other drugs, the family is destabilized. Many times this creates a crisis within the family. Sometimes other problems increase: an adolescent will begin to act out, a physical illness will become worse, or another family member's drug use will worsen. A systems approach recognizes the family's attempt at returning to balance and addresses these issues from that perspective. Just as the family learned to organize itself around the substance use, it must now reorganize itself when there is no substance use in the family. This will require the restructuring of family rituals, roles, and rules. For many families, daily routines will be significantly altered without the presence of alcohol or other drug use. In the cases of long-term substance use, families may have no concept of ways of being other than those that are centered around the abuser's behavioral shifts.

The Process of Treatment

A few general considerations should be discussed before examining the process of working with chemically dependent families. Generally, systems theorists believe that a symptomology in the child or children helps stabilize or balance a dysfunctional marital partnership. Therefore, when the child's behavior becomes healthier, the marital distress level will rise greatly. Often, to maintain the homeostasis, the partners will manipulate the child's behavior back to chemical use.

A family member is always primarily loyal to the family, no matter how dysfunctional or "crazy" the family appears to outsiders. The counselor must be cautious of criticizing or demeaning the family in any way.

There is no ideal family structure. Each family has its own personality and structure. The level of chemical use may affect the system differently based on many factors, including the learned behaviors from the family of origin. High levels of abuse may not affect one family as profoundly as lower levels affect another. Remember: each family is a unique system. All of these families, to one degree or another, operate in a crisis mode. The family moves from one crisis to another as a normal part of daily functioning (Curtis, 1999).

Families operate in an emotional field of past, present, and future. This three-tiered emotional field includes the family of origin, the present nuclear family, and the future generations of this family. Family therapy provides the unequaled opportunity to impact, or change, not only the present generation we have in treatment but, through changing the family patterns and structures, future generations as well (Buelow & Buelow, 1998).

To be effective when working with chemically dependent families, the counselor must first develop a framework or theoretical orientation within systems theories. This approach allows the counselor to organize the assessment, diagnosis, treatment planning, and goals of therapy. Since the literature on success of family therapy is somewhat divided (Buelow, 1994; Edwards & Steinglass, 1995), it does not seem to matter which theory one chooses but simply that one is competent. The basic goal of all systems theories is for the members of the family to achieve a higher level of functioning and to experience symptom relief.

Curtis (1999) discusses two important concepts when working with substance-abusing families. She states that after the presenting problems have been sorted out, many of these families have little or no understanding of the addiction process, the drug itself and its effect on the body, and the interrelatedness of the drug use with the family system. In fact, the majority of these families believe that if the drug use stops, all their problems will disappear. This view is an example of denial and rationalization that other members of the family use to protect themselves and the dependent.

Buelow and Buelow (1998) caution that families are the most difficult groups in which to create quick change because of their long history together—a history that has been successful in protecting the family from outside influences. They further state that the family has

> deeply embedded agendas . . . [with] general psychological aims (such as power) and aims in creating drug-enabling structures (such as codependence in others), [and] these manipulations also encompass tangible financial, spatial, sexual, and occupational payoffs that must be addressed in therapy. (p. 173)

Just as Kaufman (1985) describes four different types of abusing families, Buelow and Buelow (1998) discuss three stages of treatment that coincide with these four types of families. These stages are early stage, middle stage, and late stage.

Early Stage

As with Kaufman's first type of family, the families in the early dependent stage still value sobriety. They may have a family member or members who are abusing, but they continue to believe that abuse is an injurious force in the family. These families present with other problems, and the counselor must be careful not to miss the hidden or vague signs of chemical use. These are also families who, with the assistance of a competent intervention counselor, are able to develop and complete their own interventions for the dependent.

When working with these families, the counselor offers support and education. The family needs to understand how drugs fit into the family pattern of functioning. A commitment to an abstinence plan is one of the first treatment goals, followed by putting this plan into action. Skills that probably need to be addressed are communication, conflict management, parenting skills, and boundary clarification.

The counselor must be diligent in watching for compensatory mechanisms in the family. In other words, as alcohol or drugs are denied, the dependent as well as other members may begin to act out in a variety of ways. Partners may engage in extrarelational sexual behaviors, while children may begin to get in trouble at school. Also, as the family does become more functional, there is tendency to deny that the drug was the problem—in other words, to minimize the affect of the chemical on the family functioning.

Middle Stage

In the middle dependent stage, alcohol or drugs permeate the family's daily life. By this point, the chemical is part of most if not all of the family structure. Emotional dependence is higher, and compensatory behaviors are more active. Denial and blame are high. Many times these families come into treatment through the legal system, the employment system, or hospitalization for drug-related illnesses.

All of the therapeutic considerations mentioned for the early-stage families are important also with these families. In addition, the counselor must address the issues of grief and loss confronting the majority of these families. Other clinical issues include redefining a social network, uncovering relapse triggers and cues, and confronting manipulative compensatory behaviors. Blame and entitlement feelings are intense in these families, and "payment" from past debts must be made.

If the dependent has been in a structured treatment environment, it is sometimes helpful to develop a return ritual for the family. This symbolic activity will serve to ease the transition back into the family as well as confirm the family's and the dependent's commitment to sobriety.

Late Stage

Late-stage, or late-deteriorative-stage, families are often "fragmented or self absorbed" (Buelow & Buelow, 1998, p. 187). The dependent member is often physically as well as emotionally ill. All of the coping mechanisms mentioned in the previous families are intensely ingrained in this family's functioning. Often these families come into treatment through social services, the criminal justice system, or hospitalization. These families are dealing with multiple stressors including medical, legal, and economic difficulties. Independent counselors who are working with this family can be supportive and educational. They also strongly work to get the dependent member into a structured treatment facility.

Treadway (1990) offers a six-part model for working with chronic chemically dependent families:

1. *Disengagement.*   The goal of this phase is to put the responsibility of using back on the dependent. In addition, the therapist frees the partner from trying to stop the abuse. The therapist takes this role, relieving the partner of this responsibility.

2. *Differentiation.*   The goal of this phase is to assist the family through the confusion and anxiety of early recovery. Many times the therapist will use Bowenian techniques to have the clients talk through the therapist and not to each other.

3. *Negotiation.*   This phase teaches the couple problem-solving and negotiation skills. The therapist might function as an arbitrator as the family is learning these new skills.

4. *Conflict management.*   Conflict is a major problem in substance-abusing families. These families need to learn to tolerate conflict without letting it escalate out of control.

5. *Resolution of the past.*   This phase deals with the hurts, anger, and resentment from the past. The emotions built up from the prior years of being in this family plus the family of origin's (childhood's) pains and loss are brought to the surface. Treadway endeavors to unite the couple in their shared pain rather than the typical blaming that accompanies these emotions.

6. *Intimacy.*   The final phase of this model detangles sexual behavior and intimacy and discloses the part that chemicals have played in the relationship. The counselor helps couples "separate reasonable expectations from intimacy from attempts to make up for unresolved family of origin needs. Coming to terms with their old grief relationship to their original families is often a prerequisite to setting realistic expectations for their couple relationship" (p. 96). During this phase, the counselor removes him- or herself from the triangle of the relationship, empowering the couple to become more self-reliant.

Family Week

Although working with substance abuse families appears to be a long-term developmental treatment plan, many treatment programs (involving either inpatient or intensive outpatient care) are only able to offer one family week during the treatment period. The family week offers an excellent beginning for family change. The week is usually structured so that the morning meetings are with the dependent and the family and perhaps with a family group of three or so families. The afternoons are reserved for individual work with the dependent and the family, and also for leisure time.

Families must be prepared in many ways for the intensity of this week. First, they must be given the ground rules, which include the way in which the therapy will be structured (who will meet with whom and when), confidentiality limits, examples of healthy communication ("I" statements), and group norms and expectations. Furthermore, families need to understand that this is time to focus on immediate stressors and concerns. This week will be used to practice communicating honestly, expressing feelings, taking appropriate responsibility, and establishing appropriate boundaries. A relapse plan will be developed and discussed with the entire family.

Family week is usually a highly volatile and emotional week for all concerned, including the therapist. Families can observe how other families are handling their problems and learn from their strengths. They also learn from the therapists' role modeling as well as many of the interactive techniques that might be used, such as family sculpting, role playing, and reenactment (Buelow & Buelow, 1998). Family members are taught to interact more honestly and are allowed sufficient time to express their emotions.

Most families who have stayed together and get to family week usually survive family week together also. These families are then ready to continue therapy outside the treatment facility. This therapy will begin to explore the family-of-origin issues that assisted in the development of the chemical use.

HOW SUCCESSFUL IS FAMILY THERAPY?

As mentioned earlier, the literature on outcome of family therapy with substance-abusing families is mixed (see Chapter 12). We all know that individuals get better in different ways and at different rates, so many variables play into the concept of success when working with the family system. For example, how long does the dependent need to be clean and sober to claim success? How many of the family members must be using new coping skills? For how long? By what means do we measure this: self-report or outsiders' observations? Most authors agree that three criteria must be meet to consider success: the family has to value sobriety, the family has developed and implemented new problem-solving skills, and the drug-using behavior has been accepted as the primary cause of the dysfunction (Buelow & Buelow, 1998; Steinglass, 1980).

CONCLUSION

Family therapy addresses the systemic circumstances in which the individual exists. If we as clinicians believe that the etiology of substance abuse encompasses every aspect of the individual's life, then it is only reasonable that our treatment modalities mirror this belief. Family therapy not only can resolve issues in the family currently presenting for therapy but also, by addressing long-running patterns of behavior, can help prevent dysfunctionalities from arising in future generations. It therefore is a crucial part of the collaborative framework for treating substance abuse.

CASE DISCUSSIONS

Case 1 (Sandy and Pam). Neither Sandy nor Pam would be referred to residential treatment at this time. Although Pam may need detoxification, more information concerning her drug use pattern would be necessary to make this decision.

Sandy exemplifies an individual who has decided to stop drinking and now needs someone to facilitate structure and develop a plan of action to avoid a relapse. Using the biopsychosocial model of treatment, Sandy would be involved in individual therapy to address relationship issues and the possibility of posttraumatic stress disorder. Using a solution-focused model of therapy, the therapist would build on Sandy's strengths, emphasizing the fact that she has quit drinking on her own. The therapist would ask for other exceptions to times when Sandy was drinking and explore how she managed to stay sober during those times. A plan to continue these behaviors would be developed.

Since Pam and Sandy came in together to work on their relationship, the therapist would want to honor this request and continue to work with them from a systems perspective. Using the genogram previously developed, issues of transgenerational patterns of use would be explored. From a solution-focused model, the question would be how others in the family handled stress other than by drinking.

Pam would be asked to contract to decrease her drinking and not to use cocaine over a negotiated period of time and also agree not to come to a session having had alcohol or cocaine. The goal would be complete abstinence as soon as possible. It would also be effective to ask Pam to contract not to see Sam for a given period of time. During this time frame, the therapist would work with Pam on relationship issues, transgenerational patterns of coping, and alternative behaviors to using alcohol and cocaine. It would also be appropriate to work with Pam on relaxation techniques for the anxiety attacks. Referral for medication is possible but not preferable since the goal of therapy is a to learn to live productively without drugs.

The therapist would recommend that both Pam and Sandy attend AA/NA/Al-Anon meetings. The 90/90 schedule would be suggested (i.e., 90 meetings in 90 days). If an outpatient group was available, the therapist might suggest attendance for additional support and therapeutic involvement not available through a 12-step program.

Case 2 (The Smith Family).   As noted in Chapter 4, both Jane and Joe meet the criteria for substance dependence. Their chronic use of drugs spans a 23-year period. If possible, the therapist would suggest short-term residential treatment for Jane and Joe. This decision is based on the admitted inability to stop using, the environment in which Jane works, and the admitted lack of desire to quit using completely. Placing the Smiths in a setting at least to detoxify might enable the therapist to begin to develop an abstinence plan. Additionally, it would allow breathing space to work with Sarah and Karen to explore what is actually happening with them.

Residential treatment may not be practical for both adults in the family; if so, intensive outpatient treatment would be recommended. A regimen of individual, family, and group sessions would be designed. Both adults need to address transgenerational substance abuse and child abuse issues as well as parenting issues in the present. A contract to remain clean and sober should be developed and a structure constructed with the Smiths to implement the plan.

Sarah's acting-out behavior is an indication of the imbalance in the system. Also, Joe's inappropriate behavior with Sarah when drinking must be explored thoroughly. Although Karen is the quiet one, her "disappearance" from the family is also a concern for the therapist. Boundary issues and hierarchy should be discussed. Again, transgenerational patterns of abuse can be discussed and the implications for Karen and Sarah brought into the session.

The therapist must also be aware of the possibility that Sarah is already involved in drug use. Individual sessions with the girls would be an important asset in the treatment plan. The therapist would want to gather information about the day-to-day activities in the home, at school, and in other situations. Information about peers and activities would also be helpful. Referring Sarah to Alateen and Karen to a group for children would be beneficial if available.

Couples group therapy for Jane and Joe would prove extremely beneficial. In this setting, couple and family issues as well as parenting can be discussed freely and with others in the same situation as well as benefiting from the facilitation of a professional. Certainly a 12-step program would be an appropriate support for both Joe and Jane.

Case 3 (Leigh). In working with Leigh, several factors need to be considered. The first factor is Leigh's developmental stage. Normal adolescent growth includes rebellious and sometimes dangerous behavior. It most certainly includes behaviors that are unacceptable to the parents. Additionally, many changes have occurred in Leigh's life recently: her brother left for college, and she has moved to a new area and a new school. Her mother's stress appears to have increased, creating increased conflict between Leigh and her mother.

The therapist might address Leigh's drug use and acting-out behavior as a symptom of her discontent with her present situation. An additional important concern, and also a symptom, would be the fact that Leigh is overly thin. The possibility of an eating disorder combined with the other issues must be carefully evaluated. If the therapist determines that an eating disorder exists, a referral to an eating disorder specialist might be appropriate. Safety issues must be addressed in regard to all of Leigh's present behaviors.

Addressing Leigh's drug use as a symptom, rather than the problem, requires a different approach to treatment. Normalizing some of her behavior with Mom might take pressure off the situation. A "no drug" contract would be negotiated. Sessions with Mom would be scheduled to decrease the conflict and establish boundaries as well as connections. If possible, this therapist would also include the father. How to schedule these sessions would be determined after conversations with Leigh, Mom, and Dad. Mom and Dad appear to need some assistance with their relationship since Leigh feels in the middle of this situation, so parenting skills work would be one goal of therapy. Also, developing a plan in which Leigh spends quality time with her parents would be advantageous.

Leigh does not appear to need a 12-step program at this time. If a teen group were available, however, the support of other clean and sober teenagers might be beneficial.

REFERENCES

Ackerman, R. J. (1983). *Children of alcoholics: A guidebook for educators, therapists, and parents.* Holmes Beach, FL: Learning Publications.

Alexander, D. E., & Guyther, R. E. (1995). Alcoholism in adolescents and their families. *Pediatric Clinics of North America, 42,* 217–234.

Bateson, B. (1971). *Steps toward an ecology of the mind.* New York: Ballantine.

Bateson, B., Jackson, D., Haley, J., & Weakland, J. (1956). Toward a theory of schizophrenia. *Behavioral Science, 1,* 251–264.

Beavers, W. R. (1985). *Successful marriage: A family systems approach to couples therapy.* New York: Norton.

Bennett, L. A., Wolin, S. J., & Reiss, D. (1987). Couples at risk for alcoholism recurrence: Protective influences. *Family Process, 26,* 111–129.

Bertalanffy, L. von (1968). *General systems theory: Foundation, development, applications.* New York: Braziller.

Black, C. (1981). *It will never happen to me.* Denver: MAC.

Bowen, M. (1974). Alcoholism as viewed through the family systems theory and family psychotherapy. *Annals of the New York Academy of Science, 233,*115–122.

Bowen, M. (1976). Theory in the practice of psychotherapy. In P. J. Guerin, Jr. (Ed.), *Family therapy: Theory and practice.* New York: Gardner.

Brown, S., & Lewis, V. (1995). The alcoholic family: A developmental model of recovery. In S. Brown (Ed.), *Treating alcoholism.* New York: Jossey-Bass.

Buelow, G. D. (1994). Treatment of role stereotypy in severely dysfunctional and chemically dependent families. *Journal of Child and Adolescent Substance Abuse, 3,* 13–24.

Buelow, G. D., & Buelow, S. A. (1998). *Psychotherapy in chemical dependence treatment.* Pacific Grove, CA: Allyn & Bacon.

Collins, G. (1993). Reconstructing codependency using self-in-relation theory: A feminist perspective. *Social Work, 38,* 470–476.

Collins, J. J., & Messerschmidt, P. M. (1993). Epidemiology of alcohol-related violence. *Alcohol Health & Research World, 17(2),* 93–100.

Collins, R. L. (1990). Family treatment of alcohol abuse: Behavioral and systems perspectives. In R. L. Collins, K. E. Leonard, & J. S. Searles (Eds.), *Alcohol and the family: Research and clinical perspectives* (pp. 285–308). New York: Guilford.

Curtis, O. (1999). *Chemical dependency: A family affair.* Pacific Grove, CA: Brooks/Cole.

Daw, J. L. (1995, December). Alcohol problems across generations. *Family Therapy News.* Washington, D.C.: American Association for Marriage and Family Therapy.

Doweiko, H. F. (1999). *Concepts of chemical dependence* (4th ed.). Pacific Grove, CA: Brooks/Cole.

Edwards, M. E., & Steinglass, P. (1995). Family therapy treatment outcomes for alcoholism. *Journal of Marital and Family Therapy, 21,* 475–509.

Erekson, M. T., & Perkins, S. E. (1989). System dynamics in alcoholic families. Special issue. Codependency: Issues in treatment and recovery. *Alcoholism Treatment Quarterly, 6,* 59–74.

Fisher, G. L., & Harrison, T. C. (1997). *Substance abuse: Information for school counselors, social workers, therapists, and counselors.* Boston: Allyn & Bacon.

Gladding, S. (1998). *Family therapy: History, theory, and practice* (2nd ed.). Upper Saddle River, NJ: Merrill/Prentice Hall.

Goldenberg, I., & Goldenberg, H. (1999). *Family therapy: An overview.* Pacific Grove, CA: Brooks/Cole.

Gondolf, E.W., & Foster, R. A. (1991). Wife assault among VA alcohol rehabilitation patients. *Hospital and Community Psychiatry, 42,* 74–79.

Gorski, T. T. (1992). Diagnosing codependence. *Addiction and Recovery, 12(7),* 14–16.

Jackson, D. D. (1960). *The etiology of schizophrenia.* New York: Basic Books.

Jacob, T., Ritchey, P., Cvitkovic, J. F., & Blane, H. T. (1981). Communication styles of alcoholic and nonalcoholic families when drinking and not drinking. *Journal of Studies on Alcohol, 42,* 466–482.

Jacob, T., & Seilhammer, R. (1987). Alcoholism and family interaction. In T. Jacob (Ed.), *Family interaction and psychopathology: Theories, methods, and findings* (pp.535–580). New York: Plenum.

Jacobson, N. S., Holtzworth-Munroe, A., & Schmaling, K. B. (1989). Marital therapy and spouse involvement in the treatment of depression, agoraphobia, and alcoholism. *Journal of Consulting and Clinical Psychology, 57,* 5–10.

Jenkins, S. J., Fisher, G. L., & Harrison, T. C. (1993). Adult children of dysfunctional families: Childhood roles. *Journal of Mental Health Counseling, 15,* 310–319.

Kasl, C. D. (1992). *Many roads, one journey: Moving beyond the 12 steps.* New York: Harper Perennial.

Kaufman, E. (1985). Family therapy in the treatment of alcoholism. In T. E. Bratter & G. G. Forrest (Eds.), *Alcoholism and substance abuse* (pp. 376–397). New York: Free Press.

Kaufman, E., & Kaufman, P. (1992). From psychodynamic to structural to integrated family treatment of chemical dependency. In E. Kaufman & P. Kaufman (Eds.), *Family therapy of drug and alcohol abuse* (pp. 34–45). Boston: Allyn & Bacon.

Kelly, V. A., & Myers, J. E. (1996). Parental alcoholism and coping: A comparison of female children of alcoholics with female children of nonalcoholics. *Journal of Counseling and Development, 74,* 501–504.

Lawson, A., & Lawson, G. (1998). *Alcoholism and the family: A guide to treatment and prevention.* Gaithersburg, MD: Aspen.

Leonard, K. E., & Roberts, R. J. (1996). Alcohol in the early years of marriage. *Alcohol Health & Research World, 20,* 192–196.

Liepman, M. R., Nirenberg, T. D., & Begin, A. M. (1989). Evaluation of a program designed to help families and significant others to motivate resistant alcoholics into recovery. *American Journal of Drug and Alcohol Abuse, 15,* 209–221.

Lowe, R. N. (1982). Adlerian/Dreikursian family counseling. In M. A. Horne & M. M. Ohlsen (Eds.), *Family counseling and therapy* (pp. 329–359). Itasca, IL: Peacock.

McGoldrick, M. (1989). Ethnicity and the family. In B. Carter & M. McGoldrick (Eds.), *The changing family life cycle: A framework for family therapy* (pp. 70–89). Boston: Allyn & Bacon.

Meeks, D., & Kelly C. (1970). Family therapy with families of recovering alcoholics. *Quarterly Journal of Studies on Alcoholism, 31(2),* 399–413.

Miller, G. A. (1999). *Learning the language of addiction counseling.* Boston: Allyn & Bacon.

Minuchen, S. (1974). *Families and family therapy.* Cambridge, MA: Harvard University Press.

Minuchen, S. (1992). Constructing a therapeutic reality. In E. Kaufman & P. Kaufman (Eds.), *Family therapy of drug and alcohol abuse* (pp. 1–14). Boston: Allyn & Bacon.

Moos, R., Fenn, C., & Billings, A. (1989). Assessing life stressors and social resources: Applications to alcoholic patients. *Journal of Substance Abuse, 1,* 135–159.

Nichols, M. P., & Schwartz, R. C. (1995). *Family therapy: Concepts and methods.* Boston: Allyn & Bacon.

O'Connor, J., & McDermott, I. (1997). *The art of systems thinking.* London: Thorsons.

Olson, D. H., & Killorin, L. A. (1987). *Chemically dependent families and the circumplex model.* Unpublished research report, University of Minnesota, St. Paul, MN.

Owings-West, M., & Prinz, R. J. (1987). Parental alcoholism and child psychopathology. *Psychological Bulletin, 102(2),* 204–281.

Oxford, J. (1984). The prevention and management of alcohol problems in the family setting: A review of work carried out in English-speaking countries. *Alcohol, 19,* 109–122.

Pernanen, K. (1991). *Alcohol in human violence.* New York: Guilford.

Satir, V. (1967). *Conjoint family therapy.* Palo Alto, CA: Science and Behavior Books.

Schilit, R., & Gomberg E. S. L., (1991). *Drugs and behavior: A sourcebook for the helping professions.* Newbury Park, CA: Sage.

Seilhammer, R. A. (1991). Effects of addiction on the family. In D. C. Daley & M. S. Raskin (Eds.), *Treating the chemically dependent and their families* (pp. 172-194). Newbury Park, CA: Sage.

Seilhammer, R. A., & Jacob, T. (1990). Family factors and adjustment of children of alcoholics. In M. Windle & J. S. Searles (Eds.), *Children of alcoholics: Critical perspectives* (pp. 168–186). New York: Guilford.

Sheinberg, M. (1991). Navigating treatment impasses at the disclosure of incest: Combining ideas from feminism and social constructionism. *Family Process, 31,* 210–216.

Shertzer, B., & Stone, S. C. (1980). *Fundamentals of counseling.* Boston: Houghton-Mifflin.

Silverman, M. M. (1989). Children of psychiatrically ill parents: A prevention perspective. *Hospital and Community Psychiatry, 40,* 1257–1265.

Sisson, R. W., & Azrin, N. H. (1986). Family member involvement to initiate and promote treatment of problem drinkers. *Journal of Behavior Therapy and Experiential Psychiatry, 17,* 15–21.

Sonkin, D. J., Martin, D., & Walker, L. E. (1985). *The male batterer: A treatment approach.* New York: Springer.

Steinglass, P. (1976). Experimenting with family treatment approaches to alcoholism, 1950–1975: A review. *Family Process, 15,* 97–123.

Steinglass, P. (1980). A life history model of the alcoholic family. *Journal of the American Medical Association, 254,* 2614–2617.

Steinglass, P. (1994). Family therapy: Alcohol. In M. Galanter & H. D. Kleber (Eds.), *Textbook of substance abuse treatment* (pp. 315–329). Washington, DC: American Psychiatric Press.

Steinglass, P., & Robertson, A. (1983). The alcoholic family in the biology of alcoholism. In B.

Kissin & H. Begleiter (Eds.), *The pathogenesis of alcoholism: Psychosocial factors* (pp. 243–307). New York: Plenum.

Super, D. E. (1990). A life span, life-space approach to career development. In D. Brown, L. Brooks, & Associates (Eds.), *Career choice and development: Applying contemporary theories to practice* (2nd ed., pp. 197–261). San Francisco: Jossey-Bass.

Treadway, D. (1990). Codependency: Disease, metaphor, or fad? *Family Therapy Networker, 14(1),* 39–43.

Treadway, D. (1993). *Before it's too late.* New York: Norton.

U.S. Department of Health and Human Services. (1995). *Preliminary estimates from the 1994 national household survey on drug abuse.* Advance Report 10. Washington, DC: U.S. Department of Health and Human Services, Substance Abuse and Mental Health Services Administration.

Webb, S. T. (1989). Some developmental issues of adolescent children of alcoholics. *Adolescent Counselors, 1(6),* 47–48, 67.

Wegscheider, S. (1981). *Another chance: Hope and health for the alcoholic family.* Palo Alto, CA: Science and Behavior Books.

Wolin, S. J., Bennett, L. A., & Noonan, D. L. (1980). Disrupted family rituals: A factor in intergenerational transmission of alcoholism. *Journal of Studies on Alcoholism, 41,* 199–214.

Wolin, S., & Wolin, S. (1993). *The resilient self: How survivors of troubled families rise above adversity.* New York: Villard.

Zelvin, E. (1993). Treating the partners of substance abusers. In S. L. A. Straussner (Ed.), *Clinical work with substance abusing clients* (pp. 196–213). New York: Guilford.

Working with Selected Populations: Treatment Issues and Characteristics

Connie Schliebner Tait, Ph.D., and John Joseph Peregoy, Ph.D.

This chapter will address treatment issues and characteristics of five groups of individuals. The underlying criteria for selecting the groups was the power differential among these groups and the influence of societal perceptions and actions that have limited the full participation of these groups in mainstream society. Obviously, as with Chapter 9 on cultural diversity, other groups could be included in this selection, but because of space constraints, we have chosen to discuss women, the gay/lesbian/bisexual community, people with disabilities, children and adolescents, and the elderly.

WOMEN

The use of alcohol, tobacco, and other drugs (ATOD) and the misuse of prescription medications are taking a serious toll on the health and well-being of women and their families. Although women use alcohol and drugs less than men, the estimated number of women who use or abuse substances is of considerable concern. It is estimated that 21.5 million women smoke, 4.5 million are alcoholics or alcohol abusers, 3.5 million misuse prescription drugs, and 3.1 million report regularly using illicit drugs (Ford, Bales, & Califano, 1996).

Hanson and Venturelli (1998) state that to understand the impact of drug abuse on women, we must appreciate the uniqueness of female roles in our society. Women are subjected to many kinds of oppression. They are discriminated against in hiring, salary, and promotions in the workplace (Goldberg, 1995). Women are overrepresented among the poor population because of the financial difficulties faced by single mothers. The cultural environment of women may place them at risk for substance abuse owing to physical and sexual abuse, poverty, anxiety and depression resulting from multiple roles, issues of poor self-esteem, dead-end employment or no employment, and specific life stressors such as single parenthood, divorce, and loneliness (Blumenthal, 1998).

Women are also more likely than men to be subjected to sexual violence as both children and adults and to be injured in domestic violence (Goldberg, 1995; Vogeltanz & Wilsnack, 1997). Research has indicated (Wilsnack, Vogeltanz, Klassen, & Harris, 1997) a significant relationship between alcohol problems and women of childhood victimization. The use of alcohol may be used to cope with sexual dysfunction or with negative affectivity resulting from sexual abuse in childhood.

Women abusing substances are often judged by a double standard and are perceived less tolerantly compared to men (Hanson & Venturelli, 1998). They are frequently perceived as weak, deviant, or immoral, causing women to experience more guilt and anxiety about their dependence. Such stigmas discourage women from admitting their drug problems and seeking professional help.

Substance abuse among women has adverse effects on not only the individual but also their children, families, and communities. Women are still largely responsible for raising children. ATOD can intensify domestic violence, lead to child abuse and neglect, and result in foster care placement (Drug Strategies, 1998). The U.S. General Accounting Office (1998) estimates that substance abuse is a critical factor in at least three-quarters of the nation's 502,000 foster care cases. Millions more children are cared for by relatives under protective custody of the court because their parents, often single mothers, have serious alcohol and other drug problems.

In the past decade, arrests of girls for drug offenses have more than tripled (Drug Strategies, 1998). Women have been incarcerated in unprecedented numbers, largely for drug offenses. The majority of women in prison leave children under age 18 at home. The children of women in prison are at increased risk for ATOD use.

Risk Factors

Several demographic and psychosocial predictors of women's ATOD problems have been identified that support the role of environmental influences (Vogeltanz & Wilsnack, 1997). Age is a strong predictor of ATOD problems in women, with women in their 20s and 30s consistently reporting higher rates of alcohol disorders and problem drinking than women in older age groups (Grant et al., 1994). Women over age 65 report the lowest rates of alcohol disorders of any age group but have a greater likelihood of abusing prescription drugs (Graham, Carver, & Brett, 1995).

Women who are single, divorced, separated, or cohabiting are more likely to be using alcohol and drugs than married women (Gomberg, 1999). Studies have shown strong positive associations between women's drinking and their partner's drinking, with recent evidence suggesting that each partner probably influences the drinking behavior of the other (Gomberg, 1999; Roberts & Leonard, 1997).

High risk for problem drinking in the workplace is associated with nontraditional occupations, low-status jobs, part-time employment, recent layoff, or unemployment (Gomberg, 1999). Women who have fewer social roles and responsibilities are more likely to report problem drinking than women with multiple roles (Wilsnack, 1995). Studies (National Institute on Drug Abuse [NIDA], 1994) have found that at least 70% of women abusing substances have been sexually abused by the age of 16. Most of these women had at least one parent who abused alcohol or drugs. Women who use drugs risk becoming infected with HIV, especially those who inject drugs and share needles. Women who have sex with men who inject drugs are also at great risk. The NIDA (1996) reports that between 1990 and 1991, AIDS cases rose 17%. By 1994, almost 70% of AIDS cases in women are related to either injecting drugs or having sex with a man who injects drugs (see Figure 8.1).

When a pregnant woman uses drugs, she and her unborn child face serious health problems. The NIDA (1998) states that during pregnancy, the drugs used by the mother can enter the baby's bloodstream. The most serious effects on the baby can be HIV infection, AIDS, prematurity, low birth weight, sudden infant death syndrome, small head size, stunted growth, poor motor skills, and behavior problems.

Attention to women's health has been neglected particularly in biomedical and behavioral research (Blumenthal, 1998). The Center for Substance Abuse Treatment (CSAT, 1994a, 1994b) research indicates that women suffer severe physiological consequences as a result of substance abuse.

It appears that women may have even greater risks than men for certain negative physiological effects of heavy substance abuse, particularly alcohol, because of differences in the way women and men metabolize ethanol (Vogeltanz & Wilsnack,

---

FIGURE 8.1   About women, drug abuse, and AIDS

Source: From the *1996 National Household Survey on Drug Abuse* and the Substance Abuse and Mental Health Services Administration (1996).

- Nearly 1 in 3 women in the United States has used an illicit drug at least once in her life—33 million out of 110 million.

- An estimated 15% of all American women ages 15 to 44 are currently abusing alcohol or illicit drugs.

- As many as 2.7 million American females older than 12 years abuse alcohol.

- Sixteen to 21 percent of pregnant women report drinking alcohol during pregnancy.

- Research indicates that more than 4 million women need treatment for drug abuse.

- AIDS is now the fourth leading cause of death among women of childbearing age in the United States.

- In 1996, nearly 1.2 million females aged 12 and older had taken prescription drugs for a nonmedical purpose.

- In the month preceding the 1996 National Household Survey, more than 26 million women had smoked cigarettes, and more than 48.5 million had consumed alcohol.

1997). Schenker (1997) states that women alcoholics are at greater mortality risk than men and that a greater percentage of female alcoholics develop alcohol-related consequences, such as cirrhosis, hemorrhagic stroke, or brain damage. Hepatic disorder occurs more frequently among women and after a shorter duration of heavy drinking in spite of lesser consumption.

Women are more likely than men to seek assistance for non-alcohol-related problems and more often pursue services in mental health and medical settings. However, women's drug problems tend to be underrecognized in these settings as health professionals screen less for substance abuse problems in women than men (Vogeltanz & Wilsnack, 1997). Women with substance abuse problems suffer more than men from affective disorders and are more likely to experience guilt, anxiety, and depression (Kauffman, Silver, & Poulin, 1997). These presenting complaints are often treated with tranquilizing medication that does not heal the underlying cause of the distress.

Women have a greater reluctance than men to admit they have a problem with alcohol and/or drugs. They often confront barriers to finding, entering, and completing treatment programs. Society imposes some of the barriers, while others are internal within the woman herself. Many drug-using women do not seek treatment because they are afraid: they fear not being able to take care of or keep their children, they fear reprisal from their spouses or partners, and they fear punishment from authorities (NIDA, 1998). Those that have been most successful have had the help and support of significant others, family members, friends, treatment providers, and the community.

Research (CSAT, 1994a, 1994b) has indicated there are several barriers for women in the seeking of substance abuse treatment:

1. *Economic inequality.*   Women earn $0.70 for every $1.00 earned by men, are much more likely to be single heads of households, and are much more likely to live below the poverty level. The cost of treatment may be a significant obstacle to their seeking treatment.

2. *Social stigmatization.*   Women with substance abuse problems are often perceived as less socially acceptable then men. They are often considered as second-class citizens who are weak-willed and therefore are less likely to disclose their need for treatment.

3. *Lack of social and emotional support.*   Women's partners, family members, and friends often enable a woman to continue her substance abuse by denying the problem or its seriousness.

4. *Family responsibilities.*   Women are more likely to be the primary caretaker of the family and face practical considerations of adequate supervision for their children. Women entering inpatient treatment may fear losing custody of their children.

5. *Fear of rejection.*   Many women fear they will be rejected by their families or friends if they admit they are addicted to alcohol and/or other drugs because they engage in a lifestyle that is not approved of by society.

Prevention and Intervention

Understanding the social, gender, and economic barriers to treatment for women is an important step in creating programs to meet their special needs. Because the drug abuse treatment system was largely developed at a time most clients were men, there is a concern that this system is not sufficiently responsive to women's economic, social, and emotional issues (Wallen, 1998).

Research (NIDA, 1998) shows that women receive the most benefit from treatment programs that provide access to the following:

Food, clothing, shelter	Transportation
Job counseling and training	Legal assistance
Parenting training	Family therapy
Couples counseling	Medical care
Child care	Social services
Social support	Mental health care
Assertiveness training	Educational opportunities

Successful treatment programs for women build on nurturance, empowerment, and a safe environment for women to heal (Prevention Center, 1992). Within the treatment program, counselors should address the following gender-specific issues related to addiction (CSAT, 1994a):

- Low self-esteem
- Gender discrimination and harassment
- Relationships with family and significant others
- Attachments to unhealthy interpersonal relationships
- Interpersonal violence, including incest, rape, battering, and other abuse
- Eating disorders
- Sexuality, including sexual functioning and sexual orientation
- Parenting
- Work
- Life/career plan development
- Child care and child custody

Kauffman et al. (1997) state that long-term outcomes for women in recovery might be enhanced by developing follow-up services that aid women in establishing supportive relationships among friends and family as a mechanism to reduce the sense of powerlessness and to help the sense of loss that often precipitates the problem of substance abuse.

Research (NIDA, 1998) also indicates that for women in particular, a continuing relationship with a treatment provider is an important factor throughout treatment. During the recovery process, women need the support of the community and encouragement of those closest to them to assist with possible relapses. After completing treatment, women also need the services to assist them in sustaining their recovery and in rejoining the community.

THE GAY/LESBIAN/BISEXUAL COMMUNITY

The psychosocial stress of being a homosexual man or woman (hereafter also referred to as gay/lesbian/bisexual or GLB) in a society dominated by a heterosexual orientation places GLB individuals at high risk for alcohol and drug abuse. Very little research has studied the frequency of alcohol and drug use problems among GLB individuals (Hughes & Wilsnack, 1997). The limited data suggest there is a significantly higher alcoholism rate for GLB individuals than the general population. It has been estimated that 25% to 35% of the GLB population meet the criteria for a diagnosis of alcohol/drug dependency as compared to 10% to 12% of the general population (Beatty et al., 1999). Evidence suggests that more than half of all lesbians have alcohol use problems, a rate of five to seven times higher than seen in nongay women (North, 1996).

DeBord, Wood, Sher, and Good (1998) question the findings of earlier studies on ATOD use among GLB communities because of research flaws ranging from inadequate measures of sexual orientation to the sampling bias of recruiting participants from gay bars. However, estimates do exist that suggest a higher rate of ATOD use among GLB adults and GLB college students.

It is believed that factors such as stigma, denial, alienation, discrimination, and the cultural importance of bars place GLB at higher risk for developing problems with alcohol and drugs (CSAP, 1994a). Beatty et al. (1999) state that a sexual minority status may cause GLB individuals to face prejudicial attitudes, discriminatory behaviors, hatred, and verbal, emotional, or physical abuse. This discrimination can lead to loss of job and residence and rejection by family and peers. The result of living this type of existence is often immeasurable psychological stress that leads to escape with alcohol and other drugs. Alcohol use among GLBs is associated with low self-esteem, shame, guilt, depression, anxiety, anger, frustration and isolation.

Gay/Lesbian/Bisexual Identity Development

The development of a positive GLB identity can be a lengthy and difficult process. Blumenfield (1998) emphasizes that each person comes out in different ways under unique circumstances. The coming-out journey begins with an early awareness of feelings of difference to the development of an integrated identity, which takes many years. The reasons that people move from stage to stage, or fail to move, are very complex.

However, societal attitudes are important in affecting the development of a person's positive identity. Creating and maintaining a positive GLB identity and larger self-concept presents daily challenges and stresses for GLB individuals (Beatty et al., 1999).

Cass (1979, 1984) has proposed a theoretical Model of Homosexual Identity Formation for understanding six stages of development that an individual moves through in developing an integrated GLB identity. The model is based on two broad assumptions: (a) identity is acquired through a developmental process, and (b) change in behavior stems from the interaction between individuals and their environment.

The first stage of *identity confusion* is characterized by confusion, turmoil, and doubt as individuals begin to question their sexual orientation. *Identity comparison,* the second stage, occurs when they have accepted the possibility of being homosexual. In the third stage of *identity tolerance,* individuals increase their commitment to a homosexual identity but keep public and private identities separate. The fourth stage of *identity acceptance* is characterized by acceptance of a homosexual identity rather than tolerating this identity. Disclosure of homosexual identity remains selective. *Identity pride* is the fifth stage, characterized by anger, pride, and activism, which leads to immersion in the homosexual culture and rejection of the values of the heterosexual community. Finally, *identity synthesis* occurs with a fusion of the homosexual identity with all other aspects of self, as individuals no longer dichotomize the heterosexual and homosexual world.

This model can assist both clients and professionals in having a better understanding of the challenges of each developmental stage and the particular supports that might be necessary to reach an integrated identity. Blumenfield (1998) cautions that although the model represents an orderly developmental sequence, it merely depicts general patterns, and each person advances or retreats in different ways. In fact, Cass (1984) has even made revisions to the model based on a lack of empirical evidence for some of the stages. However, the model is useful in approaching the complexity of sexual orientation that occurs in the context of societal prejudice, discrimination, and lack of support (Fassinger, 1998).

The struggles of developing a GLB identity and adjusting to a stigmatized and minority sexual status can lead to low self-esteem and serious depression. Issues of being rejected by family, friends, and society can lead to internalized homophobia. Internalized homophobia is the process of internalizing and believing societal antigay attitudes, beliefs, and stereotypes that can lead to self-hatred and self-devaluation (Kus, 1995).

Risk Factors

Beatty et al. (1999) conclude that five main factors explain the etiology of problem substance use in GLBs: (a) the role of the gay bar as a primary socialization agent, (b) fewer family and societal supports, (c) socioeconomic and psychosocial conditions associated with minority status, (d) stresses related to the developmental process of GLB identity formation and coming out, and (e) internalized homophobia.

Gay bars are one of the major social institutions in the GLB community. Until recently it has provided a safe place to meet and socialize with other GLBs and openly be oneself (Murphy, 1994). Beatty et al. (1999) state that formal and informal communication and activity networks of the gay community continue to revolve around the gay bar and the accompanying use of alcohol. Thus, alcohol has been built into the social life of GLB individuals. Drinking for GLBs may not be used for escaping something but joining something. The therapist working with GLBs should be attuned to issues of potential alcohol abuse and sensitized to the fact that socialization in the bar may well be an integral part of the client's identity.

Large urban areas have a growing number of alternative places to meet and socialize: community centers, coffeehouses, clubs, organized sports teams, hiking trips, vacation tours, dancing classes, and bridge clubs (Murphy, 1994). However, for those living outside large cities, the bars may be the only alternative, and in some communities GLBs may have no public place to socialize. Professionals can work to make themselves knowledgeable of GLB community resources to help their clients locate such alternative community resources in which they can socialize with others who have similar interests.

Prevention and Intervention

The helping profession has historically been in the forefront of advocating for minority groups. "Counselors need to come forward in advocating for the dignity and human rights of all gay and lesbian people" (Morrow, 1993, p. 658). Cooley (1998) states that counselors need to become aware of their own homophobia and be willing to explore sexual orientation with their clients. Counselors need to educate themselves about the issues related to GLBs and their life struggles, which may include substance abuse.

Kus (1995) believes that therapists may incorrectly conclude that the cause of substance abuse is a client's GLB sexual orientation rather than exploring issues of depression, relationships, anxiety, and self-esteem that are related to all of areas of the person's life. The therapist's acceptance of a GLB orientation becomes crucial in treating the individual's substance use in which self-denial and self-hate are such significant factors.

Beatty et al. (1999) and Ratner (1988) believe that effective treatment, whether inpatient or outpatient, should focus on the following specific GLB concerns: (a) a treatment environment that affirms GLB lifestyles as positive alternatives to traditional heterosexual lifestyles; (b) increased self-awareness and self-acceptance as a sexual minority; (c) appropriate ways of coping with discrimination and rejection that is encountered from society, family, and others; (d) a nontraditional family network; (e) integration of their sexuality into a philosophy of life based on sobriety, quality, spirituality, and self-worth; (f) medical information that is tailored to their special needs; and (g) role models who illustrate the diversity of the GLB community.

It has been stressed (Beatty et al., 1999) that early recovery issues for GLB clients include not only the cessation of the substance abuse and the teaching of relapse prevention skills but also a self-analysis and a redefinition of oneself. To assist with behavior change, treatment needs to center on issues of identity, orientation, self-esteem, self-worth, anger, denial, and the development of coping mechanisms.

Paul, Stall, and Bloomfield (1991) recommend family therapy and aftercare treatment as vital to recovery. However, the traditional family network may not be in place for many GLBs. Identification and recognition of the nontraditional family or chosen family support system are highly advantageous for the continuance of recovery.

Issues of GLB sexuality and intimacy that are often crucial in dealing with alcohol and drug abuse are frequently not addressed in chemical dependency treatment programs (Kus, 1995). Amico and Neisen (1997) state that GLB clients are more willing to seek treatment programs that address GLB issues, have visible GLB staff members, and provide culturally relevant interventions. Alcoholic Anonymous reports over 500 GLB groups throughout the United States. Most major metropolitan communities have outpatient centers that provide chemical dependency services for GLB. The National Association of Lesbian and Gay Addictions Professionals (NALGAP) operates to create a network for support and communications among addictions professionals to educate agencies and organizations about GLB and addictions, acts as a clearinghouse for resources, raises the GLB community's consciousness and combats its denial of the problem of addictions, and strives to improve substance abuse treatment for GLB (Blumenfield, 1998). Counselors can encourage clients to establish a GLB support system, be familiar with community resources, and make the information available.

PEOPLE WITH DISABILITIES

It is estimated that at least 49 million people in the United States have one or more physical or mental disabilities and that this number is increasing as the population grows older (U.S. Bureau of Census, 1995). Estimates of people with disabilities vary, depending on how *disability* is operationally defined. People with disabilities have been identified as one of the nation's largest populations at high risk of alcohol and other drug (AOD) abuse problems (Prendergast, Austin, & Miranda, 1990). The impact of AOD among people with disabilities is estimated to be between 6 and 13 million Americans who are physically and mentally disabled and chemically dependent (Watson, Franklin, Ingram, & Eilenberg, 1998).

The words *handicapped* and *disabled* have been used synonymously, yet many in the disability community distinguish between the two. A *disability* is a medical condition that interferes with a person's development, sight, hearing, dexterity, mobility, learning, or psychological adjustment. A *handicap* is a situational or social barrier or obstacle to the person with a disability in achieving his or her maximum level of functioning. For example, "a person using a wheelchair is handicapped in traveling throughout the city not because of the wheelchair but because of the inaccessibility of buses or buildings. The disability cannot be changed, but the handicapping condition can be" (Prendergast et al., 1990, p. 2). Congress has defined *disability* "as a physical or mental impairment that substantially limits one or more major life activities of such an individual; a record of such an impairment; or being regarded as having an impairment" (Americans with Disabilities Act [ADA], 1990, Section 3, p. 2). People with disabilities include:

- those who are blind or suffer from vision impairment,
- people who have a cleft palate,
- those with a congenital disability,
- those who are deaf or hearing impaired,
- people with spinal cord injuries/those with paraplegia or quadriplegia,
- those who have mental disabilities that encompass developmental disabilities,
- people who have received head injuries/head trauma, and
- those with learning disabilities or retardation/cognitive impairment.

Psychiatric disorders covered under ADA include:

- major depression,
- bipolar disorder,
- panic and obsessive compulsive disorders,
- personality disorders,
- schizophrenia, and
- rehabilitation from drug and alcohol abuse/dependency (Sue & Sue, 1999).

It is important to note that current AOD users/abusers are not covered under ADA (Sleek, 1998). Estimates suggest that at least 50% of individuals with a psychiatric disorder also are experiencing some level of AOD problems. In addition, it is projected that at least one-third of the U.S. population will experience a mental disorder in their lifetime (Watson et al., 1998). Given that Congress recently added HIV as a disability, the number of people who qualify under ADA will continue to grow (Sue & Sue, 1999), leaving current estimates woefully short in terms of the numbers of individuals impacted with a recognized disability under ADA.

Risk Factors

One of the major issues in diagnosis of AOD issues in people with disabilities is that they are viewed as a secondary diagnosis with the disability being recognized first, if they are recognized at all. Alcohol and other drug use/dependency for this population can be masked by symptoms of psychiatric disorders such as depression or anxiety. Although studies have suggested that substance abuse is problematic, estimated to be as high as 80% among some subgroups within this population, there is still limited research on prevalence and effective intervention and prevention strategies (Watson et al., 1998).

Contributing factors to high rates of abuse include self-perception; environmental and social stress factors; myths; enabling attitudes of family, friends, and professionals in service agencies; social skills; and a general lack of knowledge by members of the abled world (Helwig & Holicky, 1994). Substance abuse behaviors need to be identified as to whether they are a consequence of or a response to the disabling event or whether individuals participated in the same behaviors prior to the disability.

All too often AOD behaviors are viewed as secondary disabilities or not recognized at all in medical settings (Watson et al., 1998). Helwig and Holicky (1994) point out that many independent living centers do not regularly ask their clients about alcohol or drug use. They further point out that the lack of assessment influences appropriate treatment and hence outcomes. One of the reasons pointed to for inadequate assessment of AOD abuse is the lack of cross training among rehabilitation counselors (Shipley, Taylor, & Falvo, 1990; *Rehabilitation Brief,* 1990; Watson et al., 1998).

Other contributing factors to AOD behaviors and lack of assessment and treatment include negative attitudes of society toward those with disabilities. These attitudes include the perception of the abled toward those with disabilities as being less than normal or as hopeless, helpless, fragile, and sick (Storti, 1997). "In a society where fitness and sports are revered, individuals with white canes, hearing aids, crutches, wheelchairs, walkers, speech problems or developmental disabilities are at best shunned, and at worst, hidden" (Helwig & Holicky, 1994, p. 227).

With these social labels of deviance, which are personally discrediting, persons with disabilities become double outcasts when identified as having AOD abuse. Helwig and Holicky (1994) have suggested that for the professional working with this population, addressing AOD issues may be viewed as an additional burden for the client, being viewed as cruel, pointless, and a waste of time.

Prevention and Intervention

Early identification of substance abuse in rehabilitation counseling or after entry into a center for independent learning is imperative. "Unless the abuse-addiction is addressed, dealing with the adjustment to a disability will most likely not occur" (Helwig & Holicky, 1994, p. 227). All too often substance abuse stands in the way of total rehabilitation and is one of the few disabilities that can be totally eliminated (Schliebner & Peregoy, 1998). This requires professionals in the field to become aware of rehabilitation concerns, substance abuse issues, and the development of the ability to address these issues openly, grounded in an informed foundation of cross training. The reader is referred to the Helwig and Holicky (1994, p. 233) article for a delineation of stress factors that may contribute to substance abuse and an assessment outline for identifying substance abuse in persons with disabilities.

People with disabilities experience the same psychological gamut of social pressures and psychological stressors that contribute to AOD abuse as do people who are not disabled. In addition, they experience the stressors related to social stigma and the additional psychological, emotional, and social problems related to their disability that can increase their risk for abuse. The etiology of AOD abuse among people with disabilities is complex (Storti, 1997). AOD abuse histories need to be evaluated in relation to the development of a disability and the onset of abuse scrutinized as to its function in the daily life of individuals with disabilities. This approach facilitates assessment with appropriate interventions applied.

Interventions need to be designed that are sensitive to the particular disability and life circumstance of the individual. Accommodations, such as American Sign Language (ASL) interpreters or educational audiotapes for the visually impaired, need to be used in psychoeducation components of therapy. When working with any person with a disability, depending on the length of the disability (congenital or traumatic), it is paramount for counselors to remember that they are working in a cross-cultural setting.

Areas for intervention that have been identified in the literature include psychoeducation on a variety of issues. Storti (1997) has suggested that clients be provided with information about specific drugs and their contraindications, independent living skills, active alternatives to AOD, parent education and involvement, counterenabling education, self-esteem, peer pressure, and the development of constructive forms of sensation and fantasy seeking. We recommend that clients be assisted in developing new social support networks in conjunction with these. While clients are working on these areas, it is also suggested that their support system receive psychoeducation on issues they may encounter owing to the traumatic demands of unexpected life changes.

CHILDREN AND ADOLESCENTS

NIDA (1997) research has shown that for most children, the vulnerable life periods are transitions, when they grow from one developmental stage to another or when they experience difficult life changes, such as moving or divorce. Exposure to risks can start even before a child is born if the mother is using drugs during pregnancy. The first main transition for children is when they leave the security of the family and enter school. When they advance from elementary school to middle school or junior high, they often face social challenges, such as learning to get along with a wider group of peers. It is at this stage, early adolescence, that children are likely to encounter drug use for the first time.

Data on substance abuse among young children have not been systematically collected (CSAP, 1998). However, the younger a child is when experimenting with ATOD begins, the more likely it is a dependency will develop later. Research conducted by the Partnership Attitude Tracking Study (Partnership for a Drug-Free America, 1998) tracked drug use and drug-related attitudes among children as young as 8 years old. The study found that the number of fourth through sixth graders (9 to 12 years old) experimenting with marijuana increased from 334,000 in 1993 to 571,000 in 1997. Almost 3 out of every 10 children (9 to 12 years old, children in fourth through sixth grades) were offered drugs in 1997, an increase of 47% since 1993.

Increasingly, research suggests that conduct disorders and other behavioral and temperament traits that increase a youth's vulnerability to drug use develop as a fairly stable pattern as early as 5 years of age (Zucker, Fitzgerald, & Moses, 1995). Characteristics of these young children that appear to developmentally lead them in the direction of a comorbid developmental psychopathology of drug abuse and other developmental problems (Alexander & Pugh, 1996) include impulsivity, attention deficit disorder, difficult temperament, below-average verbal IQ, academic under-achievement, negative affect, difficulties with emotional regulation, social incompetence, and aggression. These problem behaviors tend to cluster in children raised in dysfunctional families by parents who were likewise raised in dysfunctional or over-stressed families.

Even though there appears to be a trend toward younger substance use, 12 to 13 years of age is the turning point year (Califano & Booth, 1998). These researchers indicated that the transition from age 12 to 13 now marks the most dramatic increase in children's exposure to drugs and a decisive shift in attitude about drugs and parental involvement in their lives.

Adolescence is a developmental period that is characterized by psychological, social, and biological changes. This transition period between childhood and adult-hood is characterized by internal and external changes that are often manifested by a barrage of emotions. Johnson, Hoffman, and Gerstein (1996) state that adolescents often find themselves caught between the simplicity and security of childhood and the stress, expectations, and responsibilities of adulthood.

Although most adolescents experience transitory problems that they can resolve, others become disturbed and are unable to resolve their problems without help (Elmen & Offer, 1993). If these adolescents do not seek help, they often turn to destructive devices, such as alcohol and drugs. In conjunction with the storminess of this period, adolescents often take part in risk-taking behavior. Conger and Galam-bos (1997) state that drinking then driving, committing acts of vandalism, and engaging in unprotected sex are examples of behaviors that emerge out of adolescents' newfound autonomy and desire to participate in the peer culture. Such behaviors may have serious consequences, or they may not, depending on various factors, including how often risks are taken, the seriousness of the adolescent's actions, and sometimes luck. The consequences of adolescents' risk-taking behaviors include drug addiction, pregnancy, trouble with the law, school attrition, and sometimes death.

Youth involved with alcohol and drugs pose a major problem not only to them-selves but also to the community as a whole. Since 1975, the Monitoring the Future Study (MFT) has annually measured the extent of drug abuse among high school seniors. Among the graduating class of 1997, 54.3% of students had used an illicit drug by the time they reached their senior year of high school, continuing an upward trend since 1992 (University of Michigan, 1998; see Table 8.1). For many adolescents, the first exposure to drugs occurs at an early age (Hanson & Venturelli, 1998). MFT also found that by eighth grade, approximately 55% of children had used alcohol, 46% had used tobacco, 22% had used inhalants, and 20% had used marijuana. Furthermore, about 25% of all school-age youth are children of alcoholics.

Some of these youth may be experimenting with drugs, others attempting to ease the stress of adolescence, and others modeling the behavior of family members and peers. Regardless of the reasons, the consequences of substance abuse are serious. Routine use can contribute to school and social failures, unintended injuries,

TABLE 8.1 Percentage trends in lifetime prevalence of use of various drugs for 8th, 10th, and 12th graders (*n* = 50,000)

	1991	1992	1993	1994	1995	1996	1997	1998	1997–1998 Change
Any Illicit Drug									
8th Grade	18.7	20.6	22.5	25.7	28.5	31.2	29.4	29.0	−0.4
10th Grade	30.6	29.8	32.8	37.4	40.9	45.4	47.3	44.9	−2.4
12th Grade	44.1	40.7	42.9	45.6	48.4	50.8	54.3	54.1	−0.2
Marijuana/Hashish									
8th Grade	10.2	11.2	12.6	16.7	19.9	23.1	22.6	22.2	−0.4
10th Grade	23.4	21.4	24.4	30.4	34.1	39.8	42.3	39.6	−2.7
12th Grade	36.7	32.6	35.3	38.2	41.7	44.9	49.6	49.1	−0.5

Source: University of Michigan (1998).

criminal and violent behavior, sexual risk taking, depression, and suicide (Curry & Spregel, 1997).

Risk Factors

No single profile identifies who will or will not use alcohol and drugs. Adolescent substance abusers have different personality types, family histories, socioeconomic levels, and life experiences. However, research (NIDA, 1997) reveals that there are many risk factors for substance abuse, each representing a challenge to the psychological and social development of an individual and each having a differential impact depending on the phase of development. In general, risk factors can be seen as operating in three areas of influence: (a) individual factors of biology, behavior, and personality; (b) family factors; and (c) environmental factors (CSAP, 1998). Conclusions from the research indicate that the more risk factors an adolescent is exposed to, the higher the risk of involvement with alcohol and/or drugs.

Individual Risk Factors
- Antisocial and other problem behaviors such as stealing, vandalism, conduct disorder, attention-deficit hyperactivity disorder (ADHD), rebelliousness, and aggressiveness, particularly in boys
- Alienation
- High tolerance for deviance and strong need for independence
- Psychopathology
- Attitudes favorable to drug use
- High-risk personality factors such as sensation seeking, low harm avoidance, and poor impulse control

Family Factors

- Parental substance use and modeling
- Poor family management and parenting practices
- Poor parent-child relationships
- Family conflict
- Physical and sexual abuse

Environmental Factors

- Peer influence; peer rejection or low acceptance
- Deficient cultural and social norms
- Extreme poverty
- Neighborhood disorganization that reduces the sense of community
- Failure to achieve in school
- Low school involvement
- Negative school environment

Mathias (1996) notes that not all youth exposed to known risk factors go on to drug use and abuse during adolescence. Having protective factors in the multiple domains is what is particularly important in buffering adolescents from the effects of earlier circumstances that place them at risk. Peters and McMahon (1996) conclude that youth are less likely to engage in problematic early substance use if they are members of prosocial, supportive social networks.

Family members are a significant factor in adolescent development as they are role models and major sources of support. According to the CSAP (1998), the strongest pathway protecting youth from drug use involves positive family relations, leading to improved supervision and monitoring, and antidrug family and peer norms. Hence, family interventions that decrease family conflict and improve involvement and parental monitoring should reduce later youth problem behaviors.

The second most important socializing agent for children, after the family, is the school. What is happening or not happening in schools has an impact with youth using illicit drugs. Kumpfer and Turner (1990) hypothesize that youth who bond to prosocial institutions, such as the family and the school, are less vulnerable to the influence of negative peers. The major factor that contributes to school bonding (which entails commitment, attachment, and belief) is involvement. The degree of involvement is determined by opportunities for involvement and reinforcement for involvement in a rewarding social environment. The researchers found that students bond more readily in a positive social environment that discourages the use of drugs. Decrease in drug use is found in schools where a positive school climate exists in which students feel rewarded for achievement, perceive opportunities for involvement, feel respected and heard, and feel capable of influencing school policy and in which clear policy exists.

In addition to protective influences, factors related to resiliency also need to be explored. There are many personal characteristics that recent research (Jessor, 1993; Kumpfer, 1993) has indicated enable environmentally stressed youth to cope with adversity. Norman (1994) found the following resiliency factors:

- An easy temperament/disposition
- Intellectual capability
- A sense of self-efficacy (self-esteem, self-confidence)
- Ability to appraise the environment realistically
- Social problem-solving skills
- A sense of direction or mission
- Empathy
- Humor
- Adaptive distancing abilities when faced with a dysfunctional environment

A number of programs are attempting to incorporate resiliency ideas into adolescent substance abuse prevention programs. Norman (1994) states that each focuses on strength building and empowerment rather than pathology and risk. However, program planning needs to take into account both.

Prevention and Intervention

Effective identification and assessment of substance abuse is a crucial early step in both treatment and prevention programs. Kumpfer, Molgaard, and Spoth (1996) suggest that prevention strategies require attention to the risk factors associated with substance abuse and then focus on protective mechanisms that will inhibit the use of drugs. Prevention efforts should be interrelated activities that include the home, school, and community. These efforts need to extend beyond providing information and specifically address the individual and environmental risk factors.

Family support programs that encourage involvement of the parents in their children's lives are a major key to making adolescents less vulnerable to alcohol and drugs. Regardless of the parents' relationship to their child, they need to be involved in the solution. Kumpfer, Williams, and Baxley (1996) state that intensive, structured family interventions hold promise for the reduction of substance use in adolescents. NIDA (1997) research has indicated that prevention programs can enhance protective factors among young children by teaching parents skills for better family communication, discipline, firm and consistent limit setting, and other parenting skills. The research has shown that parents need to take a more active role in their children's lives, including talking to them about drugs, monitoring their activities, getting to know their friends, and understanding their problems and personal concerns.

Prevention programs designed to increase positive peer relationships focus on an individual's relationship to peers by developing social competency skills. These skills include improved communications, enhancement of positive peer relationships and social behaviors, and resistance skills to refuse drug offers (NIDA, 1997).

Schools are a crucial element to the prevention of substance use by youth. According to NIDA (1997) research, prevention efforts need to focus on enhancing academic performance and strengthening students' bonding to school by giving them a sense of identity and achievement and reducing the likelihood of their dropping out of school. Most curricula include the support for positive peer relationships and an education component designed to correct the misperception that most students are using drugs. The research found that when youth understand the negative effects of drugs (physical, psychological, and social) and when they perceive their friends' and families' social disapproval of drug use, they tend to avoid initiating drug use. A comprehensive drug prevention curriculum for kindergarten through grade 12 is essential to teach students that drug use is wrong and harmful and to support and strengthen resistance to drugs.

In combination with prevention efforts, effective treatment approaches need to be designed to meet adolescents' specific needs. Sanjuan and Langenbucher (1999) stress that adolescents have special needs owing to their unique developmental position: they have a dependent position in the family and community; they are constrained by their levels of physical, social, and cognitive development; they are prone to influence from peers; they are frequently victims of comorbid psychiatric disorders; and they often use many drugs at once.

In view of adolescents' developmental position, Jenson, Howard, and Yaffe (1995) recommend nontraditional treatment programs that avoid labeling youth as alcoholic or addicted and work within the framework of their culture and development. Nontraditional programs view ATOD use as an expression of the developmental process and discourage labeling. Community-based services such as outpatient counseling, recreation, education, group therapy, peer support groups, and vocational training are examples of nontraditional programs. Treatments also include family therapy, social skills training, medical and relapse prevention, school support, and attendance in a self-help group. Most programs recognize that adolescent treatment must address not only substance abuse but also its underlying causes.

THE ELDERLY

The elderly are generally defined as those people who are 55 years of age or older. Identification with this descriptor is often a personal choice when seeking out senior discounts at restaurants, for example, yet are recorded in the health and mental health delivery systems when one seeks medical or psychological services. Age definitions vary in the literature, using such age breaks as 55 and older, 60 and older, and finally 65 and older (Gurnack, 1997).

Alcohol abuse subgroups are also differently defined in the literature. Three abuse subgroups are defined according to age of onset: (a) the early-life onset group is composed of people who manifest their alcohol problems before age 40, (b) the midlife onset group ranges from 41 to 59 years of age, and (c) the late-life onset group exhibits signs of alcohol abuse at or after the age of 60 (Atkinson, Tolson, & Turner, 1990). Substance abuse among the elderly is unique, depending on the age of onset of use and the lifetime prevalence of ATOD.

The extent of alcohol use, drug misuse, and abuse among the elderly is a national concern that is rising as the nation grows older. According to the 1995 census, 33.5 million individuals, or 12.5% of the U.S. population, is 65 years of age or older (U.S. Census Bureau, 1995). By 2030, when baby boomers become senior citizens, it is estimated that 21% of the population will be 65 years of age or older. For now, 17% of adults aged 60 and older are estimated to abuse alcohol and other drugs (Guerra, 1998).

About 1.5 billion drug prescriptions are written in the United States annually, with one-third of these written for the elderly. During the past 25 years, the average number of prescriptions per person for the general population has increased from 2.4 to 7.5 annually. The elderly average 13 prescriptions per year (Stall, 1996), a higher number due to the many medications taken for a range of health conditions that surface later in life interrelated with the body's own aging process (Crawley, 1993).

A common concern for the elderly using prescription or over-the-counter (OTC) drugs is drug misuse. This can involve underuse, overuse, and erratic use leading to adverse consequences (Schliebner & Peregoy, 1998). Misuse can also take the form of medication swapping between spouses, partners, and/or peers in independent living or care facilities (Chapman, 1996; Joseph, 1997). Another concern is the interaction between prescription and OTC drugs taken concomitantly without medical supervision or knowledge.

While the use/abuse of alcohol generally declines in old age, it still remains a major problem for some elderly and is often an underreported and/or hidden problem. Hazelden (1996) reports that 20% of hospitalized older adults are diagnosed with alcoholism, and nearly 70% are hospitalized with alcohol-related problems. As with other age groups, there are more male alcoholics than female, with about two-thirds being early-onset drinkers (Liberto & Oslin 1997). This group is considered at high risk for successful treatment, while late-onset drinkers have a good chance of recovery.

The greatest proportion of abused drugs in this population, other than alcohol, continues to be OTC drugs, nicotine, and caffeine (George, 1990; Schliebner & Peregoy, 1998). The percentage of elderly abusing illegal drugs continues to be rather low unless the use of a prescription drug without proper physician direction is categorized as illegal. If so, there is a great concern about the elderly using drugs in this manner.

Risk Factors

The elderly are at risk for a number of physiological, psychological, social, and economic factors that can lead to substance abuse and/or misuse. Those abusing substances are more likely to be unmarried, undergo more stress, have more financial problems, report persistent interpersonal conflicts with others, and have fewer social resources (Brennan & Moos, 1996). Older adults rarely seek treatment for substance abuse problems because of shame, and they may feel uncomfortable in programs that also deal with drugs such as heroin or crack cocaine (Wren, 1998).

Physical changes take place in the body as it ages. Some of these changes directly relate to the body's ability to metabolize drugs. With normal aging, there is a decrease in total body water content and an increase in the proportion of body fat. Alcohol is rapidly distributed in body water after ingestion. With the decrease in body water as we age, the volume for distribution decreases and therefore the amount of alcohol that reaches the central nervous system increases.

The brain becomes more sensitive to the toxic effects of alcohol in the latter years (Goldstein, Pataki, & Webb, 1996). The parts of the brain that deal with motor skills and cognition age faster than other areas of the brain. Therefore, when these areas are affected by alcohol, the impairment is significant at lower levels of use than at an earlier age. Alcohol affects the cardiac muscle, increasing heart rate and output. Again, when coupled with normal age-related cardiovascular problems, the result can be disastrous. Other disorders that may be caused by alcohol use by older individuals include hypertension, lower resistance to infections, muscle weakness, and electrolyte and metabolic disturbances (Szwabo, 1993).

A second major risk factor is the change in social support and work-related activities for the elderly. Older adults have fewer family responsibilities and work-related duties. Many families live far apart, and when older friends begin to die, the person is left with a small or no social support network. Also, many older adults are retired, leaving the days empty of structured activity and creating the need for a substitute activity. Sometimes the activity is alcohol or other drug consumption.

Loss of family and friends coupled with loss of job (status), economic instability, and failing health creates another problem for the elderly. Reports show that more than 50% experience depression or severe anxiety. Add the possibility of dementia, and mental illness becomes a common occurrence. It is estimated that of the 21% to 24% of patients diagnosed with dementia, clear evidence exists in these cases that alcohol contributed to the cognitive impairment (Smith & Atkinson, 1997).

The elderly have a prevalence of diseases that predispose them to substance use: arthritis, osteoporosis, recurrent gout attacks, neuropathies, and cancer, among others. These diseases all involve chronic pain that must be managed every day. Most people have easy access to prescription drugs for these problems. Physicians are quick to prescribe and not so quick to evaluate medications being taken by the person before prescribing others. Managed care systems create an atmosphere where the individual is often passed from doctor to doctor. None of these professionals has a true sense of the medications or problems in the person's life. Frustration with the system and anger at being dependent on it may prompt further depression and anxiety in the elderly (Gambert, 1992). In even the best of medical circumstances, many elderly live alone, and as dementia increases, over- or undermedication is common without the supervision of a live-in partner or friend.

Diagnosing substance abuse in the elderly is complicated. Many of alcohol's effects on older adults mimic changes associated with normal aging (Doweiko, 1999). Even trained physicians find it difficult to differentiate between late-onset Korsakoff's syndrome and forms of senile dementia (Blake, 1990; Rains, 1990).

Prevention and Intervention

Many elderly people are unaware of the effects of aging in combination with the use of alcohol and other drugs. Therefore, beginning with an educational discussion may be extremely helpful. Counselors should ask specifically about the frequency and quantity of use, as well as OTC medications, prescriptions, and alcohol use. Possible symptoms of use should not be ignored. Hesitancy to confront an older adult and not wanting to take away "their last pleasure" sets the stage for denial and enabling behavior on the part of the clinician or family member.

Medical personnel should be made aware of what is happening with the person. If dietary supplements are necessary, the individual should have access to appropriate vitamins and follow an adequate diet plan.

The older adult should be engaged in a social support system. This may be a 12-step group, although resistance to attendance may be high. Other community activities such as senior citizens' groups might provide reinforcement for the individual. Family members should be educated about the dangers of substance abuse and self-medication in the elderly.

Liberto and Oslin (1997) conclude that the elderly in a treatment program respond better to more structured program policies, more flexible rules regarding discharge, more comprehensive assessment, and more outpatient mental health aftercare. Older adults who receive appropriate treatment respond well and can successfully return to their previous lifestyle.

Few studies have been undertaken of treatment for substance abuse in the elderly (Gambert, 1992). Our society's generally negative feelings about the elderly may be in part to blame for this. However, if the problem is acknowledged and treated, older adults have a very high rate of success in treatment. It is getting them into treatment that is difficult.

Also, clinicians have a moral obligation to consider the complications of aging diseases. Although substance abuse is not the answer, without other options, controlled addiction may be the only solution without "callous disregard for comfort and well-being" (Gambert, 1992, p. 850).

The goal of treatment should be the highest quality of life possible for the longest time possible. The problem must be recognized to be treated. Before that, counselors and families need to be aware of elderly persons who are at high risk. They need to be identified and counseled with as many risk factors eliminated as possible (Gambert, 1992; Hazelden Corporation, 1996).

CONCLUSION

Among women, people with disabilities, gays, lesbians, bisexuals, children and adolescents, and the aged, we are witnessing a growth in alcohol and drug use behaviors. A common theme among these groups is identification and early intervention. All these groups share the experience of being marginalized within our society, which in turn influences self-esteem as well as self-efficacy skills. These issues, then, are not only individual issues but issues of social importance. Interventions need to be designed to meet individual and group needs, and professionals must act as change agents within their communities and society. As change agents, helping professionals can assist in challenging myths and educating the community of particular individual and group needs revolving around ATOD behaviors and risk factors for the groups presented in this chapter.

REFERENCES

Alexander, J. F., & Pugh, C. A. (1996). Oppositional behavior and conduct disorders of children and youth. In F. W. Kaslow (Ed.), *Handbook of relational diagnosis and dysfunctional family patterns* (pp. 31–56). New York: Wiley.

Americans with Disabilities Act. (1990). Public Law 101-336, July 26, 1990, 104 Stat. 327 [Online]. Available: httpweb.icdi.wvu.edu/kinder/pages/ada_statute.htm.

Amico, J. M., & Neisen, J. H. (1997). *Sharing the secret: The need for gay-specific treatment.* Presentation at the National Association of Alcoholism and Drug Abuse Counselors Annual Conference.

Atkinson, R. M., Tolson, R. L., & Turner, J. A. (1990). Late versus early onset problem drinking in older men. *Alcoholism: Clinical and Experimental Research, 14,* 574–579.

Beatty, R. L., Geckle, M. O., Huggins, J., Kapner, C., Lewis, K., & Sandstrom, D. J. (1999). Gay men, lesbians, and bisexuals. In B. S. McCrady & E. E. Epstein (Eds.), *Addictions: A comprehensive guide* (pp. 542–551). New York: Oxford University Press.

Blake, R. (1990). Mental health counseling and older problem drinkers. *Journal of Mental Health Counseling, 12,* 354–367.

Blumenfield, W. J. (1998). Science, sexual orientation, and identity: An overview. *Blackboard: The Gay, Lesbian, & Straight Education Network* [Online], pp. 1–14. Available: http://www.glstn.org.

Blumenthal, S. J. (1998). Women and substance abuse: A new national focus. In C. L. Wetherington & A. B. Roman (Eds.), *Drug addiction research and the health of women.* NIH Pub. No. 98-4290. Bethesda, MD: National Institutes of Health.

Califano, J. A., & Booth, A. (1998, September). *1998 National Center on Addiction and Substance Abuse national survey of teens, teachers, and principals.* New York: Columbia University Press.

Cass, V. C. (1979). Homosexual identity formation: A theoretical model. *Journal of Homosexuality, 4,* 219–235.

Cass, V. C. (1984). Homosexual identity formation: Testing a theoretical model. *Journal of Sex Research, 20,* 143–167.

Center for Substance Abuse Prevention. (1998). *Preventing substance abuse among children and adolescents: Family-centered approaches.* DHHS Pub. No. (SMA) 3224-FY 98. Rockville, MD: Department of Health and Human Services.

Center for Substance Abuse Treatment. (1994a). *Alcohol, tobacco, and other drugs: Lesbian, gay men, and bisexuals.* Rockville, MD: Department of Health and Human Services.

Center for Substance Abuse Treatment (1994b). *Practical approaches in the treatment of women who abuse alcohol and other drugs.* Rockville, MD: Department of Health and Human Services.

Chapman, R. J. (1996, October 10). Personal communication.

Conger, J. J., & Galambos, N. L. (1997). *Adolescence and youth: Psychological development in a changing world.* New York: Longman.

Cooley, J. J. (1998). Gay and lesbian adolescents: Presenting problems and the counselor's role. *Professional School Counseling, 1,* 30–34.

Crawley, B. (1993). Self-medication and the elderly. In E. M. Freeman (Ed.), *Substance abuse treatment: A family perspective* (pp. 217–238). Newbury Park, CA: Sage.

Curry, D. G., & Spregel, I. A. (1997). Gang homicide, delinquency, and community. In G. L. Mays (Ed.), *Gangs and gang behavior* (pp. 314–336). Chicago: Nelson-Hall.

DeBord, K. A., Wood, P. K., Sher, K. J., & Good, G. E. (1998). The relevance of sexual orientation to substance abuse and psychological distress among college students. *Journal of College Student Development, 39,* 157–168.

Doweiko, H. E. (1999). *Concepts of chemical dependency.* Pacific Grove, CA: Brooks/Cole.

Drug Strategies. (1998). *Keeping score 1998.* Washington, DC: Levine & Associates.

Elmen, J., & Offer, D. (1993). Normality, turmoil, and adolescence. In P. Tolan & B. Cohler (Eds.), *Handbook of clinical research and practice with adolescents* (pp. 5–19). New York: Wiley.

Fassinger, R. E. (1998). Lesbian, gay, and bisexual identity and student development theory. In R. L. Sanlo (Ed.), *Working with lesbian, gay, bisexual, and transgender college students* (pp. 13–22). Westport, CT: Greenwood.

Ford, B., Bales, S. F., & Califano, J. (1996). *The gender gap between adolescent girls' and boys' tobacco, alcohol, and drug use has closed.* National Center on Addiction and Substance Abuse. New York: Columbia University Press.

Gambert, S. R. (1992). Substance abuse in the elderly. In J. H. Lowinson, P. Ruiz, R. B. Millman, & J. G. Langrod (Eds.), *Substance abuse: A comprehensive textbook* (pp. 843–851). Baltimore: Williams & Wilkins.

George, R. L. (1990). *Counseling the chemically dependent: Theory and practice.* Boston: Allyn & Bacon.

Goldberg, M. E. (1995). Substance-abusing women: False stereotypes and real needs. *Social Work, 40,* 789–798.

Goldstein, M. Z., Pataki, A., & Webb, M. T. (1996). Alcoholism among the elderly. *Psychiatric Services, 47,* 941–943.

Gomberg, E. S. (1999). Women. In B. S. McCrady & E. E. Epstein (Eds.), *Addictions: A comprehensive guide* (pp. 527–541). New York: Oxford University Press.

Graham, K., Carver, V., & Brett, P. J. (1995). Alcohol and drug use by older women: Results of a national survey. *Canadian Journal on Aging, 14,* 769–791.

Grant, B. F., Harford, T. C., Dawson, D. A., Chou, P., Dufour, M., & Pickering, R. (1994). Prevalence of DSM-IV alcohol abuse and dependence: United States, 1992. Epidemiologic Bulletin No. 35. *Alcohol Health and Research World, 18,* 243–248.

Gurnack, A. M. (Ed.). (1997). *Older adults' misuse of alcohol, medicines, and other drugs: Research and practice issues.* New York: Springer.

Hanson, G., & Venturelli, P. (1998). *Drugs and society.* Sudbury, MA: Jones & Bartlett.

Hazelden Corporation. (1996). Alcoholism and drug abuse: A growing problem among the elderly. *On the World Wide Web,* 1-2.

Helwig, A., & Holicky, R. (1994). Substance abuse in persons with disabilities: Treatment considerations. *Journal for Counseling and Development, 72,* 227–233.

Hughes, T. L., & Wilsnack, S. C. (1997). Use of alcohol among lesbians: Research and clinical implications. *American Journal of Orthopsychiatry, 67,* 20–36.

Jenson, J. M., Howard, M. O., & Yaffe, J. (1995). Treatment of adolescent substance abusers: Issues and practice and research. *Social Work and Health Care, 21,* 1–18.

Jessor, R. (1993). Successful adolescent development among youth in high-risk settings. *American Psychologist, 48,* 117–126.

Johnson, L. D., Hoffmann, J. P., & Gerstein, D. R. (1996). *The relationship between family structure and adolescent substance use.* Rockville, MD: SAMSHA, Office of Applied Studies.

Joseph, C. L. (1997). Misuse of alcohol and drugs in the nursing home. In A. M. Gurnack (Ed.), *Older adults' misuse of alcohol, medicines, and other drugs: Research and practice issues* (pp. 228–254). New York: Springer.

Kauffman, S. E., Silver, P., & Poulin, J. (1997). Gender differences in attitudes toward alcohol, tobacco, and other drugs. *Social Work, 42,* 231–241.

Kumpfer, K. L. (1993). *Resiliency and AOD use prevention in high risk youth.* Unpublished manuscript. Available from School of Social Work, University of Utah, Salt Lake City, UT, 84112.

Kumpfer, K. L., Molgaard, V., & Spoth, R. (1996). The strengthening families program for the prevention of delinquency and drug use. In R. D. Peters & R. J. McMahon (Eds.), *Preventing childhood disorders, substance abuse, and delinquency* (pp. 242–267). Thousand Oaks, CA: Sage.

Kumpfer, K. L., & Turner, C. W. (1990). The social ecology model of adolescent substance abuse: Implications for prevention. *International Journal of the Addictions, 25,* 435–462.

Kumpfer, K. L., Williams, M. K., & Baxley, G. (1996). *Selective prevention for children of substance abusing parents: The Strengthening Families Program.* Silver Springs, MD: National Institute on Drug Abuse, Technology Transfer Program.

Kus, R. (1995). *Addiction and recovery in gay and lesbian persons.* New York: Haworth.

Liberto, J. G., & Oslin, D. W. (1997). Early versus late onset of alcoholism in the elderly. In A. M. Gurnack (Ed.), *Older adults' misuse of alcohol, medicines, and other drugs: Research and practice issues* (pp. 54–93). New York: Springer.

Mathias, R. (1996, January–February). Students' use of marijuana, other illicit drugs, and cigarettes continued to rise. *NIDA Notes, 8,* 6–7.

Morrow, D. (1993). Social work with gay and lesbian adolescents. *Social Work, 38,* 655–660.

Murphy, B. C. (1994). Difference and diversity: Gay and lesbian couples. In L. A. Kurdek (Ed.), *Social services for gay and lesbian couples* (pp. 5–31). New York: Haworth.

National Institute on Drug Abuse. (1994). *Women and drug abuse.* NIH Pub. No. 94-3732. Rockville, MD: National Clearinghouse for Alcohol and Drug Information.

National Institute on Drug Abuse. (1996). *National pregnancy and health survey.* Washington, DC: U.S. Department of Health and Human Services, Public Health Service, National Institutes of Health.

National Institute on Drug Abuse. (1997). *Preventing drug use among children and adolescents: A research based guide.* NIH Pub. No. 97-4212. Rockville, MD: National Clearinghouse for Alcohol and Drug Information.

National Institute on Drug Abuse. (1998). *Treatment methods for women.* Washington, DC: U.S. Department of Health and Human Services, Public Health Service, National Institutes of Health.

Norman, E. (1994). Personal factors related to substance misuse: Risk abatement and/or resiliency enhancement. In T. P. Gullotta, G. R. Adams, & R. Montemayor (Eds.), *Substance misuse in adolescence* (pp. 15–35). Thousand Oaks, CA: Sage.

North, C. S. (1996). Alcoholism and women. *Postgraduate Medicine, 100,* 221–224, 230–232.

Partnership for a Drug-Free America. (1998). *The boomer-rang: Baby boomers seriously underestimate presence of drugs in their children's lives* [On-line]. Available: http://www.drugfreeamerica.org.

Paul, J. P., Stall, R., & Bloomfield, K. A. (1991). Gay and alcoholic: Epidemiologic and clinical issues. *Alcohol World, 15,* 151–160.

Peters, R. D., & McMahon, R. J. (Eds.). (1996). *Preventing childhood disorders, substance abuse, and delinquency.* Thousand Oaks, CA: Sage.

Prendergast, M., Austin, G., & Miranda, J. (1990). *Substance abuse among youth with disabilities.* Madison: Wisconsin Clearinghouse, University of Wisconsin–Madison.

Prevention Center: Center for Applied Prevention Research. (1992). *Profile of the chemically dependent woman.* Boulder, CO.

Rains, V. S. (1990). Alcoholism in the elderly—the hidden addiction. *Medical Aspects of Human Sexuality, 24,* 40–43.

Ratner, E. (1988). A model for the treatment of lesbian and gay alcohol abusers. *Alcoholism Quarterly, 5,* 25–46.

Rehabilitation Brief. (1990). Vol. 12, No. 12.

Roberts, L. J., & Leonard, K. E. (1997). Gender differences and similarities in the alcohol and marriage relationship. In R. W. Wilsnack & S. C. Wilsnack (Eds.), *Gender and alcohol: Individual and social perspectives* (pp. 289–311). New

Brunswick, NJ: Rutgers University Center of Alcohol Studies.

Sanjuan, P. M., & Langenbucher, J. W. (1999). Age-limited populations: Youth, adolescents, and older adults. In B. S. McCrady & E. E. Epstein (Eds.), *Addictions: A comprehensive guide*. New York: Oxford University Press.

Schenker, S. (1997). Medical consequences of alcohol abuse: Is gender a factor? *Alcoholism: Clinical and Experimental Research, 21,* 179–180.

Schliebner, C. T., & Peregoy, J. J. (1998). Alcohol and other drug prevention and intervention: Characteristics and issues of selected populations. In P. Stevens & R. Smith (Eds.), *Substance abuse prevention and intervention: Theory and practice*. New York: Macmillan.

Shipley, R. W., Taylor, S. M., & Falvo, D. R. (1990). Concurrent evaluation and rehabilitation of alcohol abuse and trauma. *Journal of Applied Rehabilitation Counseling, 21*(3), 37–39.

Sleek, S. (1998, July). Mental disabilities no barrier to smooth and efficient work. *Monitor,* p. 15.

Smith, D. M., & Atkinson, R. M. (1997). Alcoholism and dementia. In A. M. Gurnack (Ed.), *Older adults' misuse of alcohol, medicines, and other drugs: Research and practice issues* (pp. 132–157). New York: Springer.

Stall, R. S. (1996). Drug abuse in the elderly: Major issues. *On the World Wide Web,* 1–3.

Storti, S. A. (1997). *Alcohol, disabilities, and rehabilitation*. San Diego, CA: Singular.

Sue, D. W., & Sue, D. (1999). *Counseling the culturally different: Theory and practice*. New York: Wiley.

Szwabo, P. A. (1993). Substance abuse in older women. *Clinics in Geriatric Medicine, 9,* 197–208.

University of Michigan. (1998). *Monitoring the future study*. Ann Arbor: Institute for Social Research.

U.S. Bureau of the Census. (1995). *Population profile of the United States*. Washington, DC: U.S. Government Printing Office.

U.S. General Accounting Office. (1998). *National Institutes of Health: Problems implementing the policy on women in study populations*. Washington, DC: Superintendent of Documents, U.S. Government Printing Office.

Vogeltanz, N. D., & Wilsnack, S. C. (1997). Alcohol problems in women: Risk factors, consequences, and treatment strategies. In S. J. Gallant, G. P. Keita, & R. Royak-Schaler (Eds.), *Health care for women: Psychological, social, and behavioral influences* (pp. 75–96). Washington, DC: American Psychological Association.

Wallen, J. (1998). *Need for services research on treatment for drug abuse in women*. NIH Pub. No. 98-4290. Washington, DC: U.S. Government Printing Office.

Watson, A. L., Franklin, M. E., Ingram, M. A., & Eilenberg, L. (1998). Alcohol and other drug use among persons with disabilities. *Journal of Applied Rehabilitation Counseling, 29,* 22–29.

Wilsnack, S. C. (1995). Alcohol use and alcohol problems in women. In A. L. Stanton & S. J. Gallant (Eds.), *Psychology of women's health: Progress and challenges in research and application* (pp. 381–443). Washington, DC: American Psychological Association.

Wilsnack, S. C., Vogeltanz, N. D., Klassen, A. D., & Harris, T. R. (1997). Childhood sexual abuse and women's substance abuse: National survey findings. *Journal of Studies on Alcohol, 58,* 264–271.

Zucker, R. A., Fitzgerald, H. E., & Moses, H. D. (1995). Emergence of alcohol problems and the several alcoholisms: A developmental perspective on etiologic theory and life course trajectory. In D. Cicchetti & D. J. Cohen (Eds.), *Manual of developmental psychopathology* (Vol. 2, pp. 677–711). New York: Wiley.

Issues in Prevention and Intervention: Working with Diverse Cultures

JOHN JOSEPH PEREGOY, PH.D., AND CONNIE SCHLIEBNER TAIT, PH.D.

Our intent in this chapter is to present a background for viewing factors that affect diverse cultural groups related to substance use and abuse, prevalence, and effective prevention and intervention strategies. The diverse groups discussed in this chapter are limited to minority/ethnic cultures that are prevalent in the United States. The assumption at the foundation of this chapter is simple yet often overlooked in the implementation of individual and community alcohol and other drug interventions. Simply stated, intervention programs designed for particular groups *need* to be developed within the sociocultural worldview in which they are applied. Imposing dominant middle-class, white male interventions in communities not reflecting these values would be tantamount to changing cabins on the Titanic.

The chapter is divided into sections by sociocultural group. Each section has subsections that include a demographic overview, which may present cultural values and sociocultural perspectives; risk factors affecting each group; barriers to treatment; and, finally, considerations in prevention and intervention with each group.

AMERICAN INDIANS AND ALASKAN NATIVES

American Indians and Alaskan Natives are a heterogeneous group made up of 557 federally recognized tribes and a number of tribes that are not federally recognized (Peregoy, 1999). The most recent census data indicate that there are 2.21 million American Indians and Alaskan Natives (U.S. Bureau of the Census, 1995). According to the 1995 census, 41% of American Indians and Alaskan Natives were younger than 29 years of age compared to 29% of the total U.S. population. About 57% of the population can be considered in the childbearing years (ages 10 to 44) (Indian Health Service, 1996). It is projected that by the year 2050, the Indian/Native population will reach 4.3 million, nearly doubling today's number. High school graduation rates are low, about 66% versus 75% for the general U.S. population (Pavel, Skinner, Cahalan, Tippeconic, & Stein, 1998, October). In addition, income for Indians/Natives is about 62% of the national average, with the poverty rate being about three times the national average (U.S. Bureau of the Census, 1995).

Each tribe maintains its own unique customs, values, and religious/spiritual practices. Tribes range from very traditional, in which members speak their tribal language at home, to tribes who use English as their first language. About 67% of all American Indians and Alaskan Natives live outside a reservation. With this shift to the cities, an increase in interethnic and intertribal marriages has occurred. This diversity is also compounded by the fact that more than 60% of all Indians are of mixed background, the result of intermarriages among African American, white, Hispanic/Latino, and Asian populations (Peregoy, 1999).

The shift to the urban setting has also separated the enrolled tribal member from treaty-obligated services such as health and human services. A person who meets tribal enrollment criteria and is registered on the rolls of the tribe is entitled to services from the tribe, has voting rights within tribal elections, and has eligibility for government services provided by treaty agreements. Enrolled tribal members who have moved to the city are subject to many of the same social pressures and urban survival problems as other ethnic minorities (Trimble, Flemming, Beauvais, & Jumper-Thurman, 1996).

Alcohol use is a relatively new phenomenon in Indian/Native life. With the arrival of Columbus and the principle of Manifest Destiny, this new drug encroached upon cultural fabrics that have been put under many stresses, historically and in the present day (Abbott, 1996). Reliable data on extent and pattern of drug use (including alcohol) among American Indians have been scarce and compounded by questions about the generalizability of findings (Abbott, 1998). It has been suggested that Indians/Natives are more likely to be either abstainers or heavy drinkers than members of the general population. Among Navajo (Dine) adults, fewer drink alcohol (52%) than other people in the general population of the United States. It appears that the greatest proportion of adults who drink are between the ages of 15 and 29, and drinking behaviors decline after age 40 (May, 1994). One survey (Barker & Kramer, 1996) among an older urban population found that 72% of the elders (aged 60 and older) did not drink. The findings suggest that older urban American Indians/Alaskan Natives do not differ in their alcohol consumption from the general population. Substance abuse behaviors may taper off with age, and the data indicate that there is a slight decrease in lifetime prevalence. Yet, for those who drink heavily, it is a killing behavior.

Alcohol and other drug use in the Indian/Native communities takes a drastic toll. Many Indian/Native deaths—including accidental deaths, homicides, suicides, and health status, such as cirrhosis and other liver diseases—can be attributed to alcohol and substance abuse. Alcoholism death rates for Indians/Natives range to about six times that of the national average (Indian Health Service [IHS], 1996). In reviewing the 10 leading causes of death in the Indian/Native communities from 1983 to 1993, alcohol use was directly implicated in four: accidents, cirrhosis of the liver, homicides, and suicides. Nearly one-third of all outpatient visits to Indian Public Health Services were related to substance abuse or dependence (IHS, 1997).

A 1997 report by the Indian Health Service stated that age-adjusted mortality rates were considerably higher for Indians/Natives than for all other races. For example, the following rates were identified but are by no means exhaustive:

alcoholism—579% greater,

accidents—212% greater,

suicide—70% greater, and

homicide—41% greater (p. 6).

Nationally, crime statistics for 1998 showed that the average annual number of victimizations for Indians/Natives aged 12 and older are 248% higher than the rest of the nation. A report by the Bureau of Justice Statistics (Greenfield & Smith, 1999) states:

> Intimate and family violence involve a comparatively high level of alcohol and drug abuse by offenders as perceived by the victims. Indian/Native victims of intimate and family violence, however, are more likely than others to be injured and need hospital care. (p. 8)[1]

Data available from the 1997 *Trends in Indian Health* indicate that Indian/Native female alcoholism death rates ranged from 20.1 to 87.6 per 100,000 population, depending on the age group. The rate for all U.S. female per 100,000 never reached 10 across all age groups (IHS, 1997).

Fetal alcohol syndrome (FAS) and fetal alcohol effects (FAEs) are consequences of women consuming large amounts of alcohol during pregnancy. The child can then suffer from neurosensory and developmental disabilities. Although FAS and FAE occur in every cultural community and socioeconomic group, the occurrences vary by subpopulation. FAS is estimated to occur in the general population at about 1 in 750 live births. May (1994) found that the incidence ranged from 1.3 in 1,000 live births for the Navajo tribe to 10.3 in 1,000 live births for other Southwestern and Plains tribes.

It is a logical conclusion to reach that alcohol and drugs cause the majority of the health and psychological problems experienced by Indians/Natives. Clearly, substance abuse is a killing behavior in Indian/Native communities.

---

[1] "Intimate violence" refers to victims of former spouses, girlfriends, or boyfriends. "Family violence" refers to other relatives, and "alcohol-involved incidences" refers to those cases where the victim perceived that they could determine that the offender was using alcohol/drugs.

Risk Factors

The elements underlying Indian/Native substance abuse are complex and fall into three primary categories: biological, psychological, and sociocultural (Mail, 1989). Biological factors include physiology, or the body's response to substances that influence substance dependence. Psychological factors include an individual's and community's response to the stresses of oppression and other stressors that assist in sobriety or abuse.

Sociocultural factors encompass culturally influenced perceptions in response to larger social pressures as they relate to substance use. Educational levels are low, the average education is completion of the ninth grade (U.S. Bureau of the Census, 1995), unemployment rates exceed 90% on some reservations, and family income is about one-third of the national average (Peregoy, 1999). The comparison of family income is faulty in that it does not take into consideration cultural obligations to extended family members and is therefore an overestimate of available resources in many instances.

The literature on Indian/Native substance use often cites stress as a precipitating or causal factor in alcohol and drug abuse (Johnson, 1994). This stress has been referred to as *acculturative stress,* defined as the demands to integrate into and identify with a more dominant culture (Berry, Minde, & Mok, 1987). Simultaneously, *deculturative stress* takes place, defined as stress resulting from the loss or devaluation of historical tradition (Gloria & Peregoy, 1996). Suicide, where rates in the Indian/Native community can be 5 to 10 times higher than the national average, is thought to be partly due to acculturative and deculturative stress (EchoHawk, 1997).

Gloria and Peregoy (1996) viewed acculturation as the outcome of processes that occur at multiple levels in a society, stating that the acquisition of foreign (mainstream) beliefs and values produces stress that may be alleviated by substance use and abuse. These authors have also identified high rates of substance abuse, family disruption, criminal behavior, and mental illness as attributes of deculturative stress. "To be between two worlds forces individuals into conflicts of choice and produces casualties among those who cannot embrace either the old or new ways" (Braroe, 1988, p. 8).

Several researchers have proposed using a social integration model for understanding how communities influence substance use (Flemming, 1992; May, 1994). The assumption underlying this approach is the belief that cohesive, well-integrated communities provide mitigating influences on stress, while poorly integrated communities tend to demonstrate high levels of stress and concomitant substance abuse. Mail (1989) has pointed out that alcohol may become a primary coping response for some individuals and communities, and peer groups may be as powerful an influence as any other factor.

The costs of substance abuse go beyond the emotional and physical dangers and include the use of scarce economic resources. When money is spent on drugs and alcohol, it is unavailable for individual or family purchases. Also, reservation economies are affected by economic leakage, the drain of reservation resources being spent outside the reservation economy (Peregoy, 1999). Education is often related to potential earning power. The use of alcohol and other drugs is related to the 50% dropout rate from school by American Indian youth (Beauvais, Chavez, Oetting, Deffenbacher, & Cornell, 1996).

Barriers to Treatment

Barriers exist in the provision of services offered in the non-Indian community, including historical distrust; difficulties in cross-cultural communication stemming from a lack of shared meaning; the use of extended family systems, which can be misunderstood as child neglect or social instability within the family unit; and unfamiliarity of non-Indian counselors with Indian/Native conversational styles among traditional and transitional family groups (Peregoy, 1999; Sue & Sue, 1999; Trimble et al., 1996). These groups do not emphasize personal issues and may refer only peripherally to matters of great importance to the family.

It has also been pointed out that non-Indian agencies have not demonstrated the ability to cross-culturalize their services to benefit Indian/Native families (Robbins, 1994). There is some resistance to providing home-based services, which is interpreted by the Indian community as a fear of cultural differences on the part of non-Indian providers. This matter speaks to the need for cultural sensitivity on the part of the non-Indian service provider. For further information on Indian/Native cultures, including value orientations, refer to Courtney (1986), Peregoy (1999), and Trimble et al. (1996).

Prevention and Intervention

All programming, from prevention to rehabilitation, needs to be developed within the context of the community and the individual. Many programs aimed at American Indian clients emphasize traditional healing practices, including the sweat lodge, the talking circle, and other traditional ceremonial or religious activities (Peregoy, 1999; Robbins, 1994). These programs appear to be successful for clients who have a strong attachment to traditional Indian/Native cultures. These approaches would not be applicable to clients who do not have a strong attachment to Indian/Native culture and religion. Before implementing services for any client, it is important to understand their level of acculturation and their commitment to traditional Indian/Native religions.

Prevention programs using "educational methods" on reservations have failed when they were based on scare tactics. Such programs have actually led to increased drug use in adolescent populations (Neligh, 1990). Prevention programming could take several other paths to be effective, including offering alternatives to substance use by strengthening community projects such as recreational opportunities, cultural heritage programs, and employment opportunities and training.

Elements that run consistently through the literature for prevention and intervention programs divide programming into two areas: on-reservation and off-reservation programming (Flemming, 1992; Hayne, 1993, 1994; Lujan, 1992; Robbins, 1994). Intervention specialists and providers need to have:

- knowledge of Indian/Native characteristics, such as tribalism (an attitude toward other tribes), identity issues, level of acculturation of the client and the community they come from, and issues surrounding biculturalism, which is essential for integrating mainstream and traditional healing techniques;

- an understanding that there is no single explanation for Indian/Native substance abuse; and

- a treatment orientation based on the notion that alcoholism is a disease excludes the social and cultural aspects of drinking (Robbins, 1994).

Counselors also have a better chance of reducing the frequency of alcohol, tobacco, and other drug (ATOD) abuse if they acknowledge that substance abuse is learned in a cultural context.

Communities need to respond to ATOD issues in a comprehensive fashion (Flemming, 1992; Hayne, 1993, 1994). Communities, both urban and rural/reservation, can begin to develop a comprehensive ATOD plan by (a) forming a consensus of the problem, (b) defining safe drinking practices, (c) determining and promoting specific safety provisions, and (d) building support for a comprehensive prevention plan (Flemming, 1992). Lujan (1992) argues that strong community policies should be developed that are comprehensive, consistent, and clearly defined in relationship to alcohol. This argument describes the necessity to use a public health approach integrating all major institutions, such as the family, school, religion, law enforcement, courts, health services, and the media. These activities should include the identification of both protective and risk factors in the community.

ASIAN AMERICANS

The Asian and Pacific Islander population is growing rapidly in the United States and has been projected to reach 12.1 million, or 4% of the U.S. population, by 2000 (U.S. Bureau of the Census, 1995). The large increase is due to the changes in immigration laws that occurred in 1965 and the entry of over 1.5 million Southeast Asian refugees since 1975 (Chung, Bemak, & Okazaki, 1997). This is a diverse population, consisting of at least 40 distinct subgroups that differ in language, religion, and values (Sandhu, 1997). According to Sue and Sue (1999), they include the larger Asian groups in the United States (Chinese, Filipinos, Koreans, Asian Indians, and Japanese), refugees and immigrants from Southeast Asia (Vietnamese, Laotians, Cambodians, and Hmongs), and Pacific Islanders (Hawaiians, Guamanians, and Samoans). Between-group differences within the Asian American population may be great, but within-group differences also compound the difficulty of making any generalizations about this population. Individuals differ on variables such as migration or relocation experiences, degree of assimilation or acculturation, identification with the home country, use of their native language and English, composition and intactness, amount of education, and adherence to religious beliefs (Sue & Sue, 1999). Such diversity has made the challenge of culturally competent substance abuse treatment services a complex one for providers (National Institute on Drug Abuse [NIDA], 1995).

Research and information on alcohol and other drug use among Asian Americans is relatively small but suggests that this population uses and abuses substances less frequently than do members of other racial/ethnic groups (Zane & Kim, 1994). This observation can be partially attributed to the "model minority" stereotype held by drug researchers and mental health professionals that Asians do not have drug problems and therefore are in little need of study (Fong, 1998). Wentao, Salomon, and Chay (1999) state that the "model minority" belief only adds pressure on Asian Americans. Some Asian immigrants have found success in society, but most are still struggling for survival. This pressure finds many persons of Asian origin feeling nervous, tense, and depressed as they compete with everyone around them.

Uba (1994) conducted an in-depth review of studies and found the combination of minority status/racism, cultural conflicts, immigrant status, and refugee experiences as sources of stress that are distinct from other Americans. She notes that these stressors may serve to create a sense of anger, frustration, and self-hate that can fester and build into severe identity and mental health problems.

Prevalence of Substance Use Among Racial and Ethnic Subgroups in the United States, 1991–1993, was released by the Substance Abuse and Mental Health Services Administration (1998) to report national estimates of ATOD use. The overall rate of past-year illicit drug use for the total U.S. population (age 12 and older) was 11.9%. Relative to the total U.S. population, Asian/Pacific Islanders reported use at 6.5%. Prevalence of dependence on alcohol for those 12 and older among Asian/Pacific Islanders was 1.8%, and prevalence of cigarette use was 21.7%. However, drug use among Asian American students has been increasing at an alarming rate (Kim, Coletti, Williams, & Helper, 1995).

Cultural backgrounds and norms governing ATOD-using styles in various cultures differ. Kim et al. (1995) note that Asian drinking is thought to be more social than solitary, occurring in prescribed settings (usually with food) to enhance social interaction rather than as a method of escapism and within the context of moderate drinking norms. Asian women are expected to drink little or no alcohol. It is true that drinking attitudes and customs of the various Asian American cultures are similar in their encouragement of moderation and that no Asian American culture advocates or encourages excessive alcohol use. These views may account for a significantly lower prevalence rate of alcohol use among Asian American groups than that of whites.

Cultural Values

To fully understand the Asian American client, it is critical for a mental health professional to consider culture in the counseling process (Axelson, 1999). Although Asian immigrants and refugees form diverse groups, certain commonalities can be generalized to the Asian populations. Sue and Sue (1999) and Ho (1994) have discussed salient cultural values operating among Asian Americans:

- *Filial piety.* Filial piety is the respectful love, obligation, and duty to one's parents. Asian children are expected to comply with familial and social authority even if they must sacrifice their personal desires and ambitions. As children become acculturated into the dominant U.S. culture, pressure to meet parental obligations and expectations can lead to stress and conflict.

- *Shame as a behavioral control.*   Traditionally, shaming is used to help reinforce familial expectations and proper behavior within and outside the family. Individuals who behave inappropriately will "lose face" and may cause the family to withdraw support. With the importance of interdependence, the withdrawal of support can cause considerable anxiety in having to face life alone.

- *Self-control.*   The Confucian and Taoist philosophies emphasize the need for moderation—to maintain modesty in behavior, be humble in expectations, and restrain emotional expression. Love, respect, and affection are shown through behaviors that benefit the family and its members. Hence, the Asian American client may lack experience in identifying and communicating emotional states.

- *Awareness of social milieu.*   Asian American individuals tend to be very sensitive to the opinions of peers, allowing the social norms to define their thoughts, feelings, and actions. One subordinates to the group to maintain solidarity. Social esteem and self-respect are maintained by complying with social norms.

- *Fatalism.*   Asian Americans may accept their fate and maintain a philosophical detachment. This silent acceptance contributes to their unwillingness to seek professional help. A "what will be, will be" view of life is often misconstrued by mental health professionals as resistance to treatment.

- *Role and status.*   The hierarchy of the Asian family and community is based on cultural tradition of male dominance. Men and elders are afforded greater importance than women and youths. The father makes the major decisions, and the mother is responsible for the children. The greatest responsibility is placed on the eldest son, who is expected to be a role model for younger siblings and help raise them. Upon the death of the father, the eldest son takes on the family leadership. Fewer demands are placed on daughters, because they leave their family of origin upon marriage. Therapy with Asian Americans must take into account family hierarchy and the demands placed on each member.

- *Somatization.*   Generally Asian Americans perceive problems as difficulties with physical health. Physical illness is believed to cause psychological problems. Complaints such as headaches, stomachaches, and muscle aches are often expressed in response to stressors. Mental health professionals must take into account physical complaints as real problems to improve other aspects of the client's life.

Risk Factors

ATOD-using behavior is influenced by many cultural and situational variables pertinent to Asian groups. Kim et al. (1995) identify these factors to be (a) cultural values, traditions, attitudes, and beliefs; (b) the degree to which one is socialized to the native culture; (c) the degree of acculturation to the dominant values of the host culture, acculturation that leads to conflict, including conflict across a generation gap; (d) family conflicts; (e) role conflicts; (f) alienation and identity conflict; (g) racism; and (h) other factors related to immigration and economic stress. In addition to these risk factors, Asian Americans' personal and social problems may be caused by their immigration status:

- *Feelings of personal failure.*   For many immigrants there is great stress placed on basic survival needs and adjustment. This detracts from individual and family life just when they are needed most. Often immigrants are underemployed, reducing their social status that they held in the home country.

- *Family role reversals.*   In families in which the parents do not speak English, children may be forced to accept adult responsibilities, such as the spokesperson for the family. This is a role reversal for the father who is traditionally the family authority. Youth may lose respect for their elders because they are unable to assume the traditional roles or provide financial support. The impact on the family can be depression, alienation, family conflicts, and ATOD abuse.

- *Economic stress.*   Many immigrant Asian families are unable to support themselves financially owing to a lack of job skills, low English proficiency, and large family sizes. Several of these families are also supporting their extended family in their native countries, contributing to additional economic pressures and subsequently the risk of ATOD abuse.

Asian American mental health experts generally agree that Southeast Asian refugees are at the highest risk of these and other even more severe stressors (Fong, 1998). Van der Veer (1998) discusses the impact of refugees who experienced traumatization and uprooting. They have encountered repression, torture, violence, separation and loss, hardships, and exile. These experiences are so painful that the refugee is likely to suffer psychological dysfunction in both the short and long term. Symptoms of mental and emotional distress common among refugees include insomnia, eating disorders, moderate to severe depression, culture shock, and homesickness (Fong, 1998). Once refugees arrive in the United States, the new sources of stress that emerge are unemployment, underemployment, and poverty. The use of alcohol and drugs is seen as helpful for dealing with sadness and forgetting painful memories (Amodeo, Robb, Peou, & Tran, 1996).

Sue and Sue (1999) and Kitano and Maki (1996) propose three ways used by Asian Americans to adjust to the conflicts of acculturation. *Traditionalists* maintain loyalty to their ethnic group by retaining traditional values and living up to the expectations of the family. *Marginal persons* view their ethnicity as a handicap and attempt to become over-Westernized by rejecting traditional Asian values. This type of adjustment often leads to an identity crisis and a marginal existence, because these individuals cannot completely shed certain traditional ways. The third group, individuals who are attempting to develop a *new identity,* incorporate positive aspects of the Asian culture with the current situation. They have a need to attain self-pride by reversing the negatives of racism and discrimination in the United States. They may become politically or militantly involved to expose and change cultural racism in the United States.

Accurate assessment of an individual's acculturation level assists the therapist in data collection, analysis, interpretation, and determination of whether the client will return for future therapy (Sue & Sue, 1999). Understanding the culture of Asian Americans and potential adjustment problems is a necessary first step in providing sensitive interventions to facilitate a positive therapeutic experience.

Prevention and Intervention

The use of mental health services by Asian Americans remains quite low because of the stigma and shame of talking about one's problems (Fong, 1998; Zane & Kim, 1994). A report by the National Clearinghouse for Alcohol and Drug Information (1995) states that prevention and treatment programs for this population will be most effective if they reflect the values and norms of the population being served. To be successful, recovery programs for Asian Americans should address a variety of important issues: language, socioeconomic, cultural, and geographic barriers to treatment; status and length of time in the United States; and level of acculturation and assimilation into mainstream American culture. Addressing the following areas would lead to an increased possibility of successful treatment:

1. Acknowledge the diversity, including the conflicts, shared values, and attitudes, of the many cultures within the Asian/Pacific Islander American population.

2. Involve community members in treatment efforts whose voices command the respect of both parents and youth, such as elders, teachers, doctors, business leaders, community leaders, and youth role models.

3. Help recent immigrants adapt to the English language and American culture.

4. Acknowledge and respect prevention/healing practices of traditional cultures. Treatment should incorporate culturally based support systems in families and communities, as well as Eastern and Western wellness models.

5. Conduct outreach about important substance abuse treatment issues in newspapers, magazines, and media that provide information in Asian/Pacific Islander languages.

6. Provide education to young people on ethnic heritage and customs to promote positive cultural identity, self-esteem, and family communications. Education for parents on U.S. life and substance abuse issues will help them understand their children's acculturation and the stressors related to that process.

Sue and Sue (1999) recommend giving Asian/Pacific Islander clients an overview of the counseling process to familiarize them with roles and expectations. Chung et al. (1997) suggest the following guidelines for mental health professionals:

1. Use restraint when gathering information. Because of the stigma against mental illness, the therapist should refrain from asking too many personal questions during the initial session.

2. Do a thorough analysis of current environmental concerns, such as the need for food and shelter. Clients may need information on services that are available to them. Assess financial and social needs.

3. Assess clients' worldviews, the way they view the problem, and determine appropriate solutions.

4. Focus on the specific problem brought in by clients, and help them develop goals for treatment.

5. Take an active and directive role. Because of cultural expectations, clients will rely on the therapist to furnish direction.

6. In working with families, consider the intergenerational conflicts. Be willing to accept the hierarchical structure of the family.

7. Focus on concrete resolution of problems, and deal with the present or immediate future.

8. In the case of refugees, do a careful history and gather information on their family life in their home country, their escape, and how this was experienced. Also important to refugees are the adjustment to the new culture, their methods of coping, and any marital or family problems that have developed.

Undoubtedly, more research is needed to increase our understanding of the causes of ATOD use among various Asian/Pacific Islander groups and effective prevention and treatment approaches. Mental health professionals must educate themselves about cultural differences if they are to provide services to address the unique needs of this population. Amodeo et al. (1996) state that it will take time to develop effective models of treatment. These efforts will require the involvement of not only ATOD experts but also Asian/Pacific Islander agencies and community leaders in a process of exploration, experimentation, and evaluation.

AFRICAN AMERICANS

African Americans are currently the largest ethnic minority group in North America, constituting 12.8% of the total United States population. This percentage translates into approximately 34.2 million people of African descent in the United States today and is expected to reach 35.5 million by 2000 (U.S. Department of Commerce, 1997).

Wide gaps exist between African Americans and the general population in the arenas of education, employment, and income. According to the U.S. Bureau of the Census (1995), the poverty rate for African Americans remains nearly three times higher than that of white Americans (33.1% vs. 12.2%), with 26% of African American families with an income below the poverty level, and the unemployment rate is twice as high (11% vs. 5%). Their disadvantaged status, racism, and poverty contribute to the following statistics. Freeberg (1995) reported that a third of African American men in their twenties were in jail, on probation, or on parole; this rate increased by over 33% during a 5-year span. The life span of African Americans is 5 to 7 years shorter than that of white Americans (Felton, Parsons, Misener, & Oldaker, 1997).

Educationally, the opportunities for African American youths have yet to improve significantly, especially in urban areas (Exum, Moore, & Watt, 1999). A situation in the Oakland Unified School District illustrates many of the issues (Fields, 1997). There, African American students constitute approximately 53% of the student population and have the lowest grade point average, yet they represent 80% of all suspended students and 71% of all special education students. Currently, 64% of all students held back are African American. In Oakland middle schools, 56.3% of African American students had grade point averages below 2.0 versus 20.9% of white students. It has been suggested (Sue & Sue, 1999) that teachers are not sensitive to cultural differences, and the curriculum may also not be meaningful to the experiences of minority group children. Drug abuse may also contribute to the lack of achievement in African American children.

For many urban African American adolescents, life is complicated by problems, poverty, illiteracy, and racism (Sue & Sue, 1999). The homicide rate for African American youth between the ages of 15 and 24 was nearly 10 times that of white youth in 1989, their suicide rate increased to over twice that of other teenagers between 1980 and 1992, they are more likely to contract sexually transmitted diseases than other groups of teenagers, and unemployment can range from 37% to nearly 50% among African American teenagers (Harvey & Rauch, 1997).

The rate of illicit drug use for African Americans is 7.5% of the population. This usage rate remained somewhat higher than for whites (6.1%) and Hispanics (5.2%) in 1996 (SAMHSA, 1997). A study found that 27% of drug-related hospital emergency room visits occurred among African Americans (SAMHSA, 1997). One out of every 14 African American men is behind bars for a crime in which drugs or alcohol was involved (National Center on Addiction Substance Abuse, 1998).

Although these statistics are bleak, Ford (1997) concludes that much of our literature is based on individuals of the lower class who are on welfare or unemployed and not enough on other segments of the African American population. More than a third of African Americans are now middle-class or higher. They tend to be well educated, homeowners, and married (Hildebrand, Phenice, Gray, & Hines, 2000). The success of this portion of the population is not without frustrations, however. Sue and Sue (1999) note that many may feel bicultural stress. Middle-class African Americans can experience feelings of guilt for having made it, frustrations from the limitations of the "glass ceiling," and feelings of isolation.

Ford (1997) believes that middle- and upper-class African Americans may suffer a negative impact on mental health from issues such as believing a double standard exists (having to work twice as hard to succeed), feelings of isolation (being the only African American in an organization), powerlessness (given responsibility only on tasks pertaining to minorities), being an "expert" or "representative" on minority issues, and "survival guilt" in moving to a higher-class neighborhood. Because of this, middle- and upper-class African Americans may occupy a marginal status: not fully accepted by whites and rejected by African Americans (Sue & Sue, 1999).

Risk Factors

African Americans have been particularly vulnerable to the negative social and health consequences of substance abuse. According to Dawkins and Williams (1997), African Americans experience an earlier onset of alcoholism and other drug problems, a greater likelihood of being routed to the criminal justice system rather than to treatment for problems caused by substance abuse, and higher rates of illnesses, such as liver cirrhosis and esophageal cancer. Crack cocaine has compounded the problems associated with substance abuse in this population.

There is increasing concern that African Americans who are concentrated in urban environments may be at greater risk for the transmission of human immunodeficiency virus (HIV) infection due in part to the high level of intravenous heroin and cocaine use and the exchange of sexual favors for crack cocaine (Dawkins & Williams, 1997).

Exum et al. (1999) state that African Americans have historically been underserved by traditional counseling services. The reasons suggested for this gap in service are poverty, lack of accessible facilities, lack of awareness of service facilities or their purpose, and the absence of culturally acceptable treatment models.

Other problems that African Americans face that can lead to depression, substance use, and other mental health problems include the following (Baruth & Manning, 1999):

- Adverse effects of myths and stereotypes regarding the African American culture
- Historical and contemporary racism and discrimination
- Low self-esteem, confusion about cultural identity, and feelings of rejection from years of discrimination
- Lack of education
- Communication problems
- Differing cultural characteristics and customs
- Unequal employment and housing opportunities
- Underemployment, unemployment, and low socioeconomic status
- Increasing number of one-parent or female headed households
- Living in high-stress environments, such as low income, high rates of crime, high unemployment

Cultural Values

The African American family has been identified as having strengths that help overcome oppressive societal conditions and contribute to both family and community cohesiveness (Baruth & Manning, 1999; Hildebrand et al., 2000; McCollum, 1997; Stevenson, 1998). These strengths include (a) strong kinship bonds across a variety of households; (b) strong work, education, and achievement orientation; (c) a high level of flexibility in family roles; and (d) a strong commitment to religious values and church participation.

As a group, African Americans tend to be more group centered and sensitive to interpersonal matters and to stress community, cooperation, interdependence, and being one with nature (McCollum, 1997). In contrast, white middle-class values stress individuality, uniqueness, competition, and control over nature (Sue & Sue, 1999).

Sue and Sue (1999) note that many African Americans have an extended family network that provides emotional and economic support. Among families headed by females, the care of children is often undertaken by a large number of relatives, older children, and close friends. African American men and women value behaviors such as assertiveness, and within the family, men are more accepting of women's work and willing to share in the responsibilities traditionally assigned to women. Many African American families have instilled positive self-esteem in their children despite the problems with racism and prejudice.

Elderly persons are highly respected in the African American family. Vacc, DeVaney, and Wittmer (1995) emphasize the key roles elderly African Americans play within the family, church, and community. Younger family members experiencing difficulties are often referred to their grandparents for counsel. Many grandparents accept the responsibility for rearing their grandchildren while the parents work or acquire education. In addition, elderly African American family members play a significant role in passing on cultural values, customs, and traditions to their children.

Spirituality and religion are essential elements of the African American way of life. According to Exum et al. (1999), African American churches have always been more than houses of worship, and the African American minister has been more than a preacher. The church has historically served as a spiritual, intellectual, and political arena for the African American community, and the ministers have traditionally served as teachers, counselors, and political activists. The churches are agents for transmitting traditional values, strengthening family ties, and providing opportunities to learn about their ancestry.

Barriers to Treatment

African Americans who seek treatment are often thought to have a negative view of mental health services. Some may have a historical hostility response because of their prolonged inferior treatment in American society (Vontress & Epp, 1997). Brown, Lipford-Sanders, and Shaw (1995) contend that African Americans underuse counseling services because they perceive counselors as insensitive to their needs, believe that counselors fail to provide equal energy and time working with underrepresented groups, and feel that counselors do not accept, understand, or respect cultural differences.

Counselors also need to understand that African Americans often rely heavily on their church for help (Baruth & Manning, 1999). Mental health professionals are becoming increasingly open to the advantages of religious involvement and how a strong spiritual base can support resilience to life's problems (Hines & Boyd-Franklin, 1996).

Other barriers that contribute to underusing mental health services for the African American community include (a) the lack of a historical perspective on the development of the family and support systems within the African American community, (b) a lack of awareness and understanding of the unique characteristics of the value systems of African American families, and (c) communication barriers that hinder the development of trust between the African American client and the non-African therapist (Baruth & Manning, 1999; Sue & Sue, 1999).

Prevention and Intervention

The key to prevention with African Americans is complex and yet practical if strategies are developed to meet individual, family, and community needs. Mental health professionals must be capable of analyzing adaptive behavior patterns, the cultural rituals of alcohol and drug use, and the specific sociopolitical influences of substance abuse with African Americans (Carter & Rogers, 1996). The counselor's process, goals, and expectations should fit the worldview of the African American client.

Because of past experiences with racism and prejudice, African American clients are often distrustful of white counselors. Sue and Sue (1999) note that to make headway, the therapist must establish a trusting relationship. African American clients are especially sensitive to interpersonal processes and will test the relationship. They may directly challenge the therapist's values and qualifications or act in a very guarded and aloof manner. These behaviors are part of a protective mechanism. A relationship may develop if the counselor can respond in a straightforward manner. Self-disclosure is very difficult for many African American clients since it leaves them vulnerable to racism.

African Americans have traditionally relied on the support of the family, church, and the community (SAMHSA, 1997). Culturally sensitive and relevant treatment programs and materials specifically targeting African Americans are essential to successful programs. Aponte, Rivers, and Wohl (1995) support the inclusion of the family in the treatment process to explore the sources of strength. Spirituality is also recognized as a tool in the treatment of African Americans. A strong spiritual leader may be included as reflective of the community culture.

In working with African American youth and adults, Sue and Sue (1999) suggest the following:

1. It is often beneficial to bring up the client's reaction to a counselor of a different ethnic background.
2. If the client was referred, determine the feelings about counseling and how it can be made useful.
3. Identify the expectations and worldview of the African American client. Determine how the individual views the problem and the possible solutions.
4. Establish an egalitarian relationship. Most African Americans tend to establish a personal commonality with the counselor.

5. Determine how the client has responded to discrimination and racism in both unhealthy and healthy ways. Also examine issues around racial identity.

6. Assess the positive assets of the client, such as family, community resources, and church.

7. Determine the external factors that might be related to the presenting problem. This may involve contact with outside agencies for assistance.

8. Help the client define goals and appropriate means of attaining them. Assess ways in which the client, family members, and friends handled their problems successfully.

HISPANICS

The term *Hispanic* was generated as a U.S. government catch phrase to conveniently classify different subgroups and subcultures of people who are of Cuban, Mexican, Puerto Rican, and South or Central American descent (Gloria & Peregoy, 1996). While Hispanics do have much in common (language; religion; customs; and attitudes toward self, family, and community), the subgroups have considerable variation in ethnic origins, socioeconomic groups, dialects, immigration status, and histories (Chilman, 1993; Sue & Sue, 1999). The U.S. Bureau of the Census (1995) reported 22.8 million Hispanics in the United States. "Two thirds of the population are of Mexican descent, 10.5% from Puerto Rico, 4.8% Cuban, and about 13.6% from Latin countries" (Sue & Sue, 1999, p. 287). These numbers reflect a population increase of 65% since the 1980 census. This increase has been attributed to both immigration and high fertility rates. The census data do not reflect undocumented Hispanics who choose to "pass" because of fear of deportation or for economic, political, or personal reasons (Goffman, 1963).

The SAMHSA's (1998) report entitled *Prevalence of Substance Use among Racial and Ethnic Subgroups in the United States 1991-1993* notes that this was the first report on national estimates of illicit drug use and alcohol abuse/dependence. Prior to this publication, little information on substance abuse and Hispanics was available. What did exist failed to delineate differences among the various Hispanic subgroups. Earlier, generalizations did emerge that Hispanics were more likely to use drugs than other groups. The most recent information, however, indicates that although portions of the Hispanic community have been affected by serious drug problems, the Hispanic population as a whole is not more likely to use drugs than other groups. Variability among the seven Hispanic American subgroups was significant for substance use, alcohol dependence, and the need for illicit drug abuse treatment. Mexican Americans and Puerto Ricans exhibited higher prevalence of illicit drug use (including marijuana and cocaine), heavy alcohol use/dependence, and the need for illicit drug use treatment. Caribbean Americans, Central Americans, and Cuban Americans, however, showed lower prevalence. South Americans and other Hispanics reported prevalence close to the total population (SAMHSA, 1998). Many of the factors associated with substance abuse among other oppressed minority groups in the United States appear to operate for Hispanics as well (Felix-Ortiz, Fernandez, & Newcomb, 1998).

Research has shown that Hispanics suffer the full impact of the "culture of poverty," which has been described as living under the impact of multiple oppressions. These factors include low income, unemployment, underemployment, undereducation, poor housing, prejudice, discrimination, and cultural/linguistic barriers. In addition to the stress of the culture of poverty, many Hispanics also experience acculturation stress. The intergenerational transition from one's culture of origin to the development of bicultural abilities places stress and strain on the individual and the family system (Castro & Guitierres, 1997).

Gloria (1993) points out one pattern of acculturation known as *cultural shift,* whereby an individual substitutes one set of practices with alternative cultural characteristics. Generally, this shift occurs out of the necessity to acculturate to the dominant society and is an act of survival rather than choice. A dramatic point of stress in the acculturational process is a shift from a culture that values family unity and subordination of the individual to the welfare of the group to a highly individualistic culture predominant in U.S. society (Smart & Smart, 1994). If substance abuse is used to cope with stress, then levels of drug use will vary depending on the level of acculturation (Castro & Guitierres, 1997).

Cultural Values

Discord and family disruption have been identified as an antecedent of substance use and abuse among Hispanic adolescents and young adults (Gloria & Peregoy, 1996; Szapocznik & Kurtines, 1993). To gain insight into the Hispanic individual, investigation of *la familia* is paramount, because the family is the basis of Hispanic cultures. Often divided by generation, the immigrant's status tends to guide the adherence to the values and mores of one's culture of origin. The difference between the cultural orientation of the family and the cultural identity of the child may cause intergenerational conflicts. For example, immigrant families tend to develop a family struggle in which younger members struggle for autonomy (i.e., American value) and the older family members struggle for connectedness (i.e., Hispanic value) (Felix-Ortiz et al., 1998; Gloria & Peregoy, 1996).

The acculturation process can produce tremendous amounts of stress for the individual and place dramatic strains on the family system. Those who have immigrated alone, leaving behind their extended family support system, face the potential of adjustment problems (Nyamathi & Vasquez, 1995).

Hispanics underuse mental health services and tend to terminate therapy after one contact at a rate of more than 50% (Atkinson, Morten, & Sue, 1993; Gonzalez, 1997). Sue and Sue (1999) suggest that ineffective and inappropriate counseling approaches to the values held by this group are often reasons for early termination. Certain unifying cultural values distinguish Hispanics from the dominant culture (Gloria & Peregoy, 1996). An increased awareness of the cultural concepts can foster a positive therapeutic experience for the Hispanic client.

Gloria and Peregoy (1996) state that the Hispanic family provides support, identity, and security for its members. The strong sense of obligation ensures that the family's needs as a unit supersede individual needs. Sue and Sue (1999) note that children are expected to be obedient and are not generally consulted on family decisions, and adolescents are expected to take responsibility for younger siblings at an early age.

The Hispanic nuclear family is embedded in the extended family consisting of aunts, uncles, grandparents, cousins, godparents, and lifelong friends. During times of crisis, the family is the first resource for advice before help is sought from others. The downside, however, is that the extended family system can serve as a stressor due to the emotional involvement and obligations with a large number of family and friends (Sue & Sue, 1999). Nonetheless, this strong tie highlights the importance of enlisting the family in therapy (Gloria & Peregoy, 1996).

The cultural value of personalism defines an individual's self-worth and dignity from inner qualities that give self-respect. The Hispanic culture values the uniqueness of inner qualities that constitute personal dignity. This sense of self-respect, self-worth, and dignity in oneself and others demands showing and receiving proper respect. A therapist that conveys personalism develops trust and obligation with the Hispanic client (Gloria & Peregoy, 1996).

Sex-role norms and hierarchy within the family unit continue to influence both Hispanic men and women; however, acculturation and urbanization appear to be affecting both of these standards. Traditionally, males are expected to be strong and dominant providers, while females are more nurturant, self-sacrificing, and submissive to males. Some Hispanic women are more modern in their views of education and work but remain traditional in their personal relationships (Sue & Sue, 1999).

In addition to sex roles, a hierarchy of leadership and authority is related to gender and generation. The father's role is one of superior authority, and the mother's role can be viewed as the center of the family and purveyor of culture. "Although the father is seen by himself and others as the family leader who has power, the culture also includes a strong sense of related parental responsibility" (Chilman, as cited in McAdoo, 1993, p. 153). Roles appear to include egalitarian decision making and indirect assertion by women, which may serve to preserve the appearance of male control (Hayes, 1997). Children are expected to obey their parents, and younger children are expected to obey older siblings who are role models (Chilman, 1993). Understanding the roles and hierarchy of each Hispanic family is vital in assisting with problem solving, renegotiation, and redefinition of power relationships (Gonzalez, 1997; Hayes, 1997).

Spiritual values and the importance of religion can be a strong influence on the behavior of Hispanics (Atkinson et al., 1993). Spiritualism assumes an invisible world of good and evil spirits who influence behavior. The spirits can protect or cause illness, so an individual is expected to do charitable deeds to be protected by the good spirits (Gloria & Peregoy, 1996).

Catholicism is the primary religion for Hispanics. Traditional adherence to the religious values of enduring suffering and self-denial may prevent some Hispanics from seeking mental health treatment. Catholicism, like many other religions, has powerful moral and social influences on day-to-day living (Gloria & Peregoy, 1996).

According to Gloria and Peregoy, religion and shared spiritual beliefs and practices are built on the idea of natural and supernatural forces that link an individual to a greater power. The three main healing/spiritual systems among Hispanics in the United States include *Curanderismo* (Mexican American indigenous healers), *Espiritismo* (Puerto Rican), and *Santeria (*Cuban). Under each of these systems, life is governed by thoughts, intentions, and behaviors. Harmony is a unifying balance; failure to follow prescribed rules of belief can lead to imbalance and stress, including suffering, sickness and bad fortune (Koss-Chioino, 1995). Therapy can be augmented by enlisting other support systems, such as the church or folk healers (*curanderos/-as*). The reader is cautioned that when working with indigenous healers, traditional healing practices need to be understood. For example, *curanderas* on the California-Mexico border were prescribing dried rattlesnake meat for HIV-positive clients. Many of these clients contracted salmonella poisoning as a result (Peregoy, 1991).

Barriers to Treatment

Barriers to treatment for Hispanic groups include the disproportionate number of Hispanics enrolled in programs that emphasize pharmacological treatment rather than psychological treatment (Caetano, 1989). This barrier may be due to the economics of treatment costs or the failure of treatment programs to operate effectively across cultural milieus. The inability of service agencies to respond to the needs of Hispanics is the result of several factors.

First, cross-cultural counseling has been recognized as a viable force in the mental health field (Pedersen, 1991). The responsibility of this approach requires that mental health professionals be familiar with standard models of treatment in the field and that these models be analyzed as to how they may complement or belittle cultural beliefs and perspectives. These perspectives would include, for example, the view of alcoholism as a disease as well as the belief that an individual who abuses it is morally weak. The latter view is not consistent with the disease model of alcoholism but is a common perspective among Hispanics. Moreover, cultural perspectives, across and within groups, and gender role expectations need to be understood. The perspective in some Hispanic cultures that alcohol use/abuse for men maintains a romantic element puts abuse in a different light within a cultural lens (Gloria & Peregoy, 1996; Marin & Marin, 1997).

Cultural perspectives such as this one have implications for service delivery at all levels. As an example, working with a self-referred Hispanic male who believes these cultural values, the mental health worker may need to help him work through the shame of being morally weak within a traditional concept of machismo. In addition, an understanding of the meaning of substance abuse behaviors and their social contexts may produce an awareness of how competing values cause stress and influence substance abuse coping responses. Bilingual language ability and bicultural skills have been identified as essential elements in the provision of services to Hispanic groups, which, until the early 1980s, were vastly underrepresented in service delivery (Glick & Moore, 1990; Sue & Sue, 1999). These factors have continued to affect program service delivery. This problem speaks to the need for training programs to actively recruit and train Hispanics into the human services professions.

Immigrant legal status can also be a barrier if individuals have entered the country illegally. These individuals may not seek assistance owing to fear of deportation. This group may be at particular risk for substance abuse, especially if they do not have well-developed support systems in place (Pearson, 1990). Research-based investigation into risk factors and conceptual models of alcohol and other drug use can also act as barriers when they are based on faulty assumptions. One example of this type of barrier can be found in research that was limited to a single model. This model paralleled an early drinking model developed for African Americans (by non-African researchers) that focused on heavy drinking and alcohol problems as a product of anomie or deprivation (Caetano, 1989). Caetano (1989, 1990) has argued that the issues concerning Hispanic drinking behaviors are more complex than earlier models would indicate. When considering Hispanic substance abuse behaviors together with the effect of ethnic minority status and stresses of recent immigration to the United States, the earlier models are not sufficient to explain substance abuse behaviors of Hispanics. Acculturational stress, socioeconomic status (SES) and poverty, role strain and conflict, unemployment, and discrimination are all factors that play into drug use and abuse (Robinson & Howard-Hamilton, 2000).

Current research findings provide a better perspective on substance use patterns based on gender and age among Hispanic populations. Hispanic men are more likely to use the drugs previously mentioned than Hispanic women. Data also reveal sex differences in use and experimentation at age 35 with substance use among Hispanic populations, with males more likely to use and experiment with substances than females. One hypothesis that may contribute to this difference of use in age and sex is that older cohorts were probably raised with stronger traditional norms discouraging drug use among women, while those in younger cohorts appear to be experimenting and using at higher rates (Felix-Ortiz et al., 1998). Other possible explanations may be the level of acculturation or, for younger Hispanics, the influence of peer pressure combined with stages of development.

Contrary to popular myth, data on national drug use patterns indicate whites have the highest lifetime use of cigarettes, alcohol, hallucinogens, and stimulants, regardless of age (Rouse, 1995). Another study also revealed differences among subgroups of Hispanics. For example, Puerto Ricans between the ages of 18 and 34 had the highest rates of lifetime drug use (Booth, Castro, & Anglin, 1990). Puerto Ricans reported greater use of cocaine than whites, African Americans, or any other Hispanic subgroup. It has been documented that inhalant use is much lower among Hispanic populations than current stereotypes would suggest (Rouse, 1995). From these differences it is hypothesized that subcultural experiences may be critical to substance use and that SES and level of urbanization may be causal factors related to abuse and lifetime prevalence. It is important to note that this study did not control for differences in SES or social class that have been implicated in affecting differences in survey research. Acculturation, too, is important in assessing abuse patterns. Acculturation levels have been associated with greater lifetime rates of substance use.

Prevention and Intervention

With the dearth of research on treatment for Hispanics in general and even less known about long-term effects of intervention, the following recommendations are drawn from the literature and presented as a guide. Prevention and intervention with Hispanic groups need to be culturally sensitive to the individual client's life circumstances, including the level of acculturation, availability of natural support systems, and environmental conditions. In addition, mental health professionals working with Hispanic populations need to incorporate into the counseling process such cultural concepts as *confianza* (trust), *dignidad* (dignity), and *respeto* (respect); current time orientation; preference for action-oriented advice; and the belief that human beings are at the mercy of supernatural forces (Cuadrado & Lieberman, 1998; Gloria & Peregoy, 1996).

Primary prevention programming can use characteristics of Hispanic communities such as strong family units and extended family ties to support efforts aimed at adolescents and adults. Programming that addresses anticipated stressors or themes of conflict and that focus on strengths and skills for optimum functioning will enable individuals to combat potential negative effects of acculturational stressors. Peer pressure has been cited as a strong factor in substance abuse (Castro & Guitierres, 1997). Community and school programming that focuses on leadership skills and problem solving can be helpful if they are continuous and provide consistent opportunities for youth to explore their own creativity. In rural areas it has been suggested that community-based approaches should focus on educational systems (Castro & Guitierres, 1997).

CONCLUSION

Four themes emerge from the selected groups presented in this chapter. The first is the broad effect of stressors—environmental, social, and cultural—on, among, and within group interactions. This theme challenges us as mental health workers to expand our understanding of the interplay of populations outside the mainstream, with those who have full participation within the mainstream.

The second theme can be summed up as perception, which is influenced by culture. This theme requires investigation into cultural and environmental conditions as they relate to community perceptions of alcohol and other drug behaviors. The question that arises from this theme is how to mobilize a community against the detrimental affects of substance abuse behaviors, within a culturally relevant and meaningful approach.

The third theme speaks to acculturation and identity development. All the groups presented in this chapter, at some level, need to learn to cope with the development of bicultural skills. We believe that the learning of bicultural skills and the appreciation of diversity are not only the responsibility of selected populations but rather the necessary responsibility of us all.

Finally, the fourth theme to emerge is the multiplicity in ways of knowing, which are influenced by society, culture, socioeconomic status, age, and cultural, social, and gender identity development.

All these themes speak to the need of mental health workers to challenge their perspective of the world and develop an awareness of how one perceives culturally different clients. In developing this awareness, counselors need to gain an understanding of the history and background of their clients to address their issues within the context in which they are presented. By doing so, they will not only serve their clients needs more fully but also empower them within the process.

REFERENCES

Abbott, P. J. (1996). American Indian and Alaska Native aboriginal use of alcohol in the United States. *Journal of American Indian and Alaskan Native Mental Health Research, 7*(2), 1–13.

Abbott, P. J. (1998). Traditional and Western healing practices for alcoholism in American Indians and Alaskan Natives. *Substance Use and Misuse, 33*(13), 2605–2646.

Amodeo, M., Robb, N., Peou, S., & Tran, H. (1996). Adapting mainstream substance-abuse interventions for southeast Asian clients. *Families in Society: The Journal of Contemporary Human Services, 64,* 403–412.

Aponte, J. F., Rivers, R. Y., & Wohl, J. (1995). *Psychological interventions and cultural diversity.* Boston: Allyn & Bacon.

Atkinson, D., Morten, G., & Sue, D. W. (1993). *Counseling American minorities: A cross cultural perspective.* Madison, WI: Brown & Benchmark.

Axelson, J. A. (1999). *Counseling and development in a multicultural society.* Pacific Grove, CA: Brooks/Cole.

Barker, J. C., & Kramer, J. B. (1996). Alcohol consumption among older urban American Indians. *Journal of Studies of Alcohol, 57,* 119–124.

Baruth, L. G., & Manning, M. L. (1999). *Multicultural counseling and psychotherapy: A lifespan perspective* (2nd ed.). Upper Saddle River, NJ: Merrill/Prentice Hall.

Beauvais, F., Chavez, E. L., Oetting, E. R., Deffenbacher, J. L., & Cornell, G. R. (1996). Drug use, violence, and victimization among White American, Mexican American, and American Indian dropouts, students with academic problems, and students in good academic standing. *Journal of Counseling Psychology, 43,* 292–299.

Berry, J. W., Minde, T., & Mok, D. (1987). Comparative studies of acculturative stress. *International Migration Review, 21,* 491–511.

Booth, M. W., Castro, F. G., & Anglin, M. D. (1990). What do we know about Hispanic substance abuse? In R. Glick & J. Moore (Eds.), *Drugs in Hispanic communities* (pp. 21–44). New Brunswick, NJ: Rutgers University Press.

Braroe, M. W. (1988). *Indian and White: Self-image and interaction in a Canadian plains community.* Stanford, CA: Stanford University Press.

Brown, S. P., Lipford-Sanders, J., & Shaw, M. (1995). Kujichagulia—Uncovering the secrets of the heart: Group work with African American women on predominately White campuses. *Journal for Specialists in Group Work, 20,* 151–158.

Caetano, R. (1989). Concepts of alcoholism among Whites, Blacks, and Hispanic populations. *Journal of Studies on Alcohol, 50*(6), 580–582.

Caetano, R. (1990). Hispanic drinking in the U.S.: Thinking in new directions. *Journal of Addiction, 85,* 1231–1236.

Carter, J. H., & Rogers, C. (1996). Alcoholism and African-American women: A medical sociocultural perspective. *Journal of the National Medical Association, 88,* 81–86.

Castro, F. G., & Guitierres, S. (1997). Drug and alcohol use among rural Mexican-Americans. In E. B. Robertson, Z. Sloboda, G. M. Boyd, L. Beatty, & N. J. Kozel (Eds.), *Rural substance abuse: State of knowledge and issues.* NIDA Research Monograph 168. Washington, DC: U.S. Department of Health and Human Services.

Chilman, C. S. (1993). Hispanic families in the United States: Research perspectives. In H. P. McAdoo (Ed.), *Family ethnicity: Strength in diversity* (pp. 141–163). Newbury Park, CA: Sage.

Chung, R. C.-Y., Bemak, F., & Okazaki, S. (1997). Counseling Americans of Southeast Asian descent. In C. C. Lee (Ed.), *Multicultural issues in counseling* (2nd ed., pp. 207–231). Alexandria, VA: American Counseling Association.

Courtney, R. (1986). Islands of remorse: Amerindian education in a contemporary world. *Curriculum Inquiry, 16*(1), 43–64.

Cuadrado, M., & Lieberman, L. (1998). Traditionalism in prevention of substance misuse among Puerto Ricans. *Substance Abuse & Misuse, 33*(14), 2737–2755.

Dawkins, M. P., & Williams, M. M. (1997). Substance abuse in rural African American populations: Rural substance abuse. In E. B. Robertson, Z. Sloboda, G. M. Boyd, L. Beatty, & N. J. Kozel (Eds.), *Rural substance abuse: State of knowledge and issues.* NIDA Research Monograph 168. Washington, DC: U.S. Department of Health and Human Services.

EchoHawk, M. (1997) Suicide: The scourge of Native American people. *Suicide and Life Threatening Behavior, 27,* 60–67.

Exum, H. A., Moore, Q. L., & Watt, S. K. (1999). Transcultural counseling for African Americans revisited. In J. McFadden (Ed.), *Transcultural counseling* (2nd ed., pp. 171–219). Alexandria, VA: American Counseling Association.

Felix-Ortiz, M., Fernandez, A., & Newcomb, M. D. (1998). The role of intergenerational discrepancy of cultural orientation in drug use among Latina adolescents. *Substance Abuse & Misuse, 33*(4), 967–994.

Felton, G. M., Parsons, M. A., Misener, T. R., & Oldaker, S. (1997). Health promoting behavior of black and white college women. *Western Journal of Nursing Research, 19,* 654–664.

Fields, C. D. (1997). Ebonics 101: What have we learned? *Black Issues in Higher Education, 13,* 19–28.

Flemming, C. M. (1992). Next twenty years of prevention in Indian country. *Journal of American Indian and Alaskan Native Mental Health Research, 4*(3), 85–88.

Fong, T. P. (1998). *The contemporary Asian American experience: Beyond the model minority.* Upper Saddle River, NJ: Prentice Hall.

Ford, D. Y. (1997). Counseling middle-class African Americans. In C. C. Lee (Ed.), *Multicultural issues in counseling* (2nd ed., pp. 81–108). Alexandria, VA: American Counseling Association.

Freeberg, L. (1995, October 5). 1 of 3 Blacks in 20s has had trouble with law. *Seattle Post-Intelligencer,* pp. A1, A8.

Glick, R., & Moore, J. (1990). *Drugs in Hispanic communities.* New Brunswick, NJ: Rutgers University Press.

Gloria, A. M. (1993). *Psychosocial factors influencing the academic persistence of Chicano/a undergraduates.* Unpublished doctoral dissertation, Arizona State University, Tempe.

Gloria, A. M., & Peregoy, J. J. (1996). Counseling Latino alcohol and other substance users/abusers: Cultural considerations for counselors. *Journal for Substance Abuse Treatment, 13*(2), 1–8.

Goffman, E. (1963). *Stigma: Notes on the management of a spoiled identity.* Upper Saddle River, NJ: Prentice Hall.

Gonzalez, G. M. (1997). The emergence of Chicanos in the 21st century: Implications for counseling, research, and policy. *Journal of Multicultural Counseling and Development, 25*(2), 94–106.

Greenfield, L. A., & Smith, S. K. (1999, February). American Indians and crime. Washington, DC: U.S. Department of Justice.

Harvey, A. R., & Rauch, J. B. (1997). A comprehensive Afrocentric rites of passage program for Black male adolescents. *Health and Social Work, 22,* 32–37.

Hayes, L. L. (1997, August). The unique counseling needs of Latino clients. *Counseling Today*, pp. 1, 10.

Hayne, B. (1993, September). An eagle's view: Sharing successful American Indian/Alaskan Native alcohol and other drug prevention. N.p.: Northwest Regional Laboratory, Western Regional Center for Drug-Free Schools and Communities.

Hayne, B. (1994, September). *An eagle's view. Vol. II: Sharing successful American Indian/Alaskan Native alcohol and other drug prevention.* N.p.: Northwest Regional Laboratory, Western Regional Center for Drug-Free Schools and Communities.

Hildebrand, V., Phenice, L. A., Gray, M. M., & Hines, R. P. (2000). *Knowing and serving diverse families* (2nd ed.). Upper Saddle River, NJ: Merrill/Prentice Hall.

Hines, P. M., & Boyd-Franklin, N. (1996). African American families. In M. McGoldrick, J. Giordano, & J. K. Pearce (Eds.), *Ethnicity and family therapy* (2nd ed., pp. 66–84). New York: Guilford.

Ho, M. K. (1994). Asian American perspective. In J. U. Gordon (Ed.), *Managing multiculturalism in substance abuse services* (pp. 72–98). Thousand Oaks, CA: Sage.

Indian Health Service. (1996). *Trends in Indian Health—1996.* Washington DC: U.S. Department of Health and Human Services, Public Health Service.

Indian Health Service. (1997). *Trends in Indian Health—1997.* Washington DC: U.S. Department of Health and Human Services, Public Health Service.

Johnson, D. (1994). Stress, depression, substance abuse, and racism. *Journal of American Indian and Alaskan Native Mental Health Research, 6*(1), 29–33.

Kim, S., Coletti, S. D., Williams, C., & Hepler, N. A. (1995). Substance abuse prevention involving Asian/Pacific Islander American communities. In G. J. Botvin, S. Schinke, & M. A. Orlandi (Eds.), *Drug abuse prevention with multiethnic youth* (pp. 295–326). Thousand Oaks, CA: Sage.

Kitano, H. H. L., & Maki, M. T. (1996). Continuity, change, and diversity: Counseling Asian Americans. In P. B. Pedersen, J. G. Draguns, W. J. Lonner, & J. E. Trimble (Eds.), *Counseling across cultures* (4th ed., pp. 124–145). Thousand Oaks, CA: Sage.

Koss-Chioino, J. D. (1995). Traditional and folk approaches among ethnic minorities. In J. F. Aponte, R. Y. Rivers, & J. Wohl (Eds.), *Psychological interventions and cultural diversity* (pp. 145–163). Boston: Allyn & Bacon.

Lujan, C. C. (1992). An emphasis on solutions rather than problems. *Journal of American Indian and Alaskan Native Mental Health Research, 4*(3), 101–104.

Mail, P. D. (1989). American Indians, stress, and alcohol. *Journal of American Indian and Alaskan Native Mental Health Research, 3*(2), 21–32.

Marin, G., & Marin, M. A. (1997). Differential perceptions of drinkers of alcoholic beverages by Mexican-Americans and non-Hispanic Whites. *Substance Abuse & Misuse, 32*(10), 1369-1384.

May, P. A. (1992). Alcohol policy considerations for Indian reservations and border towns. *Journal of American Indian and Alaskan Native Mental Health Research, 4*(3), 5-59.

May, P. A. (1994). The epidemiology of alcohol abuse among American Indians: The mythical and real properties. *American Indian Culture and Research Journal, 18*(2), 121-143.

McCollum, V. J. C. (1997). Evolution of the African American family personality: Considerations for family therapy. *Journal of Multicultural Counseling and Development, 25,* 219–229.

National Center on Addiction Substance Abuse. (1998). *Behind bars: Substance abuse and America's prison population.* New York: Columbia University Press.

National Clearinghouse for Alcohol and Drug Information. (1995). *Making prevention work.* Rockville, MD: Author.

National Institute on Drug Abuse. (1995). *Promoting addiction treatment to diverse populations:*

Asian/Pacific Islander Americans. Rockville, MD: U.S. Government Printing Office.

Neligh, G. (1990). Mental health programs for American Indians: Their logic, structure and function. *Journal of the National Center of American Indian and Alaskan Native Mental Health Research Monograph, 3*(3).

Nyamathi, A., & Vasquez, R. (1995). Impact of poverty, homelessness, and drugs. In A. M. Padilla (Ed.), *Hispanic psychology: Critical issues in theory and research* (pp. 213–230). Thousand Oaks, CA: Sage.

Pavel, D. M., Skinner, R. R., Calahan, M., Tippeconic, J., & Stein, W. (1998, October). *American Indians and Alaskan Natives in postsecondary education.* U.S. Department of Education, Office of Educational Research and Improvement. Washington, DC: U.S. Government Printing Office.

Pearson, R. E. (1990). *Counseling and social support: Perspectives and practice.* Newbury Park, CA: Sage.

Pedersen, P. B. (1991). Special issue: Multiculturalism as a fourth force in counseling. *Journal of Counseling and Development, 70*(1), 4–251.

Peregoy, J. J. (1991). *Stress and the sheepskin: An exploration of the Indian/Native perspective in college.* Unpublished doctoral dissertation, Syracuse University, Syracuse, NY.

Peregoy, J. J. (1999). Revisiting transcultural counseling with American Indians/Alaskan Natives: Issues for consideration. In J. McFadden (Ed.), *Transcultural counseling* (2nd ed., pp. 137–170). Alexandria, VA: American Counseling Association.

Robbins, M. L. (1994). Native American perspective. In J. U. Gordon (Ed.), *Managing multiculturalism in substance abuse services* (pp. 148–176). Thousand Oaks, CA: Sage.

Robinson, T. L., & Howard-Hamilton, M. F. (2000). *The convergence of race, ethnicity, and gender: Multiple identities in counseling.* Upper Saddle River, NJ: Merrill/Prentice Hall.

Rouse, B. A. (Ed.). (1995). *Substance abuse and mental health statistics sourcebook.* Office of Applied Studies, Substance Abuse and Mental Health Services Administration, Public Health Service, U.S. Department of Health and Human Services. Washington, DC: U.S. Government Printing Office.

Sandhu, D. S. (1997). Psychocultural profiles of Asian and Pacific Islander Americans: Implications for counseling and psychotherapy. *Journal of Multicultural Counseling and Development, 25,* 7–22.

Smart, J. F., & Smart, D. W. (1994). The rehabilitation of Hispanics experiencing acculturative stress: Implications for practice. *Journal of Rehabilitation, 60*(4), 8–12.

Stevenson, H. C. (1998). Theoretical considerations in measuring racial identity and socialization: Extending the self further. In R. L. Jones (Ed.), *African American identity development* (pp. 217–253). Hampton, VA: Cobb & Henry.

Substance Abuse and Mental Health Services Administration. (1997). *Promoting addiction treatment to diverse populations: African Americans.* Washington, DC: National Clearinghouse for Alcohol and Drug Information.

Substance Abuse and Mental Health Services Administration. (1998). *Disparity reported in substance use among racial/ethnic subgroups.* Washington, DC: National Clearinghouse for Alcohol and Drug Information.

Sue, D. W., & Sue, D. (1999). *Counseling the culturally different: Theory and practice.* New York: Wiley.

Szapocznik, J., & Kurtines, W. M. (1993). Family psychology and cultural diversity: Opportunities for theory, research, and application. *American Psychologist, 48,* 400–407.

Trimble, J. E., Flemming, C. M., Beauvais, F., & Jumper-Thurman, P. (1996). Providing services for Native American Indians. In P. B. Pedersen, J. G. Draguns, W. J. Lonner, & J. E. Trimble (Eds.), *Counseling across cultures* (4th ed., pp. 177–209). Thousand Oaks, CA: Sage.

Uba, L. (1994). *Asian Americans: Personality patterns, identity, and mental health.* New York: Guilford.

U.S. Bureau of the Census. (1995). *Population profile of the United States.* Washington, DC: U.S. Government Printing Office.

U.S. Department of Commerce. (1997). *The Black population in the United States: Current population reports*. P20-508. Washington, DC: U.S. Bureau of the Census.

Vacc, N. A., DeVaney, S. B., & Wittmer, J. (1995). *Experiencing and counseling multicultural and diverse populations*. Bristol, PA: Accelerated Development.

van der Veer, G. (1998). *Counseling and therapy with refugees and victims of trauma*. New York: Wiley.

Vontress, C. E., & Epp, L. R. (1997). Historical hostility in the African American client: Implications for counseling. *Journal of Multicultural Counseling and Development, 25*, 170–184.

Wentao, J., Salomon, H. D., & Chay, D. M. (1999). Transcultural counseling and people of Asian origin: A developmental and therapeutic perspective. In J. McFadden (Ed.), *Transcultural counseling* (2nd ed., pp. 258–281). Alexandria, VA: American Counseling Association.

Zane, N., & Kim, J. H. (1994). Substance use and abuse. In N. W. S. Zane, D. T. Takeuchi, & K. N. J. Young (Eds.), *Confronting critical health issues of Asian and Pacific Islander Americans* (pp. 316–343). Thousand Oaks, CA: Sage.

Maintaining Behavior Change: Relapse Prevention Strategies

10

PATRICIA STEVENS, PH.D.

Individuals involved in recovery and the treatment of recovering individuals recognize that maintaining sobriety is perhaps the most difficult aspect of recovery. There is a high degree of consensus in the field that relapse is a common element in the recovery process. Some believe that the "most common treatment outcome for alcoholics and addicts is relapse" (Dimeff & Marlatt, 1995, p. 176). It is interesting to note, however, that, until recently, relapse and relapse prevention have had little research and even less attention in most treatment programs.

The meaning of a relapse has changed over the years. Relapse was originally seen as a failure of the individual in recovery. According to Alcoholics Anonymous (AA), when individuals relapse, they revert to a preabstinence level of abuse/dependency and must begin the process of recovery from the beginning. As other concepts of both etiology and maintenance of dependency have developed, the view of relapse has also changed. Many now view relapse as a normal part of the recovery process and as a learning experience for the recovering individual. In fact, after treatment most individuals still use substances on an episodic basis (DeJong, 1994). The first 90 days after treatment appear to be when clients are the most vulnerable to relapse. Clients have not developed strong coping skills this early in the process and therefore tend to be unable to make healthy decisions in regard to their life choices (DeJong, 1994; Dimeff & Marlatt, 1995; Doweiko, 1999).

Currently, *recovery* is defined not only as abstinence from mind-altering chemicals or nonproductive compulsive behaviors but also changes in physical, psychological, social, familial, and spiritual areas of functioning. These changes are a process and not an event in the recovering individual's life. It is generally accepted that the dynamics that enable an individual to maintain sobriety are as different as the factors that initiate sobriety (Buelow & Buelow, 1998). Just as there are differences in individuals in the treatment process, there are differences in individuals in the recovery process. The stage of recovery as well as unique individual differences both play a part in the process.

Some important factors in this process are (a) the length and severity of their abuse/dependency; (b) gender and ethnicity; (c) the perception of the problem; (d) the motivation to change; (e) the availability of support systems, both professional and nonprofessional; and (f) the degree of damage in each aspect of the individual's life (Daley, 1988). A recovery plan must take into account all of these aspects of the individual. It would also be fair to say that recovery, as with all changes in an individual's life, is ultimately governed by the individual's drives and motivation to change. It is well established in psychotherapy that positive treatment outcome is highly correlated with the individual's motivation to participate in treatment, understanding of the treatment process, and desire for change (Cormier & Cormier, 1985). At times, in substance abuse/dependency counseling, as in other areas of psychotherapy, the therapist's or significant others' motivation for change may be greater than the individual's motivation for change (Marion & Coleman, 1991).

Many individuals are "dry" or "clean," referring to having completed withdrawal and being physically free of alcohol, tobacco, and other drugs (ATOD). However, this state should not be confused with recovery. Being physically without ATOD but making no other lifestyle changes most frequently leads to chronic relapse. And, even if individuals do not begin to use again, their behaviors mimic their active drug-using behaviors, particularly those observed in the precontemplation stage of use. This is sometimes called "white knuckle sobriety."

Relapse has many definitions. One is a breakdown or setback in a person's attempt to change or modify a target behavior (Marlatt, 1985b). *Webster's New Collegiate Dictionary* defines relapse as "a recurrence of symptoms of a disease after a period of improvement." A simple definition would be the return to substance use or to the dysfunctional pattern of compulsive behavior. Relapse can be seen from two dimensions. The first is the "event" of resumption of use; the second is the "process" whereby attitudes and/or behaviors are exhibited that indicate a likelihood of resumption of use (Gorski, 1990). It is also true that these indicators vary widely from individual to individual and therefore may be difficult to recognize and identify.

Another aspect of the relapse process is "lapse"—the initial return to use after a period of sobriety. This may be a single episode, or it may lead to relapse—as indicated in the word itself, to lapse and lapse again. A lapse is usually temporary as opposed to a relapse, which is considered a return to uncontrolled use. Although AA defines a lapse as a failure in sobriety and indicates that the individual must begin their path to sobriety again, many mental health practitioners believe that a lapse may be used to assist the client (and the therapist) in learning what the factors are that motivate the client to return to substance use or relapse. This information can then be used to develop a plan to prevent other lapses or a return to substance use. In truth, some clients gain valuable self-information from a lapse and are strengthened by this new knowledge.

DETERMINANTS OF RELAPSE

Chiauzzi (1990) found four common elements in those individuals who relapsed:

1. Personality traits that interfered with sobriety, such as a tendency toward compulsive behavior or dependency.
2. A tendency toward substitute addictions. These individuals change one chemical for another.
3. Having a narrow view of recovery and not working toward life changes.
4. Ignoring warning signs including stimulus factors (Shiffman, 1992) of the sight, sound, or emotions connected with chemical use.

Although several models of relapse prevention will be discussed later in this chapter, it is interesting to note that all of these models incorporate common elements that are precursors of renewed substance use. The counselor should also be aware that these different elements are overlapping and integrated. They represent every aspect the client's life. Recovery, therefore, means a restructuring of one's entire life system.

Environmental

When clients are in treatment, either residential or intensive outpatient, they believe strongly that they can abstain from use. This belief has its basis in the comfort of the protected and supportive atmosphere of treatment. When they return to their own environment, many times this protection and support are not as available. Feelings of self-efficacy and control are replaced by anxiety, insecurity, and doubt (Marlatt & Gordon, 1985).

High-risk situations—incidents, occurrences, or situations that threaten the client's control—increase the likelihood of a return to use. Examples of high-risk situations would be going to a party with old friends who still use; riding by the bar, crack house, or dealer's house where the client previously purchased the substance; or frequenting locations where the client previously used substances. Dimeff and Marlatt (1995) report that 75% of all relapses involve a failure to deal with these situations successfully.

When the clients place themselves in these situations, they also put themselves in a negative emotional state. Early studies indicate that this emotional state accounts for 35% of all relapses. Interpersonal conflict, which may also be high at this time as the client endeavors to decide which behavior to engage in, accounts for 16% of relapses. Social pressures account for 20% (Cummings, Gordon, & Marlatt, 1980). As you can see from the earlier examples, all three of these components—interpersonal conflict, negative emotional state, and social pressure—exist when a client is in a high-risk situation.

Negative emotional states refer to anger, anxiety, frustration, depression, and/or boredom. Interpersonal conflict refers to arguments or confrontation with family, friends, or other significant individuals in the client's life. Social pressure is when the client responds to environmental or peer pressure to resume substance use (Lewis, Dana, & Blevins, 1994).

Urges and craving for their drug of choice are also a part of the relapse process. Craving is a cognitive state where individuals relive the positive feelings of use, while urges are behavioral impulses to get and use ATOD (Beck, Wright, Newman, & Liese, 1993). Beck et al. identify four different situations that contribute to the urge to use:

- learned response to the discomfort of withdrawal,
- unhappiness or discomfort,
- external "cues" or "triggers" (e.g., finding drug paraphernalia, going to the bar with old friends), and
- and a desire to enhance positive experiences in using.

Behavioral

Clients who have few or no coping skills to respond to these high-risk situations are more likely to return to substance use. Several studies emphasize the importance of teaching clients alternative coping skills to deal with these situations (Hawkins, Catalano, & Wells, 1986; Marlatt, 1985c). It is also important to teach the client new decision-making skills (Annis & Davis. 1991). A sober lifestyle requires integration into "normal" family life, work, recreation, diet and exercise, stress management, and handling the desire to use drugs again. This is a daily endeavor that is stressful in and of itself. Abstinence does not mean an absence of problems in one's life. Learning to deal with stress and negative emotions in a healthy way is imperative to recovery.

Dealing with daily life requires constant "minidecisions." It is these erroneous daily minidecisions, not major life decisions, that often lead the individual to relapse (Cummings et al., 1980).

Cognitive

Researchers have found a variety of cognitive variables that affect relapse. The person's attitude toward sobriety (Chalmers & Wallace, 1985), perception of their ability to cope or self-efficacy (Annis, 1986; Annis & Davis, 1987), and expectation of relapse are important factors (Annis & Davis, 1991). AA and Narcotic Anonymous (NA) refer to "stinking thinking" or the faulty thinking of substance abusers that can contribute to relapse. Irrational beliefs both about self and the present circumstances create negative emotions for the client. It may not be the actual thought or pattern of thinking but more how the abuser interprets or manages the situations that determine the outcome (Marion & Coleman, 1991).

Affective

Both negative and positive emotional states may lead to substance reuse. Depression and anxiety have been shown to be major determinants of relapse (Hatsukami, Pickens, & Svikis, 1981; Pickens, Hatsukami, Spicer, & Svikis, 1985). However, the research is unclear as to whether the depression and anxiety exist before the use resumes or as a product of the relapse.

The stress of everyday living can create negative emotions in the recovering person. Twelve-step programs use the acronym *HALT* (hungry, angry, lonely, tired) to alert individuals to emotions that lead to reuse. Individuals are told to "get off the pity pot" when they are overwhelmed by feelings of depression and hopelessness. Learning to handle these emotions positively can prevent relapse. For many clients, the purpose of using was to numb one's feelings. So, the first step in avoiding relapse needs to be learning to recognize, label, and be able to communicate feelings in a productive way (Marion & Coleman, 1991). Relaxation techniques, assertiveness skills, and other coping skills will be important to reducing the risk of relapse.

Two very strong emotions that must be dealt with in recovery are shame and guilt. Guilt is a consequence of the dependency process both for the addict and for the significant others in the addict's life. When the guilt becomes tied to "who I am" and not "what I did," it is known as shame. Dealing with guilt and shame affects an individual's self-esteem through negative feedback. These feelings can become overwhelming in recovery and easily lead to relapse in an attempt to protect one's self from a confrontation with these feelings (Marion & Coleman, 1991).

Recognizing that positive emotional states also create stress is imperative when working with this population. Positive events in daily life such as a new job, a child's wedding, and a renewal of an intimate relationship may be seen as more stressful than negative events since the abuser is "comfortable" with negative emotions. In fact, success may be the most stressful event in recovery.

Relational

The lack of a supportive family or social network has been highly correlated with a return to substance use (Daley, 1987; Hawkins & Fraser, 1987; Miller, 1992; Zackon, McAuliffe, & Ch'ien, 1985). Many times the primary significant other is also an active substance abuser, and, as noted earlier in this book, many of these individuals come from families with substance abuse problems that span generations. Lack of productive work or leisure time activities has also been shown to be a determinant of relapse (Gorski, 1990; Miller, 1992).

The family is the most significant relationship that is harmed in the process of abuse and dependency. Broken promises, hurts, isolation, and in many cases verbal, physical, and/or sexual abuse have been present. Taking responsibility for the behaviors and mending the relationships are a large part of recovery. The family must be engaged in the recovery process to minimize the possibility of relapse. Research appears to indicate that family involvement is critical as a positive correlation exists between family involvement in treatment and recovery. Families who are involved support rather than sabotage the process (Daley & Marlatt, 1992). As abusers begin to become aware of the behaviors in which they engaged when using and to move toward health, if the family is not engaged in this same process, the results could be devastating.

Work and leisure time are two other components that may create a problem in recovery. Many times the individual has lost a job or been demoted owing to the substance abuse problem. Finding satisfying work is an important component to avoid relapse. Leisure time for substance abusers has previously meant time when these individuals were either looking for their drug of choice, using the drug, or hiding the fact that they were using. Without these activities, recovering individuals find themselves with lots of time on their hands. Boredom, because of a lack of social support or activities, is a leading cause of relapse.

Summary

It is easy to see that recovery is a complex system. Every aspect of the individual's life has been affected by substance use. These aspects must now be changed, and change itself creates stress and anxiety. Stress and anxiety have previously been handled through the use of a chemical. Without this known means of coping, the individual is lost. It is imperative, then, that the learning of new skills be incorporated into the recovery process.

Several models of relapse prevention have developed through the years. The first model was Alcoholics Anonymous. This model has become the framework for a multitude of self-help/support groups including NA, Cocaine Anonymous (CA), and Overeaters Anonymous (OA). Other researchers and recovering people have developed different models of relapse prevention (e.g., Rational Recovery; Many Roads, One Journey; Women for Sobriety). Along with the AA model of recovery, a psychoeducational model, a developmental model, and a cognitive-behavioral/social learning model for maintaining sobriety will be discussed here.

ALCOHOLICS ANONYMOUS MODEL

Alcoholics Anonymous was officially founded on June 10, 1935. The groundwork for the organization was laid earlier, however, when Carl Jung, the famous psychologist, sent Ronald H. to the Oxford Group, a popular nondenominational religious group of the time, to find a spiritual awakening that therapy could not provide. Ronald H. was able to maintain his sobriety and to assist his friend, Edwin T., to do the same. Edwin T. was a friend of Bill W. At this time, Bill W. was still drinking but later was hospitalized for detoxification. After his release, he read *The Varieties of Religious Experiences* by William James that became the foundation for the Twelve Steps of AA. During a business trip at a later date, Bill W. was fighting to keep his sobriety and, being in Akron, Ohio, was referred to Dr. Robert H. Smith (Dr. Bob). Although reluctantly, Dr. Bob agreed to see him. Dr. Bob was still drinking at this time, but Bill W. found himself reaching out to Dr. Bob with the message of his own sobriety. Through their subsequent conversations and friendship, both remained sober and founded what we know today as Alcoholics Anonymous (Fisher & Harrison, 1997; Kurtz, 1979). By the fourth year after its founding, there were approximately 100 members in the groups (Nace, 1987). These early members wrote about their struggle to maintain sobriety, publishing the first edition of the book *Alcoholics Anonymous* in 1939. Included in this first edition of the "Big Book" were the Twelve Steps and Twelve Traditions of the organization. AA has developed into a fellowship of over 15 million individuals in over 500,000 groups in 114 countries (Hemfelt & Fowler, 1990). AA members often say "wherever you can find a liquor store, you can find an AA group."

The cornerstone of the AA model is the paradoxical belief that to gain control of one's life, one must give up control to a Higher Power. Although God is mentioned in AA, members believe that one's Higher Power can be many things or beings. AA distinguishes between spirituality and religion and believes that addiction is a spiritual disease as well as a physical one. By embracing spirituality, not a specific religious dogma, AA allows all individuals to embrace a Higher Power of their own choosing. AA is a "spiritual program of living" (Miller & Kurtz, 1994, p. 165).

Fundamental in the 12-step philosophy is the belief that abstinence from substance use is not enough. Individuals must be willing to make attitudinal and behavioral changes in their lifestyle. The AA model is designed to enable individuals to address every aspect of their lives—physical, emotional, social, and spiritual—and to make positive changes in each of these areas. The Twelve Steps of recovery are the foundation for these changes (see Figure 10.1). Having made these changes, the individual will then reach out to others in an effort to offer assistance in recovering from a substance using lifestyle (Marion & Coleman, 1991). The Twelve Traditions are also an important component of AA. These traditions govern the operation of AA.

AA considers five aspects of recovery as the most important in the program: (a) learning to give up control to gain control, (b) self-examination and discussion of this examination, (b) making amends, (d) group participation, and (e) daily reminders (Hoffman & Gressard, 1994). These factors work best when combined in the noncoercive atmosphere of participation that is present in AA.

Giving Up Control to Gain Control

The first three steps of AA are about recognizing and acknowledging one's limitations. These steps require that individuals accept that their resources are not enough to solve life's problems. The third step requires that they give control of the problem to a "Higher Power." The paradox of giving up control to gain control is one of the most difficult for the individual to understand (Hoffman & Gressard, 1994). It is the experience of AA members (and substance abuse counselors) that after the initial behavior change has been accomplished, individuals begin to feel they are in control of their behavior and do not need to continue with the meetings, meditations, and group support of AA. It is imperative for the counselor to watch for signs of overconfidence in the client that would indicate this belief. Statements such as "I have this under control," "I have this problem licked," "I haven't had the urge to drink/use in weeks," or "I can cut down on meetings for a while" should trigger an immediate response from the alert counselor. When these statements are made in the early

---

The Twelve Steps

1. We admitted we were powerless over alcohol—that our lives had become unmanageable.

2. Came to believe that a Power greater than ourselves could restore us to sanity.

3. Made a decision to turn our will and our lives over to the care of God *as we understood Him.*

4. Made a searching and fearless moral inventory of ourselves.

5. Admitted to God, to ourselves, and to another human being the exact nature of our wrongs.

6. Were entirely ready to have God remove all these defects of character.

7. Humbly ask Him to remove our shortcomings.

8. Made a list of all persons we had harmed, and became willing to make amends to them all.

9. Made direct amends to such people wherever possible, except when to do so would injure them or others.

10. Continued to take personal inventory and when we were wrong promptly admitted it.

11. Sought through prayer and meditation to improve our conscious contact with God *as we understood Him*, praying only for knowledge of His will for us and the power to carry that out.

12. Having had a spiritual awakening as the result of these steps, we tried to carry this message to alcoholics, and to practice these principles in all our affairs.

FIGURE 10.1   The Twelve Steps of Alcoholics Anonymous

Source: From *Alcoholics Anonymous* (pp. 59–60), 1976, New York: Alcoholics Anonymous World Services, Inc.

stages of recovery, the client should be reminded of the difficulty of behavior change maintenance and the paradox of control.

Self-Examination

Self-examination is essential in recovery. Steps 4 through 7 are about self-assessment and include a series of change-oriented activities. They require that individuals do a "searching and fearless moral inventory" of their behavior. They then discuss this inventory with another trusted individual. Steps 8 and 9 direct individuals to make amends for injuries to others, and step 10 requires an ongoing moral inventory. The consistent review of feelings and behaviors is imperative to sobriety. While using drugs, an individual represses and/or avoids feelings. Acknowledging and examining these feelings make up an important piece of "working the program" in AA.

Making Amends

Steps 8 and 9 are about making amends for past behavior. Through this inventory and the process of making amends, abusing individuals may work through the guilt and shame associated with past behaviors and recognize the limits of personal responsibility (Doweiko, 1993). Making amends is a way to alleviate guilt associated with the negative effect of the addict's past behaviors on family, friends, and associates. Not dealing with these past behaviors can strain the individual's support system as well as being a component in returning to substance use. Accepting responsibility for one's behavior and the consequences of that behavior is a step in learning a healthy behavior pattern.

Steps 10 through 12 build on the framework developed in the previous steps. Step 10 requires an ongoing inventory and admission of wrongdoing in the present. Spirituality is the focus of step 11, and the need to be involved with others is addressed in step 12.

Group Participation

The fourth powerful component of AA is the group support provided by the involvement in AA meetings. Anonymity is seen as an integral element in AA, both to protect the identity of its membership and so that no one person becomes a spokesperson for the group (Doweiko, 1993). AA sees a commitment to recovery as a commitment to or involvement in AA.

Individuals in AA are also supported by "sponsors." A sponsor is an AA member with a history of sobriety who has worked through the Twelve Steps and has a basic understanding of his or her own addiction. This individual is available 24 hours a day, 7 days a week for the newly recovering individual. Sponsors serve a variety of purposes. They listen, provide support and confrontation, are the most common recipient of the "moral inventory" information, encourage AA attendance, and may even provide recreational activities. They also serve as a spiritual guide.

An addict's sponsor is interested in the individual's recovery but is not responsible for that recovery (McCrady & Irvine, 1989). In the AA philosophy, the responsibility for recovery is on the individual. The role of the sponsor is often similar to that of a psychotherapist and, in fact, may embody many of the same characteristics (Rogers, 1961).

Daily Reminders

The fifth necessary component in the AA recovery program is the constant awareness of the disease and the recovery principles. This awareness is facilitated through the use of daily reminders. AA has developed daily meditations, slogans, readings, and prayers that keep the individual focused on these principles. It is AA's belief that without these daily reminders it is easy to forget the necessary components of recovery and thereby to relapse. It is of particular importance for sobriety to remember the "truth" of steps 1 to 3. These slogans offer practical advice to the recovering person such as "Take It Easy," "One Day at a Time," and "Let Go and Let God." AA also offers literature that is free to anyone on how to deal with the many life problems that are a part of the recovery process.

How Effective Is AA?

AA is viewed by many recovering individuals and professionals in the field as the single most important component of recovery. Yet critics of the program suggest caution, stating that those people who join AA and remain members may not be a representative sample of the substance-abusing population (Emrick, Tonigan, Montgomery, & Little, 1993). The fact that these people remain members separates them from those who do not join or who join and do not remain active. Additionally, research is difficult since the groups have a high degree of variability (McCrady & Irvine, 1989). No well-designed research outcome study has been completed on the effectiveness of AA. An interesting note is that it is from the early membership of AA that Jellinek's original work on the stages of alcoholism was drawn. This research is limited because the population studied was composed of white middle-class males. This obviously limits the use of this research with other populations (Doweiko, 1999).

Criticism about the AA program has also been leveled by women's groups and minority groups who feel disenfranchised by AA. Many women believe AA perpetuates the powerlessness of women in steps 1 through 3. A feminist version of the Twelve Steps has been written to address this issue (Figure 10.2). Minority groups belief that AA serves the white middle class and does not address ethnic issues in their philosophy. It would appear that some research supports this theory—that AA is most effective with "socially stable white males over 40 years of age, who are physically dependent on alcohol and prone to guilt, and who are the first born or only child" (Doweiko, 1993, p. 368). However, little evidence supports this research, and most believe that this conclusion is not reliable in predicting successful membership in AA.

Some evidence also indicates that AA is not effective with individuals who are coerced into attendance. People who are sentenced to jail or to educational programs for driving under the influence appear to have better subsequent driving records than those who are court ordered to attend AA. (Peele, Brodsky, & Arnold, 1991). This outcome may be associated with either motivation or the concept of self-efficacy.

The answer to effectiveness may be far too complex to answer by a simple study. Effectiveness research in the field of substance abuse, for AA or any recovery program, is limited (see Chapter 12 for a review of research). It serves the mental health practitioner to be aware that some individuals are best served by AA, and some individuals might be better served through other approaches.

AA Associated 12-Step Programs

Using the AA model of recovery as a basis, several 12-step programs have been developed (e.g., NA, CA, OA). All are based on the AA philosophy and use a varia-

1. We acknowledge we were out of control with our addiction but have the power to take charge of our lives and stop being dependent on others for our self-esteem and security.

2. We came to believe that the Universe/Goddess/Great Spirit would awaken the healing wisdom within us if we opened ourselves to that power.

3. We declared ourselves willing to tune into our inner wisdom. To listen and act based upon these truths.

4. Made a searching and fearless inventory of how the culture has mired us down with guilt and shame, recognizing how hierarchy has harmed us, and how we have been complicit in harming ourselves—and only then look at how we have harmed others.

5. We examined our behavior and beliefs in the context of living in a hierarchical, male-dominated culture.

6. We shared with others the way we have been harmed, harmed ourselves and others, striving to forgive ourselves and to change our behavior.

7. We admitted to our talents, strengths, and accomplishments, agreeing not to hide these qualities to protect others' egos.

8. We became willing to let go of our shame, guilt, and other behavior that prevents us from taking control of our lives and loving ourselves.

9. We took steps to clear out all negative feelings between us and other people by sharing grievances in a respectful way and making amends when appropriate.

10. Continued to trust our reality and when we were right, promptly admitted it and refused to back down. We do not take responsibility for, analyze, or cover up the shortcomings of others.

11. Sought through meditation and inner awareness the ability to listen to our inward calling and gain the will and wisdom to follow it.

12. Having learned to care for and love ourselves as a result of these steps, we give to others out of choice and seek to practice these principles in all our affairs.

FIGURE 10.2   The feminist alternative to the Twelve Steps
Source: From *CoAcoAA Newsletter, 4*(3) (Spring 1991), pp. 2–3.

tion of the Twelve Steps of AA. The difference in these groups is their scope. NA, for example is all-inclusive with its definition of addiction. It includes any mood-changing, mind-altering substance. CA limits its membership to individuals who identify cocaine as their primary drug or drug of choice, while OA is directed toward individuals who have compulsive eating habits.

Al-Anon, Alateen, and Nar-Anon are examples of support groups for families of substance users. Al-Anon and Nar-Anon are for the partners and families of users. Al-Anon was founded by Lois W. (Bill W.'s wife) in 1954. While the substance abuser is in AA or NA, families meet to share experiences and discuss problems. These groups use the same Twelve Steps as they work toward their own recovery process.

Alateen, which began in 1957, is for teenagers who live in alcoholic or drug-abusing families and for substance-using teenagers. It also uses the 12-step model and has its own Big Book. It was started to create an opportunity for youth to come together for support, to share experiences, learn about dependency, and to develop problem-solving skills. The model has been used to develop Twelve Steps for even very young children (see Figure 10.3).

A PSYCHOEDUCATIONAL MODEL: RATIONAL RECOVERY

Rational Recovery (RR) developed as an alternative for individuals who had difficulty with the spiritual aspect of AA. This program was developed beginning in 1988 by Jack Trimpey (1996) and is based on the work of Albert Ellis. RR uses the framework of rational emotive therapy to combat the irrational thoughts and beliefs of recovering

---

1. I am powerless over alcohol, drugs and other people's behavior, and my life got really messed up because of it.
2. I need help. I can't do it alone anymore.
3. I've made a decision to reach out for a Power greater than me to help out.
4. I wrote down all the things that bother me about myself and others, and all the things I like, too.
5. I shared these with someone I trust because I don't have to keep them secret anymore.
6. My Higher Power helps me with this, too.
7. The more I trust myself and my Higher Power, the more I learn to trust others.
8. I made a list of all the people I hurt and the ways I hurt myself. I can now forgive myself and others.
9. I talked with these people even if I was scared to because I knew that it would help me feel better about myself.
10. I keep on discovering more things about myself each day and if I hurt someone, I apologize.
11. When I am patient and pray, I get closer to my Higher Power, and that helps me to know myself better.
12. By using these steps, I've become a new person. I don't have to feel alone anymore, and I can help others.

FIGURE 10.3   Twelve Steps for Kids

Source: From *Kids' Power* (p. 61) by J. Moe and D. Pohlman, 1989, Deerfield Beach, FL: Health Communications, Inc.

individuals. Trimpey takes the irrational beliefs about alcoholism and drug use and reframes them into rational beliefs and ideas. These irrational thoughts are labeled as "the Beast," and individuals use a "Sobriety Spreadsheet" to combat the Beast.

There is some research on the effectiveness of RR that indicates a high (73%) abstinence rate for 3 months following attendance. One limitation of this study is that the population was largely well educated and employed, creating concern about the generalizability of the results to other populations (Gallant, Egelko, & Edwards, 1993).

A DEVELOPMENTAL MODEL

The developmental theorists integrate concepts of the disease model with a developmental model of recovery. Gorski and Miller (1982, 1986) have developed a six-stage/nine-step model of recovery. Known as the CENAPS Model of Relapse Prevention (Gorski, 1989, 1990, 1992, 1993), it is based on the belief that substance abuse creates dysfunction at every level in an individual's life (Gorksi, 1990). It is, therefore, imperative in relapse prevention to focus on treatment at each of these levels.

This model takes into consideration that relapse is a progression of behaviors that allows the substance use to be reactivated if intervention does not take place. Gorski and Miller (1982, 1986) view addiction as a chronic and progressive disease and advocate for change in all aspects of an individual's life for recovery to happen. Another aspect of this developmental model, which borrows from the AA model, is the belief that the individuals must admit they have a problem and then abstain from substance use. Gorski and Miller believe that this model works best for patients who have been in treatment and relapsed.

The six stages of the developmental model are as follows:

1. *Transition.* The individual begins to experience more severe symptoms and dependency and recognizes the need for treatment and seeks it.
2. *Stabilization.* This is the beginning stage of treatment and may include detoxification. The individual is stabilized, and immediate problems are solved to facilitate the termination of substance use.
3. *Early recovery.* The client is becoming aware of how the use of substances affected thinking and begins to manage feelings without use.
4. *Middle recovery.* A balanced lifestyle change begins.
5. *Late recovery.* The client has used the counseling process to understand core psychological issues that might create relapse potential.
6. *Maintenance.* Maintenance is a life-long process of sharpening coping skills to deal with life problems (Gorski, 1989).

Gorski and Miller (1982, 1986) and later Gorski (1990, 1992, 1993) developed nine steps or principles to facilitate relapse prevention. Skills are needed at each stage of recovery, and the role of the counselor is to assist client with each of these steps or principles:

1. The first step is to stabilize the client or assist the client to develop a daily structure. This is a mechanism to solve immediate problems and to assist the client to begin to live without substance use.

2. The second principle is teaching the client continual self-assessment. This provides a means to understand the previous relapse pattern and to intervene in that pattern.

3. Educational information is given concerning the disease and the biopsychosocial models of dependency.

4. The counselor helps the client identify the warning signs of an impending relapse.

5. After identification of warning signs, the counselor facilitates the client's ability to manage his or her own warning signs.

6. The client creates a set of activities to use when these warning signs appear to avoid relapse.

7. The relapse dynamic is interrupted. Problems that are associated with the warning signs are discussed and solved.

8. The counselor may well have been working throughout this process with family and friends. At this point, significant others become involved in the relapse planning program.

9. The final step is a consistent follow-up over a minimum of 2 years and reinforcement by the counselor of the client's progress during this time.

Similar to the AA model, the developmental model is structured with the assumption that relapse problems and warning signs will change as the individual progresses through the stages of recovery. These changes will necessitate the reworking of these steps or principles with each developmental stage of recovery.

A COGNITIVE-BEHAVIORAL/SOCIAL LEARNING MODEL

The cognitive-behavioral model (Annis, 1986, 1990; Annis & Davis, 1991; Cummings et al., 1980; Mackay & Marlatt, 1991; Marlatt, 1985a) is based on social learning theory (Bandura, 1969). Social learning theory holds that substance use and abuse are learned behaviors in which use has been increased in frequency, duration, and intensity for psychological benefit (Lewis et al., 1994). In other words, use is associated with reinforcement, either immediate or delayed.

Social Learning Theories

Drive reduction theory states that internal tension creates a drive state. A chemical substance is used to reduce the drive. This use reduces tension, which is reinforcing to the individual. This reinforcement strengthens the substance use behavior. The substance will then be used more frequently in response to the need to reduce the drive.

Drive reduction theory takes into account the individual's continued use in the face of negative effects from using. If the drive is intense, the immediate reinforcement—or drive reduction effect—will overshadow the negative effects created by continued use (Hull, 1943; Thorndike, 1932).

Another social learning theory perspective examines the effect of environmental stressors on substance use. This theory asserts that substance use is a mechanism, learned through reinforcement and modeling, to reduce stress. As substance use continues, the individual may use more frequently and at higher dosages to avoid withdrawal (Lewis et al., 1994).

The importance of self-efficacy must not be overlooked in any discussion of social learning theory (Bandura, 1969). Research substantiates the validity that low self-efficacy or perceived ability to cope with high-stress situations is correlated with a return to drinking behavior and smoking (Condiotte & Lichtenstein, 1981). Therefore, if high self-efficacy is positively correlated with abstinence, then a crucial element in relapse prevention would be the development of a strong sense of capacity to handle situations. Self-efficacy theory provides that "hands-on" practice handling situations of ever-increasing difficulty creates this sense of ability to handle situations. Certain criteria are important in these practice sessions, however, to increase confidence (Bandura, 1978):

1. The exposure to substance use was challenging to the client.
2. Only a moderate degree of effort was needed to experience success.
3. Little external aid was necessary.
4. The success was part of a pattern of improvement.
5. An increase in personal control was demonstrated.
6. The successful performance was relevant to the client's own life situations.

In relapse prevention planning, it is important for clients and counselors to monitor situations in an ongoing manner. It is helpful for the client to make a record of problem situations; behaviors, thoughts and feelings immediately before the situation and after the situation; and any means used to cope with the situation. This log will facilitate the client's awareness of any unique triggers to substance use and allow for the client and the counselor to plan for realistic situations in the client's life.

This planning also allows for anticipation of problem situations. The client should be encouraged to look at the days or weeks ahead and anticipate situations that might prompt a desire a return to substance use. With forewarning of possible difficulties, the counselor and client can successfully plan an appropriate relapse prevention technique for each situation (see Figure 10.4).

A significant factor in self-efficacy theory is the rehearsal or practice of using methods before the difficulty is encountered. These practice sessions lead to increased perceived ability or self-efficacy on the part of the client. Whenever possible, practice within a therapy session or group can be used.

The client should not only plan intervention techniques to avoid a return to substance use but should also work with the counselor to determine how a lapse will be

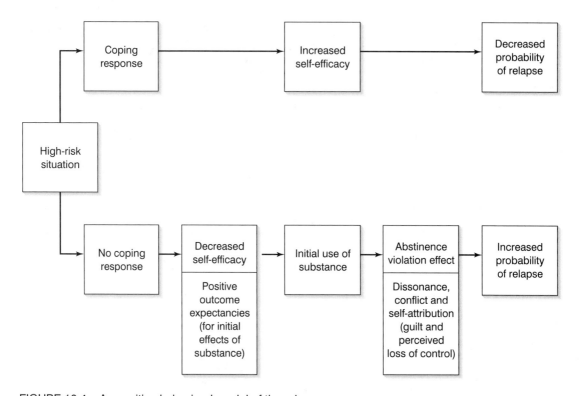

FIGURE 10.4   A cognitive-behavioral model of the relapse process

Source: From *Relapse Prevention* (p. 38) by G. Alan Marlatt and Judith E. Gordon (Eds.), 1985, New York: Guilford Press. Copyright 1985 by Guilford Press.

handled in the most constructive manner possible. Plans for interruption of a relapse should also be considered. Support and intervention are imperative at these times not only to interrupt the return to substance use but also to deal with any negative feelings the client may experience owing to the return to substance use.

Reviewing with the client how behavior has changed is an important reinforcement technique. It encourages the client to continue improvement but also allows the client to examine the substance use in a multidimensional way. Improvement in each aspect of the client's life can be discussed and reinforced (Annis & Davis, 1991).

Cognitive-Behavioral Model

Marlatt and his colleagues have developed the most widely used cognitive behavioral model of relapse prevention. Marlatt bases this theory on the belief that "[t]he goal of relapse prevention is to teach individuals who are trying to change their behavior how to anticipate and cope with the problem of relapse" (Marlatt & Gordon, 1985, p. 3). Although we will address the use of this model with substance abusers, the model appears to be advantageous with many other compulsive or addictive behavior patterns. In any situation, it is most effective with individuals who are motivated to change their behavior and who have expressed a commitment to do so. Individuals who are changing because of external motivational influences, such as court-ordered clients or clients responding to a work or marital crisis, may not respond as well.

This relapse prevention model is based on three assumptions:

1. The etiology of addictive behaviors and the process of change "may be governed by different factors or learning principles."
2. "The process of changing a habit involves at least three separate stages": commitment and motivation, implementation of change, and long-term maintenance of behavior change.
3. The maintenance stage of behavior change "accounts for the greatest proportion of variance associated with long-term treatment outcomes" (Marlatt & Gordon, 1985, p. 21).

A fourth assumption may be added to the list. Relapse may be viewed as a "transitional process . . . [or] . . . a fork in the road . . . with one path returning to the former problem level . . . and the other continuing in the direction of positive change" (pp. 32–33). In other words, in contrast to the AA model, relapse is not seen as a failure but as a learning tool for the individual. The lapse is used as a means to assess the antecedents to the lapse and to formulate a more successful coping strategy for the future. One of the most important factors in determining whether the individual will return to substance use is the individual's perception of the lapse. Does the client see this as a failure or as a way to learn and develop stronger skills (Marlatt, 1985a)?

This approach stresses the need for lifestyle change. Exercise, biofeedback, meditation, stress management techniques, relaxation training, and cognitive restructuring are a few examples of these changes. Self-monitoring is important. Clients must learn new coping skills to deal with high-risk situations. However, Marlatt (1985a) believes that new coping skills alone are not sufficient to maintain sobriety. He believes that positive addictions and substitute indulgences are also necessary.

The cognitive-behavioral model assumes a collaborative relationship between the client and the therapist. Together they will identify, assess, and plan for situations that may prove problematic for the client. These situations can be interpersonal or intrapersonal and fall into three categories: (a) negative emotional states, (b) interpersonal conflict, and (c) social pressures (Cummings et al., 1980). For clients to become aware of these situations, daily self-monitoring is encouraged.

The next step for the client is to develop new coping skills for handling these situations without a return to substance use. Each client needs to learn, in cooperation with the therapist, a unique set of skills that are appropriate to the client's situation. New cognitive and behavioral skills can be learned. Behavioral skills would include assertiveness training and alternative behaviors such as exercise or meditation. Cognitive restructuring, imagery, and self-talk might also be implemented.

A balanced lifestyle is emphasized throughout this model. Clients must learn to replace negative addictions with positive addictions such as aerobics, running, walking, relaxation, or other pleasurable activities. An equality between what one should do and what one wants to do is another aspect of a healthy lifestyle. Too many "shoulds" lead to a feeling of deprivation that could be an antecedent to relapse. All of these skills combined are designed to decrease the individual's frequency of desire to return to substance use and to increase the client's overall coping capacity (Marlatt, 1985c). This model is flexible and manageable. Its success is based in the fact that it responds to the unique and individualized needs of clients.

THE CONCEPT OF RE-JOYMENT

Zackon (1988) writes about the role of joy in the recovery process. Zackon makes the point that definitions of relapse have something in common. It is a

> subdynamic of addiction . . . stimulated by conditioned drug-craving responses to internal and environmental cues or the result of inadequate preparation for stressful situations . . . such as social relationships . . . intensified by faculty thinking . . . and inadequate external intervention. (p. 68)

Relapse prevention models also incorporate similar concepts and skills. Zackon states that the "various methods . . . proposed . . . to prevent these problems could usually coexist peaceably in the same program, likely with addictive value" (p. 68). Having made these two observations, Zackon then proposes that the question we forget to ask is "What is the relationship between joylessness and relapse?" (p. 69).

In our diligent and caring quest to teach the individual all the cognitive and behavioral skills necessary to stay clean and sober, we may be overlooking an intrinsically important aspect of recovery. Becoming clean and sober requires the substance abuser to give up a lifestyle that is "psychologically comfortable" and to enter unfamiliar territory. Abusers must leave friends who shared a value system and created a sense of community for them. Recovery requires that the person "abandon an entire universe of feelings for another" (p. 71).

The world of the substance abuser is one of high stakes and high risk. Adrenaline runs high. Risk-taking behavior is common. Entering a world of "mundane" pleasures creates boredom and joylessness. The recovering individual does not remember how to experience joy or enjoyment with everyday living. Many common social situations are uncomfortable. Friends are few, if they exist at all. Addicts must learn to lower their "pleasure threshold" (Zackon, 1988, p. 75)—in other words, learn to enjoy more moderate stimulation than that experienced while using in everything from food to fun to sexual activity.

Also, early recovery means detoxification and withdrawal symptoms that may linger. It also means facing the pain of one's life both before, during, and now after the drug use. Destroyed relationships, financial problems, legal problems, expectations from everyone, physical pain, and the consistent—and sometimes strong—drug cravings create a heavy burden of unhappiness that drains energy and prolongs the lack of joyfulness in the individual's life.

So it becomes incumbent upon the counselor not to overlook the relearning of pleasure in the recovery process. Relearning takes time, and counselors need to remember that this relearning can be blocked by guilt and shame or simply by lack of money to participate in activities. Counselors should also remember that many individuals began using "for want of pleasure in a mean world" (Zackon, 1988, p. 76) and that the world is still as mean as ever.

In relapse prevention models and programs, counselors should emphasize and systematically support "re-joyment." This may mean that counselors take the nontherapeutic role of "coach" in these activities. Aftercare groups, AA, NA, and other social support groups can provide much needed activities for recovering individuals.

CONCLUSION

In summary, the determinants of relapse and prevention models share commonalties. Relapse prevention skills, cognitive and behavioral, are important in creating a clean and sober lifestyle. However, simply put, the intentionality and joy with which the individual is living life may be a much more powerful deterrent to relapse than the so-called living skills taught in a conventional relapse prevention program.

REFERENCES

Annis, H. M. (1986). A relapse prevention model for treatment of alcoholics. In W. R. Miller & N. Heather (Eds.), *Treating addictive behaviors: Process of change* (pp. 407–421). New York: Plenum.

Annis, H. M. (1990). Relapse to substance abuse: Empirical findings within a cognitive-social learning approach. *Journal of Psychoactive Drugs, 22,* 117–124.

Annis, H. M., & Davis, C. (1987). Assessment of expectancies in alcoholic dependent clients. In G. A. Marlatt & D. Donovan (Eds.), *Assessment of addictive behaviors*. New York: Guilford.

Annis, H. M., & Davis, C. S. (1991). Relapse prevention. *Alcohol Health & Research World, 15*(3), 204–212.

Bandura, A. (1969). *Principles of behavior modification*. New York: Holt, Rinehart, & Winston.

Bandura, A. (1978). Reflections on self-efficacy. *Advances in Behavioral Research and Therapy, 1,* 237–269.

Beck, A. T., Wright, F. D., Newman, C. F., & Liese, R. S. (1993). *Cognitive therapy of substance abuse*. New York: Guilford.

Buelow, G. D., & Buelow, S. A. (1998). *Chemical dependence treatment: A practical and integrative approach*. Pacific Grove, CA: Brooks/Cole.

Chalmers, D., & Wallace, J. (1985). Evaluation of patient progress. In S. Zimberg, J. Wallach, S. B. Blume, & J. Wallace (Eds.), *Practical approaches to alcoholism psychotherapy* (pp. 174–185). New York: Plenum.

Chiauzzi, E. (1990). Breaking the patterns that lead to relapse. *Psychology Today, 307,* 1374.

Condiotte, M. M., & Lichtenstein, E. (1981). Self-efficacy and relapse in smoking cessation programs. *Journal of Consulting and Clinical Psychology, 49,* 648–658.

Cormier, W. H., & Cormier, L. S. (1985). *Interviewing strategies for helpers* (2nd ed.). Belmont, CA: Brooks/Cole.

Cummings, C., Gordon, J., & Marlatt, G. (1980). Relapse: Prevention and prediction. In W. Miller (Ed.), *Addictive behaviors: Treatment of alcoholism, drug abuse, smoking and obesity* (pp. 62–74). New York: Pergamon.

Daley, D. C. (1987). Relapse prevention with substance abusers: Clinical issues and myths. *Social Work, 45*(2), 38–42.

Daley, D. C. (1988). *Surviving addiction: A guide for alcoholics, drug addicts and their families.* New York: Gardner.

Daley, D. C., & Marlatt, G. A. (1992). Relapse prevention: Cognitive and behavioral interventions. In J. H. Lowinson, P. Ruiz, R. M. Millman, & J. G. Langrod (Eds.), *Substance abuse: A comprehensive textbook* (2nd ed., pp. 533–542). Baltimore: Williams & Watkins.

DeJong, W. (1994). Relapse prevention: An emerging technology for promoting long term abstinence. *International Journal of the Addictions, 29,* 681–785.

Dimeff, L. A., & Marlatt, G. A. (1995). Relapse prevention. In R. K. Hester & W. R. Miller (Eds.), *Handbook of alcoholism treatment approaches* (2nd ed.). New York: Allyn & Bacon.

Doweiko, H. F. (1999). *Concepts of chemical dependency* (4th ed.). Pacific Grove, CA: Brooks/Cole.

Emrick, C. D., Tonigan, J. S., Montgomery, H., & Little, L. (1993). Alcoholics Anonymous: What is currently known? In B. S. McCrady & W. R. Miller (Eds.), *Research on Alcoholics Anonymous* (pp. 23–28). New Brunswick, NJ: Rutgers Center for Alcoholic Studies.

Fisher, G. L., & Harrison, T. C. (1997). *Substance abuse: Information for school counselors, social workers, therapists, and counselors.* Boston: Allyn & Bacon.

Gallant, M., Egelko, S., & Edwards, H. (1993). Rational Recovery: Alternative to AA for addiction? *American Journal of Drug and Alcohol Abuse, 19,* 499–510.

Gorski, T. T. (1989). *Passages through recovery: An action plan for preventing relapse.* Center City, MN: Hazelden.

Gorski, T. T. (1990). The CENAPS model of relapse prevention: Basic principles and procedure. *Journal of Psychoactive Drugs, 22,* 125–133.

Gorski, T. T. (1992, July/August). Creating a relapse prevention program in your treatment center. *Addiction & Recovery,* pp. 16–17.

Gorski, T. T. (1993, March/April). Relapse prevention: A state of the art overview. *Addiction & Recovery,* pp. 25–27.

Gorski, T., & Miller, M. (1982). *Counseling for relapse prevention.* Independence, MI: Independence Press.

Gorski, T. T., & Miller, M. M. (1986). *Staying sober: Guide to relapse prevention.* Independence, MO: Herald House.

Hatsukami, D., Pickens, R., & Svikis, D. (1981). Post-treatment depressive symptoms and relapse to drug use in different age groups of an alcohol and other drug use population. *Drug and Alcohol Dependence, 8*(4), 271–277.

Hawkins, J. D., Catalano, R., & Wells, E. (1986). Measuring effects of a skills training intervention for drug abusers. *Journal of Consulting and Clinical Psychology, 54*(5), 661–664.

Hawkins, J. D., & Fraser, M. W. (1987). The social networks of drug abusers before and after treatment. *International Journal of Addictions, 22*(4), 343–355.

Hemfelt, R., & Fowler, R. (1990). *Serenity: A companion for 12 step recovery, complete with New Testament, Psalms, Proverbs.* Nashville, TN: Nelson.

Hoffman, F. J., & Gressard, C. F. (1994). Maintaining change in addictive behaviors. In J. A. Lewis (Ed.), *Addictions: Concepts and strategies for treatment* (pp. 143–160). Gaithersburg, MD: Aspen.

Hull, C. (1943). *Principles of behavior.* New York: Appleton-Century-Crofts.

Kurtz, E. (1979). *Not-God: A history of Alcoholics Anonymous.* Center City, MN: Hazelden.

Lewis, J. A., Dana, R., & Blevins, G. A. (1994). *Substance abuse counseling: An individualized approach* (2nd ed.). Pacific Grove, CA: Brooks/Cole.

MacKay, P. W., & Marlatt, G. A. (1991). Maintaining sobriety: Stopping is starting. *International Journal of Addictions, 25,* 1257–1276.

Marion, T. R., & Coleman, K. (1991). Recovery issues and treatment resources. In D. C. Daley

& M. S. Raskin (Eds.), *Treating the chemically dependent and their families* (pp. 100–127). Newbury Park, CA: Sage.

Marlatt, G. A. (1985a). Cognitive assessment and intervention procedures for relapse prevention. In G. A. Marlatt & J. Gordon (Eds.), *Relapse prevention: A self-control strategy for the maintenance of behavior change* (pp. 201–209). New York: Guilford.

Marlatt, G. A. (1985b). Lifestyle modification. In G. A. Marlatt & J. Gordon (Eds.), *Relapse prevention: A self-control strategy for the maintenance of behavior change* (pp. 280–350). New York: Guilford.

Marlatt, G. A. (1985c). Relapse prevention: Theoretical rationale and overview of the model. In G. A. Marlatt & J. R. Gordon (Eds.), *Relapse prevention: Maintenance strategies in the treatment of addictive behavior* (pp. 104–105). New York: Guilford.

Marlatt, G. A., & Gordon, J. (1985). (Eds.). *Relapse prevention: A self-control strategy for the maintenance of behavior change*. New York: Guilford.

McCrady, B. S., & Irvine, S. (1989). Self-help groups. In R. K. Hester & W. R. Miller (Eds.), *Handbook of alcoholism treatment approaches: Effective alternatives* (pp. 153–169). Elmsford, NY: Pergamon.

Miller, W. R. (1992). The effectiveness of treatment for substance abuse: Reasons for optimism. *Journal of Substance Abuse, 9*, 93–102.

Miller, W. R., & Kurtz, E. (1994). Models of alcoholism used in treatment: Contrasting AA and other perspectives with which it is often confused. *Journal of Studies on Alcohol, 55*, 159–166.

Nace, E. P. (1987). *The treatment of alcoholism*. New York: Brunner/Mazel.

Peele, S., Brodsky, A., & Arnold, M. (1991). *The truth about addiction and recovery*. New York: Simon & Schuster.

Pickens, R., Hatsukami, D., Spicer, L., & Svikis, D. (1985). Relapse by alcohol abusers. *Alcoholism: Clinical and Experimental Research, 9*(3), 244–247.

Rogers, C. R. (1961). *On becoming a person*. Boston: Houghton Mifflin.

Shiffman, S. (1992). Relapse process and relapse prevention in addictive behaviors. *Behavior Therapist, 15(1)*, 99–110.

Thorndike, E. (1932). *The fundamentals of learning*. New York: Teachers College Press.

Trimpey, J. (1996). *Rational Recovery: The new cure for substance addiction*. New York: Simon & Schuster.

Zackon, F. N. (1988). Relapse and "re-joyment": Observations and reflections. In D. C. Daley (Ed.), *Relapse: Conceptual, research and clinical perspectives* (pp. 67–78). New York: Haworth.

Zackon, F., McAuliffe, W., & Ch'ien, J. (1985). *Addict aftercare: Recovery training and self-help*. DHHS Pub. No. (ADM) 85-1341. Rockville, MD: National Institute of Drug Abuse.

Prevention

OLIVER J. MORGAN, PH.D., NCC[1]

Drug abuse is a preventable behavior. Drug addiction is a treatable disease.[2]

Misuse and abuse of psychoactive substances is a fact of American life as we enter the 21st century. Alcohol, tobacco, and other drug (ATOD) abuse touches every level of our culture and national experience: individual, family, school, and community. Legal drugs such as caffeine, alcohol, and tobacco are commonly used by adults—and often by children as well—despite evidence of adverse health outcomes. Illegal drugs, such as marijuana, cocaine, and heroin, as well as over-the-counter and prescription drugs, are used for purposes of recreation or self-medication despite the known health risks and potential legal and financial penalties. Every age group is affected; no one— not children, teens, adults, or elders—seems immune.

Chapter 1 of this text presents some of the costs of ATOD abuse. Other information regarding use and its negative consequences is clear and compelling (Center for Substance Abuse Prevention [CSAP], 1995). The Youth Risk Behavior Surveillance System (YRBSS), sponsored by the Centers for Disease Control (CDC), provides important data on risk for youthful users.[3]

For example:

---

[1] The author wishes to thank the students in HS 422/COUN 561: Substance Abuse Prevention and Education for their contributions to this text, which is a summary of the course.

[2] Partnership for a Drug-Free America, quoted in National Institute on Drug Abuse (1997, p. 18).

[3] YRBSS data and research procedures may be obtained by contacting the CDC Web site at www.cdc.gov for more information.

- 50.8% of students surveyed had had at least one drink of alcohol on 1 or more of the 30 days preceding the survey, while 33.4% of students had had five or more drinks during the same period.

- 47.1% of students surveyed had used marijuana during their lifetime; 26.2% of students acknowledged current marijuana use. Almost 10% of students had tried marijuana before 13 years of age.

- 8.2% of students had used some form of cocaine during their lifetime, 4.7% of students had used crack or freebase forms of cocaine during their lifetime, and 3.3% acknowledged current cocaine use.

- 17% of students surveyed had used other illegal drugs (e.g., LSD, "ecstasy," mushrooms, "ice," heroin) during their lifetime.

- 16% of students had sniffed glue, breathed the contents of aerosol sprays, or inhaled paint sprays with the intent to become intoxicated during their lifetime. Students in grade 9 were significantly more likely than students in grade 12 to report inhalant use.

- 36.4% of students had smoked cigarettes on 1 or more of the 30 days preceding the survey, while 16.7% had smoked cigarettes on 20 or more of the 30 days preceding.

- Among students reporting current cigarette use, 66.7% of those under 18 years of age who purchased cigarettes in a store or gas station had not been asked to show proof of age.

As families, schools, and communities focus on the consequences of ATOD abuse and addiction, counselors will increasingly be called on to help in addressing these difficult problems. Not only will counselors be asked to help in assessing and treating affected individuals and their families; they will also become involved in efforts to *prevent* abuse and the consequences that inevitably result.

This chapter is intended to help those who are concerned with this problem and are ready to work in the area of prevention/education. It is designed to give a broad introduction to foundational terms, concepts, and currently accepted approaches in the ATOD prevention field. Resources and a basic way to proceed with effective, state-of-the-art prevention will be presented. Guidelines will be offered for those counselors who may wish to establish or collaborate in an effective program of prevention in their schools or communities.

Programs of prevention can be targeted to many different problems, age groups, and populations. Drunk driving programs, HIV/AIDS prevention programs, antismoking programs in the early school years, and cancer awareness programs of various kinds all indicate the range of possible prevention efforts. This chapter, however, will focus mainly on prevention of ATOD abuse among children, teens, and young adults. Nevertheless, the basic principles are applicable across the range of prevention initiatives. The basic perspective of the chapter will be the public health model of prevention.

CASE DISCUSSION

Case 3 (Leigh). Imagine that you are Leigh's counselor at the new school she is attending. You are called to a "special" evening meeting at the invitation of the principal; a number of concerned parents and community representatives are also attending. The topic is a perceived rise in drug use among students at the school. The goal is to formulate some way to address the problem.

You have gotten to know Leigh only recently. Her acknowledgment of "smoking some dope" every so often and drinking with friends rings true to you; you know that she is "hanging out" with other students about whom you are increasingly concerned. You are also aware of too many students in the school who live with ongoing parental conflict or are struggling with marital separation or divorce. You know other students who seem withdrawn and isolated or who are experiencing academic difficulty for no apparent reason. You have come to think of Leigh, her new friends, and these other students as "at risk" for a whole variety of problems. Your hope is that the meeting will shed some light on these concerns.

The meeting begins with the principal and several community leaders presenting anecdotal evidence of drug use among students at several other schools in the region. The local police chief and a juvenile officer speak about increased incidences of drug sales and arrests within the community. Several teachers address their concerns about students in academic difficulty and a growing sense that some of the students are distracted and uninvolved in the classroom. Several parents speak to their worries about peer pressure and their children's "friends." They demand that something be done.

As the meeting progresses, there are calls for more drug information to students, student assemblies at which the police warn of impending trouble for students caught using or selling drugs, and classroom presentations by recovering addicts who can portray the perils of drug addiction. There are calls for action by law enforcement against street dealers and even against bar owners and alcohol distributors who are suspected of providing alcohol to underage persons. While many of the parents seem unwilling to acknowledge a potential problem with their own daughters or sons, they do insist that the school and community agencies do "something" about the problem.

The principal turns to you as the school counselor to help provide a "way forward." He asks you to chair a working group of teachers and parents, charged with constructing a prevention program to be implemented in the fall. Where would you begin? What resources are available to you and the working group? What approaches make the most sense? What students would you target for intervention? How can you find out what is most likely to work? What do you do?

TYPES OF PREVENTION

ATOD use, and the problems that result from it, are best viewed on a continuum that ranges from incidents of misuse, through a pattern of increasing or chronic abuse, moving toward ATOD dependence (see Figure 11.1). Each individual has a different history of involvement with and use of drugs. For example, some use can remain chronic at a point along the continuum, while other use seems to progress. Each person's history and pattern of use presents an individualized picture of inter-

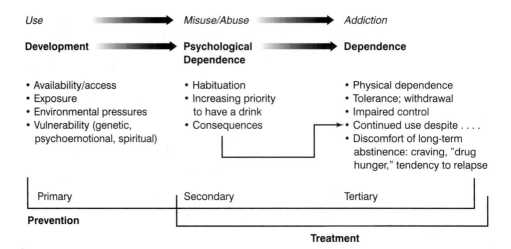

FIGURE 11.1   Natural history of alcoholism/addiction

Source: Adapted with permission of Enoch Gordts, M.D., director, National Institute on Alcohol Abuse and Alcoholism (1999).

acting factors, including environmental and social influences along with genetic, constitutional, and biological vulnerabilities (Institute of Medicine [IOM], 1989). This *individualized expression of differential factors* presents complications and important implications for assessment, treatment, and prevention (see Chapter 1).

Once there is a perceived need for prevention, initial questions involve *who* should be the targeted audience and *what goals* should be set. Understanding some basic classifications can help in formulating a response to those questions. That is, these classifications, as they relate to ATOD abuse, can help in clarifying the goals and objectives of prevention efforts.

The traditional and widely accepted public health model of prevention speaks of three important classifications: primary, secondary, and tertiary prevention (Hanson & Venturelli, 1998; IOM, 1989; McNeece & DiNitto, 1998; Ray & Ksir, 1993). *Primary* prevention is targeted at those with little or no experience with alcohol, tobacco, or other drugs. The goal of primary prevention is to prevent or delay the beginning of use by this population. Persuading young school-age children not to smoke is one example. Identifying those who may be at risk for ATOD use and helping mitigate the elements of risk in their lives is another goal. *Secondary* prevention is for novice or experienced users and those who may already be showing signs of difficulty. Identifying those who are experimenting with ATOD and helping them discontinue or limit their use encompass one form of secondary prevention; "harm reduction" strategies that diminish the type or frequency of negative consequences from ATOD use is another. Alcohol abuse prevention programs in college settings are examples of secondary prevention. *Tertiary* prevention addresses persons at the more advanced stages of ATOD abuse and/or addiction. It encompasses the same goals as treatment and relapse prevention.

The IOM (1989) has developed a slightly different classification scheme that is also helpful in prevention planning (McNeece & DiNitto, 1998). At the *universal* level, ATOD education and prevention efforts are targeted to the general population, while specifically defined at-risk populations are addressed at the *selective* level of prevention. Persons or groups who already show problems as a result of ATOD use and who require intervention to halt or ameliorate these difficulties are targeted at the *indicated* level.

Today, as we shall see, the accepted prevention paradigm is a *comprehensive* delivery of programs and services.

SINGLE-FOCUS APPROACHES

Early prevention efforts in the 1960s and 1970s focused on classroom education, dissemination of information to potential users, and scare tactics. The rationale for these efforts was a basic belief: If potential or experimenting users received accurate information about the perils and consequences of drug use, their attitudes toward use and abuse would change, and they would modify their behavior (Goode, 1999; Ray & Ksir, 1993). This *knowledge-attitudes-behavior (KAB) model* took several forms. Lectures by physicians, law enforcement officers, pharmacists, and recovering persons, sometimes bolstered by displays of various drugs and drug paraphernalia, were mainstays of these early prevention efforts. Presentations were sometimes supplemented by an array of scary antidrug films, descendants of the famous *Reefer Madness* of the 1930s. Often these lectures were accompanied by dire warnings of possible consequences, stereotypes of users, overstatements about the likely addiction that would follow from experimentation, and moralizations about the destructive lifestyle that would affect those who used (see Resnick, 1978). It is not uncommon even today to hear parents or school personnel recommend variations of this same approach as they become aware of abuse in their community.

Although well intentioned, these early efforts were based more on fear, zeal, and moralistic attitudes than on scientific knowledge. Evaluations of program effectiveness were rarely conducted; those involved were content to believe that the right thing had been done and the proper messages communicated (Moskowitz, 1989). Most prevention specialists today, however, acknowledge that this early approach was unproductive at best and potentially counterproductive (Blane, 1976, 1986; Kinney & Leaton, 1987; McNeece & DiNitto, 1998; Wallack & Corbett, 1990). Nevertheless, providing accurate information to potential drug users continues to be one element of ATOD prevention (Wallack & Corbett, 1990). As part of a more comprehensive prevention effort, providing information may be important depending on the kinds of information presented, the characteristics and needs of those targeted for information, and the context within which this information is given (Bangert-Downs, 1988).

The 1970s and 1980s saw the development of a variety of newer approaches to drug prevention and education (Wallack & Corbett, 1990). Moving beyond the traditional information-based approaches, these newer methods included *affective education* (helping students identify and express their feelings; helping them feel valued and accepted; building self-esteem), *values clarification* (assisting students in decision-making skills), teaching *alternatives* to drug use (e.g., relaxation, meditation, exercise, involvement with the arts), and development of personal and social *skills* (e.g., problem-solving, self-management, and leadership skills; recognition of peer pressure and methods of resistance). The basic belief undergirding these programs was that adolescents and others would be deterred from using drugs if their self-esteem, social and communication skills, and decision-making, problem-solving, and resistance tools were improved.

Many of these approaches showed some initial promise, but rigorous evaluation was still spotty or gave ambiguous results (Braucht & Braucht, 1984). A 1984 review of prevention programs suggested the need for more adequate evaluation, again debunked the supposed benefits of KAB models, and criticized existing approaches for lack of success in actually preventing substance abuse (National Institute on Drug Abuse [NIDA], 1984). Nevertheless, these approaches may also be important today when integrated into a more thorough and long-term approach to prevention.

The ongoing debate about effectiveness of these approaches can be seen in the case study of Project DARE (Drug Abuse Resistance Education). Begun in 1983 as a joint project of the Los Angeles Police Department and local school districts, DARE features uniformed police officers presenting a multisession program of information and affective prevention to fifth and sixth graders (McNeece & DiNitto, 1998; Ray & Ksir, 1993). The program spread rapidly across the country during the 1980s and 1990s. Many of the theoretically important prevention components are incorporated: building self-esteem, helping students recognize and resist peer pressure, practicing specific strategies for resistance and using alternative ways of coping, and emphasizing information about the consequences of ATOD use (U.S. Department of Health and Human Services, 1997). Nevertheless, evaluation of DARE's effectiveness is mixed (Aniskiewicz & Wysong, 1990; Clayton, Cattarello, & Johnstone, 1996; DeJong, 1987; Ennett et al., 1994; Gopelrud, 1991; Ringwalt et al., 1994). It may be more effective in helping parents, school, and community leaders meet the need for programming than in actually preventing ATOD abuse over the long term (Ray & Ksir, 1993).

In the 1980s, prevention efforts began to shift toward intervention into the *environment* of (potential) users (Goode, 1999). Based on "social inoculation" and "social influence" theories, this approach focused on the social environment in which students and potential users live and the temptations that they face (Goode, 1999; Ray & Ksir, 1993). Programs that were undertaken using this view included sensitivity to the social and interpersonal environment of students (e.g., family, school, neighborhood, peers), exploration of risk and protective factors that are important in these environments and are related to individual development and life transitions, training in "refusal" skills, and "normative education" (or social marketing) that was intended to correct misperceptions about the social norms governing use within peer and social groups. One example of an environmental approach that continues to show promise, and which is easily incorporated into a wider, more comprehensive strategy of ATOD prevention, is *normative education*.

A variety of social influences affect drug use. All communities or groupings of people have social norms about a variety of things from acceptable language and dress, to rules of proper conduct, values, and beliefs about ATOD use. "Norms" are perceived rules of behavior or values that influence a person's attitudes and actions. In prevention terms, norms set limits or establish guidelines that are the background or framework for ATOD use/abuse (Goode, 1999). These social norms are properties of large communities as well as of small subgroups, and the norms may conflict between groups. While norms can influence a person's behavior and attitudes directly, they can also be misperceived and still exert influence.

For example, teens tend to overestimate the number of their peers who smoke, drink, use drugs, or engage in sex. This inflated sense of what their peers are doing can powerfully influence an individual's attitudes toward ATOD use and open the doorway to his or her own experimentation and drug use (Ray & Ksir, 1993; U.S. Department of Health and Human Services, 1997). Normative education attempts to present factual information about students' social environments, creating a more realistic picture of social norms as they actually exist and reducing the "everybody does it" belief and pro-drug attitude (Ray & Ksir, 1993). When combined with other prevention strategies (e.g., resistance training, parent education), normative education to correct students' erroneous beliefs about the prevalence and acceptability of alcohol use among their peers has been shown to be an effective strategy (Hansen, 1993; U.S. Department of Health and Human Services, 1997).

Research into prevention strategies and ATOD abuse by college students also suggests the importance of this approach as part of an overall prevention plan (Berkowitz, 1997; Haines, 1996; Perkins, 1991; Perkins & Berkowitz, 1986). Using accurate survey data to correct misperceptions about campus ATOD use, attitudes, and values and tailoring programs to selected and at-risk populations, prevention specialists have achieved some important successes (Berkowitz, 1997; Hanson & Venturelli, 1998). The ongoing development of a "proactive prevention model" on college campuses indicates the importance of normative education within the context of comprehensive approaches:

> The proactive prevention model incorporates strategies of earlier models of AOD prevention, providing services to prevent abuse among non-users (primary prevention), reducing the likelihood that at-risk individuals will develop problems (secondary prevention), and helping abusers into recovery (tertiary prevention). Thus, the proactive prevention model utilizes many strategies and approaches associated with other models, but incorporates these activities into a more comprehensive, campus-wide program which emphasizes the strengthening of already existent healthy behaviors. . . .
>
> The proactive prevention model is distinguished from previous approaches by its two main components: emphasizing the importance of providing accurate information about communities and normative environments, and focusing on healthy, positive attitudes and behaviors of community members. One of the goals of this approach is to empower abstainers and responsible drinkers to take a more visible role in shaping campus ecology and modeling healthy behaviors. (Berkowitz, 1997, pp. 119–120, 124)

An example of an environmental approach carried to an extreme, however, is the "Just Say No" campaign of the Reagan administration, coupled with the strategy laid out in the 1987 publication of *What Works: Schools without Drugs* by the U.S. Department of Education. Rooted in a "zero-tolerance" approach to use in the school environment, it discusses no educational curricula or affective strategies; rather, it "stresses policies such as locker searches, suspension, and expulsion of drug-using students" (Goode, 1999, p. 366). This approach was typical of the more hard-line approaches encouraged by the "war on drugs" in the late 1980s and early 1990s, which emphasized the role of law enforcement and supply reduction tactics (e.g., increasingly harsh legal penalties for drug-related offenses, forfeiture laws, interdiction of drugs at the nation's borders) over the use of more long-term demand reduction strategies (prevention and education, treatment).

Of course, throughout this brief history of efforts at ATOD education and prevention, a focus on drug *availability*—another form of the environmental approach—has been woven into the mix, having its roots as far back as the early temperance efforts of the mid- to late 1800s. This group of prevention efforts has involved legal, law enforcement, and policy initiatives intended to limit the access of youthful and other users to a variety of substances. These efforts involve such initiatives as the pricing of some substances (e.g., taxation of cigarettes and alcohol), regulation of distribution outlets (e.g., state stores and licensing systems for wholesale and retail purchase of alcohol), minimum drinking age laws, warnings in advertisements and labeling on alcohol and cigarettes, and "dram shop" or "social host" liability (i.e., the legal and financial liability of alcohol servers for the damage that intoxicated or underage patrons may inflict on themselves or others). These efforts at limiting availability and access have also met with mixed success, when used as stand-alone prevention efforts (U.S. Department of Health and Human Services, 1997).

While many of these basic approaches—information-based, affective, environmental—may have limited effectiveness when used in isolation, they nevertheless show promise as part of an overall comprehensive strategy. Integration of these approaches into a coherent prevention strategy, directed toward clearly defined populations and having appropriate goals, is the more accepted way of proceeding today (CSAP, 1995).

In 1986, with the assistance of the federal government in its new "drug-free schools and communities" initiative, many school districts and local communities received financial assistance to enhance prevention efforts, and a number of research efforts began to evaluate the effectiveness of drug prevention programs (Ray & Ksir, 1993). Since then, a number of promising approaches to prevention have been studied and a consensus about the need for "comprehensive" prevention programming has grown:

> The most important conclusion to be reached after 20 years of organized prevention programming is that no single strategy has demonstrated a long-term impact, and many of the experts now believe that it may be a mistake to think in terms of a single-strategy solution. In many respects, life has become more complicated for the current generation. . . . Prevention efforts, therefore, must become more *comprehensive*. (McNeece & DiNitto, 1998, p. 170; my emphasis)

COMPREHENSIVE PREVENTION

Many prevention experts today emphasize the need for a comprehensive approach to ATOD prevention (Berkowitz, 1997; CSAP, 1995; Gonzalez, 1993–94; Office of Substance Abuse Prevention [OSAP], 1989; Petosa, 1992; Tobler, 1986, 1992). As Figure 11.2 shows, a comprehensive approach to prevention incorporates a number of unique characteristics compared with previous single-focus efforts.

A comprehensive prevention strategy attempts to address *multiple levels of intervention* and *multiple populations*. Depending on the context and the ATOD issues at hand, all levels of prevention—primary, secondary, and tertiary; universal, selected, and indicated—are considered and a variety of affected populations are addressed. All the possible constituencies who are involved—for example, at-risk populations, secondary-effects sufferers, and "special" populations (e.g., minorities, persons with disabilities, women)—are targeted for prevention efforts. A comprehensive strategy takes into account the variety of factors that may be involved in the problem and the available theories for addressing these factors, integrating *multiple strategies* that may be helpful in meeting current needs (e.g., information dissemination, affective programming, self-esteem building, skill development, normative education, etc.). In this effort, the strategy will envision using a number of different resources and personnel in a wide *collaborative* effort (CSAP, 1995).

A comprehensive prevention strategy will also incorporate a view of the wider *environment* and ecology within which the problem resides; community-based assessment and delivery of prevention services will be actively encouraged (CSAP, 1995). It will also be important here to consider issues of *diversity* in the planning and implementation of programs (see Chapters 8 and 9 of this text). Prevention efforts will be *developmentally appropriate*. A comprehensive strategy also attends to the *effects and consequences* of ATOD abuse on other areas of living, including on the community's values and resources. It understands that the impact of abuse is multiple and consequently so are the needs.

Finally, comprehensiveness presumes that prevention is a *long-term effort* and requires exposure to health-based messages over time. There is no such thing as a

FIGURE 11.2   Characteristics of comprehensive prevention

Comprehensive ATOD prevention strategies integrate . . .

- Multiple levels of intervention (primary, secondary, tertiary)
- Multiple populations (universal, selected, indicated)
- Multiple strategies (informational, affective, environmental)
- Networks of resources (collaborative)
- Variety of environmental factors
- Sensitivity to diversity and developmentally appropriate
- Multiple effects and consequences of use/abuse
- Need for long-term effort

"quick fix" or magic solution. Rather, a long-term commitment is required along with flexibility and the ability to adapt to changes, build on successes, and respond to failures. This requires particular attention to initial goal setting that is clear and outcome based as well as to ongoing evaluation that is tied to ongoing program revision. In this way prevention will become second nature in the environment and context of need.

In its National Structured Evaluation (NSE) of over 600 prevention modules and published results, the CSAP (1995) arrived at an important conclusion: "The delivery of a *comprehensive, coordinated, and complementary set of strategies* is likely to lead to levels of effectiveness that are much greater than could be achieved with single strategies carried out in isolation" (p. 13; my emphasis).

Comprehensive Prevention in Practice: Project HOPE

What is meant in ATOD prevention by a "comprehensive, coordinated and complementary set of strategies"? An example would be the planning and implementation of Project HOPE (Stevenson, McMillan, Mitchell, & Blanco, 1998).

With the aid of a CSAP grant, prevention specialists set out to address problems of ATOD abuse among Latino students. Survey and other data indicated that Latino youth in Rhode Island's urban centers were at high risk for substance abuse and related problems. The researchers chose to implement a multidimensional and multidisciplinary strategy of intervention targeted to seventh and eighth graders in ESL (English as a Second Language) classes at middle school sites with high numbers of Latino youth. Their goals were to increase "protective" factors (discussed later) against abuse at individual, family, and school levels and to produce actual reductions in rates of the use of alcohol, cigarettes, and marijuana.

Prevention programmers wove together several important themes into a multicomponent, comprehensive strategy:

> Recognizing the special role of the family in Latino cultural life, the project sought to strengthen parenting as well as increase parents' investment in the school institutions influencing their children's lives. Although the risks associated with parental substance abuse and inconsistent parenting are generally acknowledged, these factors become exacerbated in families experiencing the strain of adjusting to a new culture that has different norms about the role of the family. . . . On the other hand, effective parents can buffer external stresses on their children by serving as sources of support and healthy development, promoting respect for cultural traditions, supporting personal identity development, and challenging both children and school personnel to work toward school success and career direction. Family bonding is often seen as a protective factor, and this is particularly true for Latino youth. . . .
>
> The project also sought to improve the bonding between child and school more directly, recognizing the special needs growing out of a distinctive culture and language background. . . . The HOPE creators saw the school environment itself as a potential part of the problem and of the solution. (Stevenson et al., 1998, pp. 290–291)

Three major components comprise this comprehensive strategy. The Youth component consisted of three interventions: (a) a 12-session school-based ATOD prevention (e.g., risks, peer pressure and refusal skills) and career opportunity curriculum; (b) a peer leadership/positive peer culture program delivered through retreats and after-school programs and designed to empower youth for positive values, attitudes, and behaviors; and (c) a bilingual/bicultural counseling, referral, and advocacy effort within the schools. Counselors "acted as advocates for the students, and mediated with teachers and parents in order to promote school bonding" (Stevenson et al., 1998, p. 288).

The parent component consisted of a nine-session, culturally sensitive parenting skills workshop and home-based advocacy training to "increase parents' ability to be advocates for their children with the school system" (Stevenson et al., 1998, p. 288). A school component was also designed to increase teachers' and administrators' sensitivities to Latino needs, including ongoing conversation with Latino community leaders.

Using a variety of evaluation measures, the Project HOPE programmers documented positive changes in school attendance, cultural pride, and peer culture; in parents' engagement with the school institutions and students' perceptions of the school environment; and in measurable reductions in alcohol use. These prevention researchers believe that "the multi-component nature of the project was essential for impact" (Stevenson et al., 1998, p. 315). Integrating several theory-based interventions into a comprehensive strategy with a known at-risk population appears to have increased the effectiveness of this prevention effort.

RISK AND PROTECTIVE FACTORS

Multiple and individually expressed factors that interact in the etiology and maintenance of ATOD use and abuse suggest the need for multiple, integrated strategies to combat abuse. As we have seen, this point argues for the need for comprehensive prevention. One contemporary approach that is receiving a lot of attention, and that includes a comprehensive understanding of factors in prevention, is the study of risk and protective factors as they relate to ATOD use and abuse (Acuda & Alexander, 1998; Botvin, Malgady, Griffin, Scheier, & Epstein, 1998; CSAP, 1995; Florida Alcohol and Drug Abuse Association, 1996; Hawkins, Catalano, & Miller, 1992; Liepman, Keller, Botelho, Monroe, & Sloane, 1998; NIDA, 1997). Reviews of this important approach, as it relates to culturally diverse groups, are reported in Bhattacharya (1998), Cherry et al. (1998), LeMaster (1998), and Stevenson et al. (1998). Reports of factor differences between urban and rural youth appear in Botvin et al. (1998) and Farrell and White (1998).

In constructing or evaluating ATOD prevention programs, particularly those aimed at youth and young adults, it is important to have some knowledge of the *risk* factors that may predispose vulnerable individuals or groups to use/abuse and of the *protective* factors that may inoculate individuals or groups from use or problems of abuse. A brief summary of such factors is given in Table 11.1.

Again using the public health model, an understanding of ATOD prevention ought to encompass the *agent* (e.g., alcohol or marijuana) involved, the *individual*

TABLE 11.1 Risk and protective factors: ATOD abuse*

Levels	Risk Factors	Protective Factors
I. Agent	Early onset of use Choice of drug Experimentation "Gateway" effect	Delayed onset of use
II. Host 1. Biomedical	Genetic vulnerability Physiological vulnerability Age Sex Race/ethnicity	
2. Personality/character	Novelty and thrill seeking/risk taking Alienation and rebelliousness Poor impulse control Poor coping skills Co-occurrence of psychiatric disorders High stress (inter- or intrapersonal, life transitions) Misperceptions of peer use Particular life challenges (e.g., homosexuality, disability, oppression)	Self-esteem and internal locus of control Self-discipline Problem-solving and critical thinking skills Sense of humor
3. Behavioral/attitudinal	Social marginalization ("failure to fit in") Early antisocial behavior Perceived "invulnerability" Favorable attitudes toward ATOD use Susceptibility to peer influence Friends who use ATOD Perceived benefits (e.g., social acceptance, anxiety reduction, performance enhancement) Other risky behaviors (e.g., risky driving, violence)	Positive peer influence Effectiveness in work, play, and relationships Perceived dangers of ATOD use and consequences Healthy expectations and positive assessment of future Relationship with caring adult Positive moral values Opportunities to contribute positively Religious involvement

III. Environment

	Risk Factors	Protective Factors
1. Family	Family dysfunction/trauma/major loss Lack of caring Lack of clear behavioral expectations Poor supervision Inconsistent or excessive discipline Low expectations for individual success Permissive parental attitudes re ATOD use Influence of older siblings History of ATOD use	Family bonding ("nurturing attachments") Clear and high expectations Parent communication and involvement Consistent praise/low criticism "Quality" time "Responsible decisions" message Influence of older siblings Healthy stress management Sharing responsibilities
2. School	Alienation Poor performance Learning problems (e.g., ADHD) School dropout	Involvement (e.g., athletics, extracurriculars) School performance Positive school climate
3. Community	Availability Unhealthy/ambivalent social norms	Access barriers (e.g., pricing, age restrictions) Clear messages re use Drug-free alternatives Opportunities for prosocial action (e.g., mentoring, peer support, community service)
4. Other	Media/advertising portrayals of ATOD Societal institutions disintegrating, ignoring youth needs, or having lack of appeal	Healthy norms in larger community (e.g., media) Cultural focus on healthy decisions Honest and comprehensive ATOD education Religious involvement

*No single risk factor is determinative; multiple factors interact in an additive manner.

(host) who uses, and the *environment* (social context, immediate surroundings, local community, society) in which an individual obtains or uses psychoactive substances (CSAP, 1995). The model emphasizes the interactive nature of these elements (IOM, 1989) and suggests interventions at any of these three levels that may address or reduce risk (Committee to Identify Research Opportunities, 1992). Our examination of risk and protective factors in ATOD prevention follows these three categories.[4]

Risk factors are "characteristics that occur statistically more often for those who develop ATOD problems, either as adolescents or as adults" (CSAP, 1995, p. 24). They are "indicators" of potential trouble and may be helpful in identifying those who are vulnerable to developing ATOD difficulties. One way to utilize Table 11.1 is to review the column of risk factors, organized according to agent, host, and environment.

CASE DISCUSSION

Case 3 (Leigh).   Leigh is already "experimenting" with pot and alcohol (agent). While she may or may not have a biomedical vulnerability to ATOD use, she may well be experiencing high levels of stress due to her family situation and move to a new school; she has found new friends who use and is likely to have favorable attitudes toward ATOD use as well as a sense of perceived benefits that result from use (host). Her difficulties with several important social systems such as family and school, as well as the potential availability of ATOD in her environment, are also some of the factors (environment) in her at-risk picture.

While no one risk factor can predict a person's ATOD use or abuse, the cumulative effect of a number of risk factors—and the timing of their occurrence in individual and family development across the life span—may help counselors and others identify those who are vulnerable and begin to think through how to help.

The risk-based approach suggests that there will be some benefit to addressing certain risk "targets" for prevention intervention, such as family relationships, school environment, peer relationships, and the wider community. Individual risk characteristics may also be addressed, such as social marginalization, misperceptions of wider peer use, stress, coping skills, and the like. Prevention planners must be prepared to address these targets through a variety of appropriate interventions. Sharing accurate information, developing self-esteem and resistance skills, providing normative education, building effective parent networks, working with community leaders to change

---

[4] A concise yet thorough review of this material, organized in a similar way, may be obtained in the CSAP (1995) report *Making Prevention Work* (DHHS Publication No. [SMA] 95-120). A copy may be ordered free of charge through the Substance Abuse and Mental Health Services Administration or The National Clearinghouse on Alcohol and Drug Information: (800) 729-6686.

the availability and access to alcohol and other drugs—any one of these strategies may be appropriate in meeting the needs of those involved.

"Prevention efforts can enhance protective factors and move toward reversing or reducing risk factors" (NIDA, 1997, p. 4). A comprehensive approach to ATOD prevention suggests that reducing risks can be complemented by a strategy of enhancing resiliency (CSAP, 1995). Here the value of "protective" factors comes to the fore. These factors tend to inoculate potential users against the need, desire, or social influence that lead to use/abuse; they are associated with reduced potential for use. A review of the column labeled "Protective Factors" in Table 11.1 will suggest a number of potential strategies for enhancing personal and social resiliency.

Project HOPE, referred to earlier in this chapter, is one example of a comprehensive prevention program that integrated risk reduction and resiliency building into its approach. Each of the strategies used in its Youth, Parent, and School components was intended to achieve this dual purpose.

CASE DISCUSSION

Case 3 (Leigh).   A comprehensive prevention program in Leigh's school may begin to take shape as the counselor's working group considers a set of complementary and integrated strategies. Informed by the risk and protective factors approach, these strategies might include the following:

- Identification of those already using and assessment of the risk factors that may be most powerfully operative. Establishment of peer intervention and peer support programs (e.g., Student Assistance Programs [SAPs], children-of-divorce support groups) to address risks and to establish positive connections among youth, and between students and school (secondary prevention; selected level) may be needed.

- Assessment of the needs of the general student population and provision of accurate information about the risks and consequences of ATOD use/abuse (primary prevention; universal level)

- Parent programs that share accurate ATOD information, address parent concerns about how to discuss drug use with their children, and connect parents with one another in a caring network of mutual support (primary and secondary prevention; universal level)

- Identification of students and families experiencing dysfunction, undergoing high levels of stress or conflict, and/or having histories of ATOD abuse; provision of services for counseling or intervention (tertiary prevention; indicated level)

- Creating school policies and teacher in-service programming to help in identifying at-risk students and creating involvement of school personnel in "student success- and support-oriented" initiatives, such as peer education, personal relationships with caring adults, and student service organizations with opportunities to make positive contributions to the community (primary prevention; universal level)

These strategies and more may become part of an overall comprehensive prevention plan in Leigh's school that is sensitive to risk and protective factors in the lives of youth.

STEPS TO AN EFFECTIVE PREVENTION PROGRAM

At a practical level, it is important to understand that prevention strategies must be built on a sound planning process. For a comprehensive strategy to succeed, it is essential that this planning be conducted and/or affirmed by a representative group of stakeholders, members of the community who represent various important constituencies—for example, schools, law enforcement, media, health service organizations, families, churches, and so forth. A number of important questions ought to be addressed as the core considerations of the planning process. Table 11.2, taken from the Office of Substance Abuse prevention guide (OSAP, 1989), *Planning Plus II*, shows these questions.

Notice that effective prevention planning begins with needs assessment and the development of goals and "measurable" objectives. These first three steps are essen-

TABLE 11.2   Basic prevention planning questions

Planning Step	Prevention Planning Issue
1. Needs assessment	What ATOD problems does the community need to address?
2. Development of goals	What should be achieved in the short term? Long-term?
3. Development of objectives	What *measurable* results can be realistically achieved? On what timetable? Be as specific as possible!
4. Identification of resources	What resources (financial, personnel, etc.) does the strategy need to achieve the objectives?
5. Identification of funding sources	Where will the money come from?
6. Assignment of leadership tasks	Who is best equipped and responsible for each part of the prevention strategy?
7. Implementation	What procedures will keep the program/strategy on track?
8. Evaluation	How can the community determine whether the objectives are met? Is there a commitment to do so?
9. Program revision	What (ongoing) changes are needed to improve the program/strategy?

Source: Adapted from OSAP (1989).

tial, and prevention planners must be willing to take the time and energy to pursue them thoroughly. Affirmation and acceptance by community leaders ("gatekeepers," such as school administrators and parents) of the needs, goals, and objectives that are developed in these first three steps are essential for program success. Notice, too, that these steps are tied to evaluation (step 8) and program revision (step 9). Without clear and measurable objectives, effective evaluation is nearly impossible.

Prevention planners should have no illusions, however, about the ease or time frame required to achieve these first three steps. School personnel, and even parents, can be hesitant about conducting a thorough needs assessment. While it may seem obvious that prevention initiatives require a sound understanding of the extent and scope of the problem in a particular setting, this information can also be disquieting and may be perceived as damaging in the short term from a public relations point of view. In addition, gatekeepers themselves may need to be educated about the approaches and underlying assumptions that guide selection of specific goals and objectives. Here, prevention planners may have to confront misperceptions about the effectiveness of some "common-sense" strategies (e.g., information dissemination and scare tactics) and will have to address potential strongly held value positions among gatekeepers to win their assent and support (see, e.g., Goodstadt, 1989; Milgram, 1987; Moskowitz, 1989). Discussions of issues such as the (potential) objective of zero tolerance versus responsible decisions, or abstinence versus harm reduction, will inevitably have to occur. Winning the support of gatekeepers will take time in such cases but is critical for long-term program support, gathering resources, implementation, and effectiveness.

In addition, having clearly held and affirmed goals and objectives will be necessary for evaluation of program effectiveness. A well-thought-out plan of evaluation can help in assessing program successes, addressing program failures, and revising program delivery to increase positive outcomes. This, too, will take time and energy but is essential in achieving prevention goals.

A sound planning process is only the first step, however, in constructing an effective and comprehensive prevention program. Based on the best research available, the OSAP (1989) has constructed a listing of 12 "attributes" of successful prevention programs (see Table 11.3). Planning, implementation, evaluation, and ongoing program revision are the hallmarks of the best programs. Prevention providers will benefit from a careful review of these important attributes.

IMPLICATIONS FOR COUNSELING

Counselors are increasingly called on to be agents of change (Lee & Walz, 1998) in today's world. This "mandate" includes involvement in formulating and collaborating with strategies of prevention that benefit communities. Working with high-risk youth and preventing ATOD abuse is one important way in which counselors can help (Capuzzi, 1998).

As counselors move into the 21st century, it is critical that they have the knowledge base and skills necessary for prevention work. The task of training tomorrow's

TABLE 11.3   Twelve attributes of effective prevention programs

Attributes	Brief Descriptions
1. Program planning process	Comprehensive and integrated Theory based Conducted or affirmed by community stakeholders
2. Goals and objectives	Based on community needs assessment Specific, measurable goals and outcomes Matches specific action plans to target groups
3. Multiple activities	Strategically integrated multiple actions (e.g., information, skills development, alternatives, public policy) Actions delivered in sufficient quantity to affect targets
4. Multiple targets/populations	Includes all affected elements of community or population served
5. Evaluation base	Mechanism for data collection on ongoing basis Method of cost analysis/effectiveness Focus on behavior change Tied back to planning process/revision
6. Sensitive to needs of all	Sensitive to issues of diversity (e.g., minority, ethnicity, immigrant, disability, lifestyle, age, sex)
7. Part of overall health promotion/system	Collaborates with other programs/systems to increase community health
8. Community involvement and ownership	Shared responsibility/grassroots ownership
9. Long-term programming	No "quick fix" Long-term commitment that is flexible, adaptable, and responsive
10. Multiple systems/levels	Collaborative effort of multiple social systems (e.g., family, church, school, recreation, law enforcement, media)
11. Marketing/promotion	Showcase positive efforts of prevention
12. Replicability/generalizability	Sufficient documentation and clarity to permit development of related programming

Source: Adapted from OSAP (1989, pp. 297–299).

professional counselors, particularly in the areas of social change, advocacy, and prevention, is the responsibility of today's counselor educators (Capuzzi, 1998; Collison et al., 1998). While training standards for the best counselor education programs (e.g., those approved by the Council for the Accreditation of Counseling and Related Educational Programs [CACREP]) include provisions for overall health promotion and prevention, recent studies indicate that a gap still persists in the preparation of counselors in the area of ATOD abuse, addiction, intervention, and prevention (Morgan, Toloczko, & Comly, 1997; Toloczko et al., 1998). This gap must be addressed.

Counselors will need to be thoroughly grounded in the principles and techniques of prevention and systemic change and have the self-esteem and advocacy skills to implement these changes. . . . [C]ounselors need to be trained to do both developmental counseling and preventive program planning as well as diagnosis and treatment planning. . . . A comprehensive knowledge and skills base must be delivered via every counselor education program in the country. (Capuzzi, 1998, p. 113)

CONCLUSION

This chapter has been designed to provide experienced counselors and counselors in training with the foundational concepts, trends, and knowledge that will enable them to participate in ATOD prevention and education programming. This work is both exciting and challenging. It is an essential element in the modern counselor's role as an agent of change.

Building on lessons learned from the past, today's prevention efforts need to be comprehensive, collaborative, and based on current knowledge about what works. The most effective prevention programs are an integrated and coordinated set of strategies, constructed to enhance the health and well-being of persons and to reduce the risk of abusive behavior and its consequences.

For the student or experienced professional who wants to learn more, a number of prevention-related Internet Web sites are provided here. These are only a small sampling of the information and resources that are available, yet they will help concerned counselors to continue their own development in this important area of professional work.

SELECT INTERNET WEB SITES ON ATOD PREVENTION AND EDUCATION

Government Sites
National Clearinghouse for Alcohol and Drug Information (NCADI)
http://www.health.org/

National Institute on Alcohol Abuse and Alcoholism (NIAAA)
http://www.niaaa.nih.gov/

National Institute on Drug Abuse (NIDA)
http://www.nida.nih.gov/

Substance Abuse and Mental Health Services Administration (SAMSHA),
Department of Health and Human Services
http://www.samsha.gov/

University-Based Sites
Center for Alcohol and Addiction Studies (CAAS) at Brown University
http://center.butler.brown.edu/

Higher Education Center for Alcohol and Other Drug Prevention
http://www.edc.org/hec/

The National Center on Addiction and Substance Abuse (CASA) at Columbia University
http://www.casacolumbia.org/home.htm

School of Public Health, Harvard University/ College Alcohol Study
http://www.hsph.harvard.edu/cas/

Miscellaneous
American Society of Addiction Medicine (ASAM)
http://207.201.181.5/asam50.htm

Lindesmith Center
http://www.lindesmith.org/

Partnership for a Drug-Free America (PDFA)
http://www.drugfreeamerica.org/

Partnership for Responsible Drug Information
http://www.prdi.org/

REFERENCES

Acuda, W., & Alexander, B. (1998). Individual characteristics and drinking patterns. In M. Grant & J. Litvak (Eds.), *Drinking patterns and their consequences* (pp. 43–62). Washington, DC: Taylor & Francis.

Aniskiewicz, R., & Wysong, E. (1990). Evaluating DARE: Drug education and the multiple meanings of success. *Policy Studies Review, 9,* 727.

Bangert-Downs, R. L. (1988). The effectiveness of school-based substance abuse education—A meta-analysis. *Journal of Drug Education, 18*(3), 243–265.

Berkowitz, A. D. (1997). From reactive to proactive prevention: Promoting an ecology of health on campus. In P. C. Rivers & E. R. Shore (Eds.), *Substance abuse on campus: A handbook for college and university personnel* (pp. 119–139). Westport, CT: Greenwood.

Bhattacharya, G. (1998). Drug use among Asian-Indian adolescents: Identifying protective/risk factors. *Adolescence, 33*(129), 169–184.

Blane, H. T. (1976). Education and prevention of alcoholism. In B. Kissin & H. Begleiter (Eds.), *The biology of alcoholism* (Vol. 4, Chap. 12). New York: Plenum.

Blane, H. T. (1986). Preventing alcohol problems. In N. J. Estes & M. E. Heinemann (Eds.), *Alcoholism: Development, consequences, and interventions* (3rd ed., pp. 78–90). St. Louis: Mosby.

Botvin, G. J., Malgady, R. G., Griffin, K. W., Scheier, L. M., & Epstein, J. A. (1998). Alcohol and marijuana use among rural youth: Interaction of social and intrapersonal influences. *Addictive Behaviors, 23*(3), 379–387.

Braucht, G. N., & Braucht, B. (1984). Prevention of problem drinking among youth: Evaluation of educational strategies. In P. M. Miller & T. D. Nirenberg (Eds.), *Prevention of alcohol abuse* (pp. 253–279). New York: Plenum.

Capuzzi, D. (1998). Addressing the needs of at-risk youth: Early prevention and systemic intervention. In C. C. Lee & G. R. Walz (Eds.), *Social action: A mandate for counselors* (pp. 99–116). Alexandria, VA, and Greensboro, NC: American Counseling Association and the ERIC Counseling and Student Services Clearinghouse.

Center for Substance Abuse Prevention. (1995). *Making prevention work.* DHHS Publication No. (SMA) 95-120. Washington, DC: U.S. Department of Health and Human Services.

Cherry, V. R., Belgrave, F. Z., Jones, W., Kennon, D. K., Gray, F. S., & Phillips, F. (1998). NTU: An Africentric approach to substance abuse prevention among African American youth. *Journal of Primary Prevention, 18*(3), 319–339.

Clayton, R. R., Cattarello, A. M., & Johnstone, B. M. (1996). The effectiveness of Drug Abuse Resistance Education (Project DARE): 5-year follow-up results. *Preventive Medicine, 25,* 307–318.

Collison, B. B., Osborne, J. L., Gray, L. A., House, R. M., Firth, J., & Lou, M. (1998). Preparing counselors for social action. In C. C. Lee and G. R. Walz (Eds.), *Social action: A mandate for counselors* (pp. 263–277). Alexandria, VA, and Greensboro, NC: American Counseling Association and the ERIC Counseling and Student Services Clearinghouse.

Committee to Identify Research Opportunities in the Prevention and Treatment of Alcohol-Related Problems, Institute of Medicine. (1992). Prevention and treatment of alcohol-related problems: Research opportunities. *Journal of Studies on Alcohol, 53*(1), 5–16.

DeJong, W. (1987). A short-term evaluation of Project DARE (Drug Abuse Resistance Education): Preliminary indications of effectiveness. *Journal of Drug Education, 17*(4), 279–294.

Ennett, S. T., Rosenbaum, D. P., Flewelling, R. L., Bieler, G. S., Ringwalt, C. L., & Bailey, S. L. (1994). Long-term evaluation of drug abuse resistance education. *Addictive Behaviors, 19*(2), 113–125.

Farrell, A. D., & White, K. S. (1998). Peer influences and drug use among urban adolescents: Family structure and parent-adolescent relationship as protective factors. *Journal of Consulting and Clinical Psychology, 66*(2), 248–258.

Florida Alcohol and Drug Abuse Association. (1996). *Just the facts: Family risk and protective factors*. Educational Fact Sheet available from FADAA Resource Center, 1030 E. Lafayette St., Suite 100, Tallahassee, FL 32301.

Gonzalez, G. (1993–1994). Can colleges reduce student drinking? *Planning for Higher Education, 22*(2), 14–21.

Goode, E. (1999). *Drugs in American society* (5th ed.). Boston: McGraw-Hill.

Goodstadt, M. S. (1989). Drug education: The prevention issues. *Journal of Drug Education, 19*(3), 197–208.

Gopelrud, E. N. (Ed.). (1991). *Preventing adolescent drug use: From theory to practice*. Monograph 8, DHHS Publication No. (ADM) 91-1725. Rockville, MD: Office of Substance Abuse Prevention.

Haines, M. P. (1996). *A social norms approach to preventing binge drinking at colleges and universities*. Newton, MA: Higher Education Center for Alcohol and Other Drug Prevention.

Hansen, W. B. (1993). School-based alcohol prevention programs. *Alcohol Health and Research World, 17*(1), 54–60.

Hanson, G., & Venturelli, P. (1998). *Drugs and society* (5th ed.). Sudbury, MA: Jones & Bartlett.

Hawkins, J. D., Catalano, R. F., & Miller, J. Y. (1992, July). Risk and protective factors for alcohol and other drug problems in adolescence and early adulthood: Implications for substance abuse prevention. *Psychological Bulletin, 112*(1), 64–105.

Institute of Medicine. (1989). *Prevention and treatment of alcohol problems: Research opportunities*. Washington, DC: National Academy Press.

Kinney, J., & Leaton, G. (1987). *Loosening the grip: A handbook of alcohol information*. St. Louis, MO: Times Mirror/Mosby College.

Lee, C. C., & Walz, G. R. (Eds.). (1998). *Social action: A mandate for counselors*. Alexandria, VA, and Greensboro, NC: American Counseling Association and the ERIC Counseling and Student Services Clearinghouse.

LeMaster, P. L. (1998). Protective and risk factors for problem health behaviors among American Indian adolescents. *Dissertation Abstracts International, 58*(10), 5353-B.

Liepman, M. R., Keller, D. M., Botelho, R. J., Monroe, A. D., and Sloane, M. A. (1998). Understanding and preventing substance abuse by adolescents: A guide for primary care clinicians. *Primary Care, 25*(1), 137–162.

McNeece, C. A., & DiNitto, D. M. (1998). *Chemical dependency: A systems approach* (2nd ed.). Boston: Allyn & Bacon.

Milgram, G. G. (1987). Alcohol and drug education programs. *Journal of Drug Education, 17*(1), 43–57.

Morgan, O. J., Toloczko, A. M., & Comly, E. (1997). Graduate training of counselors in the addictions: A study of CACREP-approved programs. *Journal of Addictions & Offender Counseling, 17*(2), 66–76.

Moskowitz, J. M. (1989). The primary prevention of alcohol problems: A critical review of the research literature. *Journal of Studies on Alcohol, 50*(1), 54–88.

National Institute on Drug Abuse. (1984). *Drug abuse and drug abuse research*. DHHS Publication No. (ADM) 85-1372. [First in a series of triennial reports to Congress from the Secretary, Department of Health and Human Services]. Washington, DC: U.S. Department of Health and Human Services.

National Institute on Drug Abuse. (1997). *Preventing drug use among children and adolescents: A research-based guide*. NIH Publication No. 97-4212. Washington, DC: Author.

Office of Substance Abuse Prevention. (1989). *Prevention plus II: Tools for creating and sustaining drug-free communities*. DHHS Publication No. (ADM) 89-1649. Washington, DC: Author.

Perkins, H. W. (1991). Confronting misperceptions of peer use norms among college students: An alternative approach for alcohol and other drug education programs. In *The Higher Education Leaders/Peers Network Peer Prevention Program Resource Manual* (pp. 18–32). Washington, DC: Texas Christian University, U.S. Department of Education, Fund for the Improvement of Post-Secondary Education.

Perkins, H. W., & Berkowitz, A. D. (1986). Perceiving the community norms of alcohol use among students: Some research implications for campus alcohol education programming. *International Journal of the Addictions, 21*(9/10), 961–976.

Petosa, R. (1992). Developing a comprehensive health promotion program to prevent adolescent drug abuse. In G. W. Lawson & A. W. Lawson (Eds.), *Adolescent substance abuse: Etiology, treatment, and prevention* (pp. 431–449). Gaithersburg, MD: Aspen.

Ray, O., & Ksir, C. (1993). *Drugs, society and human behavior* (6th ed.). St. Louis, MO: Mosby–Year Book.

Resnick, H. S. (1978). *It starts with people: Experiences in drug abuse prevention*. Washington, DC: U.S. Department of Health, Education, and Welfare.

Ringwalt, C. L., Green, J. M., Ennett, S. T., Iachan, R., Clayton, R. R., & Leukfeld, C. G. (1994, June). *Past and future directions of the D.A.R.E. Program: Draft final report*. Research Triangle Park, NC: Research Triangle Institute.

Stevenson, J. F., McMillan, B., Mitchell, R. E., & Blanco, M. (1998). Project HOPE: Altering risk and protective factors among high risk Hispanic youth and their families. *Journal of Primary Prevention, 18*(3), 287–317.

Tobler, N. S. (1986). Meta-analysis of 143 adolescent drug prevention programs: Qualitative outcome results of program participants compared to a control or comparison group. *Journal of Drug Issues, 16*(4), 537–567.

Tobler, N. S. (1992). Drug prevention programs can work: Research findings. *Journal of Addictive Diseases, 11*(3), 1–28.

Toloczko, A. M., Morgan, O. J., Hall, D., Bruch, L. A., Mullane, J., & Walck, C. (1998). Graduate training of rehabilitation counselors in the addictions: A study of CORE-approved programs. *Rehabilitation Education, 12*(2), 115–127.

U.S. Department of Health and Human Services. (1997). *Ninth special report to the U.S. Congress on alcohol and health*. NIH Publication No. 97-4017. Washington, DC: Author.

Wallack, L., & Corbett, K. (1990). Illicit drug, tobacco and alcohol use among youth: Trends and promising approaches in prevention. In H. Resnik, S. E. Gardner, R. P. Lorian, & C. E. Marcus (Eds.), *Youth and drugs: Society's mixed messages* (pp. 5–29). OSAP Prevention Monograph No. 6, Alcohol, Drug Abuse, and Mental Health Administration, Office for Substance Abuse Prevention. Rockville, MD: U.S. Department of Health and Human Services, Public Health Service.

Research and Contemporary Issues

ROBERT L. SMITH, PH.D.

There remains a demand for greater emphasis on research concerning alcohol, tobacco, and other drugs (ATOD), specifically concerning the efficacy of programs designed to minimize their abuse. This chapter reviews major problems that have prevented concise, well-focused research in treating substance abuse, followed by a summary of relevant research concerning the effectiveness of many present day treatment models. The second section of this chapter examines several contemporary issues in the field of substance abuse counseling and treatment. The issues covered also demand further investigation and professional discussion.

RESEARCH

Problems with Substance Abuse Research

Research attempts in substance abuse treatment have produced a sparse number of controlled studies that can be replicated and clinically applied. Despite an ongoing interest in research and a concern for "what works" in the field, few definitive answers to this widespread phenomenon have evolved. However, after reviewing treatment for alcohol problems, Hester and Miller (1995) do conclude the following:

1. Persuasive evidence in the treatment research literature indicates that a number of different approaches are significantly better than no intervention.

2. No single approach stands out as superior to all others.

3. The answer to effective treatment seems to be selecting the right approach for the individual from a large array of effective alternatives.

Despite recent optimism, there are still few well-designed studies on substance abuse treatment. A major variable preventing clearly definable research in this field is the fact that substance abuse is a phenomenon usually not attributed to a singe cause or even a small number of events. Why one engages in the abuse of a substance in the first place is affected by a number of social, psychological, cultural, and biological factors. The degree to which each of these influence and eventually affect the long-term use of substances often compounds the study.

Treatment methods that have been used to remedy substance abuse have been wide ranging. In some cases, treatment methods are limited to the therapist's own training and/or experiences. Treatment centers or agencies can also obscure well-designed studies by advocating only one theoretical stance or treatment, making it impossible to do comparative studies involving several effective methods.

Often, treatment centers using multidimensional approaches with substance abuse clients are unable to determine what specific treatment modalities are responsible for producing a specific change (Walden House Day Treatment Program, 1995). For example, many substance abuse clients participate in concurrent programs such as cognitive therapy, family systems therapy, AA groups, education seminars, and peer consultation groups. When successful, the combination of these treatment modalities can be seen as the change agent. Nevertheless, the specific treatment modalities considered most significant to the change process itself are rarely identified.

Additional research concerns in substance abuse treatment include a lack of standardized measures used to gather information concerning substance abuse clients. Measures used to obtain the health history of clients vary widely and are often germane only to a particular center or agency, thus producing independent sets of non-standardized data. Comparative analyses in these cases are impossible. There is also minimal consistency concerning the use of standardized instruments that attempt to measure treatment change. Because of these inconsistencies, a comparative analysis of outcome research findings has been impossible.

However, general research findings have produced a few conclusions concerning substance abuse treatment. For example, research evidence (Doweiko, 1999) suggests that for many the use of outpatient drug addictions treatment is as effective as inpatient programs. This becomes relevant in today's climate when considering health care delivery costs. Miller et al. (1995) found a significant negative correlation between the strength of efficacy evidence for modalities and their cost; that is, the more expensive the treatment method, the less the scientific evidence documenting its efficacy. In addition, Miller et al. (1995), after conducting a meta-analysis of treatment modalities used with alcohol problems, found brief interventions to have one of the largest databases and to be most positive in its results.

Alcoholism Outcome Research

Significantly more research investigations have examined the effects of treatment on alcohol abuse as compared to other drugs. Also, alcohol treatment programs have yielded better results as compared to other drug abuse treatment programs. One of the most comprehensive studies of outcome research on alcoholism was provided by Hester (1994). This study reviewed the following variables: (a) evidence of effectiveness, (b) insufficient evidence of effectiveness, (c) indeterminate evidence of effectiveness, (d) fair evidence of effectiveness, and (e) good evidence of effectiveness. For a treatment program to be considered effective, it had to show significant reduction in intake of alcohol as compared to a control group. This is one of the few reviews that as its standard included control or comparison groups. Summarized findings from 250 studies are examined as follows:

Treatments of Alcoholism with No Evidence of Effectiveness (a review of control group studies only)

- Antianxiety medications
- Cognitive therapy
- Confrontational interventions
- Educational lectures/films
- Electrical aversion therapies
- General counseling
- Group therapies
- Insight-oriented psychotherapy
- Nausea aversion therapies
- Residential milieu therapies

It should be made clear that effectiveness in this review is based on whether controlled or comparison groups were used. Therefore, a special note concerning general counseling and group therapy deserves mention. Often in treatment, general counseling and group therapies are defined in global terms, hence not rendering themselves to research possibilities. Therefore, one should not conclude general ineffectiveness of these treatment models based on the criteria used by the investigator.

The following treatments have a minimal number of studies that fit Hester's criteria for scientific rigor:

Insufficient Evidence of Effectiveness

- Alcoholics Anonymous
- Minnesota Model of residential treatment
- Halfway houses
- Acupuncture
- Calcium carbide (an antidipsotropic medication not available in the United States)

A special notation needs to be made concerning the AA model of treatment. Because of the lack of controlled studies, this model is placed in this category. Like many other treatment models AA can identify a significant number of individuals that will attest to its effectiveness in dealing with alcohol abuse. Research on the AA model is presented later in this chapter.

A minimal number of controlled or comparison studies have been located using the following treatments, making it difficult to determine their effectiveness.

Indeterminate Evidence of Effectiveness

- Nonbehavior marital therapy
- Hypnosis
- Lithium

Structural and strategic approaches are included in the list of nonbehavioral marital therapies studied.

Hester (1994) found four or more controlled studies that reasonably supported the following treatment modalities indicating a fair level of effectiveness with alcohol abuse problems:

Fair Evidence of Effectiveness

- Antidepressant medication
- Behavior contracting
- Covert sensitization
- Oral and implant disulfiram

The following treatment models have produced enough control studies to report good evidence of effectiveness, according to Hester:

Good Evidence of Effectiveness

- Behavioral marital therapy
- Brief interventions
- Community reinforcement approach (CRA)
- Self-control training
- Social skills/training
- Stress management

Behavioral marital therapy includes increasing the frequency of positive reinforcements given in a relationship. Both conjoint therapy and couple's therapy use communication skill building and problem solving, reflecting a behavioral approach producing significant results (Hester, 1995). Manuals describing this approach are available (McCrady, 1982; O'Farrell, 1986; O'Farrell & Cowles, 1989; O'Farrell &

Cutter, 1984). Many of the other approaches listed in this category are also behavioral in nature.

An example of a brief intervention model is FRAMES, elements of which are described by Miller and Rollnick (1991):

*F*eedback regarding a patient's drinking that is individualized and objective

*R*esponsibility that is placed on the patient for deciding what to do regarding drinking

Clear *A*dvice to change

A *M*enu of interventions and options for change, including a willingness to negotiate the goals of change

An *E*mpathic style of counseling

*S*elf-efficacy

Outcome research on methadone maintenance programs, outpatient programs, and residential programs are examined next. Results are often reported in terms of degrees of improvement over time and the extent to which clients relapse.

Methadone Maintenance Outcome Research

Methadone maintenance (MM) programs, specifically designed for narcotic analgesic dependence, have been widely discussed (Booth, 1995; O'Brien, 1996; Levy & Rutter, 1992). Used mainly for the treatment of heroin addiction, the foundation of the methadone maintenance program is that all narcotic analgesics may be substituted for one another. The use of methadone in this regard has been extensive owing to minimal clinical side effects (Gerstein & Harwood, 1994).

Using methadone maintenance programs offers a number of benefits. One has been cost-effectiveness, particularly when considering clients' reduction in criminal activity. A second benefit has been that methadone maintenance programs seem to help reduce the spread of HIV-1 infection (DeMaria & Weinstein, 1995).

Early research findings on the methadone maintenance programs (Dole & Nyswander, 1965) found that most patients using this approach would remain in treatment when compared to others experiencing outpatient psychotherapy and that behavior by patients in the community drastically improved. In addition, early findings showed criminal behavior as decreasing along with a decline in the use of other drugs. A well-designed study in Sweden (Gunne & Grombladh, 1984) revealed significant findings on the use of methadone with 34 heroin-dependent individuals. In this study, 17 individuals were randomly assigned to MM, and a second 17 were given outpatient nonmethadone treatment. A 2-year follow-up revealed that 71% of the MM patients were doing well compared to 6% from the control group. A 5-year follow-up found 13 methadone patients remaining in treatment and not using heroin. For the control group, 9 patients subsequently entered MM, with 8 not using heroin. Of the 8 control patients not applying for MM, 5 were reported dead of an overdose of drugs, 2 were in prison, and 1 was drug-free. Other studies in which MM was used in either public or private settings (owing to the closure of many clinics) have produced similar results (Anglin et. al, 1989; McGlothlin & Anglin, 1981).

An issue raised in relation to the effectiveness of methadone treatment involves clinic policies and counselor characteristics. Programs committed to low average doses of methadone for patients, as a result of clinic philosophy or influence from state regulators, have revealed lower retention rates and greater drug use by patients. It has been documented (Hargraves, 1983) that higher dose levels of methadone are significantly more successful than lower ones in controlling drug consumption during treatment. The dose level of methadone has been shown to be the most discriminate factor in predicting success as determined by drug use. Gerstein and Harwood (1994) also report that programs with high illicit drug consumption used low methadone dosage. These programs had high rates of staff turnover along with poor relationships between staff and patients. These factors may be considered as additional reasons for lower levels of effectiveness.

Although MM programs have been quite effective, they have aroused controversy, too. For example, several programs have had a significant dropout rate along with some abuse potential, indicating that these programs should not be seen as the final answer to problems of narcotics addiction. Also, little evidence has supported the original theory of why a MM program would work as related to narcotics addiction. However, methadone maintenance, combined with a wide range of other support services (individual counseling, group, career, etc.) is seen as effective when properly administered.

Cocaine Studies

Only recently has published research on the treatment of substances outside of alcohol began to appear. Of the illicit drugs, cocaine has been of great concern since it was documented as the only illicit substance whose use increased through the mid-1980s (National Institute on Drug Abuse [NIDA], 1994). Cocaine as a drug of abuse seems to have peaked around 1986, with casual use declining since (Kleber, 1991). Few cocaine treatment programs have been studied. However, Hall, Havassy, and Wasserman (1991) found that cocaine addicts who made a commitment to full abstinence following treatment were most likely to avoid further cocaine use. Yet, the pharmacological, behavioral, and environmental factors related to cocaine still present special problems of treatment and the study of cocaine treatment programs.

Randomized clinical studies on psychotherapeutic approaches used with cocaine abusers are rare. One study (Carroll et al., 1994), however, did examine psychotherapeutic treatments for cocaine abuse. In this investigation, 42 ambulatory cocaine abusers were randomly assigned to (a) a relapse prevention (RP) group, using a cognitive behavioral approach, or (b) an interpersonal psychotherapy (IPT) group, using a short-term psychodynamic approach. Although the dropout rate was high for each group following a 12-week treatment, it was significantly higher for the IPT group (62%) as compared to the RP group (33%). Abstinence was significantly higher for the high-severity subjects in the RP group when compared to the IPT group. The high attrition rate of this study revealed at least some success with cocaine abusers who are treated psychotherapeutically, with better results using a cognitive-behavioral approach adapted for cocaine abusers.

Other studies have used or modified Washton's (1989) program design for the treatment of cocaine and crack addiction, with an emphasis on structure, intensity, and frequency. This usually has meant a highly structured outpatient regimen combining individual, group, and family counseling; education; urine testing; and self-help (Washton & Stone-Washton, 1991). Earlier studies by Washton (1989) indicated that employed cocaine and crack addicts can be treated successfully in inpatient or outpatient programs that are followed by intensive aftercare treatment emphasizing relapse prevention, and intensive outpatient treatment can be a cost-effective alternative to inpatient care. Results reported by Washton showed a 77% abstinence rate for inpatient clients and a 74% abstinence rate for outpatient clients at the end of treatment. In a 6- to 24-month follow-up, 68% of the outpatients and 64% of the inpatients were abstinent.

Washton's recommendation and findings on treating cocaine abusers are supported by Kang et al. (1991), also reporting a need for an intensive level of outpatient contact or residential treatment followed by aftercare with patients who were attempting to sustain abstinence. In a related study examining cocaine, as well as opiate and alcohol treatment, McLellan et al. (1994) found that the same factors predict outcomes of cocaine treatment as they do in opiate and alcohol treatment. In all cases, higher levels of severity at intake predicted greater substance abuse at follow-up. Better social adjustment at follow-up was predicated by diminished employment and mental and family problems.

Outpatient Programs Research

As early as 1956, outpatient (day treatment) programs have been used to address alcohol-related problems (Fox & Lowe, 1967). Outpatient programs are wide-ranging in duration and treatment methods. They vary from one-session assessment followed by a referral, to 3- to 6-month programs including psychotherapy weekly, to 1- to 2-year programs with psychotherapy combined with other treatment activities. This wide variance in outpatient programs has made studying treatment effectiveness difficult. However, research conducted by the Drug Abuse Reporting Program (DARP) and the Treatment Outcome Prospective Study (TOPS) (Hubbard et al., 1975; Sells, 1974; Simpson, Savage, & Lloyd, 1979) enables one to make some general conclusions concerning outpatient programs.

One conclusion is that the longer patients remain in outpatient treatment, the better the outcome (Gerstein & Harwood, 1994). Patients staying in treatment fewer than 90 days showed negligible improvement when compared to 90-day-plus groups of patients. The TOPS study (Hubbard et al., 1975) suggests that the critical retention threshold for patients is 6 months. Patients involved in outpatient program activities past the 6-month date significantly improved as related to drug abstinence and quality-of-life factors.

A few descriptive reports of full-day outpatient programs are available (Alterman & McLellan, 1993), with some evidence of the effectiveness of programs that include counseling, group therapy, psychoeducation, vocational training, and other helping services (Alterman, O'Brien, & Droba, 1993; Feigelman, Hymany, Amann, & Feigelman, 1990). Recent findings (Guydish, Werdegar, Chan, Nebelkopf, & Acampora, 1995) suggest that such programs can also be used effectively as a precursor to residential treatment and that some clients can be treated effectively in day treatment alone. Six-month follow-ups show that clients who enter outpatient full-day treatment with severe alcohol and other related substance abuse problems and remain for at least 2 weeks report significantly decreased substance abuse and fewer legal and psychiatric problems. An increase in levels of social support is also found. These programs most often have multiple components, including person structure, daily contact, intensive therapeutic contact (individual and group), and psychoeducational services.

Controlled studies examining the effectiveness of different treatment models with alcohol abuse have reported some significant outcome differences, with about half of all studies reflecting reliable differences (Miller et al., 1995). The 219 studies included in Miller et al.'s meta-analysis described treatment more in terms of managing and changing current problems of addiction and less on working with intrapsychic facets. Individual treatment concentrated on the addicts' problems and addictive supporting behaviors. Treatment often was concrete and specific. However, because of the high level of comorbidity between substance use disorders and a wide range of psychiatric symptoms as characterized by DSM-IV (depression, dysthymia, and anxiety disorders), it is believed that individuals treated can gain from approaches that combine addictions counseling and more intense psychotherapy. Washton (1989) previously had advocated such a treatment consisting of structured abstinence oriented activities, drug education, family involvement, 12-step participation, group therapy, and individual psychotherapy. In Washton's program, often the same person provided both drug-focused counseling and psychotherapy.

Supportive expressive psychotherapy (psychoanalytic therapy), interpersonal psychotherapy (psychoanalytic therapy), cognitive treatment (cognitive therapy), behavioral therapy, and family systems therapy have all been used alone or in combinations with addicted patients. Only in the last two decades have these approaches been subject to scientific investigation of their efficacy with substance abusing patients (Hester & Miller, 1995). The 43 treatment modalities studied by Miller et al. (1995) included brief interventions, behavioral contracting, cognitive therapy, marital/family therapy, psychotherapy, and a variety of other processes. The controlled studies of group or individual psychotherapy included in this research yielded negative findings with remarkable consistency. The one exception was client-centered therapy, which compared favorably with alternative approaches in three of four studies. The greatest success rates were found in studies using brief interventions and social skills training. These more recent findings are contradictory to earlier reports (Carroll, Rounsaville, & Treece, 1991; LaRosa, Lipsius, & LaRosa, 1974; Resnick et al., 1981; Woody et al., 1983), stating there is enough evidence to support psychotherapy as an effective treatment model for substance abuse disorders in outpatient programs. Implications from the meta-analysis work by Miller et al. (1995) and previous studies point to certain conditions needing to be met for positive outcomes to occur. Included within these conditions are a need for brief interventions, frequent visits for treatment, the use of less confrontational approaches, and combining approaches, often customized for patients. Traditional psychotherapeutic methods, as expected, would seem to be more effective with patients experiencing clinical problems along with addictions. At present research has not found any one psychotherapeutic treatment method in outpatient treatment programs to be superior to any other forms of treatment.

Inpatient Programs Research

Structure, intensity, and high costs characterize inpatient programs for chemical dependency (CD). The typical inpatient for years was described as being 40 years old, white, and alcohol-dependent. Programs have changed to a large degree by including patients with varied drug problems, multiple substance abuse issues, and a large number of adolescents. Chemical dependency treatment has often been referred to as the Minnesota Model, 28-day, 12-step, or Hazelden-type treatment (Gerstein & Harwood, 1994).

The inpatient chemical dependency programs for treating alcohol abuse, according to a number of studies, have been more successful than programs treating other drugs or multiple substances. Moos, King, and Patterson (1996) studied 2,190 males who were initially treated at a Veterans Administration (VA) medical facility for alcohol abuse. For patients with a coexisting mental health issue, inpatient treatment at a hospital-based program, combined with outpatient care, resulted in reduced remission rates. However, patients who remained in care for 2 weeks or less experienced high remission rates. Adelman and Weiss (1989) found that 77% of alcoholics they studied eventually required some form of inpatient treatment and that treatment programs in medical settings had lower dropout rates than patients in nonmedical settings. Earlier studies (Peluso & Peluso, 1988) sampled 1,000 adult patients with at least a 5-day stay. Follow-up studies found 61% classified as recovering.

In addition, it has been found that users of illicit drugs have had a recovery rate of 10% points lower than alcohol abuse patients (Gerstein & Harwood, 1994). The same results were previously supported by the Hazelden studies (Gilmore, 1985; Laundergan, 1982). Inpatient chemical dependency treatment programs for cocaine have been limited. In one study, Rawson et al. (1986) reported effectiveness of an inpatient cocaine treatment program as compared to outpatient and no treatment. However, current research is more supportive of inpatient CD programs in treating alcoholism, as compared to their effectiveness with other drug usage.

SPECIFIC PRACTICE EFFECTIVENESS

A number of studies examining the efficacy of specific practices with substance abuse deserve mention. Certain substance abuse practices or programs have been reported as successful, either alone or along with other treatment modalities. Treatment programs discussed here include the 12-step AA approach to substance abuse, individual outpatient counseling programs, group counseling programs, family therapy, and multidimensional programs.

The 12-Step Programs

In the 1990s there was reported to be over 94,000 Alcoholics Anonymous groups, 22,000 Narcotics Anonymous groups, more than 32,000 Al-Anon groups, as well as thousands of other related groups across the country. Groups like these have expanded significantly during the past decade. Because of widespread availability, the 12-step programs have been seen by many as the best hope in stopping the continued growth of substance abuse. Outcome studies on the effectiveness of AA, although sparse, have been conducted (Dorsman, 1996; Humphreys & Moos, 1996; Watson et al., 1997). Some of the earlier studies (Alibrandi, 1978) found about half of newcomers to AA did not relapse during the first year of AA membership. Nace (1987) found that 70% of those who stayed sober for 1 year while attending AA meetings remained sober at the end of the second year, while 90% of those who stayed sober at the end of the second year remained sober at the end of their third year. However, Ogborne and Glaser (1985), in a review of several AA research investigations, concluded that AA was effective only with certain populations, such as white males over 40 who were physically dependent on alcohol and possessed certain characteristics. Hester (1994), in agreement with Ogborne and Glaser, challenged the effectiveness of mandatory attendance programs such as AA and NA. Hester states that after studying 600 AA/NA programs, insufficient evidence was found demonstrating their overall effectiveness despite indications that relapse was significantly affected. Yet, Emerick, Tonigan, Montgomery, and Little (1993) suggest that AA/NA meetings were effective since relapse is more likely to occur when clients do not participate in AA meetings.

Studies designed to evaluate/review AA groups and their effectiveness have been burdened with scientific design problems. Most of these studies did not include control groups. The two controlled AA studies included in the Miller et al. (1995) meta-analysis both revealed no beneficial effect of this modality. However, this conclusion is contradictory to earlier findings, with their limitations, that have generally shown positive results (Bebbington, 1976; Leach & Norris, 1977; Madsen, 1974). Leach (1973) reports four studies involving AA treatment in New York, London, Finland, the United States, and Canada. The results from the United States and Canada ($N = 11,355$) report 38% of the sample were abstinent from 1 to 5 years. Madsen (1974) compared AA treatment with other approaches in California. From responses to questionnaires in an ethnographic study, AA showed outstanding gains when compared to a variety of other treatment modalities.

Findings concerning AA's effectiveness are still mixed owing to a wide range of uncontrolled variables: an inability to use control groups, questions of mandatory versus voluntary participation, and the wide variance found among AA meetings conducted across the country. Positive findings (Emerick et al., 1993) have correlated AA attendance and participation with positive outcomes. The meta-analysis of AA studies (Emerick et al., 1993) found that individuals most likely to affiliate with AA had a history of (a) using external supports to stop drinking, (b) losing control of drinking and of behavior when drinking, (c) consuming a high quantity of alcohol, (d) expressing distress about their drinking, (e) being obsessively/compulsively involved with alcohol, (f) believing that drinking enhances mental functioning, and (g) engaging in religious/spiritual activities (Montgomery, Miller, & Tonigan, 1995).

Emerick et al. (1993) also found participation in AA prior to treatment not to be a significant factor when predicting treatment outcome. However, AA attendance during and/or after treatment was found to be positively associated with successful outcomes (Emerick, 1989; Emerick et al., 1993). Montgomery et al. (1995), supported in part by grants from the National Institute on Alcohol Abuse and Alcoholism, studied whether AA involvement would predict treatment outcome. Their findings, supported by previous research (Emerick et al., 1993), suggest that it is the extent of involvement or active participation in the AA process, rather than mere attendance at AA meetings, that predicts more favorable outcomes after treatment. These findings are also consistent with discussions centered on mandated versus voluntary AA meetings. When attendance by members is voluntary and when such members actively participate in AA meetings, there is strong evidence of successful outcomes.

One has to wonder whether the same axiom holds true for other treatment modalities used with substance abuse clients. Watson, Hancock, Malovrh, Gearhart, and Raden (1996) studied a sample of 150 men who had been treated on an inpatient basis. The researchers found a positive relationship between the number of AA meetings attended and abstinence rate from chemicals. However, Humphreys and Moos (1996) found that a group of patients who entered into outpatient counseling had the same percentage of abstinent members as did subjects from the group that joined AA.

These studies point to some powerful aspects of AA, as well as ongoing questions concerning its overall effectiveness (Doweiko, 1999). One suggestion about future AA research is that meetings need to be more closely examined. Studies need to be conducted that look at aspects of AA believed to be effective, for whom, and under what conditions. I believe this direction of research can be most promising, recognizing existing evidence indicating both the value and overall effectiveness of AA/NA programs and their underlying concepts. For now there seems to be a consensus concerning the value of AA as an important, often necessary, adjunct to other treatment modalities (Bloise & Holder, 1991; Clark, 1995; Gallegos, Lubin, & Bowers, 1992; Hoffman & Miller, 1992; Humphreys & Moos, 1996; McLellan et al., 1992; Zweben, 1987).

Individual Counseling Programs

Individual counseling programs remain a viable option for many addicted patients. The outpatient-counseling model offers the individual a chance to live at home and in most cases continue working. There is a belief that for many patients, individual outpatient drug addiction counseling is as effective as inpatient chemically dependent programs (Doweiko, 1999). Individual counseling approaches for drug use are viewed as heterogeneous in nature (Institute of Medicine, 1990) and often serve clients who have less severe drug-related problems.

The goals of individual outpatient substance abuse counseling programs include abstinence from alcohol and other drugs. In addition, counseling focuses on (a) social relational stabilization (e.g., marital/family), (b) employment stabilization, (c) physical health, (d) emotional health, (e) legal problem resolution, and (f) spiritual strengthening (Lewis, Dana, & Blevins, 1994).

Thousands of clients who used drug abuse counseling programs were studied through the classic research: the Treatment Outcome Prospective Study (TOPS) in 1989, funded by the Research Triangle Institute. Results indicated that individual counseling programs were effective in two areas: (a) reducing drug use and (b) improving employment. Because of a low rate of retention in these programs, the TOPS findings have been questioned. Yet, the Drug Abuse Reporting Program (DARP), conducted by the Institute for Behavior Research at Texas Christian University, supported many of the TOPS findings. Conclusions drawn from this research indicated that individual counseling approaches in outpatient drug abuse programs were generally effective. But there was also a call for clearer descriptions of specific counseling interventions and individual treatment modalities used.

Findings from the Institute of Medicine as early as 1990 concluded that only a minimum amount of research exists pointing to effective individual counseling interventions used with drug abusing clients. Findings by the institute, published in *Broadening the Base of Treatment for Alcohol Problems* (1990), included the following:

1. Among young problem drinkers, about 50% to 60% of men and 70% of women experience improvement without formal treatment.

2. For middle-aged drinkers in trouble with alcohol, the rate of improvement without formal treatment is 30% to 40% for men and 30% for women.

3. In older drinkers, the rate for improvement without formal treatment is about 60% to 80% for men and 50% to 60% for women.

Additional conclusions drawn were that the wise health care provider will seek to activate or enhance "naturally" occurring factors that facilitate the remission of alcohol problems (Institute of Medicine, 1990, p. 158).

A number of earlier studies attempted to examine individual therapeutic techniques used with drug abuse clients and their families. Approaches investigated included behavior therapy (Leiser, 1976; Ulmer, 1977), reality therapy (Schuster, 1978–1979), autogenic training (Roszell & Chaney, 1982), and counseling in general (Schilit & Gomberg, 1991; Weiner, 1975). Evidence concerning effectiveness of these approaches has been inconclusive, but conclusions point to the need for controlled studies examining the effects of individual counseling programs as compared to controlled populations not undergoing treatment.

Counseling, listed as one of the four most common forms of drug abuse treatment, was most recently seen as effective in reducing drug use (NIDA, 1994). The

Drug Abuse Treatment Outcome Study (DATOS) tracked 10,010 drug abusers in nearly 100 treatment programs in 11 cities who entered treatment between 1991 and 1993. Results showed that counseling was effective in reducing the use of substance for clients who remained in treatment. Support for both client-centered counseling and behavioral contracting was recently reported through a methodological analysis of the alcohol treatment outcome literature (Miller et al., 1995).

Group Counseling Programs

Interpersonal relationships and social interactions are major factors affecting substance abuse clients. Because of this phenomenon, the group counseling process has been historically considered as a viable approach to use with substance abusers, either alone or in conjunction with other treatment methods. Group programs attempt to help substance abuse clients alter distorted concepts of self, learn from others, regain hope, and reduce isolation. Despite the generally stated advantages of using group counseling approaches with substance-abusing clients, these programs have been sparsely researched. Miller and Hester (1986), after reviewing studies on the efficacy of group counseling programs with substance abuse clients, concluded that we have yet to consistently demonstrate measurable effective outcomes. Yet the general view has been that group therapy programs are effective with adolescent substance abusers.

Fram (1990) believes that the use of groups with exclusively chemically dependent clients will maximize treatment efforts. Small-group treatment methods with substance abusers have been so effective that most drug rehabilitation centers now use them as the core of their program. As early as 1971, Stein and Friedman stated that group psychotherapy is, in most instances, the treatment of choice for the psychological problems of alcoholism. They estimated that 60% to 70% of patients in group psychotherapy improve, versus 20% to 40% of patients receiving individual psychotherapy alone. Yet, over the last three decades no controlled outcome studies have supported these claims. Although research is still lacking to scientifically support group counseling in general, specific group programs and modules have shown to be effective with alcohol abuse clients.

Miller et al. (1995) have stated the important contributions of coping/social skills training (CSST) groups by identifying 11 controlled studies supporting the beneficial effects of this treatment modality. Although the specific content of CSST groups are variable, major themes or domains include (a) interpersonal skills for building better relationships, (b) cognitive-emotional coping for mood regulation, (c) coping skills for improving daily living and dealing with stressful life events, and (d) coping in the context of substance use cues (Monti et al., 1996). Research findings strongly suggest that this treatment modality should become a significant component of treatment for alcohol problems and dependence.

Family Therapy

Family therapy over the years has been viewed as a promising treatment approach for substance abusers (Kaufman, 1979). Such treatment may include the substance abuser and his or her spouse/partner, the substance abuser and family of origin, or the substance abuser and children. In certain occasions three generations may be involved in the treatment process. Family therapy treatment is seen as an active process that involves family members along with the substance abuser.

When therapy includes family members, it has been believed that its impact can be significant when working with alcoholic patients (Liepman, Nirenberg, & Begiw, 1989). Despite few controlled studies to validate this belief, Stanton and Todd (1982) report family therapy to be effective when compared to certain individual approaches used by themselves with clients. An earlier report by Hendricks (1971) found that narcotic addicts receiving family therapy treatment were significantly more likely to remain in treatment than those who did not participate in family treatment.

Todd and Selekman (1991) found that when family therapy was used with substance abuse cases, individuals tended to stay longer in treatment and maintain sobriety for longer periods of time. McCrady (1986) also found that alcoholic abusing clients were more likely to stay in treatment, comply with abstinent behavior, and maintain marital satisfaction when marital therapy was part of their treatment.

The number of family members involved in substance abuse treatment seems to affect the outcome of substance abuse counseling in a positive direction. Additional studies, such as the Purdue Brief Therapy Model (Lewis, Piercy, Sprenkle, & Trepper, 1991), found that a family therapy intervention model with adolescents was significantly more effective in reducing adolescent drug use than a straight family education intervention program. Joanning, Quinn, Thomas, and Mullen (1992), in a study funded by the NIDA, examined the effectiveness of Family System Drug Education (FSDA) with adolescent drug abusers. The FSDA approach, involving families and focusing on education and information, was reported as effective in reducing adolescent drug abuse.

More recent research on whether marital/family therapy (MFT) makes a difference with substance abuse clients has distinguished between MFT behavioral and MFT nonbehavioral methodology. More controlled MFT studies using a behavioral methodology (four vs. three) revealed supporting evidence of effectiveness (Miller et al., 1995), while more MFT studies using a nonbehavioral methodology (four vs. three) showed no beneficial treatment effects. This has led O'Farrell (1995), to conclude that the behavioral approach in MFT is most promising when focusing on the drinking and drinking-related interactions plus work on more general marital relationship issues. However, the more popular family systems and family disease models in MFT (O'Farrell, 1995) have shown to have little or no research support for their effectiveness.

Multidimensional Programs

Research in substance abuse counseling often fails to identify specific treatment methods, approaches, or techniques that produce change with identified drug abuse problems. Today most substance abuse treatment programs favor a multidimensional approach when dealing with addictions.

Multidimensional or multimodality treatment approaches include a variety of interventions, such as detoxification, individual counseling, group counseling, family therapy, inpatient treatment, and education. Multidimensional models are beginning to be more widely used both by outpatient and inpatient programs. They have been recommended as the treatment model of choice to counteract addictions (Doweiko, 1999). Yet, research studies demonstrating treatment combinations that might work best as a multidimensional model are nonexistent. However, some generalizations can be made such as combining AA/NA programs with individual counseling and family therapy modalities. What treatment modalities work with specific addiction problems needs to be researched, leading to the possibility of being able to predict "what works" under which circumstances with substance abuse clients.

Summary

Can substance abuse treatments be effective? A certain amount of evidence suggests substance abuse treatments can be effective in reducing substance use and in bringing about improvements in the areas of employment, criminal activity, social adjustment, and use of health care activities (Anglin & Hser, 1990; Ball & Ross, 1991; Doweiko, 1999; Institute of Medicine, 1990; McLellan et al., 1994). Yet, success has been mixed with outcome studies identifying large numbers of clients even from the successful studies who broke the law or were readmitted for additional care. Results of these studies have led researchers to investigate pretreatment variables that might predict outcome of substance abuse treatment. Variables being studied (McLellan et al., 1994) include severity of dependence, family and social supports, psychiatric symptoms, personality type, and so forth. However, this remains a difficult process that is confounded by differences in substance being studied and by variances in treatment.

Both inpatient and outpatient programs have reported success in dealing with alcohol abuse and cocaine abuse patients. As a result, some very clear guidelines and program recommendations for the treatment have evolved (Washton, 1992). There have been reports that individual counseling and certain types of group counseling, when used alone, are at times effective with substance abuse clients. However, only a few studies of this nature have been done, and currently most treatment programs combine these modalities with other methods of treatment. More information is being obtained on the successful use of AA programs, particularly as related to mandated versus voluntary attendance. Level of participation, rather then simply the number of meetings attended, is a significant variable in predicting abstinence. Perhaps we are approaching a time when enough studies are available examining the treatment of cocaine abuse and other illicit drugs to conduct meta-analysis research in these areas similar to studies by Miller et al. (1995) and Emrick et al. (1993) on alcohol abuse.

CONTEMPORARY ISSUES

Many of the contemporary issues involving substance abuse counseling directly or indirectly relate to research—research as to "what works" with specific presenting problems, substance abuse etiology, predictability of substance abuse, adolescent substance abuse, gender differences, and programs for minorities. Several of these areas are briefly mentioned in this closing section in an attempt to stimulate further discussion, additional reading, and future investigation.

The Disease Concept of Alcoholism: Still Questions

Most physicians, counselors, and psychologists still view alcoholism according to the disease model. Alcoholism is seen as a disease with treatment emphasizing total abstinence. This concept was challenged by the decision of the Supreme Court in *Traynor v. Turnage* (1988). The court ruled against a plaintiff who was seeking an extension of education benefits due to alcohol abuse. The client's condition of abusing alcohol was argued to be a disease that prevented the plaintiff from using educational benefits granted by the military. The Court ruled against the plaintiff in this case, stating that consumption of alcohol is not regarded as totally "involuntary." Many professionals thought this ruling would affect the widely held belief in the disease model of substance abuse. However, this was not been the case.

Today, the full endorsement of the disease model is questioned and is being challenged. Some counselors and treatment centers have advocated gradual reductions of alcohol consumption by their clients, and some use a "safe amount" of drinking as part of their treatment. A view widely discussed is the conceptualization of alcoholism and substance abuse along a continuum from nonproblematic to highly problematic (Lewis, Dana, & Blevins, 1994). Treatment according to this concept stresses working with the client in terms of where he or she is and does not assume progression according to the disease model. It is predicted that treatment approaches and ideas about treatment will continue to be examined and implemented and that they will often not align with a particular set of beliefs as the disease model of alcohol abuse. However, the concept of "controlled drinking" is very controversial. Research suggests that less than 2% of individuals identified as alcoholics might safely return to social drinking (Helzer et al., 1985; Vaillant & Hiller-Sturmhofel, 1996).

It should be noted that controlled drinking is seen as a possibility for only those individuals who are not clearly addicted and who have not experienced problems associated with addiction (Hester & Miller, 1989). Research findings (Watson et al., 1996) clearly indicate that controlled drinking is impossible once one is physically dependent on alcohol.

Defining Abuse within the Context of Diagnosis

Debate continues as to the definition of abuse when discussing the use of substances. While the term *substance* can generally be agreed on as a drug of abuse, a medication, or a toxin (DSM-IV), the term *abuse* seems to be defined more in terms of degree of use and often as part of a value or belief system. Despite the development of more specific criteria identifying substance abuse, as per the DSM-IV, questions of labeling and definition persist. Should someone who takes a substance that leads to a physically hazardous situation be labeled as a substance abuser, or should the context in which this behavior occurred be considered? In cases where several psychosocial factors are present leading to the use of substance and creating impairment or distress, should the substance abuse classification take preference, or should commingling factors enter into the diagnosis? Is it possible that systemic factors lead to the use of the substance, and therefore should they be given first priority? Is one drinking episode followed by social or employment problems enough to warrant a substance abuse classification, or is a more lengthy history needed? It is believed that such classifications or labels need to be continually discussed so they are not aligned with a preconceived belief and value system surrounding substance in general.

Dual-diagnosis or comorbidity issues complicate substance abuse definitions. This dilemma creates an additional challenge to the practitioner. For years it has been known that individuals addicted to various substances often manifest psychiatric symptomology. In many cases, substance abuse disorders are linked to affective disorders (Mayfield, 1985), sociopathy (Kay, 1985), schizophrenia (Alterman, 1985), depression (Hesselbrock et al., 1986), and other conditions. Questions of diagnosis and treatment under these conditions become extremely complex (see Chapter 4).

Determining Treatment Goals

Related to the aforementioned matters is the issue of determining proper treatment goals. Treatment goals in the substance abuse field vary greatly. For example, the question of moderate, "acceptable" drinking versus complete sobriety continues to be discussed. Advocates of the latter include AA, clinics, hospitals, and supporters of the disease model. Others have felt that some individuals can learn to control their drinking and operate at more moderate levels of alcohol consumption (Lewis et al., 1991). This controversy is negated by a lack of data from nontreated problem drinkers, who generally recover through what has been termed "spontaneous recovery." Many have also raised the question of whether abstinence is a realistic goal.

Other issues have surfaced over treatment goals with drugs such as cocaine, heroin, and marijuana. Even less documentation is available showing permanent or long-term abstinence in patients using these drugs. Research has also shown high levels of relapse. Goals of treatment are therefore being revisited in relation to the particular drug being treated and to relapse predictability. Many therapists and treatment facilities have begun to reexamine the treatment process and now keep statistics on relapse. Relapse is seen by many in the field as part of the therapeutic process, with complete withdrawal from one's drug habit viewed as unrealistic for certain clients.

Concepts such as these are disturbing for agencies that want to prove efficacy and for legislators who want to have the problems of substance abuse quickly fixed. Yet, government agencies and practicing professionals have to wrestle with indefinite solutions and change that is difficult. Unfortunately, the etiology of drug abuse and its complications are multifaceted, demanding diversity of treatment and intermittent goal setting.

Gender Issues and the Use of Drugs

Although gender and gender issues as related to substance abuse have been covered elsewhere in this text, brief comments need to be made in this chapter. Studies have shown major differences between men and women who are treated for alcohol and drug abuse (George, 1990). George (1990) states that male alcoholics possess the following characteristics when compared to women:

- are younger at the time of the first drink,
- participate in more morning drinking,
- have more extensive histories of delirium tremens,
- experience more blackouts,
- more frequently lose jobs and friends because of drinking,
- have more histories of school problems,
- have more alcohol-related arrests, and
- make fewer suicide attempts.

George (1990) further cites work by Horn and Wanberg (1973) stating differences between men and women who abuse alcohol:

- women began to drink later in life,
- women drink more often at home alone,
- women have shorter drinking binges,
- women often use alcohol in an attempt to improve job performance,
- women are less gregarious drinkers,
- women are more often solitary drinkers, and
- women more often perceive their alcoholism as becoming worse.

Despite these findings, treatment differences according to gender are seldom discussed and often not implemented. Research conducted on alcohol abuse and drug abuse treatment has excluded large samples of women. Traditional stereotypes of men and women alcoholics persist even today, with views of a male drunk as one who is accepted and often seen as humorous, while the female alcoholic or drug user is seen in disdain, exhibiting behavior that is unacceptable or disgraceful.

Gender in terms of the therapist-client relationship is a related issue. Some findings show that same-gender therapists and clients work best. Issues also have been raised about gender bias. Sensitivity to the client's gender and research on the role of gender in therapy around substance abuse is long overdue.

Researchers have found that women usually obtain their drug of choice in different ways than do men (Doweiko, 1999). There are also some indications that sedatives and "diet pills" have become more closely associated to addictions of women. These drugs are often initially obtained from their physician. There also appears to be differences in how males and females use a drug of choice, as well as how they react to the drug. Observation and investigation need to continue on this topic. Findings in this area may lead to addiction prevention and treatment strategies that may differ for women and men.

Training and Background of Substance Abuse Counselors

The question of who is best qualified to work with substance abuse issues continues to be debated. Many agencies are split in terms of background, experience, and training needed in order for one to work effectively in this field. For years a large segment of substance abuse helpers believed that to be an effective substance abuse counselor, one must have abused a substance and recovered. According to this belief, one must have gone through the substance-abusing process and treatment to understand and work with others. By having gone through this process, the counselor would be accepted by clients.

As the field of substance abuse counseling has evolved, others have advocated a professional training "education" approach to preparing substance abuse counselors, with an emphasis on formal training, including clinical work with drug users. In some cases, state departments have set standards for training for a Certified Addiction Counselor (CAC). The CAC must meet certain standards set forth by the state, including coursework and supervised experiences in the field. In addition, one often completes a master's degree in counseling, social work, or psychology with an emphasis in substance abuse counseling, including a clinical supervised internship.

George (1990) suggests it is important that substance abuse counselors have certain minimum skills and knowledge to maximize the therapeutic effect on clients. Such individuals would possess a working knowledge of chemical dependency. The International Association for Addictions and Offenders Counselors (IAAOC) has developed a knowledge base for substance abuse counselors. These standards have been implemented as Specialty Certification Standards for Substance Abuse Counselors with the National Board for Certified Counselors (NBCC). Under this substance abuse specialty, individuals qualify by completing a master's degree with designated coursework and experiences in substance abuse counseling. The Master Addiction Counselor (MAC) certification developed jointly by the NAADAC and NBCC is considered by some (Cahillane, 1996) to be the most widely regarded certification in the field. Other existing boards, such as the National Board of Addiction Examiners, offer certification at the baccalaureate, master, and doctoral levels, as well as a skill-based level.

Parallel to certification has been the evolution of master's-level training programs with specialties in substance abuse counseling. An example of one of the first complete master's programs in substance abuse counseling was started at Northeast Louisiana University (Locke, 1992), offering graduates the opportunity to matriculate in a program and become degreed in substance abuse counseling. Other such programs include those at East Carolina University and Penn State University.

Despite differences of opinion as to how one enters the field of substance abuse counseling, through direct experience as a recovered alcohol or drug user and/or through formal training, most would agree that continued training and experiences are necessary in this field. With multiple diagnosis cases, the need for family treatment, use of medication, and so forth, substance abuse counselors will need continually to update both their skills and knowledge base.

Ethical Issues and Substance Abuse Counseling

The area of substance abuse counseling has recently developed more complete codes of ethics helpful to practicing counselors who are working with a variety of drug-abusing clients. Despite such codes, developed by the National Association of Alcoholism and Drug Abuse Counselors (NAADAC) and the IAAOC, all potential ethical dilemmas cannot be covered by a set of predetermined standards. Of particular relevance with ATOD abuse cases is the issue of confidentiality.

Occurring issues include confidentiality around drug use, slippage in alcohol intake, and/or drug supplying. The counselor is caught between confidentiality when serving the client, the referring agency, the client's workplace, the employee assistance program (EAP), and the client's family network. Breach of confidentiality—when it might be appropriate and under what circumstances—needs to be carefully thought out and clearly articulated to each client and his or her family.

As multidimensional approaches become more frequently implemented, numerous problems will evolve about the sharing of information. How much information is to be shared from individual counseling sessions, family sessions, and other client experiences? Under what circumstances and according to what conditions does one share professional information with others who are working with or close to the client? Are federal guidelines also an issue here in terms of clarity, and do they exacerbate the problem?

Each incident is now taken on a case-by-case basis, with a decision of what to do based on (a) what is best for the client, (b) what the agency's policies are, and (c) how these points fit with the rule of no harm to self and others. Until further precedent is established examining a wide range of cases, counselors will be left with making decisions based on their own personal experiences and their best judgment.

Burnout

The mental health profession has a history of high levels of burnout. Lack of clear results, case overload, unrealistic expectations, minimal agency support, and funding reductions are some of the reasons for burnout. Many counselors are unable to remove themselves from the job and establish the necessary distance from their clients. Often counselors are unable to detach from the problems and pain expressed by their clients. A feeling of helplessness is present with difficult cases.

ATOD abuse counselors seem to be more prone to experience these emotions and are therefore more susceptible to burnout (George, 1990). Counselors who work with court-mandated cases may be particularly vulnerable. There is often a sense of a loss of control, particularly in treatment centers that seem chaotic as clients began treatment only to terminate in the first few weeks. Little time is allowed for consultation with peers, and often few opportunities exist either to support or seek the support from others. Caseloads in many clinics are exhausting. Mortality rates of severe drug cases are high, and each death from drug overdose takes its toll on the counselor.

Because substance abuse counseling is a difficult job, there is a high level of turnover in substance abuse treatment clinics. Many professionals start out as substance abuse counselors and then move to other positions in the counseling profession where clear-cut results can be seen and where caseloads might be more reasonable.

Suggestions for preventing burnout of substance abuse counselors have been made (George, 1990): (a) maintaining an appropriate workload, (b) leaving one's work at the office, (c) setting boundaries with clients and staff, (d) developing and maintaining an independent personal life away from the job, and (e) attending conferences and workshops that provide opportunities for both skill building and sharing with colleagues.

Burnout will continue to be an issue with substance abuse counselors as cases become more complex. As this occurs, the suggestions to cope and prevent burnout will take on greater relevance.

Ethnic Minorities and Substance Abuse

Special attention is needed as related to ethnic minorities and the use of substances, as noted previously in this text (see Chapter 9). Although the general health of Americans has improved over the last two decades, many minorities have not experienced these improvements. Most of the minorities continue to have higher death rates from chronic diseases and lower life expectancies when compared to white populations (Schilit & Gomberg, 1991). There have been few studies and very little written on the treatment of ethnic minority drug and alcohol abusers. Despite this, some believe that culture-specific treatment programs need to be explored to meet the needs of varied ethnic groups.

Suggestions have been made of building on the church's role with substance abusers of African Americans or Hispanic descent. For many ethnic minorities, the church, rather than AA or another treatment facility, is seen as a place to share problems outside the family. Spanish-speaking substance abuse counselors who are culturally sensitive to ethnic minority issues also need to be employed in treatment centers.

Limited information has been published about the use of alcohol and drugs in Asian and Pacific American populations. We know that a stigma is placed on substance abuse with this minority group, causing them to be overlooked when writing in this area. In comparison, American Indians and the use of substances, particularly alcohol, have received much attention. It has been reported (Heath, 1989) that alcohol contributes to 4 of the 10 leading causes of death for this ethnic minority group. At the same time, studies (Walker, Benjamin, Kwlahan, & Walker, 1989) reveal that alcohol treatment programs for Indians have yielded poor results.

Continued study is needed concerning ethnic minority groups and related issues of substance abuse and treatment. Basic statistics are no longer enough. Attention first needs to be devoted to methods of encouraging minority groups to seek treatment. An examination of the best methods of treatment, sensitive to cultural differences, can than be studied.

Medications and Alcohol, Tobacco, and Other Drugs

Medications in the treatment of alcoholism, narcotic addiction, cocaine, and nicotine dependence have and continue to be used with mixed results. Benzodiazepines, for example, have a history of use to treat symptoms associated with alcohol withdrawal. Yet, it has been found that this treatment must be used judiciously, based on the case presented. Antabuse (disulfiram) combined with alcohol has long been used to produce unpleasant effects for the problem drinker. However, disulfiram combined with alcohol can cause a number of side effects, including being fatal for the client (Doweiko, 1999). Other chemicals such as buprenorphine have been used to block the euphoric effects of intravenously administered narcotics. Yet, because of its abuse potential, this drug too has been used with caution. A number of agents have been used that showed initial promise in the treatment of cocaine withdrawal craving. This includes imipramine, bupropion, bromocriptine, flupenthixol, and buprenorphine. Although some have helped in the control of post-cocaine craving, there is no evidence of an elimination of such.

A number of pharmacological treatment modalities have been used in the treatment of nicotine dependence. Included in this list is the use of nicotine-containing gum, transdermal nicotine patches, nasal spray, clonidine, silver acetate, and buspirone. Although research does exist concerning the use of these treatments, no single substance has proven effective in treating the symptoms of nicotine withdrawal beyond any reasonable doubt (Doweiko, 1999).

One can be assured that new pharmacological treatment modalities will evolve and be tried with the different addictions. It is suggested that careful study and prudent use be made of their use.

CONCLUSION

A number of additional issues could be raised in this chapter related to substance abuse counseling. Of particular concern is the treatment of substance abuse with young children and adolescents, only briefly discussed in this text. Other issues such as addressing drugs and violence, responding to a changing managed care system, and working within and outside the workplace in treating addiction problems need our continued focus. However, it is the evolution of these issues and thoughtful responses to them that make substance abuse counseling a challenging, albeit often frustrating, professional area.

REFERENCES

Adelman, S. A., & Weiss, R. D. (1989). What is therapeutic about inpatient alcoholism treatment? *Hospital and Community Psychiatry, 40*(5), 515–519.

Alibrandi, L. A. (1978). The folk psychotherapy of Alcoholics Anonymous. In S. Zimberg, J. Wallace, & S. Blume (Eds.), *Practical approaches to alcoholism psychotherapy*. New York: Plenum.

Alterman, A. I. (1985). Substance abuse in psychiatric patients: Etiological, development and treatment considerations. In A. I. Alterman (Ed.), *Substance abuse and psychopathology* (pp. 121–136). New York: Plenum.

Alterman, A. I., & McLellan, A. T. (1993). Inpatient and day hospital treatment services for cocaine and alcohol dependence. *Journal of Substance Abuse Treatment, 10,* 269–275.

Alterman, A. I., O'Brien, C. P., & Droba, M. (1993). Day hospital vs. inpatient rehabilitation of cocaine abusers: An interim report. In F. M. Tims & C. G. Luekenfeld (Eds.), *Cocaine treatment: Research and clinical perspectives.* NIDA Research Monograph 135 (pp. 150–162). NIH Publication No. 93-3639. Washington, DC: U.S. Government Printing Office.

Anglin, M. D., & Hser, Y. (1990). Legal coercion and drug abuse treatment. In J. Inciardi (Ed.), *Handbook on drug control in the United States* (pp. 235–247). Westport, CT: Greenwood.

Anglin, M. D., Speckart, G. S., Booth, M. W., et al. (1989). Consequences and costs of shutting off methadone. *Addictive Behavior, 14,* 307–326.

Ball, J. C., & Ross, A. (1991). *The effectiveness of methadone maintenance treatment.* New York: Springer.

Bebbington, P. E. (1976). The efficacy of Alcoholics Anonymous: The elusiveness of hard data. *British Journal of Psychiatry, 128,* 572–580.

Bloise, J. O., & Holder, H. D. (1991). Utilization of medical care by treated alcoholics: Longitudinal patterns by age, gender, and type of care. *Journal of Substance Abuse, 3*(1), 13–27.

Booth, M. (1995). The quiet addiction. *Denver Post Magazine, 103*(353), 12–15, 18.

Cahillane, B. (1996, July 1). Certification information. *International Association for Addictions and Offender Counselors Newsletter,* 22.

Carroll, K. M., Rounsaville, B. J., Nich, C., Gordon, L. T., Wirtz, P. W., & Gawin, F. (1994). One year follow-up of psychotherapy and pharmacotherapy for cocaine dependence. *Archives of General Psychiatry, 51,* 989–997.

Carroll, K. M., Rounsaville, B. J., & Treece, F. H. (1991). A comparative trial of psychotherapies for ambulatory cocaine abusers: Relapse prevention and interpersonal psychotherapy. *American Journal of Drug and Alcohol Abuse, 17,* 229–247.

Clark, C. M. (1995). Alcoholics Anonymous. *Addictions Newsletter, 2*(3), 9, 22.

Counseling the adolescent substance abuser. (1994). Thousand Oaks, CA: Sage.

DeMaria, P. A., & Weinstein, S. P. (1995). Methadone maintenance treatment. *Postgraduate Medicine, 97*(3), 83–92.

Dole, V. P., & Nyswander, M. A. (1965). Medical treatment for diacetylmorphine (heroin) addiction. *Journal of the American Medical Association, 193,* 645–656.

Dorsman, J. (1996). Improving alcoholism treatment: An overview. *Behavioral Health Management, 16*(1), 26–29.

Doweiko, H. E. (1999). *Concepts of chemical dependency* (4th ed.). Pacific Grove, CA: Brooks/Cole.

Emerick, C. D. (1989). Alcoholics Anonymous: Membership characteristics and effectiveness as treatment. In M. Galaner (Ed.), *Recent developments in alcoholism: Treatment research* (Vol. 7, pp. 37–53). New York: Plenum.

Emerick, C. D., Tonigan, J. S., Montgomery, H. A., & Little, L. (1993). Alcoholics Anonymous: What is currently known? In B. S. McCrady & W. R. Miller (Eds.), *Research on Alcoholics Anonymous: Opportunities and alternatives.* Piscataway, NJ: Rutgers Center of Alcohol Studies.

Feigelman, W., Hymany, M. M., Amann, K., & Feigelman, B. (1990). Correlates of persisting drug use among former youth multiple drug abuse patients. *Journal of Psychoactive Drugs, 22,* 634–641.

Fox, V., & Lowe, G. D. (1967). Day-hospital treatment of the alcoholic patient. *Quarterly Journal of Studies on Alcohol, 29,* 634–641.

Fram, D. H. (1990). Group methods in the treatment of substance abusers. *Psychiatric Annals, 20*(7), 385–388.

Gallegos, K. V., Lubin, B. H., & Bowers, C. (1992). Relapse and recovery: Five to 10 year follow-up study of chemically dependent physicians—The Georgia Experience. *MMJ 41*(4), 284–318.

George, R. L. (1990). *Counseling the chemically dependent: Theory and practice.* Upper Saddle River, NJ: Prentice Hall.

Gerstein, D. R., & Harwood, H. J. (Eds.). (1994). *Treating drug problems: Vol. 2.* Washington, DC: National Academy Press.

Gilmore, K. M. (1985). *Hazelden primary residential treatment program: Profile and patient outcome.* Center City, MN: Hazelden.

Gunne, L., & Grombladh, L. (1984). The Swedish methadone maintenance program. In G. Serban (Ed.), *The social and medical aspects of drug abuse* (pp. 205–213). Jamaica, NY: Spectrum.

Guydish, J., Werdegar, D., Chan, M., Nebelkopf, E., & Acampora, A. (1995). Challenges in developing a drug abuse day treatment program. In B. Fletcher, J. Inciardi, & A. Horton (Eds.), *Drug abuse treatment: The implementation of innovative approaches* (pp. 195–207). Westport, CT: Greenwood.

Hall, S. M., Havassy, B. E., & Wasserman, D. A. (1991). Effects of commitment to abstinence, positive moods, stress and coping on relapse to cocaine use. *Journal of Consulting and Clinical Psychology, 59,* 526–532.

Hargraves, W. A. (1983). Methadone dose and duration for methadone treatment. In J. R. Cooper, F. Altman, B. S. Brown, et al. (Eds.), *Research on the treatment of narcotic addiction: State of the art.* NIDA Treatment Research Monograph (pp. 19–79). DHHS Publication No. ADM 83-1281. Washington, DC: U.S. Government Printing Office.

Heath, D. B. (1989). American Indians and alcohol: Epidemiological and sociocultural relevance. In D. L. Spiegler, D. A. Tate, S. S. Aitken, & C. M. Christian (Eds.), *Alcohol use among U.S. Ethnic minorities* (pp. 207–222). NIAAA Research Monograph No. 18. Washington, DC: U.S. Government Printing Office.

Helzer, J. I., Robbins, L. N., Taylor, J. R., Carey, K., Miller, R. H., Combs-Orme, T., & Farmer, A. (1985). The extent of long-term drinking among alcoholics discharged from medical and psychiatric treatment facilities. *New England Journal of Medicine, 312,* 1678–1682.

Hendricks, W. J. (1971). Use of multifamily counseling groups in treatment of male narcotic addicts. *International Journal of Group Psychotherapy, 21,* 34–90.

Hesselbrock, M. N., Hesselbrock, V. N., Babor, T. F., et al. (1986). Antisocial behavior, psychopathology and problem drinking in the natural history of alcoholism. In D. W. Goodwin, K. T. Van Dusen, & S. A. Mednick (Eds.), *Longitudinal research in alcoholism* (pp. 197–214). Boston: Kluwer-Nijhoff.

Hester, R. K. (1994). Outcome research: Alcoholism. In *Textbook of substance abuse treatment.* Washington, DC: American Psychiatric Press.

Hester, R. K. (1995). Self-control training. In R. K. Hester & W. R. Miller (Eds.), *Handbook of alcoholism treatment approaches.* New York: Allyn & Bacon.

Hester, R. K., & Miller, W. R. (1989). Self-control training. In R. K. Hester & W. R. Miller (Eds.), *Handbook of alcoholism treatment approaches: Effective alternatives* (pp. 141–150). Elmsford, NY: Pergamon.

Hester, R. K., & Miller, W. R. (Eds.). (1995). *Handbook of alcoholism treatment approaches.* New York: Allyn & Bacon.

Hoffman, N. G., & Miller, N. S. (1992). Treatment outcomes for abstinence-based programs. *Psychiatric Annals, 22.*

Horn, J. L., & Wanberg, K. (1973). Females are different: On the diagnosis of alcoholism in women. In *Proceedings of the first annual alcoholism conference of the National Institute on*

Alcohol Abuse and Alcoholism. Washington, DC: U.S. Government Printing Office.

Hubbard, R. L., Marsden, M. E., Rachal, J. V., et al. (1975). *Drug abuse treatment: A national study of effectiveness*. Chapel Hill: University of North Carolina Press.

Humphreys, K., & Moos, R. H. (1996). Reduced substance-abuse-related health care costs among voluntary participants in Alcoholics Anonymous. *Psychiatric Services, 47,* 709–713.

Institute of Medicine. (1990). *Prevention and treatment of alcohol problems: Research opportunities*. Washington, DC: National Academy Press.

Joanning, H., Quinn, W., Thomas, F., & Mullen, R. (1992). Treating adolescent drug abuse: A comparison of family systems therapy, group therapy, and family drug education. *Journal of Marital and Family Therapy, 18*(2).

Kang, S.-Y., Kleinman, P. H., Woody, G. E., Millman, R. B., Todd, T. C., Kemp, J., & Lipton, D. S. (1991). Outcomes for cocaine abusers after once-a-week psychosocial therapy. *American Journal of Psychiatry, 148*(5), 630–635.

Kaufman, E. (1979). The application of the basic principles of family therapy to the treatment of drug and alcohol abusers. In E. Kaufman & P. Kaufman (Eds.), *Family therapy of drug and alcohol abuse*. New York: Gardner.

Kay, D.C. (1985). Substance abuse in psychopathic states and sociopathic individuals. In A. I. Altenman (Ed.), *Substance abuse and psychopathology* (pp. 91–120). New York: Plenum.

Kleber, H. D. (1991). Tracking the cocaine epidemic. *Journal of the American Medical Association, 266,* 2272–2273.

LaRosa, J. C., Lipsius, J. H., & LaRosa, J. H. (1974). Experience with a combination of group therapy and methadone maintenance in the treatment of heroin addiction. *International Journal of Addiction, 9,* 605–617.

Laundergan, J. C. (1982). *Easy does it! Alcoholism treatment outcomes, Hazelden and the Minnesota Model*. Center City, MN: Hazelden.

Leach, B. (1973). Does AA really work? In P. G. Bourne & R. Fox (Eds.), *Alcoholism: Progress in research and treatment* (pp. 245–284). New York: Academic Press.

Leach, B., & Norris, J. L. (1977). Factors in the development of Alcoholics Anonymous (AA). In B. Kissiw & H. Beglerter (Eds.), *The biology of alcoholism: Treatment and rehabilitation of the chronic alcoholic* (Vol. 5, pp. 441–543). New York: Plenum.

Leiser, E. (1976). Behavior therapy with a narcotics user: A case report: Ten-year follow-up. *Behavior Research and Therapy, 14*(5), 381.

Levy, S. J., & Rutter, E. (1992). *Children of drug abusers*. New York: Lexington.

Lewis, J. A., Dana, R. Q., & Blevins, G. A. (1994). *Substance abuse counseling: An individualized approach*. Pacific Grove, CA: Brooks/Cole.

Lewis, R. A., Piercy, F. P., Sprenkle, D. H., & Trepper, T. S. (1991). The Purdue brief family therapy model for adolescent substance abusers. In T. Todd & M. Selekman (Eds.), *Family therapy approaches with substance abusers* (pp. 29–48). Needham Heights, MA: Allyn & Bacon.

Liepman, M. R., Nirenberg, T. D., & Begiw, A. M. (1989). Evaluation of a program designed to help families and significant others to motivate resistant alcoholics into recovery. *American Journal of Drug and Alcohol Abuse, 15,* 209–221.

Locke, D. W. (1992, July). Personal communication.

Madsen, W. (1974). *The American alcoholic*. Springfield, IL: Thomas.

Mayfield, D. (1985). Substance abuse in the affective disorders. In A. I. Alterman (Ed.), *Substance abuse and psychopathology* (pp. 69–90). New York: Plenum.

McCrady, B. S. (1982). Conjoint behavioral treatment of an alcoholic and his spouse. In W. M. Hay & P. E. Nathan (Eds.), *Clinical case studies in the behavior treatment of alcoholism* (pp. 127–156). New York: Plenum.

McCrady, B. S. (1986). The family in the change process. In W. R. Miller & N. H. Heather (Eds.), *Treating addictive behaviors: Processes of change* (pp. 305–318). New York: Plenum.

McGlothlin, W. H., & Anglin, M. D. (1981). Shutting off methadone: Costs and benefits. *Archives of General Psychiatry, 38,* 885–892.

McLellan, A. T., Alterman, A. I., Metzger, D. S., Grissom, G. R., Woody, G. E., Luborsky, L., & O'Brien, C. P. (1994). Similarity of outcome predictors across opiate, cocaine, and alcohol treatments: Role of treatment services. *Journal of Consulting and Clinical Psychology, 62*(6), 1141–1158.

McLellan, A. T., O'Brien, C. P., Metzger, D., et al. (1992). How effective is substance abuse treatment-compared to what? In C. P. O'Brien & J. J. Jaffe (Eds.), *Addictive states* (pp. 231–251). New York: Raven.

Miller, W. R., Brown, J. M., Simpson, T. S., Handmaker, N. S., Bien, T. H., Luckie, L. F., Montgomery, H. A., Hester, R. K., & Tonigan, J. S. (1995). What works? A method analysis of the alcohol treatment outcome literature. In R. K. Hester & W. R. Miller (Eds.), *Handbook of alcoholism treatment approaches* (2nd ed., pp. 12–44). Boston: Allyn & Bacon.

Miller, W. R., & Hester, R. K. (1986). The effectiveness of alcoholism treatment methods: What research reveals. In W. R. Miller & N. Heather (Eds.), *Treating addictive behaviors: Processes of change*. New York: Plenum.

Miller, W. R., & Rollnick, S. (1991). *Motivational interviewing*. New York: Guilford.

Montgomery, H. A., Miller, W. R., & Tonigan, J. S. (1995). Does Alcoholics Anonymous involvement predict treatment outcomes? *Journal of Substance Abuse Treatment, 12*(4), 241–246.

Moos, R. H., King, M. J., & Patterson, M. A. (1996). Outcomes of residential treatment of substance abuse in hospital and community-based programs. *Psychiatric Services, 46*, 66–72.

Nace, E. P. (1987). *The treatment of alcoholism*. New York: Brunner/Mazel.

National Institute on Drug Abuse. (1994). *Monitoring the future study, 1975–1994*. Rockville, MD: U.S. Government Printing Office.

O'Brien, C. P. (1996). Recent developments in the pharmacotherapy of substance abuse. *Journal of Consulting and Clinical Psychology, 64*, 677–686.

O'Farrell, T. J. (1986). Marital therapy in the treatment of alcoholism. In N. S. Jacobson & A. S. Gurman (Eds.), *Clinical handbook of marital therapy* (pp. 513–535). New York: Guilford.

O'Farrell, T. J. (1995). Marital and family therapy. In R. K. Hester & W. R. Miller (Eds.), *Handbook of alcoholism treatment approaches* (2nd ed., New York: Allyn & Bacon.

O'Farrell, T. J., & Cowles, K. S. (1989). Behavioral marital therapy. In R. K. Hester & W. R. Miller (Eds.), *Handbook of alcoholism treatment* (pp. 183–205). Elmsford, NY: Pergamon.

O'Farrell, T. J., & Cutter, H. S. G. (1984). Behavioral marital therapy couples groups for male alcoholics and their wives. *Journal of Substance Abuse Treatment, 1*, 191–204.

Ogborne, A. C., & Glaser, F. B. (1985). Evaluating Alcoholics Anonymous. In T. E. Bratter & G. G. Forrest (Eds.), *Alcoholism and substance abuse: Strategies for clinical intervention*. New York: Free Press.

Peluso, E., & Peluso, L. S. (1988). *Women and drugs*. Minneapolis, MN: CompCare.

Rawson, R. A., Obert, J. L., McEann, M. J., & Mann, A. J. (1986). Cocaine treatment outcome: Cocaine use following inpatient, outpatient, and no treatment. In L. S. Harris (Ed.), *Problems of drug dependence: Proceedings of the 47th annual scientific meeting, the Committee on Problems of Drug Dependence, Inc.* NIDA Research Monograph 67, 271-277, DHHS Pub. No. (ADM) 86-1448. Washington, DC: U.S. Government Printing Office.

Resnick, R. B., Washton, A. M., Stone-Washton, W., et al. (1981). Psychotherapy and naltresone in opioid dependence. In L. S. Harris (Ed.), *Problems of drug dependence*. NIDA Research Monograph 37, 109–115. Rockville, MD: U.S. Department of Health and Human Services.

Roszell, D. K., & Chaney, E. F. (1982). Autogenic training in a drug abuse program. *International Journal of the Addictions, 17*(8), 1337–1350.

Schilit, R., & Gomberg, E. S. (1991). *Drugs and behavior*. Newbury Park, CA: Sage.

Schuster, R. (1978–1979). Evaluation of a reality therapy stratification system in a residential drug rehabilitation center. *Drug Forum, 7(1)*, 59–67.

Sells, S. B. (Ed.). (1974). *Studies of the effectiveness of treatments for drug abuse: Evaluation of treatments* (Vol. 1). Cambridge, MA: Ballinger.

Simpson, D. D., Savage, L. J., & Lloyd, M. R. (1979). Follow-up evaluation of treatment of drug abuse during 1969 to 1972. *Archives of General Psychiatry, 36,* 772–780.

Stanton, M. D., & Todd, T. C. (1982). *The family therapy of drug abuse and addiction.* New York: Guilford.

Stein, A., & Friedman, E. (1971). Group therapy with alcoholics. In H. I. Kaplan & B. J. Sadock (Eds.), *Comprehensive group psychotherapy.* Baltimore, MD: Williams & Wilkins.

Taylor, J. R. (1986–1987). Controlled drinking studies: Methodological issues. *Drugs and Society, 1,* 83–107.

Todd, T. C., & Selekman, M. (1991). *Family therapy with adolescent substance abusers.* Needham Heights, MA: Allyn & Bacon.

Ulmer, R. A. (1977). Behavior therapy: A promising drug abuse treatment and research approach of choice. *International Journal of the Addictions, 12*(6), 777–784.

Vaillant, G. E., & Hiller-Sturmhofel, S. (1996). The natural history of alcoholism. *Alcohol Health and Research World, 20,* 152–161.

Walden House Day Treatment Program. (1995). A day treatment program in a therapeutic community setting: Six-month outcomes. *Journal of Substance Abuse Treatment, 12*(6), 441–447.

Walker, R. D., Benjamin, G. A., Kwlahan, D., & Walker, P. S. (1989). American Indian alcohol misuse and treatment outcome. In D. L.

Spiegler, D. A. Tate, S. S. Aitken, & C. M. Christian (Eds.), *Alcohol use among U.S. Ethnic minorities.* NIAAA Research Monograph 18, pp. 301–311. Washington, DC: U.S. Government Printing Office.

Washton, A. M. (1989). *Cocaine addiction: Treatment, recovery, and relapse prevention.* New York: Norton.

Washton, A. M. (1992). *Cocaine recovery workbooks.* Center City, MN: Hazelden Educational Materials.

Washton, A. M., & Stone-Washton, N. S. (1991). *Step zero: Getting to recovery.* Center City, MN: Hazelden Educational Materials.

Watson, C. G., Hancock, M., Gearhart, L. P., Mendez, C. M., Malovrh, P., & Raden, M. (1997). A comparative outcome study of frequent, moderate, occasional, and nonattenders of Alcoholics Anonymous. *Journal of Clinical Psychology, 53,* 209–214.

Watson, C. G., Hancock, M., Malovrh, P., Gearhart, L., & Raden, M. (1996). A 48-week natural history follow-up of alcoholics who do and do not engage in limited drinking after treatment. *Journal of Nervous and Mental Disease, 184*(10), 623–627.

Weiner, H. (1975). Methadone counseling: A social work challenge. *Journal of Psychedelic Drugs, 7*(4), 381–387.

Woody, G. E., Luborsky, L., McLellan, A. T., et al. (1983). Psychotherapy for opiate addicts: Does it help? *Archives of General Psychiatry 40,* 639–648.

Zweben, J. E. (1987). Recovery-oriented psychotherapy: Facilitating the use of 12-step programs. *Journal of Psychoactive Drugs, 19,* 243–251.

Index